RUSSIAN FOR BEGINNERS

учебник

ABOUT THE AUTHORS

CHARLES DUFF (1894–1966) had wide experience in the practical use of Russian. After serving with the French Army as an interpreter, he was employed for many years as Press Officer by the British Foreign Office. Thereafter, he devoted his time to teaching, writing, and translating. He served as lecturer at the Institute of Education, London University, and as Professor of Occidental Languages at Nanyang University.

Mr. Duff pioneered in developing and applying modern methods of teaching foreign languages, using them in classroom work and as a basis for his popular volumes of self-instruction. His many books include *How to Learn a Language*; and the Everyday Handbooks *Spanish for Beginners*, *Italian for Beginners*, and *German for Beginners* (with Paul Stamford).

DMITRI MAKAROFF is not only an experienced teacher of Russian, his native language, but also the distinguished translator into English of Mayakovski's famous play *The Bed Bug* and of Chekhov's early play *Platonov*. Both plays were produced in London. He has served as instructor at the Joint Services School for Linguists. His collaboration with the late Mr. Duff produced a happy result: the completion of a thorough book that is realistic in the practical sense, one that teaches first things first and is closely related to everyday life.

EVERYDAY HANDBOOKS

R U S S I A N
FOR BEGINNERS

by CHARLES DUFF
and DMITRI MAKAROFF

Collins

An Imprint of HarperCollins Publishers

INTRODUCING THE COURSE

THIS is a comprehensive course in Russian, which provides necessary grammar, carefully chosen vocabulary, and common idioms, with sufficient practice material and reading matter to enable the adult of average intelligence to assimilate the essential elements of the language. In one important respect *Russian for Beginners* differs from the other books in this series. It allows for a fact that is too often overlooked in textbooks: that the first stage of learning Russian is generally found by absolute beginners to be more difficult than the first stage of learning, say, Spanish, French, or German.

Unlike our delightfully simple English, Russian is a highly "inflected" language. In it meanings are changed by changing the forms of words rather than by adding, as we do, other words. This involves from the outset a different way of thinking from ours. Russian has much more of elementary and of more difficult grammar than we have in English, which tends to play havoc with the enthusiasm of many beginners. Then there is the "strange" alphabet, not to dwell on certain difficulties of pronunciation! All this can be rather forbidding, but if the early stage be taken gently—never hurriedly or impatiently—and if the Russian be presented in a simplified form, in small quantities, any normal person can learn it. In the first stage it demands from us all a certain amount of what many regard as drudgery. But, when this first stage is passed, enlightenment increases, and with this comes a fascination for the language.

Therefore one must have a textbook which goes as far as possible in the simplified presentation of that first stage. And this is what we have attempted to do in Part I of this book. In Part I we have it strongly in mind that no details of explanation can be too elementary for the beginner: especially for the beginner whose English grammar may be weak or totally forgotten. Here he will learn English grammar as he goes along. We do not apologize for what some others may regard as over-simplification, or for the repetition of words already met, or for re-stating in some places what has already been given of grammar, the idea of this being that it is the basis of some further expansion of grammar now to be given. Such features are deliberate in the interests of many beginners, and calculated to save time.

When Part I has been mastered, the learner's horizon will begin to expand considerably with Part II. He will still have to work at his Russian grammar, but the work becomes more interesting. He will find himself dealing with Russian that has been written for Russians. The texts for Reading—graded in difficulty—include: (1) extracts (usually self-contained for interest) from Russian folk and classical literature; and (2) extracts from Soviet writers and popular modern publications. This is all "guided" reading with full notes and a literal (*not* "literary") translation, sufficient to introduce the beginner to both classical and Soviet Russian prose. We have endeavored to make the Soviet reading matter as light as possible, so that, after it has been worked through carefully, the task of reading contemporary Soviet writing will be easier and require only help from a dictionary. Study is aided by the provision of tables and of diagrams of knotty points of grammar. Material for reference is relegated to Appendixes.

In preparing the book we have taken into account—with gratitude for an excellent piece of work—*The Russian Word Count* * by Josselson. But we have not followed it slavishly. This Count is based on *written* Russian (from early nineteenth century to 1953) and, within this field, can be a most useful guide to the frequency of words and forms. But no adequate study of the frequencies of the contemporary *spoken* language has yet become available, nor, so far as we know, scientifically attempted, nor on a scale to provide required results. So we

* Its sub-title is: Frequency Analyses of Grammatical Categories of Standard Literary Russian.

must therefore rely on empirical methods for most of the vocabulary required for "active" use in speech. Our total vocabulary consists of 5000 words, which (excepting such "active" certainties as numeral words) are contained in the Vocabulary on pages 322–368. As examples of very common "active" words which do not come into the literary *Word Count* made by Josselson one may cite **щи** (= *cabbage soup*) and **борщ** (= *a widely consumed soup made with beet*). These words must be used daily by innumerable people in the Soviet Union, but there is *no* statistical guide to their frequency! Such words are given in this book as "active" vocabulary to be memorized.

When this book is used for private Lessons or class-work, the teacher will determine the apportionment of tasks. A very few items of grammar and a vocabulary of at first a dozen Russian words, increasing to 20–30 or even more, is sufficient for a Lesson lasting one hour. The self-taught will make their own pace, and our advice to them is to "hasten slowly" and make sure of knowing each Lesson before passing on to the next. For both, constant review is necessary. It may be of interest to note that, although the workings of the normal human memory are not yet fully understood, one can be fairly sure of at least two important factors in: (1) *Motivation*—that is keenness or otherwise to learn; and (2) *Concentration of attention while learning*. Motivation is of primary importance. The learner must be keen to learn if he is to learn well and quickly. And he must concentrate while learning. Study that is spaced out at regular intervals and uninterrupted by distractions always gives the best results. Morning study is said to be better than study which comes after a day's work; and review best left for the evening. These are matters for individual choice. Final hints: (1) never let a day pass during the first six months without doing a daily stint at Russian; (2) always regard accuracy as of more importance than speed in learning; (3) if you feel that you are getting bogged down or confused or frustrated, stop attempting new Lessons, and go back again over what has been done.

Grateful acknowledgements are due to our publishers for

their help and encouragement in the preparation of this book, and to the skilful and patient printers who have dealt with its many technical problems. Grateful acknowledgements are also due to the Soviet magazines and other publications quoted; to the artists and writers whose work is included here; and to Mr Horne Shepheard for the pages of Russian handwriting.

Extracts from contemporary Russian writers whose work is used here come from **Огонёк**; **Культура и жизнь**; **Наука и жизнь**; **Советский Союз**; **Весёлые картинки**; **Крокодил**; **Неделя**; **Женский календарь 1960**; **Календарь для школьника**—and all are from the period July 1959 to December 1960. Our cartoons are from the same sources.

We have also used the following Russian textbooks: **РУССКИЙ ЯЗЫК** (**Учебное пособие для нерусских педагогических училищ**): **часть первая — Лексика, Фонетика и Морфология** (**Москва, 1951**). **Справочник по глагольному управлению в русском языке** (**Москва, Учпедгиз 1957.**) Also useful has been I. M. Pulkina's *A Short Russian Reference Grammar* (Moscow, 1960); and *Die Russischen Verben* by E. Daum and W. Schenk (Leipzig, 1954).

Finally, we are grateful to Maria Pupko, Consulting Editor, and Dr. Samuel Smith, Editor-in-Chief, of Barnes and Noble, Inc. for numerous suggestions and emendations adapting the original text to the needs of the American reader.

CHARLES DUFF
DMITRI MAKAROFF

TABLE OF CONTENTS

PART I: First Principles

PART II: The Fundamentals of the Language

DIAGRAMS

WHY LEARN RUSSIAN?

Because:

It is to-day one of the three most important languages in the world.

It is the governmental and administrative language of the peoples of the Soviet Union: over 200,000,000; and one-sixth of the globe in area.

It is now, with English and German, an essential language for those interested in any branch of science and technology. The Soviet Union publishes an immense body of publications relating to these and many other subjects.

A knowledge of this language is steadily spreading to countries whose languages are rarely known by English-speaking people. Russian is becoming an increasingly important "travel-language".

It is an error for the foreigner to believe that he can "understand the Russians" without knowing their language—the key to their psychology. Such knowledge is not merely a help: it is an essential factor.

It is a language with a great literature which has many works in prose and poetry to rank with the best in world literature. Gogol, Tolstoy and Dostoyevsky are not surpassed as novelists by any in their range or humanity. And there are many modern Russian writers whose works are as yet almost unknown among us.

A study of Russian—a rich, highly flexible and inflected language—provides the foreigner with a training for the intelligence and memory at least equal to that provided by Latin and Greek. And Russian is very much alive!

It is, furthermore, a very beautiful language, one which almost invariably fascinates those who persist with it far enough to become familiar with its elements.

It is worth learning for its own sake alone, if only because it opens vistas of ways of thinking and life that are quite different from ours.

ABBREVIATIONS USED IN THIS BOOK

ac = active
acc = accusative
adj = adjective
an = animate
car = cardinal
Cl = class
coll = colloquial
comp = comparative
com = compound
cond = conditional
cond/sub = conditional-
   subjunctive
conj = conjugate, -tion
dec = decline, declension
dat = dative
det = determinate
dim = diminutive
dr = direct(ly)
ex = example
fam = familiar
$\left.\begin{array}{l} f \\ fem \end{array}\right\}$ = feminine
fl = fleeting
fut = future
gen = genitive
Gr = group
imp = imperative
impers = impersonal
indec = indeclinable
indet = indeterminate
indr = indirect
inf = infinitive
ins = instrumental

intr = intransitive
ipf = imperfective
irr = irregular
$\left.\begin{array}{l} m \\ masc \end{array}\right\}$ = masculine
$\left.\begin{array}{l} n \\ neut \end{array}\right\}$ = neuter
no = noun
num = numeral
obj = object(ive)
ord = ordinal
pa = past
par = particle
part = participle
pass = passive
pf = perfective
pl = plural
poss = possessive
prf = prefix
pres = present
pr = pronunciation
pron = pronoun
prp = preposition(al)
ref = refer to
reg = regular
rfx = reflexive
sim = similar(ly)
sing = singular
sub = subjunctive
tr = transitive
v = verb
v-adv = verbal adverb

After verbs $\left\{\begin{array}{l} (I) = \text{Verb of 1st ("e") conjugation} \\ (II) = \quad " \quad " \quad \text{2nd ("и")} \quad " \end{array}\right.$

PART I

FIRST PRINCIPLES

> **Тише е́дешь — да́льше бу́дешь.**
> *Russian proverb*

BEFORE BEGINNING THE LESSONS

Before beginning to study the Lessons, the absolute beginner must study pages 3–17.   This preliminary part contains a somewhat detailed statement of the Russian alphabet, the pronunciation of the letters, and especially of the vowels, stress and other principles which the beginner must grasp clearly in order to be able to deal intelligently with the Lessons. By reading through pages 3–17 several times until the essentials are understood and memorized, what follows will be very much easier.

RUSSIAN ALPHABET

Names of the letters and their primary sounds

Letters	Russian Names		Approximately equivalent sounds in English
А, а	ah	*a*	is like English *a* in *father,* but short; or like French *a* in *rat* or Italian *a* in *Italia.*
Б, б	be	*б*	like *b* in *bet.* Now pronounce *bet* without *t,* and the *be* is close to the Russian name of the letter. This *e* is pronounced the same in *ve, ghe,* etc.
В, в	ve	*в*	*v* as in *vat.*
Г, г	ghe	*г*	*g* (hard) as in *go, get.* Never like (soft) *g* in *gem.*
Д, д	de	*д (g)*	*d* in *dam, sad.*
Е, е	ye	*е*	*ye* in *yet.*
Ё, ё	yo	*ё*	almost like *yaw* in *yawl,* but shorter as if written *yol.* *ё* is always stressed.
Ж, ж	zhe	*ж*	like *s* in *pleasure* or *z* in *azure.* French *je.*
З, з	ze	*з*	*z* in *zone* or *s* in *rose.*
И, и	ee	*и*	like *i* in *machine;* or French *i.*
Й, й	и с кра́ткой =ee *with* short mark	*й*	like и but short. This й is used to form diphthongs after another vowel, like our *y* in *boy.* Example: **мой,** pronounce *moy.*
К, к	ka	*к*	*k* in *kick.*
Л, л	el	*л*	hard Russian л resembles our *ll* in *ill, tell;* soft ль 1 like *lli* in *million.* See pages 5, 11.
М, м	em	*м*	*m* in *met.*
Н, н	en	*н*	*n* in *net.*

3

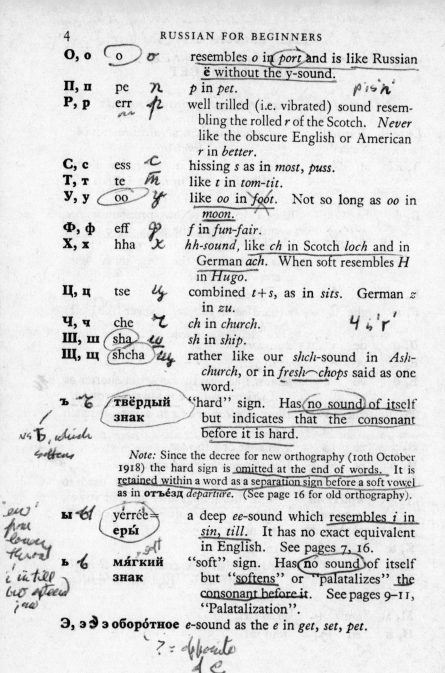

О, о   o   *σ*   resembles *o* in *port* and is like Russian ё without the y-sound.

П, п   pe   *n*   *p* in *pet*.

Р, р   err   *p*   well trilled (i.e. vibrated) sound resembling the rolled *r* of the Scotch. *Never* like the obscure English or American *r* in *better*.

С, с   ess   *c*   hissing *s* as in *most, puss*.

Т, т   te   *m*   like *t* in *tom-tit*.

У, у   oo   *y*   like *oo* in *foot*. Not so long as *oo* in *moon*.

Ф, ф   eff   *φ*   *f* in *fun-fair*.

Х, х   hha   *x*   *hh-sound*, like *ch* in Scotch *loch* and in German *ach*. When soft resembles *H* in *Hugo*.

Ц, ц   tse   *у*   combined *t*+*s*, as in *sits*. German *z* in *zu*.

Ч, ч   che   *ч*   *ch* in *church*.

Ш, ш   sha   *ш*   *sh* in *ship*.

Щ, щ   shcha   *щ*   rather like our *shch*-sound in *Ashchurch*, or in *fresh chops* said as one word.

ъ   твёрдый знак   "hard" sign. Has no sound of itself but indicates that the consonant before it is hard.

Note: Since the decree for new orthography (10th October 1918) the hard sign is omitted at the end of words. It is retained within a word as a separation sign before a soft vowel as in **отъéзд** *departure*. (See page 16 for old orthography).

ы   yérrée= еры   a deep *ee*-sound which resembles *i* in *sin, till*. It has no exact equivalent in English. See pages 7, 16.

ь   мягкий знак   "soft" sign. Has no sound of itself but "softens" or "palatalizes" the consonant before it. See pages 9–11, "Palatalization".

Э, э   э оборóтное   *e*-sound as the *e* in *get, set, pet*.

Ю, ю   yu *Ю*   *yu*-sound like *u* in *unity* or *yu* in *yule*.

Я, я   ya *Я*   *ya* in *yard*.

Approximate equivalents: Russian sounds are not easy for the English-speaking learner, who would be well advised to regard the "approximate equivalents" given above as mostly makeshifts. No book can replace oral teaching of Russian sounds, but it can help. The absolute beginner should try to find a native speaker of Russian, who should be asked to make the sounds, which the beginner must *mimick* carefully.

Difficult sounds for English-speaking learners

(1) Hard **л**
    Guttural **x**   *There are no exact equivalents for these*
    Hard vowel **ы**   *sounds in English. They must be heard.*

(2) Palatalization of consonants before soft vowels and before soft sign **ь**. This demands very close attention and to make the sounds well requires practice.

(3) Making a clear distinction between the sounds of hard and soft vowels and between some long and short vowels. This also demands close attention and practice.

Memorizing the letters

Your first task is to learn to *recognize* the letters and to know the sounds which they represent. The alphabet will later have to be known in the order of letters—for looking up words in the Vocabulary at the end of this book or in dictionaries. You may learn to recognize the letters by first taking them in groups as follows:

I. Five letters correspond to five of ours:

А К М О Т

II. Three letters are not unlike ours:

Б Д З

III. Eight letters look like some of ours but represent *other* letters in Russian:

B=V. **H**=N. **P**=R. **E**=YE. **Ë**=YO. **C**=S. **У**=U. **X**=guttural *hh*.

IV. Thirteen letters are unlike ours:

Г = G. **Ж** = Zh. **И** = I (as in ma*chi*ne). **Л** = L. **П** = P.
Ф = F. **Ц** = *ts* in *bits*. **Ш** = Sh. **Щ** = *shch* in *Ash-church*. **Ч** = *ch* in *church*. **Э** = *e* in *end*. **Ю** = *yu*-sound.
Я = *ya*-sound.

V. Four Russian letters which at first seem rather peculiar:
й = short **и**-sound, like our *y* in *boy*. It is used to form diphthongs: **мой** = *moi*-sound. Note **Нью-Йо́рк** = *New York*.

ы = the hard vowel-sound peculiar to Russian.
ь = the soft sign which indicates palatalization of the preceding consonant. We have something like it in *onion* in which the *i* softens and almost palatalizes the *n*.
ъ = the hard sign, which makes the consonant before it hard.
Both **ь** and **ъ** are mute of themselves and are often called "separation signs". They merely affect the sound of the consonant which precedes them.

THE RUSSIAN VOWELS

From the outset you must distinguish between "hard" and "soft" vowels. Each hard vowel has a soft one to correspond:

Hard vowels: **а   ы   э   о   у**
Soft vowels: **я   и, й   е   ё (е)   ю**

Russian **й** may be regarded as a semi-vowel, its commonest use being after another vowel to make a diphthong (i.e. a combination of two vowel-sounds):

мой   чай   до́брый   трамва́й

Go over the vowel-sounds as given in the alphabet until you know their approximate equivalents, which represent stressed vowels. You will learn more about these on page 8; and also about *un*stressed vowels.

Hard vowel : ы

We have no vowel-sound in English which is the exact equivalent of this Russian vowel. The *i* in such words as *sin, tin, will, ill* is only an approximation to the Russian sound. When you say stable, cradle, ladle, table, fable, the half-suppressed sound between *b* or *d* and *l* is much closer to **ы**. You should now make this sound in *stable*, etc., and it will indicate to you that the middle part of the tongue is *raised*

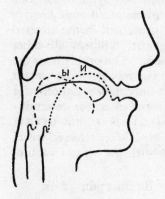

while making it—as it is in **ы**. Now say *sin, tin, will, ill* with the middle part of the tongue raised, and then repeat the words without the last consonant-sounds: *si-, ti-, wi-* and finally the *i* of *ill* by itself. This should give you Russian **ы** near enough. The tip of the tongue is *not* used in making **ы**: it lies back from the teeth while the centre part of the tongue is raised. See this diagram for the position of the tongue while making **ы**. Practise assiduously until you can make the sound without great effort. Listening to a Russian making the sound and mimicking it—as in learning *all* Russian sounds—is the best way.

Make sure that you distinguish clearly between the sounds of **ы** and **и**: *meaning* often depends on sound. **ы** always follows a hard consonant (see pages 8–9). Therefore it can never appear at the beginning of a word. Practise these Russian words:

ты мы вы сын фру́кты ры́ба

Semi-vowel : Й й

This resembles the *y*-sound of *yeast* when it is used initially as in **Йорк** in **Нью-Йорк** = *New York*. It is like our *y*-sound in *boy* when it forms a diphthong, and then it is a very slight sound.   Practise the following sounds:

     Hard: чай   —   ста́рый вой дуй
     Soft: валя́й клей си́ний   —   вою́й

This й is not a difficult sound, but it often occurs between vowels and at the end of words, and should be correctly pronounced.

STRESS

Every Russian word of more than one syllable has **one** particular syllable which must be pronounced *more forcibly* than the others, that is, the vowel contained in the stressed syllable is pronounced with emphasis, whereas all other vowels in that word remain unstressed.   The problem for the beginner is to know which syllable is stressed.   The correct stressing of a word is of the greatest importance, not only for correct pronunciation, but also, in some cases, for determining the meaning of a word (thus, мука́ = flour, but му́ка = torment).   In the first stage of this book *every* stressed vowel in the Russian text will be marked with the acute (= tonic) accent (′).   Thus:

     хорошо́ кни́га Москва́ Ленингра́д я́ма

But remember that Russians themselves never mark these stresses, so eventually you must be prepared to meet Russian texts where no stresses are given at all.   The best preparation for this is to memorize from the outset the *sound* pattern as well as the visual pattern of each new word you learn.

Warning: It is most important to remember that the double stress, which is such a distinctive feature of English pronunciation, is almost completely absent in Russian.   The English learner will instinctively try to introduce a second or "subsidiary" stress in Russian words of three or more syllables.   You should make a particular effort to avoid this.

Hard and soft consonants

It is necessary from the outset to distinguish between "hard" and "soft" Russian consonants.   No written description can convey the distinction so well as *hearing* the difference, but, as a preliminary, this must be your first rough guide:

Consonants generally hard are ж, ш, ц.   See page 16.

Consonants always soft are ч, щ, й.

Consonants soft before е and и are г, к, х.   *as in* МЯГКИЙ

Consonants which are hard but can also be softened by "palatalization", for which see below. } б, п, д, т, в, ф, з, с, л, м, н, р.

PALATALIZATION

This is the most difficult problem of Russian pronunciation for the foreigner, and it must be repeated that no textbook description can replace *careful listening* to a good Russian speaker and *mimicking the difficult sounds* repeatedly until the tongue and other organs of speech can make them reasonably well.   What is given here must therefore be regarded as merely an introductory guide which, if followed, will serve the self-taught learner until such time as he or she may find the opportunity of hearing the sounds from a good speaker.

In written or printed Russian, palatalization is indicated by the soft sign ь after a consonant.   But it also occurs—that is, a hard consonant becomes soft—when a consonant is followed by one of the soft vowels и, е, ё, я, ю.   Of this, account must always be taken.   Now you may begin to study

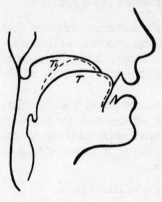

the diagram, from which you will see that, when a consonant is palatalized, the tip of the tongue is turned *down* towards the lower front teeth and the part of the tongue immediately behind the tip is *raised* and made to touch the front of the roof of the mouth or palate.   Try this movement a few times before attempting to make the sound of ть.

Next you may begin to make sounds.   The English words

given below—pronounced as by an educated *English*** person (*not* as by an American, for English and American pronunciation of English often differ considerably)—provide a fairly close approximation to the palatalization of the consonants listed on the left.   When you can make these sounds, then start again at the top of the list and try slowly to make the sounds of the Russian words *but* never forgetting that the Russian vowels have quite different values from the English.

Russian soft consonants	*English approximations*		*Russian words to exemplify palatalization*
бь	Bute	b'	бес (*demon*)
пь	pure, pew	p'	пьеса (*a play*)
дь	duke	d'	дядя (я softens д) (*uncle*)
ть	tune	t'	Татьяна *a woman's first name.*
вь	view	v'	видеть (и softens в, ь softens т) (*to see*)
фь	future	f'	физик (*physicist*)
зь	zebra	z'	земля (*earth, land*)
сь	suit	s'	семь (*seven*)
ль	lure (=*lyur*)	l'	лес (*forest*)
мь	mural	m'	семья (*family*)
нь	onion	n'	Нью-Йорк (*New York*)
рь	*memorial	r'	рюмка (*wine glass*)

* said quickly, the *r* trilled as by a Scotsman, this is as near as one can get.   There is no absolute equivalent in English.

The English letters with an apostrophe after them are to remind you that the Russian palatalization is *part of the consonant*.

There still remain ч, щ, й, г, к, х to be dealt with.   The first three are *always* soft by their nature and, for practical purposes, ч is equivalent to our *ch* in *church*, щ is equivalent to our *shch* in *Ashchurch* and, used as a consonant, й is equivalent to our *y* in *York* (**Йорк**).

*See An English Pronouncing Dictionary, by Daniel Jones.

[handwritten annotations at top: г, к, х (all gutterals) become soft before e and и (never appear w/ ъ)]

The second three may be considered as follows:

Soft sign **ь** is *never* written after these three. They become soft before **-e** and **-и**,

г as *g* in argue	g'	**гигие́на** (*pr* **г'иг'и-е́на**) (*hygiene*)
к as *c* in { cute, cube	k'	**кем** (*pr* **к'эм**) (*by whom*)
x as *h* in { *H*ugo, hew	h'	**хини́н** (*pr* **х'ин'ин**) (*quinine*)

General warning! Do not be satisfied with your palatalized consonants until you have had your pronunciation of all the Russian words given checked by a good Russian speaker.

Hard л

To make Russian hard **л**, place the tip of the tongue along the ridge of the upper teeth (which leaves a space between gums and teeth ridge) and say a prolonged l-l-l. The remainder of the tongue usually lies flat in the mouth, allowing the breath to go out at the sides. If care is taken to maintain the position of the tip of the tongue correctly, this sound "makes itself". Do this a few times and then pronounce:

ла́мпа	Во́лга	вол	луна́
lamp	Volga	ox	moon

Ж Ш Ц

These are completely hard consonants and cannot be palatalized or softened. You will find a number of instances where **ж** and **ш** are followed by **ь**, but this is simply an orthographical device and does not represent any change in pronunciation. As you will see **ж**, **ш** and **ц** cannot be followed by **я** or **ю**, which have to be changed to **a** and **y**. When the soft vowels **и** and **e** follow **ж**, **ш** or **ц** they must be pronounced as though they were the hard **ы** and **э**. Practise the following:

жир жёнский ши́на шесть цирк це́лый

The pronunciation of **и** as **ы** after **ж** and **ш**, the very letters after which **ы** cannot be written (see page 16), represents one of the few inconsistencies of Russian orthography.

Voiced and unvoiced consonants

A consonant is said to be "voiced" when the outgoing breath vibrates the vocal cords, thereby making a sound such as can be heard when we say *b, v, d, g* (in *go*), *z*.

A consonant is said to be "unvoiced" when it is uttered without vibration of the vocal cords, as in *p, f, t, k* and others.   In Russian there are:

Voiced: б   в   д   г   ж — — з —

Unvoiced: п   ф   т   к   х   ш   ч   щ   с   ц

Unvoiced without corresponding voiced are **щ, ч, ц.**   The distinction between voiced and unvoiced is necessary, as you will see.

End of word consonants: The final consonant of a Russian word tends to have a faint sound and, if it is a voiced consonant, it becomes like its corresponding unvoiced one. Thus хлеб (*pronounce* хлеп). Макáров (*pr* Макáроф). обéд (*pr* обéт).   раз (*pr* рас).   рож (*pr* рош).   And so with the others.   The change takes place whether the final consonant is hard or soft.

Beginning or middle of a word: The change from voiced to unvoiced also happens when a voiced consonant precedes an unvoiced one.   Thus в is pronounced ф in the word всё (= *all*).   The ж in лóжка is pronounced ш.   Thus, one says фсё, лóшка.

Unvoiced consonants before б, д, г, ж, з are pronounced voiced: сдéлать *pr* здéлать.   отдáть *pr* оддáть.

Before к and ч one pronounces г as х: *pr* лёгкий as лёхкий.

The combinations сч, зч, жч are all pronounced as щ: счáстье *pr* щáстье.   извóзчик *pr* извóщик.   мужчú-на *pr* мущúна.

The combinations сш and зш are pronounced шш.   сж and зж are pronounced жж.

Stressed and unstressed vowels

For our purpose here, we may consider Russian words of more than one syllable as consisting of stressed and unstressed syllables. This is helpful, especially for unstressed vowels **a** and **o**, because the pronunciation of these vowels depends on their *position* in a word.

Vowels **a** *and* **o** *unstressed:* Unstressed **a** in the syllable immediately before the stressed syllable is pronounced like the half suppressed *u* in English *cut, but, bud* (a difficult sound for those whose mother tongue is not English and represented phonetically by the IPA* symbol ʌ). Thus **балéт, вагóн.**

Unstressed **o** in the syllable *immediately* before the stressed syllable is also pronounced almost like the half-suppressed *u* in English *bud, cut* (IPA symbol ʌ):

онá — онó — водá — Москвá

In *all* other syllables preceding the stressed syllable, both **a** and **o** are pronounced like the *-o-* in our words which end in *-tion:* destination, for example. This is not a real *o*-sound, but is close to a short English *e* (IPA symbol ə). Examples:

карандáш — головá — разговóр

In *all* unstressed syllables after the stressed syllable, both **a** and **o** are pronounced like **a** and **o** in syllables *other than* that immediately before the stressed syllable: like the **o** in *destination.* Thus:

гóрод — бѝтва — прѝгорода

Other unstressed vowels: Unstressed **я** and **е** are usually pronounced as **и**:

язы́к — яйцó — перевóд — сестрá

Yet, at the end of a word they can be pronounced like the *o* in *destination* preceded by the palatal *y*-sound:

мóре — поля́ — бéлая — стáрое

*IPA = International Phonetic Alphabet. The symbols are given for teachers or others who may be acquainted with them. Refer to *An English Pronouncing Dictionary*, by Daniel Jones, Professor of Phonetics, University College, London.

Unstressed **a** after **ч** and **щ** is pronounced **и**:

watch, clock

<u>часы — щадить</u> *to spare*

Unstressed **a** after **ж** and **ш** is pronounced **ы**:

жакéт — шарлатáн

In general: These are the most important points to be noted by absolute beginners.   But, once again, it must be emphasized that the pronunciation of the Russian vowels is best learnt by listening carefully to a good Russian speaker, saying them after the teacher and correcting oneself until all the tricky sounds have been mastered.   From that point onwards accuracy in speech can be maintained by the foreigner by regular practice with Russians or very good foreign speakers of Russian.

Здрáвствуйте! — Пожáлуйста!

Здрáвствуйте!: This is a greeting which corresponds to several words and phrases of ours.   It is used for "*Good morning*", "*Good afternoon*", and even for "*Good evening*".   Also for "*Hello*", "*How goes it?*—the point being that it is used as an opening when one meets a friend or acquaintance or even a stranger.   The <u>first</u> **в** is <u>silent</u> as if the word were written **здрáствуйте**.   <u>Popular pronunciation is</u> **Здрáсте!**

Пожáлуйста!: Pronounced as if written **пожáлста** or **пожá'ста**.   The primary meaning is "*<u>Please</u>*" or "*If you please*", but it has a much wider application.   One uses it for "I beg you" on stepping aside to make way for somebody to pass.   Or <u>for "Don't mention it" in reply to</u> "Thanks".   We have no exact equivalent in English, but the word corresponds to French *Plaît-il*, German "*Bitte*", Spanish "*No hay de que*" and Italian "*Prego*". . . .

PRACTICE: **УПРАЖНÉНИЯ** (= Exercises)

Alphabet — Sounds — Stressed syllable

Бакýнин Bakunin	**ёлка** fir-tree
вóдка vodka (**д** *pr* **т**)	**журнáл** journal, magazine
генерáл general	**газéта** newspaper
дрáма drama	**зóна** zone
идиóт idiot	**Ленингрáд** Leningrad
Йéмен Yemen (river)	(*pronounce* **д** as **т**)

му́зыка music
на́ция nation (и *pr* ы)
о́пера opera
парк park
ру́бль rouble
Аме́рика America
А́нглия England
Ки́ев Kiev (в *pr* ф)
Пари́ж Paris (ж *pr* ш)
Го́голь Gogol
Шо́лохов Sholokhov (в= ф)
брат brother
стол table
каранда́ш pencil
да́ма lady
ко́мната room
ру́сский (*adj*) Russian
сове́т soviet (=advice, *or* council)
Толсто́й Tolstoy
Ура́л Urals (mountains)
филосо́фия philosophy
Че́хов Chekov (в *pr* ф)

Пу́шкин Pushkin
вы *vy* (*y*=deep *i*) you (*pl*)
Го́рький Gorky
элеме́нт element
Ю́кон Yukon (river)
Я́лта Yalta (place)
Ло́ндон London
Нью-Йо́рк New York
Кавка́з Caucasus (в *pr* ф, з *pr* с)
кни́га book
письмо́ letter
сло́во word
э́тот ⎫
э́та ⎬ this   *different pronunciation?*
э́то ⎭
да yes
нет no
не not
хлеб bread
са́хар sugar
Уро́к но́мер оди́н = Lesson No. 1
Уро́к No. 2 = Lesson No. 2

Go over the words in this list, taking them in groups of ten. You do not have to memorize the meanings at this stage. The PRACTICE is to enable you to recognize the letters and to make the sounds correctly.

Be very careful with Russian words which closely resemble their English equivalents: the pronunciation of the Russian word will usually be different *and* its stressed syllable may be quite different! For this reason be sure to memorize such words in their correct Russian pronunciation. With every new word that you meet, *first look for the stressed syllable,* make sure to pronounce it *forcibly* and that all other syllables are lightly pronounced. Practise with these words:

а́дрес — Аме́рика — Толсто́й — объе́кт   *object*
филосо́фия — актёр — ко́фе — телефо́н — генера́л

ё is always stressed, so stress not marked

Remember that **ё** is *always* stressed. (Only in Russian texts for learners is it marked with the diaeresis.)

Some rules of stress will be given on page 152–3. Until then all stressed syllables will be marked. Towards the end of this book there will be Russian text with few stress markings, and finally without any markings—as in Russian books and newspapers, etc.

BASIC RULES OF SPELLING

These rules apply throughout the language and must be mastered in the very early stage—say, by Lesson V in Part I of this book.

I. After the four hissing sounds **ж, ч, ш, щ** and the three guttural (throat) sounds **г, к, х** the hard vowel **ы** is *never* written: it is replaced by its soft vowel **и**. After the three gutturals the soft sign **ь** is *never* written.

II. After the hissing sounds **ж, ч, ш, щ, ц,** and the gutturals **г, к, х** the soft vowels **я** and **ю** are *never* written. **а** replaces **я** and **у** replaces **ю**.

III. After **ж, ч, ш, щ, ц,** a stressed **о** remains unchanged but an unstressed **о** usually changes to **е**.

THE OLD ORTHOGRAPHY

In books published before the 1917 Revolution and in some emigré publications you will find that the type also includes the following letters:

Ii equivalent to **Ии** (used when followed by another vowel)

Ѣѣ equivalent to **Ее** (used in certain roots and for some grammatical endings)

Ѳѳ equivalent to **Фф** (used to replace the Greek letter θ (*theta*) in some words of Greek origin: **Ѳеодо́сія**, Theodosia)

Vv equivalent to **Ии** (only rarely used in some ecclesiastical words of Greek origin to replace the Greek letter Yv (*upsilon*): **сѵнóдъ,** synod)

RUSSIAN HANDWRITING: THE ITALIC ALPHABET

Three pages of Russian handwriting are given (pp. 18–20) and every student who is taking the language seriously should learn this script as soon as possible. Study and practice of the script need not be begun before Lesson VI of Part I. You should be perfectly familiar with the printed alphabet before starting on the script.

Begin by copying out the letters in groups as instructed on page 18. When the letters can be written one by one, then copy out page 19 at least twice. Page 20 is for helping you to learn to read a normally clear Russian handwriting.

On page 21 you will find the Russian italic alphabet, which should be known before finishing this book. You will find that most of the italic letters are almost the same as those corresponding to them in the handwritten alphabet.

Russians do not make great use of written block letters, but there is no reason why the foreign beginner should not use them, at least in the first five Lessons, for copying out words to be memorized or to help in memorizing the printed alphabet.

PUNCTUATION: For reference

Russian punctuation is the same as in English, with a few variations. The *comma* is more often used in Russian and is governed by certain rules. It is used (1) after **да,** *yes,* and **нет,** *no,* when they are followed by other words; (2) before and after short phrases in parenthesis; (3) before conjunctions such as **но, а,** *but,* **что,** *that,* **чтóбы,** *in order that,* **потомý что,** *because;* (4) dependent and relative clauses are separated from principal clauses by a comma; (5) to separate similar parts of speech. You will notice that the use of the comma in Russian is more a matter of *grammar* than for marking pauses or to govern rhythm of speech. Pay attention to commas in the Russian text as you meet them.

Exclamation mark (!): This also is more used in Russian than in English, and always after an imperative: **Возьмúте!** *Take (this).* And after greetings: **Дóброе ýтро!** *Good morning.*

Colon and semi-colon (:, ;): independent clauses related in content but *not* joined by a conjunction are separated by a colon. The semi-colon is used to separate long sentences related in content. You will meet examples of both in the READING, Part II.

RUSSIAN HANDWRITING

1 *Аа*   2 *Бб*   3 *Вв*   4 *Гг*   5 *Дд*

6 *Ее*   7 *Ёё*   8 *Жж*   9 *Зз*   10 *Ии*

11 *Йй*   12 *Кк*   13 *Лл*   14 *Мм*   15 *Нн*

16 *Оо*   17 *Пп*   18 *Рр*   19 *Сс*   20 *Тт*

21 *Уу*   22 *Фф*   23 *Хх*   24 *Цц*   25 *Чч*

26 *Шш*   27 *Щщ*   28 *ъ*   29 *ы*   30 *ь*

31 *Ээ*   32 *Юю*   33 *Яя*

DISTINGUISH BETWEEN 2 AND 5 *б* - *д*
AFTER 16 *о* THE SMALL LETTERS 13.14.33 *Л, М, Я*
ARE NOT JOINED TO THE *о* : *Толстой*
FIRST COPY OUT LETTERS 1 - 30, MEMORISING THEM
IN GROUPS OF FIVE, AND THEN 31 - 33 :
PRACTISE 8, 15, 20, 22, 24, AND 26 TO 33 :

Жж, Мм, Тт, Фф, Цц, Шш,
Щщ, ъ ы, ь, Ээ, Юю, Яя.

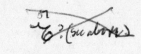

Здра́вствуйте! уче́бник, кни́га, сло́во, *textbook*

каранда́ш, стул, стол, доска́, мел, и, *board chalk and*

учи́тель, да, нет, не, и́ли, Что э́то? *teacher*

Мы в кла́ссе.

SOME NAMES OF PLACES AND PERSONS

А́нглия - Росси́я, С.С.С.Р. - Во́лга - Дон -

Ки́ев - Нева́ - Сталингра́д - Ло́ндон -

Нью Йо́рк - Гла́сго - Манче́стер - *Glasgow Manchester*

Пу́шкин - Турге́нев - Толсто́й - Че́хов -

Чайко́вский - теа́тр - Пастерна́к -

Шо́лохов - Как вы пожива́ете? -

Проко́фьев - Хорошо́ - спаси́бо.

И в са́мом ма́лом
челове́к
с большо́й бу́квы.

*And in the small self
people
with many letters*

Москва,
13го января 1960 г.

Многоуважаемый Георгий Петрович!
    Я получил Ваше любезное письмо с приложением партитуры моего „Кузнеца", переложенную на тоник соль-фа. Я с величайшим увлечением пытался изучить эту табула—туру, — но поскольку я не имею опыта в быстром её прочтении, я не могу высказать Вам моего поло—жительного или отрицательного

See page 293.

CAPITALS AND SMALL LETTERS

Я = I, when not at the beginning of a sentence is always written with a small letter.

Capital letters are used for the first word of a sentence, for the names of persons, and for geographical names. (*ulesos*)

Small letters are used for names of nationalities, whether nouns or adjectives, days of the week, months, seasons and points of the compass.

THE RUSSIAN ITALIC ALPHABET

Аа	*Кк*	*Хх*
Бб	*Лл*	*Цц*
Вв	*Мм*	*Чч*
Гг★	*Нн*	*Шш*
Дд	*Оо*	*Щщ*
Ее	*Пп*	*ъ*
Ёё	*Рр*	*Ыы*
Жж	*Сс*	*ь*
Зз	*Тт*★	*Ээ*
Ии	*Уу*	*Юю*
Йй	*Фф*	*Яя*

★Note italic *г* (**г**)   ★Note italic *т* (**т**)

★With the exception of *г* and *т*, which resemble the same letters in the written alphabet (see pages 18–19), these italics are almost the same as those of the printed alphabet on pages 3–4.

The Russian italic alphabet is used where we would use italics in English: for emphasis or to mark some contrast. In one sense it is much more often used than our English italics: in Russian newspapers and magazines, and in textbooks. Here we often find whole paragraphs in italics where we should prefer normal letters.

HOW TO STUDY LESSONS IN PART I

These hints are chiefly for the benefit of those who are using this book without a teacher. Such learners must realize that they cannot learn to speak Russian unless they hear it spoken. They should get a good Russian speaker to go through pages 3–17 with them, until they can at least make the Russian sounds correctly and recognize them when they hear them spoken. If only a reading knowledge of Russian is aimed at, this should suffice. If the book is studied without a teacher, progress will be helped by following these hints:

(1) Keep two note-books from the outset, one for noting difficult points of grammar, and one for noting words, phrases or idioms which may be found difficult to memorize. Make a habit of going over the two note-books constantly. Use Vocabulary at end of book to check words.

(2) Always make sure that you understand clearly how the grammar *works* before memorizing it. In memorizing words pay particular attention to pronunciation and stress.

(3) One hour of study per day should be the maximum. Do not set yourself a certain amount to learn in a period of study. Be content for some time to take in just what you feel you can master; and no more. Because Russian grammar in the first stage is not easy for the foreign beginner, *get into the habit of regarding accuracy as more important than speed.* Quickness in learning will come as you grow accustomed to the language.

(4) Make a habit of reading aloud all new words as you meet them. Before proceeding to a new Lesson, read aloud two or three times the PRACTICE (**УПРАЖНÉНИЯ**).

(5) Know each Lesson well before proceeding to the next.

(6) Stop at the end of every fifth Lesson and go quickly over *all* the preceding Lessons, making notes of grammar and vocabulary that have not been assimilated. Review these notes constantly until they are known.

(7) At *any* time, when you feel that you are becoming baffled or frustrated, do not get impatient or alarmed. It is merely a sign that you are going too fast. The remedy is not to proceed further but go over back Lessons once again with patience and care. When you feel satisfied and confident you may proceed: not before.

(8) *Basic principles of progress are:* (*a*) an understanding of the grammar and how it applies; (*b*) a knowledge of words and phrases; (*c*) constant practice in (*a*) and (*b*). For those whose aim it is to speak and understand spoken Russian: (*d*) the language must be practised *in speech* as well as in writing.

Finally:

DO NOT MIND SLOW PROGRESS — ESPECIALLY IN THE FIRST STAGE — SO LONG AS YOU KEEP GOING. THE STEADY DAILY EFFORT GIVES THE BEST RESULTS.

LESSON No. 1   УРÓК НÓМЕР ОДИ́Н

Masculine nouns	Feminine nouns	Neuter nouns
брат brother	**дáма** lady	**мя́со** meat
a brother	a lady	a meat
the brother	the lady	the meat
стол table	**кóмната** room	**письмó** letter
a table	a room	a letter
the table	the room	the letter
карандáш pencil	**кни́га** book	**слóво** word
a pencil	a book	a word
the pencil	the book	the word

Masculines	Feminines	Neuters
он HE	**онá** SHE	**онó** IT
тот that (one)	**та** that (one)	**то** that (one)
э́тот this (one)	**э́та** this (one)	**э́то** this (one)
кто? Who?	**что?** What?	**где?** Where? **там** there,
вот Here is,	**да,** yes	**нет,** no over there
are ...	**и** and	**a** but, and **тут** here,
		just here

Ивáн = John.   **Вéра** = Vera.

NOUNS: A noun is a word used for the name of a person, place, thing or state. *Brother, book, room* are nouns. Russian nouns are:

Animate: Those nouns which represent *the living*, whether human beings or animals, are called animate nouns. *Brother, lady* are animate nouns. *Dog, cat, horse* are also animate nouns in Russian.

Inanimate: Those which represent *the lifeless* are called inanimate nouns. *Table, room, word* are inanimate nouns.

GENDER: Russian nouns have three genders: masculine, feminine and neuter. But the gender of a Russian noun does not always correspond to that of its English equivalent. As you see above, **брат** is masculine and **дáма** is feminine.

But **стол** is masculine, **книга** is feminine and **слóво** is neuter. We now come to two rules for the gender of Russian nouns:

> *Rule* 1: **The sex of the living creature determines the gender of animate nouns.**
>
> *Rule* 2: **The gender of an inanimate noun is mostly determined by its final letter.** And so:

Masculine are: nouns ending in *a consonant.*
　　Examples: **стол,** *table* **карандáш,** *pencil.*
Feminine are: nouns which end in **-a.**
　　Examples: **кóмната,** *room* **книга,** *book*
Neuter are: nouns ending in **-o.**
　　Examples: **письмó,** *letter* **слóво,** *word*

These endings are easily memorized from **он, онá, онó:**

> **он** = HE: ends in a consonant and is masculine.
> **онá** = SHE: ends in the letter **-a** and is feminine.
> **онó** = IT: ends in the letter **-o** and is neuter.

Note: It is highly important from the outset to make sure of (*a*) the distinction between animate and inanimate nouns; and (*b*) the gender of *each noun* when you meet it. The two rules given above cover most nouns, and when you come upon a new noun you may assume that it fits one of the rules. But if not, it will be an exception and marked (*m*), (*f*), or (*n*) representing masculine, feminine or neuter, whichever it is. Note this well.

он, онá, онó are personal pronouns. A pronoun is a word used to replace a noun or the name of a person already used, or implied.

тот and **этот** in their various forms are demonstrative adjectives. When used alone they are pronouns:

> **тот** = that man (or *that* referring to a masculine noun).
> **та** = that woman (or *that* referring to a feminine noun).
> **то** = that thing (referring to a neuter noun).

AGREEMENT: When **тот, та, то** and **этот, эта, это** are used with a noun they are used in the gender of that noun.

In this they are said to "agree" with their noun. When so used they are adjectives. An adjective is a word which describes a noun more fully. And so:

тот брат   that brother   **та ко́мната**   that room
то сло́во   that word

and:

э́тот стол   this table   **э́та кни́га**   this book
э́то письмо́   this letter

ARTICLES OMITTED: The English words *a, an* and *the* (which we call "articles") have no equivalents in Russian. Each noun means either *a (an)* or *the* whatever the noun may be, or just the noun without any qualification. **кни́га** = either *book, a book,* or *the book.*

IS and ARE: The words *is* and *are* (present tense of the verb *to be*) are usually omitted in Russian. One says:

брат там = (*a* or *the*) brother (is) there.
кни́га тут = (*a* or *the*) book (is) here.
э́то стол = this (is) *or* it (is) (*a* or *the*) table.

The words in brackets are omitted in Russian.

э́то and то: these neuter forms of **э́тот** and **тот** are also used as demonstrative pronouns. One says: *with these & feminines*

Что э́то? = What (is) this?   *i.e.*
Э́то кни́га = This (is a, the) book.   *Это = this or it is*
Э́то стол = This (is a, the) table.
Где э́то? = Where (is) it?
Э́то там = It (is) over there.

Distinguish carefully between: *menu*

э́тот брат = this brother ⎱ **э́то брат** ⎰ = this (is a, the)
                              ⎰ *AND* ⎱ brother.
э́та да́ма = this lady ⎰ **э́то да́ма** ⎱ = this (is a, the) lady.

э́то сло́во can mean either *this word* or *this (is a, the) word* ⎰* according to the context.

To ask a question: Questions are asked with such words as **кто? что? где?** But a question can be asked by a direct statement such as **Э́то стол?** spoken with the intonation of a

Is this a table?

question. When the answer is **да,** or **нет,** these words are clearly separated from the remainder of the sentence by a comma. **Нет, э́то письмо́.**

Stressed syllable: This is always marked with the accent ('). See page 8. Stress in Russian is highly important.

Pronunciation: There is no difference in the pronunciation of **э́то** and **э́та:** both are pronounced **э́та.** The letter **и-** beginning a word after a word ending in a hard consonant is pronounced **ы** when the two words are joined together in normal speech: **там Ива́н = та́мыва́н.**

How to practise: When you have memorized the Russian words given at the head of the Lesson, and have mastered the explanation of how they are used (the *grammar,* that is), you may proceed to the PRACTICE but not before. Cover up the English translation and do your best to make sense of the Russian text. Then, and not before, refer to the English translation. To make sure of everything, reverse the process and try to make good Russian of the English. If you do this, from the very beginning, it will greatly help your progress. Until you know Russian handwriting, you may print out Russian words in block letters.

PRACTICE: **УПРАЖНЕ́НИЯ**

Take the PRACTICE slowly at first. Be sure that you understand it all before proceeding to the next Lesson. Print out in block letters sentences that you find difficult. Don't attempt Russian handwriting before Lesson 6. The self-taught beginner should try to find a friend to help with pronunciation. If one can be found, read the Russian text aloud and have your pronunciation corrected.

Note: The pronunciation of vowels and consonants given on pages 6–14 is the accepted standard of Moscow and Leningrad. There are some slight deviations from this standard that are permissible:

что is widely pronounced as **што.**

Что э́то?	What is this?
Э́то каранда́ш.	This is a pencil.
А э́то?	And this?
Э́то кни́га.	This is a book.
Э́то ко́мната, а э́то стол.	This is a room and (whereas) this is a table.

Это письмо́, а вот сло́во.	This is a letter and (whereas) this is a word.
Это письмо́?	Is this a letter?
Нет, э́то сло́во.	No, this is a word.
Это кни́га?	Is this a book?
Нет, э́то стол.	No, this is a table.
Это да́ма?	Is this a lady?
Нет, э́то Ве́ра.	No, this is Vera.
Кто э́то?	Who is this? OR Who is it? OR Who is there?
Это да́ма.	This is a (or the) lady. OR It's a (or the) lady.
Эта да́ма?	Is it this lady?
Нет, та.	No, it's that one.
Кто там?	Who is there?
Ива́н.	Ivan.
Где Ива́н?	Where is Ivan?
Там Ива́н.	Ivan is there. OR There's Ivan.
Ива́н тут?	Is Ivan here?
Нет, он там.	No, he's (over) there.
Где Ива́н и Ве́ра?	Where are Ivan and Vera?
Ива́н тут, а Ве́ра там.	Ivan's here and Vera's (over) there.
Он тут, а она́ там.	He's here and (but) she's there.
Да́ма там?	Is the lady there?
Да, она́ там.	Yes, she's there.
Вот где да́ма!	So that's where she (the lady) is!
Где тот каранда́ш?	Where is that pencil?
Этот каранда́ш?	This pencil?
Нет, тот.	No, that (the other) one.
Вот он.	Here it is.
Вот он где, каранда́ш!	So that's where it (the pencil) is!

LESSON No. 2   УРÓК № ДВА (2)

рестора́н	restaurant	таре́лка	plate
хлеб	bread	салфе́тка	table napkin
са́хар	sugar	ма́сло	butter
стул	chair	молоко́	milk
стака́н	glass, tumbler	пи́во	beer
ры́ба	fish	вино́	wine
жена́	wife	кино́ (*indec*)	cinema
же́нщина	woman		

ко́фе = *coffee*. This word is masculine and *indeclinable* in Russian: its form never changes.

INFLEXION: "To inflect" a word means to change some part of it (usually the ending) in order either to modify its meaning or to indicate its relationship with some other word or words. When we say *man, men, man's, men's*, the modifications are "inflexions" of the noun *man*. English has few inflexions; and they are simple.

Russian an "inflected" language: Russian, on the contrary, has many inflexions: it relies on these inflexions to express changes in the meaning of words or the relationship of a word to other words. The inflexions of nouns, pronouns, adjectives and numerals are called "declension"; those of verbs are called "conjugation". These inflexions represent the principal "mechanics" (so to speak) of the Russian language. You will begin by learning the inflexions of nouns, but first of all you must know some terms that are used in grammar.

CASES: When we say "The man has a hat", *man* is the subject and *hat* is the direct object of the verb *has*. When we say "*the man's hat*", *man's* is possessive case of *man*. When we say "the man gave the hat to me", *hat* is direct object of *gives*, and *to me* is the indirect object of the same verb. In Russian it is usual to refer to these "cases" as nominative (= subject case), genitive (= possessive case), accusative (= direct object case) and dative (= indirect object case). In Russian, all these modifications are expressed in the endings of nouns. But there are two more cases in Russian which have to be known: the instrumental and the prepositional cases. Russian has these six cases for the singular of nouns, and six similar cases for the plural.

THE SIX RUSSIAN CASES

Name of the case	What it represents	Answers the question:	
(1) Nominative	the subject; the doer or speaker	Who? кто?	What? что?
(2) Genitive	possession, source of ownership, part of, of	(a) Of whom? Whose? кого?*	(b) Of what? чего?*
(3) Dative	indirect object, indirect recipient of act	(a) to whom? кому?	(b) to what? чему?
(4) Accusative	direct object, direct recipient of action	(a) Whom? кого?	(b) What? что?
(5) Instrumental	the instrument, means or agency by which	(a) By whom? кем?	(b) By what? чем?
(6) Prepositional (often called the locative)	always used after a preposition: for place also for concerning	(a) About whom? о ком? где?	(b) About what? о чём? (c) Where?

In the following sentences, the numeral *after* a word indicates what its case would be in Russian:

> I (1) gave the hat (4) to John (3).
> It(1) was his(2) hat.
> The hat was made by machine(5).
> It is now in the hall(6).

The explanation given here is for the primary or basic signification of each of the six Russian cases, and it must be mastered and always kept in mind.

The *nominative* is the primary (or basic) case of the Russian

*г pronounced as в in -го genitive endings.

noun, and is the case in which every noun is found in vocabularies or dictionaries. All the others (often referred to as the "oblique" cases) are formed from the nominative by means of *endings* which have to be memorized—and memorized so well that one day they will come to you almost without effort, just as we say *man, men, man's, men's*, etc.

DECLENSION OF NOUNS: The system of modifying Russian nouns to indicate their different cases (that is, shades of meaning) is called declension. Very few Russian nouns are indeclinable and these will be marked: (*indec*). You have already met two:

ко́фе (*m*) = coffee. **кино́** (*n*) = cinema.

Nouns indeclinable in Russian are always of foreign origin.

Note: All this about declension may seem a little frightening to the absolute beginner, and reasonably so. Russian children, who already speak their own language fluently, have to master the system of declensions: otherwise they would grow up speaking incorrect (that is, bad) Russian. The foreign student of the language, who does not hear the language all round him, day in and day out, suffers a still greater handicap. The best way for him to learn the Russian declensions is to take them case by case, a little at a time, and *practise assiduously*. In this book they will be simplified down as far as possible, beginning with the next Lesson. Before beginning it make sure that you know what the cases represent.

PRACTICE: **УПРАЖНЕ́НИЯ**

Method of practising: Before you start a new piece, you should *always* run quickly through the Practice in the previous Lesson and, after every four or five Lessons, go through *all* of those four or five PRACTICES. If you feel at any time uncertain about any earlier feature of grammar that you thought you had mastered, go carefully over it again and do the relevant practice again. This may seem laborious, but nothing retards progress in Russian more than pushing ahead in this first stage before words and grammar have been thoroughly assimilated. The self-taught *must* observe some such method as this now suggested. In classwork the teacher will be your guide.

Где рестора́н ?	Where is the restaurant ?
Вот он.	Here it is.
Э́то стол ?	Is this a table ?

Нет, э́то стул, а вот э́то стол.	No, this is a chair and (whereas) this is a table.
Э́тот стол?	Is it this table? (Is this our table?)
Нет, тот.	No, that one.
Вот хлеб, а ма́сло там.	Here is the bread and the butter is over there.
Э́то хлеб, а то ма́сло.	This is bread and that is butter.
Э́то вино́, а э́то пи́во.	This is wine and this is beer.
Э́то вино́?	Is this wine?
Нет, э́то пи́во.	No, this is beer.
Э́то вино́?	Is it this wine?
Нет, то.	No, (it's) that one.
Э́то же́нщина?	Is this a woman?
(Да, э́то) же́нщина.	Yes, it is.
Э́та же́нщина?	Is it this woman?
Нет, та.	No, that one.
Где тут рестора́н?	Where is there a restaurant here? *or* Where is the restaurant here (i.e. which I believe should be here)?

see ✱ p.25

Pronunciation: When pronouncing words of more than two syllables, such as **каранда́ш** and **рестора́н**, be particularly careful to avoid the double stress to which English speakers are naturally prone, and which is completely alien to Russian speech. In the two words quoted, the first syllable should be very short with hardly any distinct vowel sound at all, the second is somewhat longer (although **o**, being unstressed, is pronounced as **a**) and the full stress falls on the final syllable.

К вопросу о репке...   **Рисунок Д. Донева**, Болгария.

LESSON No. 3   УРÓК № ТРИ (3)

билéт	ticket	гостѝница	hotel
багáж	luggage	кáсса	cash desk *cashier*
пóезд	train	дéло	business
вокзáл	station	селó	village
фунт	pound (*lb. and £*)	крéсло	armchair
газéта	newspaper	перó	pen, feather
ýлица	street	мя́со	meat
телегрáмма	telegram		

Nominatives: кто? Who?   что? What?
Genitives: когó? of whom?   чегó? of what?

NOMINATIVE CASE: The nominative is the primary case in all declinable words: nouns, pronouns, adjectives and numerals. From it all other cases can be formed. It answers the questions *Who?* and *What?* The nominative case represents the subject in a sentence (that is, the *doer* or *speaker*). The name of a person addressed is also in the nominative, as: Ivan, where is the luggage?=**Ивáн, где багáж?**

Possessive pronouns, nominatives:

Masculines	*Feminines*	*Neuters*
мой =my	моя́ =my	моё =my
ваш =your	вáша =your	вáше =your

The masculine forms are used before masculine nouns in the nominative, the feminines before feminine nouns, the neuters before neuter nouns:

мой билéт=my ticket.   моя́ газéта=my newspaper.
моё дéло=my business.
ваш багáж=your luggage.
вáша гостѝница=your hotel.
вáше крéсло=your armchair.

GENITIVE CASE: The Russian genitive corresponds to our English possessive case and answers the questions *Whose? Of whom? Of what?*

It is used (1) to indicate *possession* or *ownership*.
          (2) to indicate *relationship*.
          (3) to indicate *quantity of.*

Examples: (1) **багáж дáмы** = the lady's luggage
          (2) **женá брáта** = the brother's wife
          (3) **фунт мя́са** = a pound of meat

FORMATION OF THE GENITIVE OF NOUNS: To form the genitive case of a noun, drop the nominative ending and add:

-**a** for *masculine* nouns. -**ы** for *feminine* nouns.
        -**a** for *neuter* nouns.

(*Note:* Masculine and neuter genitives are the same.)

Examples of the genitive of nouns

	Masculine nouns	Feminines	Neuters
Nominatives:	**стол**	**кóмната**	**слóво**
Genitives:	**столá** (*note stress*)	**кóмнаты**	**слóва**

RULES OF ORTHOGRAPHY: In Russian great importance is attached to the sounds of words, and certain combinations of letters are not tolerated on grounds of incompatibility. This is so general a principle that it is provided for by the following Rules of Spelling:

1. *After* { **г к х / ж ч ш щ** } *write* -**и** *and never* -**ы**

2. *After* { **г к х / ж ч ш щ / ц** } *write* -**а**, -**у** *and never* -**я**, -**ю**

3. If the syllable is unstressed:
  After { **ж ч ш щ / ц** } *write* -**е** *and not* -**о**

These rules are simple to memorize, but in practice may at first cause the beginner some trouble. They are highly important for, as will be appreciated as you proceed, they apply throughout the language, and affect pronunciation (see

MUTATIONS, page 165). You may now take nouns already known and see how the rules are applied in the formation of the genitive case:

feminine

	Nominatives	Genitives
book	кни́га	кни́ги
plate	таре́лка	таре́лки
table napkin (serviette) }	салфе́тка	салфе́тки

} *rule 1, p. 33*

These are the only nouns given up to this point in which the RULES OF ORTHOGRAPHY apply. All others form their genitives in accordance with the simple rule given for formation on page 33. Thus:

MASCULINES:

Nominatives: брат   каранда́ш   рестора́н
Genitives: бра́та   карандаша́   рестора́на
Nominatives: хлеб   са́хар
Genitives: хле́ба   са́хара

FEMININES:

Nominatives: ры́ба   жена́   же́нщина
Genitives: ры́бы   жены́   же́нщины
Nominatives: гости́ница   газе́та
Genitives: гости́ницы   газе́ты

NEUTERS:

Nominatives: мя́со   молоко́   письмо́   вино́
Genitives: мя́са   молока́   письма́   вина́
Nominatives: пи́во   село́   кре́сло
Genitives: пи́ва   села́   кре́сла

FULL DECLENSION OF NOUNS: The changes you have learnt in this Lesson for the formation of the genitive case are your first step towards learning the full declensions of nouns. The full declension of a noun or other word consists of all six cases in the singular and plural. You will learn the whole system a little at a time.

PRACTICE: **УПРАЖНЕНИЯ**

Вот моя жена.	Here is my wife.
Эта дама — ваша жена?	Is this lady your wife?
Где мой багаж?	Where is my luggage?
Вот он.	Here it is.
Что это, ваш билет?	What is this, is it your ticket?
Это ваша газета?	Is this your newspaper?
(Да, это) моя (газета).	It is.
Это книга жены.	This is my wife's book.
Вот комната брата.	Here is my brother's room.
Вера — жена Ивана.	Vera is Ivan's wife.
Где салфетка Веры?	Where is Vera's table-napkin?
Где тут вокзал?	Where is the railway station here?
Вот ваш поезд.	Here is your train.
Это ваш стакан.	This is your glass.
Этот стакан — ваш?	Is this your glass? or Is this glass yours?
Этот стакан вина — мой.	This glass of wine is mine.
Вот стакан пива.	Here is a glass of beer.
Где ваше кресло?	Where is your armchair?
Это моё дело.	That's my affair.

Pronunciation: Remember the rules for the pronunciation of voiced and voiceless consonants (p. 12): **багаж** is pronounced as **багаш**, **поезд** as **поист**, **вокзал** as **вагзал.**

LESSON No. 4   УРОК № ЧЕТЫРЕ (4)

господин	Mr, gentleman	**госпожа**	Mrs, Miss
мальчик	boy	**девочка**	(little) girl
студент	student	**школа**	school
ключ	key	**доска**	blackboard
табак	tobacco	**шляпа**	hat

дерево   tree; wood (*material*)

отечество   fatherland

хорошо (*adv*)   well; all right; fine!

читайте!   Read (it)!

пишите!   Write (it)!

здра́вствуйте! This word is used as a general greeting, and can be used on most occasions at any time of the day or night. It can be used for *Good morning, good day, good afternoon, good evening*, but it is used when meeting somebody, and not when taking leave. It has in it something of the friendly *Hello!* and *How are you?* or *How are things?* Pronounce as if written: **здра́ссте.**

ACCUSATIVE CASE: This answers the questions *Whom?* and *What* (when this is direct object).

> *Nominatives:* **кто?** = Who?   **что?** = What?
> *Genitives:*   **кого́?** = Whose?   **чего́?** = Of what?
> *Accusatives:* **кого́?** = Whom?   **что?**   = What?

The accusative case of the noun is used for the *direct* object of a transitive verb. This must be explained:

A verb is a word which expresses action, motion or being.

A verb is said to be *transitive* when the action does not stop with the doer but *passes on* to some person or thing. Thus: John *struck* William. The mouse *ate* the cheese. I *wind* my watch. The words *struck, ate* and *wind* are transitive verbs.

An *intransitive* verb is one in which the action does *not* pass on from the doer. Thus John *writes* nicely. William *sat* still. Mary *sings* beautifully. The words *writes, sat,* and *sings* are intransitive verbs.

Some verbs can be used either transitively or intransitively: *eat* and *sing* are examples. When you say *I eat meat,* here *eat* is transitive, and *meat* is its direct object. *Mary then sang a song:* here *sang* is transitive and *song* is its direct object. But when you say *I eat, I sing* no object is named: the action does not pass on but remains with the doer. Hence, *eat* and *sing* are here intransitive verbs.

Subject and direct object: In Russian, the subject is in the nominative case, the *direct* object is in the accusative. You will require verbs to illustrate this, and we shall come to them very soon. Meanwhile, you will learn to form the accusative case of nouns.

Formation of the accusative of masculine nouns: There are two simple rules:

(1) *Masculine animate nouns* have their accusative the same as their genitive.

(2) *Masculine inanimate nouns* have their accusative the same as their nominative. And so:

	Masculine animate			Masculine inanimate	
Nominative:	студе́нт	} acc	стол	} acc	
Genitive:	студе́нта	} like	стола́	} like	
Accusative:	студе́нта	} gen	стол	} nom	

Accusative of feminine nouns : These form their accusative by changing the ending of the nominative to **-y**, irrespective of whether they are animates or inanimates. Thus:

	Feminine animate		Feminine inanimate
Nom:	да́ма	animates and inanimates the same	шля́па
Gen:	да́мы		шля́пы
Acc:	да́му		шля́пу

Accusative of neuter nouns : The accusative of neuter nouns is the same as the nominative. Thus:

Nom:	сло́во	село́
Gen:	сло́ва	села́
Acc:	сло́во	село́

Rule of Orthography : See Lesson No. 3. Do not ever forget that it always applies.

Stress : You will have noted that there is sometimes a change of stress in declension. Always make a careful note of it.

PRACTICE: **УПРАЖНЕ́НИЯ**

Где моя́ шля́па ?	Where is my hat ?
Вот она́.	Here it is.
Кто э́тот господи́н ?	Who is this (*or* that) gentleman ?
Э́то господи́н Бра́ун.	That (*or* this) is Mr. Brown.
Кто э́та да́ма ?	Who is this (*or* that) lady ?
Э́то госпожа́ Уа́йт.	That (*or* this) is Mrs White.
Где ваш таба́к ?	Where is your tobacco ?

Вот фунт табака́.	Here is a pound of tobacco.
Э́то ва́ше письмо́ ?	Is this your letter ?
Чита́йте ва́ше письмо́!	Read your letter.
Пиши́те письмо́!	Write the letter.
Вот кни́га господи́на Бра́у-на.	Here is Mr Brown's book.
Нет, э́то кни́га госпожи́ Уа́йт.*	No, this is Mrs White's book.
Чита́йте кни́гу!	Read the book.

*Women's surnames of non-Russian form are not declined.

Pronunciation: **ва́ше** is pronounced as **ва́ша.** In **пиши́те** and **госпожи́,** remember that **и** after **ж** and **ш** is pronounced as **ы.**

LESSON No. 5　　　　　　УРОК № ПЯТЬ (5)

First names: men		First names: women	
Алексе́й	Alexis	**А́нна** Anna, Anne	
Бори́с	Boris	**Ли́дия** Lydia	
Влади́мир	Vladimir	**Мари́я** Mary	
Григо́рий	Gregory	**Татья́на** Tatyana	
Па́вел	Paul	**Ната́лия** Natalia	
Пётр	Peter	**Тама́ра** Tamara	
Гео́ргий **Ю́рий** } George		**Людми́ла** Ludmila	

Surnames

Тю́тчев
Голови́н
Маяко́вский
Баже́нов
Короле́нко
Трубецко́й
Усти́нов

RUSSIAN NAMES OF PERSONS: In Russian there are:

(1) the first (*or* Christian) name—**и́мя**, *gen* **и́мени.**

(2) the patronymic, made from the father's name—
о́тчество.

(3) the family name (surname)—**фами́лия.**

Examples: **Ива́н Ива́нович Ове́чкин** = John, son of
John, Ovechkin.

Мари́я Серге́евна Кондра́тьева = Mary,
daughter of Sergei, Kondrat'ev.

Russian adults usually address one another by their first
name and patronymic. This is the commonly accepted
formal mode of address and does not necessarily imply any
intimacy. In the above examples, Mrs Kondrat'ev would
address Mr Ovechkin as **Ива́н Ива́нович** and he would call
her **Ма́рия Серге́евна.** And so the first thing one has to
find out when meeting Russians (either socially or in business) is their first name and patronymic (**и́мя-о́тчество**).
You ask the question:

Как ва́ше и́мя-о́тчество? = What is your name and
patronymic?

Pronunciation: The **и́мя - о́тчество** are pronounced together as one word and inevitably some slurring occurs.
Thus:

Ива́н Ива́нович is usually pronounced as **ванва́нч.**

Пётр Па́влович is usually pronounced as **пётпалч.**

Алекса́ндр Алексе́евич is usually pronounced as
са́нликсе́ич.

А́нна Ива́новна is usually pronounced as **а́ныва́нна.**

Мари́я Никола́евна is usually pronounced as **ма́рь-
никола́вна.**

Ли́дия Миха́йловна is usually pronounced as **ли́дь-
миха́лна.**

Memorize the names given in this Lesson.

Russian surnames: Most of these have a masculine and a
feminine form. The commonest masculine forms end in
-ов, -ев, -ин which have respectively the feminine forms

-ова, -ева, -ина to correspond. A smaller number of surnames have forms like those of adjectives:

Толсто́й, Толста́я ; Го́рький, Достое́вский.

Surnames of origin other than Russian have no feminine forms.

Russian names of persons are declined, and this will be dealt with later. Sufficient has been given here to show the beginner how the system works. (The whole subject will be dealt with at greater length in Part II, Lesson 31).

PRACTICE: **УПРАЖНЕ́НИЯ**

Кто э́та да́ма ?	Who is that lady ?
Э́та да́ма — госпожа́ Усти́нова.	That lady is Mrs Ustinov.
Э́то А́нна Ива́новна Усти́нова.	That's Anna Ivanovna Ustinov.
Здра́вствуйте, А́нна Ива́новна!	How do you do, Anna Ivanovna.
Чита́йте письмо́, Пётр Па́влович!	Read the letter, Pyotr Pavlovich.
Хорошо́, Мари́я Никола́евна.	Very well, Marya Nikolaevna. _this_
Кто э́тот господи́н ?	Who is that gentleman ?
Э́тот господи́н — Алекса́ндр Ива́нович Голови́н.	That gentleman is Alexander Ivanovich Golovin.
Вот Ната́лия Петро́вна, моя́ жена́.	This is my wife — Natalia Petrovna.
Брат Алекса́ндра Алексе́евича — студе́нт.	Alexander Alekseyvitch's brother is a student.
Пётр Алексе́евич, где Людми́ла Григо́риевна ?	Pyotr Alekseyevich, where is Ludmila Grigorievna ?
Она́ тут. Вот она́ где!	She's here. So that's where she is!
Тама́ра Влади́мировна, пиши́те письмо́!	Write the letter, Tamara Vladimirovna.
Кто э́тот студе́нт ?	Who is that student ?

А э́то брат Татья́ны Бори́совны.	Oh, that's Tatyana Borisovna's brother.
А как его́ и́мя-о́тчество?	And what is he called? (*or* How does one address him?)
И́мя-о́тчество господи́на Кондра́тьева — Гео́ргий Бори́сович	Mr Kondrat'ev is called George Borisovich.

LESSON No. 6   УРОК № ШЕСТЬ (6)

граждани́н (*m*) citizen	гражда́нка (*f*) citizeness
това́рищ (*m & f*) comrade	бума́га paper
по-ру́сски (*adv*) in Russian	ка́рта map
пожа́луйста please	карти́на picture
спаси́бо thank you, thanks	по-англи́йски (*adv*) in English

a and, but, whole
но but (**a**=a difference, **но**=a contrast)
не not
ничего́ nothing (**г** pronounced as **в**)
когда́ when
никогда́ never

я	ты	он	она́	оно́	мы	вы	они́
I	thou	he	she	it	we	you	they

чита́ть (I) to read   **знать** (I) to know

PERSONAL PRONOUNS: *I, thou, he, she, it, we, you, they* are the personal pronouns, for which Russian equivalents are given above. *I, thou, he, she, it* are singular (representing one person) and *we, you, they* are plural (representing more than one person). By usage in both Russian and English, *you* **(вы)** which are plural in form, are commonly used in addressing either one person or more.

I and *we* are first person, singular and plural. *Thou* and *you* are second person, singular and plural. *He, she, it* are third person singular; and *they* is third person plural.

The Russian pronoun **ты**=*thou* is very much more used than the archaic English *thou*. **ты** is used among friends, colleagues, intimates, relations and children, but should never be used by the foreigner when addressing Russians (unless they are *very* well known, and they have first used the second person singular when addressing him or her). **вы** must be the general rule.

CONJUGATION OF VERBS: The system of inflexion of verbs (called "conjugation") is the change of endings according to person (1st, 2nd, and 3rd) and number (singular and plural) and this is found only in verbs. ("Declension", as you know, is the changing of ending according to case, number and gender: nouns, adjectives, numerals, pronouns. Some verbal forms are declined in Russian.)

As you will see, when a Russian verb is conjugated, the endings of the present tense change for *each person* in the singular and plural. There are other changes which you will learn, each representing a change of meaning.

The simplicity of Russian verbs: In languages such as French, German, Spanish, Latin and Greek, *each* of the many tenses of a verb has a conjugation of its own. But in Russian each verb has only *one* tense that is conjugated. In the basic verbs that you will use in Part I of this book (they are verbs of the "imperfective aspect", of which you will learn later; see diagram on page 192) this conjugated tense is always *present in meaning*. That is, it refers only to something that is now happening.

VERBS OF THE FIRST CONJUGATION: The first conjugation verbs are characterized by the presence of the letter **"е"** in all persons other than the 1st person singular and the third person plural of the conjugated tense.

In the simplest type of first conjugation verb, when you cut off the **-ть** of the infinitive this leaves a *stem* which always ends in a vowel. Thus, the infinitive **читáть** gives the stem **читá-**. To this stem are added the endings **-ю, -ешь, -ет, -ем, -ете, -ют,** and in this way the conjugated tense of the verb is formed.

Model verbs of Conjugation (I): **-ать** *in the infinitive, with* **е** *in the second person singular of present tense:*

$$Infinitives \begin{cases} \textbf{читáть} \text{ (I) to read} \\ \textbf{знать} \quad \text{ (I) to know} \end{cases}$$

Affirmative

я	чита́ю	I read, do read, am reading
ты	чита́ешь	you (*thou*) read, are reading
он, она́ } оно́ }	чита́ет	he, she } it } reads, is reading
мы	чита́ем	we read, are reading
вы	чита́ете	you read, are reading
они́	чита́ют	they read, are reading

Negative

я	не зна́ю	I do not know
ты	не зна́ешь	you (=*thou*) do not know
он } она́ } не зна́ет оно́ }		he } she } does not know it }
мы	не зна́ем	we do not know
вы	не зна́ете	you do not know
они́	не зна́ют	they do not know

Note that in this conjugated tense (which in future, for convenience in referring to these basic (or "imperfective") verbs shall be called the "present" tense) the one Russian form can have three equivalents in English, as in *I read, do read, am reading*, etc.

Note also in the negative form that **не** always comes immediately before the verb.

Formation of 3rd person plural, conjugation (I): The 3rd person plural of any first conjugation verb is made by adding **т** to the first person singular. There are no exceptions to this rule.

ACCUMULATIVE NEGATIVE IN RUSSIAN: The negative **не** (called the "negative particle"—for particles see page 275) is the essential hard core of any negative phrase in Russian. One can increase its negative force (or amplify it) by adding other negative words such as **никогда́**=*never* and **ничего́**=*nothing*, but remember that **не** must always retain its place immediately before the verb. Thus:

я никогда́ не чита́ю = I never read.

он ничего́ не зна́ет = He knows nothing (does not know anything).

вы никогда́ ничего́ не чита́ете = You never read anything.

In this, Russian permits (indeed *insists on*) something that is not permissible in English grammar: the "double negative".

Omission of Russian personal pronoun: The inflexions of the conjugated (present) tense indicate the persons but, in the 3rd person singular, *he, she* or *it* may have to be written or spoken to avoid confusion. In all other persons, singular or plural, the personal pronoun is very often omitted. **не чита́ю** = *I don't read* or *am not reading*. But: **он, она́ не чита́ет** = *he, she doesn't read, is not reading*.

Pronunciation: Although "**e**" is the mark of conjugation (I) verbs, it is never pronounced **e** in these endings. Mostly the endings are unstressed, and then **e** is pronounced **и**. *When stressed it is pronounced* **ё**.

не being a particle has no stress of its own. In the majority of instances it is pronounced **ни** (unstressed) *and* run on to the following word:

> **я не чита́ю** pronounce as **я "ничита́ю"**

Very occasionally the stress of the verb is thrown back to the **не**. When this occurs attention will be drawn to it.

*

    (1) **господи́н; госпожа́** = Mr., Mrs.; Miss.
    (2) **граждани́н, гражда́нка** = citizen, citizeness.
    (3) **това́рищ** = Comrade. *Also* pal, mate etc.

(1) are used for Mr, Mrs and Miss among emigrés but never among citizens of the USSR, where they are used in referring to foreigners. The singular forms are used only in the 3rd person. The plural forms **господа́** ("gentlemen" or "ladies and gentlemen") is commonly used in the 2nd person, even somewhat facetiously, in the USSR.

(2) These are in common use in the USSR, and are the forms the foreigner should use.

(3) is used in one form for masculine and feminine and, strictly, among members of the Communist Party. But its use has been extended to include colleagues and respected, though not necessarily intimate friends.

PRACTICE: **УПРАЖНЕ́НИЯ**

Я чита́ю кни́гу, а вы (чита́ете) письмо́.	I am reading a book, but (whereas) you (are reading) a letter.

Мы читáем по-рýсски, а они́ по-англи́йски.	We read Russian, but they read English.
Я не знáю этого слóва.	I don't know this word.
Онá не знáет э́того слóва.	She doesn't know this word.
Э́тот господи́н хорошó знáет брáта.	This gentleman knows (my) brother well.
Я не знáю, где ваш багáж.	I don't know where your luggage is.
Вéра Ивáновна не знáет, когдá урóк.	Vera Ivanovna doesn't know when the lesson is.
Ли́дия Петрóвна хорошó читáет по-англи́йски.	Lydia Petrovna reads English well.
Мы знáем, кто хорошó читáет по-рýсски, а кто нет.	We know who reads Russian well and who doesn't.
Они́ никогдá ничегó не читáют.	They never read anything.
Я никогдá не знáю, где моя́ шля́па.	I never know where my hat is.
Кто знáет, где вокзáл?	Who knows where the railway station is?
Кто знáет, когдá урóк?	Who knows when the lesson is?
Кто э́то читáет газéту?	Who is that reading a newspaper?
Э́то товáрищ Мóлотов читáет газéту.	That's Comrade Molotov reading a (his) newspaper.
Граждани́н Ойстрáх не знáет, где гости́ница.	Citizen Oistrakh doesn't know where the (his) hotel is.
Господи́н Усти́нов знáет, где э́та ýлица.	Mr Ustinov knows where this (that) street is.
Товáрищ Улáнова хорошó читáет по-англи́йски.	Comrade Ulanova reads English well.
Господá, читáйте телегрáмму!	(Ladies and) gentlemen, read the telegram.
Господá, вы никогдá ничегó не знáете!	(Ladies and) gentlemen, you never know anything!

Russian handwriting: All learners should now begin to practise the written alphabet on pages 18 and 19, taking about five capitals and small letters at a time. When you know them all, copy out carefully the words on page 19. By Lesson 10 you should be able to write Russian words to be memorized. Keep a note book for this purpose.

LESSON No. 7　　　　УРОК № СЕМЬ (7)

де́лать (I)　to do, make	**пиани́но** (*indec*)　piano
ду́мать (I)　to think	**сего́дня**　to-day
жела́ть (I)　to wish, desire	(*pr* сиво́дни)
игра́ть (I)　to play	**ещё**　yet, still, again *more*
начина́ть (I)　to begin	**ещё не . . .**　not yet . . .
конча́ть (I)　to end, finish	(*with verb only*)
спра́шивать (I)　to ask	**раз**　one; once (*adv*); *also a*
отвеча́ть (I)　to answer	*noun* time (*m*)
ку́шать (I)　to eat	**уже́**　already
понима́ть (I)　to under-	**ча́сто**　often
stand	**до́ма** (*adv*)　at home
футбо́л　football	**и́ли**　or
те́ннис　tennis	

как (*adv*) = how.	**так** = so, like this, this way.
так как = as	**ли** = interrogative particle.

CONJ. (I) "e" VERBS: All the verbs given above are conjugated like the model **чита́ть** (I) *to read.*

жела́ть (I) *to wish, desire* when followed by a noun has that noun (or pronoun) in the genitive case.

PARTICLES: In the last Lesson you had the negative particle **не.** Now you have the interrogative particle **ли.** A particle is a word that is neither noun, adjective, pronoun or verb but is used to impart a particular meaning to some other word, phrase or sentence. It need not necessarily have any meaning of itself, as in **ли,** for example.

Interrogative particle ли: So called because it is used only in asking questions, as in: **тут ли он ?** = *Is he here ?*

ли is placed immediately *after* the word to be emphasized:

там ли он ? = Is he *there* ?

он ли там ? = Is *he* there ?

читáет ли он ? = Is he *reading* ?   Does he *read* ?

If the verb is in the negative, the negative is placed *first*, then the verb, then ли:

не читáете ли вы ? = Do you not read ?

Note (a): As you have seen, questions can be asked in Russian by merely making a statement and raising the voice:

он там ? = Is he there ?

Note (b): When the question is *indirect* as in *I wish to know whether Vera is there*, the interrogative particle ли *must* be used:

Я желáю знать, там ли Вéра.

—to which the answer is either да, or merely там (= she is); or нет, or не там (= she is not).

Note (c): The use of the interrogative particle is optional except in (*b*) and in negative interrogatives.

PUNCTUATION: You have seen that after the word знать in the example of an indirect question there is a comma. In Russian a comma is *always* used to separate closely related clauses in a sentence, often where we do not use one in English. Note also the comma after да, and нет, which mean *yes* and *no* only when followed by a punctuation mark and then other words.

ACCUSATIVE CASE = DIRECT OBJECT: The direct object of a transitive verb *in the affirmative* is always in the accusative case.   Thus:

я читáю кнѝгу = I read a book.

However, certain transitive verbs take a direct object in a case other than the accusative.   These should be carefully memorized, for instance, желáть, which takes its direct object in the genitive:

чегó вы желáете ? = What do you want ?

(част 4то)

GENITIVE CASE AFTER NEGATION:

After verbs in the negative the direct object is generally in the genitive case and not in the accusative. Thus:

я не читаю письма = I am not reading the (a) letter.
она не кушает мяса = She doesn't eat meat.

нет not only means *no* but also *is not, is no* or *there is no, there is not.* When used in this way, the noun following is always in the genitive:

нет книги = There is no book.
нет карандаша = There is no pencil.

OBJECT OF THE VERB ИГРАТЬ to play:

In English we say "to play tennis", "to play the piano", with the game or the instrument forming the direct object of the verb, but in similar instances in Russian one must say "to play at . . .", "to play on . . .": the game or the instrument must be preceded by a preposition either **в** "at", or **на** "on":

Он играет в футбол = He plays (at) football.

Она играет на пианино = She is playing (on) the piano.

в is used of games and **на** of musical instruments.

PRACTICE: УПРАЖНЕНИЯ

Вера Александровна хорошо понимает по-английски.	Vera Alexandrovna understands English well.
Я уже понимаю по-русски.	I already understand Russian.
Понимаете ли вы по-русски?	Do you understand Russian?
Они ещё не понимают, как играть в теннис.	They do not yet understand how to play tennis. (They still can't understand . . .)
Я не понимаю письма брата.	I don't (can't) understand my brother's letter.
Что вы тут делаете?	What are you doing here?
Что она там делает?	What is she doing there?
Она начинает играть на пианино.	She is beginning to play the piano.

Хорошо́ ли она́ игра́ет на пиани́но?	Does she play the piano well?
Игра́ете ли вы на пиани́но?	Do you play the piano?
Э́тот ма́льчик никогда́ не игра́ет в футбо́л.	This (that) boy never plays football.
Моя́ жена́ никогда́ не ку́шает ры́бы.	My wife never eats fish.
Сего́дня мы ничего́ не де́лаем.	We're not doing anything to-day.
Они́ жела́ют знать, когда́ уро́к.	They want to know when the lesson is.
Как вы ду́маете, где Ива́н Бори́сович?	What do you think (= What's your opinion), where is Ivan Borisovich?
Сего́дня он до́ма.	He's at home to-day.
Он уже́ до́ма. До́ма ли она́?	He's already at home. Is she at home?
Он ничего́ не отвеча́ет.	He doesn't answer anything.
Как она́ э́то де́лает?	How does she do this (it)?
Я не зна́ю, как он э́то де́лает.	I don't know how he does this (it).
Я не зна́ю, как э́то де́лать.	I don't know how to do this.
Вы э́то де́лаете так, а я так.	You do it that way and I do it this way.
Он отвеча́ет так, а она́ так.	He answers this way and she that way.
Ча́сто ли он игра́ет в футбо́л?	Does he *often* play football?
Он ли ча́сто игра́ет в футбо́л?	Does *he* play football often?
Как ча́сто вы игра́ете в те́ннис?	How often do you play tennis?
Жела́ете ли мя́са или ры́бы?	Do you want (Will you have) meat or fish?
Жела́ете ли ещё?	Do you want (Will you have) (some) more?
Ещё, пожа́луйста.	Some more, please.
Ещё раз, пожа́луйста.	Once more please.

Читáйте ещё раз!   Read (it) once more.

Они́ начинáют урóк, а мы   They are starting their lesson,
уже́ кончáем.   whereas we are already finishing ours.

Pronunciation of particles and prepositions: It is important to remember that these have no stress of their own and are always pronounced as if part of the following word (ли, however, is pronounced as if part of the preceding word). в футбóл as ффутбóл ; в тéннис as фтéннис.

— Электрóнная пáмять, где мои́ очки?!

LESSON No. 8   УРОК № ВÓСЕМЬ (8)

англичáнин   Englishman
англичáнка   Englishwoman
америкáнец   American (*m*)   (*gen* америкáнца)
америкáнка   American (*f*)
магази́н   store, shop
учени́к   pupil (*m*)
учéбник   textbook
автóбус   bus, omnibus

водá   water
учени́ца   pupil (*f*)
контóра   office
буты́лка   bottle
чтó-то   something
почему́?   Why?
потому́ что   because
тóже   also
тóлько   only
плóхо (*adv*)   badly

сигарета=*cigarette*, American or English type.
папироса=*cigarette*, Russian type, with card mouthpiece.
дайте мне . . .=Give me . . .

PERSONAL PRONOUNS—DECLENSION: Personal pronouns are fully declined in Russian: they have six cases in the singular and plural. Let us begin with:

	I	thou	he	she	it
Nominatives:	я	ты	он	она	оно
Genitives:	меня	тебя	его	её	его
Accusatives:	меня	тебя	его	её	его

[handwritten: ⎫ same]

You see that the genitives and accusatives of these pronouns are the same.

Pronunciation: The **г** in the genitive and accusative endings of these pronouns is pronounced as **в : его = иво**. (The feminine genitive is often pronounced as **ия**.)

PREPOSITIONS: A preposition is a word placed before a noun or pronoun to make clear its relation (especially in regard to direction or place) to another word. A Russian preposition may "govern" any case except the nominative. In practice, this means that every preposition must be followed by its pronoun or noun in the case which the preposition governs. Take, for example:

для+*genitive*=*for*, **без**+*gen*=*without*.

у+*gen*=*near; at, at the house of;* and *possession.*

These three prepositions "govern" the genitive case. Thus:

для меня=for me. **без работы**=without work.

у дома=near, at (my) house. *[handwritten: that's N, not H]*

[handwritten: nom: dom]

Prepositions before third person personal pronouns: After a governing preposition, the letter **н-** is added before all cases except the nominative of third person pronouns. Thus:

его his **её** her **его** its *[handwritten: he, she, it]*

become: **него** **неё** **него** after a preposition.

"TO HAVE" in Russian: There is a verb (**иметь**) for *to have,* but its use is rather specialized and it will be dealt with later. By far the commonest form, the one which you will use for some time, is the preposition **y**+the pronoun in the *genitive*+the word **есть** (third person singular of **быть**=*to be (irregular)*. The idiom is **y меня́ есть,** etc., which means *by* or *at me is*, etc. Hence, using this formula, you get the following:

I have	=	у меня́ есть	or	у меня́
(familiar) you have	=	у тебя́ есть	or	у тебя́
he has	=	у него́ есть	or	у него́
she has	=	у неё есть	or	у неё
it has	=	у него́ есть	or	у него́

Note that **есть** may be omitted, as it generally is in conversation. If you remember the literal meaning of this formula, and know that the verb *to be* is intransitive, it follows that the noun which follows will be in the *nominative*. Thus:

у меня́ (есть) кни́га   = I have a book.
у него́ (есть) каранда́ш = he has a pencil.
у неё (есть) шля́па   = she has a hat.

—and so on.

TO HAVE in the negative: You must use **нет** (=*no, not, a*) with the genitive. Thus:

у меня́ нет кни́ги   = I have no book.
у тебя́ нет карандаша́ = you *(fam)* have no pencil.
у него́ нет шля́пы   = he has no hat.

—and so on.   ← *nom:* ШЛЯПА

INTERROGATIVES: Questions may be asked either with or without the interrogative particle **ли:**

у меня́?
or: у меня́ есть?   } Have I?
or: есть ли у меня́?

It need hardly be emphasized that the verb *to have* occurs as frequently in Russian as in English. It is therefore important for you to become quite familiar with this idiomatic way of expressing it. This requires careful practice.

PRACTICE: **УПРАЖНÉНИЯ**

Вы понимáете меня́?	Do you understand me?
Понимáет ли онá егó?	Does she understand him?
Как по-рýсски . . . ?	What is the Russian for . . . ?
Онá меня́ чáсто спрáшивает, как э́то слóво по-рýсски.	She often asks me the Russian for this word.
Почемý э́тот ученúк так плóхо понимáет по-англúйски?	Why does this pupil understand English so badly?
У негó есть учéбник? Есть.	Has he a textbook? Yes (he has).
У негó ли учéбник? У негó.	Has he the textbook? He has.
Учéбник у неё? У неё.	Has she (got) the textbook? She has.
Дáйте мне папирóсу, пожáлуйста.	Give me a cigarette, please.
Э́то не папирóса, а сигарéта.	This isn't a Russian cigarette, but an English-type cigarette.
У негó нет папирóсы.	He hasn't got a Russian cigarette.
У англичáнина тóлько одúн карандáш.	The Englishman has only one pencil.
Есть ли у америкáнки брат?	Has the American woman a brother?
Нет ли газéты у америкáнца?	Hasn't the American a newspaper?
У англичáнки сегóдня ничегó нет.	The Englishwoman hasn't got anything to-day.
Сегóдня у неё тóлько одúн урóк.	She has only one lesson to-day
Англичáнин чтó-то читáет.	The Englishman is reading something.
Егó сегóдня нет дóма. Почемý?	He isn't at home to-day (He's out . . .). Why?

Потому́ что сего́дня он игра́ет в футбо́л.	Because he's playing football to-day.
Так вы игра́ете на пиани́но! Я то́же.	So you play the piano! So do I.
У тебя́ ли бума́га? Нет, у него́.	Have you got the (writing) paper? No, he has.
Как пло́хо она́ игра́ет на пиани́но! А он тоже!	How badly she plays the piano! And so does he!
У меня́ нет пиани́но. А у вас есть?	I haven't a piano. Have you?

LESSON No. 9   УРОК № ДЕ́ВЯТЬ (9)

слон elephant
осёл donkey, ass
счёт bill, account (сч pronounced as щ)
ру́сский язы́к (pr изы́к) (the) Russian language
повтори́те! Repeat (it)!
ко́шка cat
соба́ка dog
рад (m) ⎫
ра́да (f) ⎬ glad

рабо́та work
здесь (adv) here
бы́стро (adv) quickly
изуча́ть (I) to study
слу́шать (I) to listen
забыва́ть (I) to forget
рабо́тать (I) to work
тепе́рь now
ме́дленно slowly

Prepositions: без + *genitive* = without. с + *gen* = from, down from, since. до + *gen* = to, up to, until. из + *gen* = out of.

Phrases: я так рад(а) = I'm so glad
я так рад(а), что = I'm so glad that   ⎱ ра́да *if*
до свида́ния = until we meet (*au revoir*)   ⎰ *speaker is fem.*

PERSONAL PRONOUNS: DECLENSION contd.:
The plural forms of the personal pronouns given in Lesson No. 8 are:

	we	you	they
Nom:	мы	вы	они́
Gen:	нас	вас	их
Acc:	нас	вас	их

Note that the genitive and accusative forms of these pronouns are the same. **вы** (=*you* plural form of **ты**) takes the verb in the second person plural, even when a singular meaning is intended.

With these (in the genitive) the present tense of the verb *to have* can be completed:

We have = **у нас** (**есть**)
You have = **у вас** (**есть**)
They have = **у них** (**есть**)

POSSESSIVE PRONOUNS: DECLENSION: These words are declined as follows:

singular

	masc	*fem*	*neut*	
Nom:	мой	моя́	моё	⎫
Gen:	моего́ (г=в)	мое́й	моего́	⎬ =my
Acc:	моего́ *or* мой	мою́	моё	⎭
Nom:	ваш	ва́ша	ва́ше	⎫
Gen:	ва́шего	ва́шей	ва́шего	⎬ =your
Acc:	ва́шего *or* ваш	ва́шу	ва́ше	⎭

You see that two forms are given for the masculine accusatives. The short forms (**мой, ваш**) are used when the noun following is inanimate, the longer form when it is animate: the possessives before an animate noun have accusative the same as the genitive, before an inanimate noun, they have the same form as the nominative.

Stress: All cases of **мой** except the nominative have the stress on the ending; all cases of **ваш** have the stress on the first syllable.

Accusatives: **моего́ бра́та** = my brother
ваш дом = your house

Genitives: **моего́ бра́та** = of my brother
ва́шего до́ма = of your house

Memorize these examples.

Agreement: Possessive pronouns agree with their nouns in gender, case and number.

PAST TENSE OF VERBS : You will find that the past tense of verbs is easier than the present. It is formed simply by dropping the infinitive ending (generally **-ть**) putting in its place the following endings:

> *Singular:*   *Plural:*
> *masc* **-л,** *fem* **-ла,** *neut* **-ло.**   *all genders* **-ли.**

These forms are, strictly speaking, adjectival. They agree with the subject, which, of course, is always nominative, in gender and number. Thus, to form the past tense of

читáть (I)   to read

drop the infinitive ending **-ть,** leaving **читá-.**

Now add the endings just given and you will have:

я читáл(а) = I was reading, I read, I did read
ты читáл(а) = you (*fam*) read, were reading
он читáл = he read, was reading
онá читáла = she read, was reading
мы читáли = we read, were reading   ⎫
вы читáли = you (*pl*) read, were reading ⎬ = all gen-
они читáли = they read, were reading   ⎭   ders **-и**

With this verb no neuter form (ending in **-о**) is given because it is unlikely that a neuter could read.

A male person says: **читáл.**   A female says: **читáла.**

Stress: Note the stress on these words, and always note the stress on the past tense, which sometimes varies.

Meaning of the Russian past tense : It can be the equivalent of several forms which we use in English. Thus:

я читáл(а)
can be
translated:
  ⎧ I read
⎪ I was reading
⎨ I did read
⎪ I have read
⎩ I had read

This makes it easy to translate our English past into Russian, but you must be careful when translating from Russian into English. It is advisable always to consider the whole <u>Russian sentence</u>, for this will indicate which English equivalent would best translate the Russian past tense in the particular circumstances.

Drill: Before proceeding to the PRACTICE given below, make up some combinations of possessive pronouns + nouns, and also write out the past tense of some of the verbs given with Lesson N. 7.

PRACTICE: **УПРАЖНЕ́НИЯ**

Я рад, что вы чита́ли моё письмо́.	I'm glad that you (have) read my letter.
Как я ра́да, что Ива́н Сер- ге́евич так хорошо́ чита́ет по-англи́йски!	How glad I am that Ivan Sergeyevich reads English so well!
Америка́нец рад, что вы изуча́ете ру́сский язы́к.	The American is glad that you are studying Russian.
Повтори́те э́то сло́во!	Repeat this word!
Повтори́те э́тот уро́к!	Repeat this lesson!
Она́ так ра́да, что вы бы́стро рабо́таете.	She's so glad that you work quickly.
У мое́й жены́ нет биле́та.	My wife hasn't a ticket.
Есть ли у ва́шего бра́та соба́ка?	Has your brother (got) a dog?
Зна́ете ли вы его́? Мы вас зна́ем.	Do you know him? We know you.
Они́ никогда́ не слу́шают нас.	They never listen to us.
Они́ никогда́ не конча́ли рабо́ты.	Thay never used to finish their work.
У ва́шей соба́ки нет воды́.	Your dog hasn't any water.
Пиши́те бы́стро письмо́!	Write the letter quickly! (Hurry up and write the letter).
Англича́нка так ме́дленно чита́ет по-ру́сски!	The Englishwoman reads Russian so slowly!
Он меня́ спра́шивал, зна́ю ли я вас.	He was asking me whether I knew you.

Америка́нка спра́шивает студе́нта, где вокза́л.

The American woman is asking the student the way to the railway station.

Тепе́рь вы хорошо́ понима́ете, почему́ они́ так пло́хо игра́ют в те́ннис.

Now you can understand why they played tennis so badly.

Нет ли у них буты́лки вина́?

Haven't they got a bottle of wine?

Я не зна́ю, есть ли у них э́та кни́га, потому́ что их нет до́ма.

I don't know if they've got this (that) book, because they're out.

Англича́нин чита́л бы́стро, но пло́хо.

The Englishman read quickly, but badly.

Ве́ра Па́вловна по-англи́йски чита́ла ме́дленно, но хорошо́.

Vera Pavlovna read English slowly, but well.

LESSON No. 10

УРОК № ДЕ́СЯТЬ (10)

автомоби́ль (*m*) motor-car, automobile
карто́фель (*m*) potato; (*pl*) potatoes
конь (*m*) horse
словáрь (*m*) vocabulary, dictionary
корáбль (*m*) ship, vessel
геро́й (*m*) hero
сарáй (*m*) shed
трамвáй (*m*) streetcar

музе́й (*m*) museum
писáть (I) to write
идти́ (I) to go *on foot*
идти́ в шко́лу to go to school (*once*)
мно́го (*adv*) much, many
немно́го (*adv*) not much, slightly, little
в + *acc* = *motion towards;* to, into
из + *gen* = out of, away from

MASCULINE NOUNS ending ь and й: A limited number of masculine nouns have these endings. *All* nouns ending in **й** are masculine. Some nouns ending in **ь** are masculine and some are feminine, and this means that you have to be careful of the gender of all of them. In this book, the letter (*m*) or (*f*) will be placed after every noun ending in ь when it appears in the vocabulary at the head of a Lesson, and you must make a special list of these nouns and their gender as you go along. (A comprehensive list will be found on page 316). Nouns ending in ь or й include animates and inanimates. Their declension must be carefully noted.

DECLENSION OF MASCULINES in ь and й :

	animates		inanimates	
Nom:	конь	герой	словарь	трамвай
Gen:	коня	героя	словаря	трамвая
Acc:	коня	героя	словарь	трамвай

Masculine animates: accusative is the same as the genitive.

Masculine inanimates: accusative is the same as the nominative.

Stress: When the stress of a masculine noun is not on the *gen sing* ending, that stress generally remains on that syllable throughout the whole singular declension. The stress of the genitive singular usually indicates the stress on the other cases of the singular, apart from the nominative. But as there are exceptions, *it is advisable to memorize stress as you learn all declensions.*

CONJ. (I) VERBS contd.: The conjugated (present) tense of some first conjugation verbs differs slightly from that of **читáть** (I) *to read*, given in Lesson 6. Examples of these verbs are **писáть** (I) *to write* and the common verb of motion **идти́** (I) which means both *to come* and *to go* and always means *on foot*, or by the mover's own agency. In learning to conjugate these verbs the Rules of Orthography (*see* page 33) must always be kept in mind. Now consider these two verbs:

писáть (I) to write. **идти́** (I) to go *or* come *on foot*

Person

(1) я пишу́   мы пи́шем   я иду́   мы идём
(2) ты пи́шешь вы пи́шете   ты идёшь   вы идёте
(3) он ⎫   они́ пи́шут   он ⎫   они́ иду́т
    онá ⎬ пи́шет   онá ⎬ идёт
                                         онó ⎭

There are not many verbs ending in **-ти,** and they are all conjugation I. They are all infinitives with the stem ending in a consonant, as in **ид-ти́.**

The principal difference between the endings of verbs like (2) **писа́ть** and (3) **идти́** and (1) **чита́ть** is that the stem to which the endings are added ends in a *consonant.* When this occurs in the first conjugation, the endings of the 1st person singular and 3rd person plural change—almost invariably— to **-у** and **-ут.** *(not able change from ю and ют)*

In verbs like **писа́ть** (I) *to write,* it is the last *three* letters of the infinitive (**-ать**) that are removed to obtain the stem. We are therefore left with **пис-,** but this is not yet the actual stem of the present tense. The reason is that the final consonant of the stem is always changed in accordance with the Rules of Orthography (see Lesson No. 3, and also MUTATIONS, page 165). Consequently we have the present tense stem **пиш-.** And so you have the conjugation of the present tense of **писа́ть** as given a little earlier.

In regard to verbs like **идти́** (I)—with the combination consonant + **ти** in the infinitive—the removal of **ти** gives us the stem of the present tense without any further change.

All verbs marked (I) will follow the models of (1) **чита́ть,** (2) **писа́ть** or (3) **идти́.** Any variations from these forms will be indicated in the Lessons as you proceed.

It will save you much trouble if all this is fully understood and memorized. The three sets of endings of conjugation (I) verbs are summarized for reference:

SUMMARY OF PRESENT TENSE ENDINGS CONJUGATION (I):

(1) **ЧИТА́ТЬ** чита́- -ю -ешь -ет -ем -ете -ют
(2) **ПИСА́ТЬ** пиш- -у́ -ешь -ет -ем -ете -ут
(3) **ИДТИ́** ид- -у́ -ёшь -ёт -ём -ёте -у́т

Stress: Note that in (3) as the stress falls on the ending, the **-е-** becomes **-ё-** and is pronounced accordingly.

The stressed syllable of the present tense of conjugation (I) verbs is not always uniform. In the many verbs like **чита́ть** the stress remains on the stem (**чита́-**) throughout. In verbs like **писа́ть** the stress is on the ending of the first person singular (**-ý**), and on the stem in other forms of the present tense. In verbs like **идти́,** which have the stress on the final syllable, it remains on that syllable throughout the present.

MEMORIZING VERBS: If you know the infinitive and the first and second persons singular of the present tense, you can usually make all other parts of the present; and all other parts of regular verbs. Therefore, when memorizing a new verb, do it in this way:

(1) **чита́ть, чита́ю, чита́ешь** to read.
(2) **писа́ть, пишу́, пи́шешь** to write.
(3) **идти́, иду́, идёшь** to go or come *on foot.*

These parts will always be given with verbs where mistakes can be made.

PRACTICE: **УПРАЖНЕ́НИЯ**

Сего́дня учени́к идёт в шко́лу.	The pupil is going to school to-day.
Мы мно́го пи́шем по-ру́сски.	We write a lot of (much) Russian.
Как хорошо́ вы тепе́рь пи́шете по-ру́сски!	How well you write Russian now!
Тепе́рь я пишу́ по-ру́сски без словаря́.	Now I (can) write Russian without a dictionary.
Как хорошо́, что они́ так мно́го пи́шут по-ру́сски!	What a good thing that they should be writing so much Russian!
Он пи́шет, что геро́й чита́л её кни́гу.	He writes that the hero has read her book.
Чита́ли ли вы мою́ кни́гу? Чита́л.	Have you read my book? I have.
Мою́ ли кни́гу вы чита́ли? Ва́шу.	Was it my book that you read (were reading)? It was.
У меня́ нет автомоби́ля. А у вас есть?	I haven't a car. Have you?
Жена́ пи́шет, что до́ма карто́феля нет.	My wife writes that there aren't any potatoes at home (in the house).

Да́йте мне мой слова́рь!	Give me my dictionary.
Никогда́ у вас нет словаря́.	You never have a (the) dictionary.
В шко́лу они́ ме́дленно иду́т, а из шко́лы бы́стро.	They're slow going to school, but quick coming away.
Как бы́стро идёт ваш автомоби́ль!	How fast your car goes (is)!
Ваш автомоби́ль идёт так бы́стро?	Does your car go so fast?
У ва́шего геро́я нет коня́.	Your hero has no steed.
Э́тот по́езд идёт в Ло́ндон?	Does this train go to London?
Как ме́дленно он идёт, э́тот по́езд!	How slow it is, this train!
Как ча́сто он пи́шет э́то сло́во?	How often does he write this word?
Сего́дня мы идём ку́шать в рестора́н.	To-day we're going to eat in a restaurant.
Ро́берт Петро́вич по-ру́сски мно́го не понима́ет.	Robert Petrovich doesn't understand much Russian.
Вы понима́ете, что она́ пи́шет по-ру́сски?	Do you understand what she's writing in Russian?
Немно́го понима́ю.	I understand a little.

VOCABULARY: From Lesson 10 onwards you must learn to use the Vocabulary at the end of the book. This means that you will have to know the Russian alphabet in the order of the letters: otherwise much time is lost looking up words. In each of the **упражне́ния** there may from now be words not already given at the beginning of the Lessons, or in the grammatical explanation. You must look up these new words and memorize them with their meanings — noting at the same time how they have been used. Note particularly differences in Russian word-order from our English word-order. The final test always is to see whether you can write correctly the Russian for any English sentence in these PRACTICES.

LESSON No. 11   УРО́К № ОДИ́ННАДЦАТЬ (11)

ня́ня nursemaid, nanny	**исто́рия** history
тётя aunt	**ста́нция** station
а́рмия army	**ло́шадь** (f) horse

вещь (*f*) thing   **ночь** (*f*) night
кровáть (*f*) bed; bedstead   **пóмощь** (*f*) help, aid

        мóре sea
        пóле field
        здáние building
        желáние wish, desire
        плáтье dress, clothing

Prepositions : **от** + *genitive* = away from
            на + *accusative* = onto, to (*suggesting motion towards*)
            за + *accusative* = after, behind, beyond (*suggesting motion*)

FEMININE NOUNS IN -Я, -ИЯ and -Ь : In addition to the large number of feminine nouns ending in **-a,** there are others which have the soft endings given above. The ending in **-ь** is more common to feminine than to masculine nouns. These nouns are declined in the singular in their three most important cases as follows:

Nom:	нáня	áрмия	лóшадь	ночь
Gen:	нáни	áрмии	лóшади	нóчи
Acc:	нáню	áрмию	лóшадь	ночь

Compare these endings with the endings of **дáма** and **шляпа** in Lesson 4. You will note that the soft endings of the nouns in **-я** correspond with the hard endings of the nouns in **-a.**

With feminine nouns ending in **-ь,** the accusative is always the same as the nominative.

Note that the principle of "animation", so important for the formation of the accusative of masculine nouns, *does not apply to feminine nouns in the singular.*

NEUTER NOUNS IN -Е, -ИЕ and -ЬЕ : In addition to the neuter nouns in **-o** (see Lesson 3), there are many neuters with soft endings. They are declined as follows:

Nom:	мóре	здáние	плáтье
Gen:	мóря	здáния	плáтья
Acc:	мóре	здáние	плáтье

Compare these with the neuter nouns in **-o** in Lesson 3 and you will see that the soft endings correspond with the hard endings as with the feminine nouns given above. By their nature neuters are inanimates.

Pronunciation: In the examples of neuter nouns given above (when the stress falls on the stem) there is no difference at all in the pronunciation of the nominative/accusative and the genitive. The unstressed vowel of the ending has an indeterminate sound somewhere between stressed **e** and **я**.

With these neuters you have reached the end of nominative forms of Russian nouns. (There is also a small group of neuters ending in **-мя**, but they stand by themselves and will be dealt with later; see page 126.) The forms always indicate (1) the gender and; (2) the way the nouns are to be declined.

SUMMARY OF NOMINATIVE ENDINGS OF NOUNS

Masc. endings consonant   **-ь**   **-й**
Examples   стол   словáрь   сарáй

Fem. endings   **-а**   **-я**   **-ия**   **-ь**
Examples   дáма   нйня   стáнция   лóшадь

Neut. endings   **-о**   **-е**   **-ие**   **-ье**
Examples   слóво   мóре   желáние   плáтье

HARD AND SOFT ENDINGS: Always keep in mind the correspondence of hard and soft vowels:

> Hard vowels: **а э ы о у**
> Soft vowels: **я е и е ё ю**

CHANGE OF VOWEL WITH INFLECTION: It often happens that the last letter of the stem is one of the consonants that may require a change in the following vowel in accordance with the Rules of Orthography given in Lesson 3. It is of the utmost importance to bear these rules in mind *constantly*.

СТÁНЦИЯ and **ВОКЗÁЛ :** Вокзáл (said to be derived from the English *Vauxhall*) is only used of main and/or terminus railway stations in large towns. **Стáнция** is used of smaller railway stations, also of broadcasting stations, telephone exchanges, etc.

УПРАЖНЕНИЯ

Де́вочка идёт в шко́лу. Что она́ там изуча́ет? На́ша Ве́ра изуча́ет исто́рию. Ня́ня пи́шет, что ваш ма́льчик не жела́ет рабо́тать. Жела́ете ли вы мое́й по́мощи? Я уже́ пишу́ по-ру́сски без ва́шей по́мощи. Я ча́сто слу́шаю, как ня́ня игра́ет на пиани́но. У тёти сего́дня нет мя́са. Нет ли у вас карто́феля? Нет ли у неё ло́шади? Мы идём рабо́тать на по́ле. Этот трамва́й идёт за вокза́л/за ста́нцию.

LESSON No. 12   УРОК № ДВЕНА́ДЦАТЬ (12)

лимона́д lemonade
сыр cheese
чай tea
челове́к person; man (*species*)
друг friend (*m* or *f*)
обе́д dinner
обе́дать (I) to dine, have dinner
ча́шка cup

дере́вня village; the country (*as opposed to town*)
подру́га girl friend
благодари́ть (II) to thank
говори́ть (II) to speak, say, tell
держа́ть (II) to hold; keep
по́мнить (II) to remember
учи́ть (II) to learn, study
смотре́ть (II) to look

Phrases:
Как (вы) пожива́ете? = How are you?
О́чень хорошо́, спаси́бо. = Very well, thank you.
Жаль! = A pity!   Как жаль, (что) = What a pity (that)
Мне жаль + *acc* = I'm sorry for . . .

"И" VERBS—CONJUGATION (II): With very few exceptions Russian verbs are conjugated according to one of two basic conjugations. In Lessons 6 and 10 we saw the basic conjugation patterns of the 1st ("e") conjugation. The 2nd conjugation is marked by the presence of "и" where the 1st conjugation has "e" and the 3rd person plural ends in -ят instead of -ют. To obtain the stem of a 2nd conjugation

verb one *always* cuts off the *last three* letters of the infinitive
(=*vowel*+**ть**). To this stem are added the endings **-ю,
-ишь, -ит, -им, -ите, -ят**. Thus:

Infinitive: **говори́ть** (II) to speak. (*Stem:* **говор-**)

Present tense

я говорю́	I speak	**мы говори́м**	we speak
ты говори́шь (*fam*)	you speak	**вы говори́те**	you speak
он ⎱ **говори́т**	he, she	**они́ говоря́т**	they speak
она́ ⎰	speaks		

Note that the close connection between 1st person singular
and 3rd person plural in the 1st conjugation (see Lesson 6)
does not exist in the 2nd conjugation.

Many 2nd conjugation verbs have stems ending in conso-
nants which require **-ю** and **-ят** to be changed to **-у** and **-ат**.
(See Rules of Orthography, Lesson 3). Thus:

учи́ть (II) *to learn:* **учу́, у́чишь, у́чит,
у́чим, у́чите, у́чат.**

Note that the stress pattern of this verb is exactly the same
as that of **писа́ть** (I) (see Lesson 10). The verbs **держа́ть**
(II) *to hold*, and **смотре́ть** (II) *to look*, follow the same
pattern:

**держу́, де́ржишь, де́ржит, де́ржим, де́ржите,
де́ржат.**

**смотрю́, смо́тришь, смо́трит, смо́трим, смо́трите,
смо́трят.**

The two most important things to remember in learning
each new verb are (1) the conjugation to which it belongs and;
(2) the stress pattern followed in the conjugated tense.
Memorize each new verb like this:

to dine: **обе́дать** (I), **обе́даю,
обе́даешь.**   ⎫
to hold: **держа́ть** (II), **держу́,
де́ржишь.**   ⎬ From these parts all
           other parts of regular
to write: **писа́ть** (I), **пишу́,
пи́шешь.**   ⎭ verbs can be formed.

In this way you will know to which of the two conjugations the verb belongs, whether there are any peculiarities in the formation of the stem and the stress pattern followed in the conjugated tense. The formation of the past tense from the infinitive usually presents no difficulties (see Lesson 9) and the stress in most cases is the same as that of the infinitive.

THE OBJECT OF **смотре́ть** (II) TO LOOK: Just as in English one says "to look *at* something", so also the Russian verb **смотре́ть** is followed by the preposition **на** taking the accusative case:

Он смо́трит на мою́ кни́гу. He is looking at my book.

Она́ смо́трит на ва́шу карти́ну. She is looking at your picture.

благодари́ть (II), TO THANK: This verb is often followed by the preposition **за** (= *for*) taking the accusative:

Он благодари́т её за письмо́. He is thanking her *for* her/the letter.

УПРАЖНЕНИЯ

Как вы пожива́ете сего́дня? Вы по́мните меня́? Жаль, что вы не по́мните ва́шего уро́ка. Как жаль, что ваш друг не жела́ет учи́ть ру́сский язы́к! Мне жаль ва́шего дру́га. Почему́ вы смо́трите на меня́? Я на вас не смотрю́. По́мните ли вы, где вокза́л? Нет, я ничего́ не по́мню. Вы никогда́ ничего́ не по́мните! Говори́те ли вы по-ру́сски? Нет, по-ру́сски не говорю́, говорю́ то́лько по-англи́йски. Как жаль! Что она́ там де́ржит, ва́ша подру́га? Э́то она́ ча́шку ча́я де́ржит. Жела́ете ли говори́ть по-ру́сски, и́ли по-англи́йски? По-ру́сски мы говори́м пло́хо, пи́шем ме́дленно, но понима́ем хорошо́.

LESSON No. 13	УРОК № ТРИНА́ДЦАТЬ (13)

пе́рвый	first	**но́вый**	new
второ́й	second	**дорого́й**	dear
си́ний	dark blue	**молодо́й**	young

ру́сский   Russian
англи́йский   English
америка́нский   American
сад   garden
язы́к   language, tongue
аэропла́н   aeroplane
наве́рно (*adv*)   probably

гро́мко (*adv*)   loudly
ти́хо (*adv*)   quietly, softly
свобо́дно   freely, fluently
покупа́ть (I)   to buy (по-
     купа́ю, покупа́ешь)
люби́ть (II)   to like, love
     (люблю́, лю́бишь)

ADJECTIVES : An adjective is a word which defines the quality of a noun. Thus: a *good* man, a *bad* boy, *a silly* girl; *good*, *bad* and *silly* are adjectives.

Attributive and predicative : An attributive adjective denotes the quality (also called the attribute) of a noun *directly*, as in a *good* man, a *bad* boy, a *silly* girl—in which the adjective is usually placed before the noun.

A predicative adjective also denotes the quality of the noun, but does so *indirectly*—through a verb, expressed or implied. *Thus :* the man is *good*, the boy was *bad*, the girl wished to be *silly*. Here, *good*, *bad* and *silly* are predicative adjectives. These usually come after their noun.

The distinction between Russian attributive and predicative adjectives is of great importance. In this Lesson we shall begin to examine the attributive adjectives. The predicatives will come later (Lesson 28).

Attributive adjectives: These are also known as "full" or "long form adjectives". Most commonly they precede the noun with which they must agree in gender, number and case, thus:

но́вый каранда́ш, но́вая кни́га, но́вое перо́

The nominative singular endings of adjectives like **но́вый** are **-ый** for the masculine, **-ая** for the feminine and **-ое** for the neuter. The masculine nominative singular in **-о́й** indicates that the stress must be placed on the first vowel of the ending throughout:

второ́й аэропла́н, втора́я у́лица, второ́е письмо́

If the last letter of the stem is **г, к, х, ж, ч, ш, щ** or **ц** the Rules of Orthography (see Lesson 3) must be observed:

англи́йский сад, ру́сская же́нщина, америка́нское пи́во

There are also certain adjectives such as **си́ний** which have *soft* endings throughout, corresponding with the hard endings given above:

си́ний автомоби́ль, си́няя пти́ца, си́нее кре́сло

Summary: Nominative singular endings of hard and soft attributive adjectives:

	Hard		Soft
Masculine:	-ый	-о́й	-ий
Feminine:	-ая	-а́я	-яя
Neuter:	-ое	-о́е	-ее

Interrogative pronoun: како́й? кака́я? како́е?
This useful word is adjectival in form. It means *Which? What? What kind of?* or *What a!* Examples:

Како́й э́то го́род? What town is this?
Кака́я э́то кни́га? What book is this?
Кака́я кни́га! What a book!
Како́е пла́тье! What a dress!

Possessive pronouns твой and наш: твой *thy* (= your *fam*) is declined exactly like **мой** (*my*) and **наш** (*our*) is declined exactly like **ваш** (*your*) (see Lessons 3 and 9). Note that in Russian these adjectival possessive pronouns exist *only* in the 1st and 2nd persons, singular and plural. For the 3rd person one must use simply the genitive of the appropriate personal pronoun, **его́, её** or **их**. Examples:

моя́ кни́га	my book	**его́ кни́га**	his book
мое́й кни́ги	of my book	**его́ кни́ги**	of his book
твоё перо́	your pen (*fam*)	**её перо́**	her pen
твоего́ пера́	of your pen (*fam*)	**её пера́**	of her pen
наш дом	our house	**их дом**	their house
на́шего до́ма	of our house	**их до́ма**	of their house

ЛЮБИ́ТЬ (II) *to love*, *like :* Note the conjugation of this verb :

люблю́, лю́бишь, лю́бит, лю́бим, лю́бите, лю́бят.

You will see that the letter **-л** has been inserted before the ending (**-ю**) of the 1st person singular. This is because of a rule that applies to *all second conjugation verbs* with the stem ending in a labial (lip consonant), that is **б, в, м, п** and **ф.** Such verbs always insert **-л** before the ending **-ю** of the 1st person singular. See MUTATIONS p. 165

УПРАЖНЕНИЯ

Лю́бите ли вы ру́сский язы́к? Она́ лю́бит чита́ть по-ру́сски. Сего́дня америка́нец покупа́ет но́вый автомоби́ль. Это дорого́й автомоби́ль. У на́шей де́вочки нет жела́ния учи́ть ру́сский язы́к. Почему́ вы никогда́ не жела́ете говори́ть по-ру́сски? Како́й здесь трамва́й идёт на вокза́л? Како́й автомоби́ль ваш брат покупа́ет, англи́йский и́ли америка́нский? Како́е перо́ у твое́й тёти? У на́шей тёти си́нее перо́. Это о́чень дорого́е перо́. Дорога́я на́ша тётя никогда́ не покупа́ет молока́. Но́вый учени́к смо́трит на твою́ кни́гу. Кака́я э́то кни́га, пе́рвая или втора́я? Она́ свобо́дно говори́т по-ру́сски, и́ли нет? Вы наве́рно по́мните, како́й у студе́нта автомоби́ль. Почему́ вы так ти́хо говори́те? Я не люблю́ говори́ть гро́мко. Этот америка́нец лю́бит жену́. Я люблю́ твою́ подру́гу. Мы лю́бим смотре́ть на ва́шу карти́ну. Он лю́бит игра́ть в футбо́л, а я в те́ннис.

LESSON No. 14   УРОК № ЧЕТЫ́РНАДЦАТЬ (14)

соль (*f*) salt	**зуб** tooth
соло́нка salt-cellar	**щётка** brush
ма́сло butter	**зубна́я щётка** toothbrush
маслёнка butter-dish	**зе́ркало** looking-glass
шкаф cupboard, wardrobe	**запреща́ть** (I) to forbid
ме́сто place, seat	**замеча́ть** (I) to notice
портмоне́ (*n indec*) purse	**слу́шать** (I) to listen

слы́шать (II) to hear
почему́? why?
потому́ что . . . because . . .
поэ́тому therefore, and so
по-мо́ему in my opinion
по-ва́шему in your opinion
по у́лице along the street
наро́чно (adv) on purpose
неча́янно (adv) by mistake, accidentally

Слу́шаю! *I'm listening* = our 'Hello!' when speaking on the telephone.

THE DATIVE CASE: See Lesson 2. The dative case of nouns and pronouns, when used without a preposition, indicates the indirect object of a verb. It answers the questions кому́ = *to whom?* чему́? = *to what?*, кому́ and чему́ being the datives of кто and что. Thus, when we say "*I give the book to my father*", the word *book* is the direct object and *father* is the indirect object. In other words *book* is accusative and *father* dative. In English we generally have the preposition *to* before the indirect object. Russian indicates the dative by a case ending.

DATIVE OF PERSONAL PRONOUNS: You already know the nominative, genitive and accusative of the personal pronouns (see Lessons 8 and 9). Now you may add the dative:

Nom:	я	ты	он	она́	оно́	мы	вы	они́
Gen:	меня́	тебя́	его́	её	его́	нас	вас	их
Dat:	мне	тебе́	ему́	ей	ему́	нам	вам	им
Acc:	меня́	тебя́	его́	её	его́	нас	вас	их

FORMATION OF THE DATIVE SINGULAR OF NOUNS: In masculine and neuter nouns the dative singular ending is in **-у** if the ending is hard, in **-ю** if the ending is soft. Thus:

	Hard		Soft		
	masc	*neut*	*masc*		*neut*
Nom:	студе́нт	письмо́	чай	автомоби́ль	мо́ре
Gen:	студе́нта	письма́	ча́я	автомоби́ля	мо́ря
Dat:	студе́нту	письму́	ча́ю	автомоби́лю	мо́рю
Acc:	студе́нта	письмо́	чай	автомоби́ль	мо́ре

Feminine nouns both in -a and -я make their dative singular in -e, nouns in -ия make their dative in -ии, and feminine nouns in -ь make their dative in -и. Thus:

	Hard		Soft	
Nom:	да́ма	тётя	а́рмия	ло́шадь
Gen:	да́мы	тёти	а́рмии	ло́шади
Dat:	да́ме	тёте	а́рмии	ло́шади
Acc:	да́му	тётю	а́рмию	ло́шадь

Stress: In nouns of all genders the stress for the dative singular is the same as that of the genitive singular.

DATIVE OF POSSESSIVE PRONOUNS: As with nouns, the same form serves as dative singular for both masculine and neuter. Thus:

мой, моё, *dat:* моему́. твой, твоё, *dat:* твоему́ ; наш, на́ше, *dat:* на́шему. ваш, ва́ше, *dat:* ва́шему.

For the feminine the dative has the same form as the genitive: мое́й, твое́й, на́шей, ва́шей.

USE OF DATIVE AFTER CERTAIN VERBS: Here are examples of the use of this case after verbs taking two objects, one direct and the other indirect (accusative and dative), as explained at the beginning of this Lesson:

Она́ пи́шет ему́ письмо́.   She is writing (to) him a letter.

Тётя покупа́ет мне шля́пу.   (My) aunt is buying (for) me a hat.

Often a whole clause can play the part of a direct object:

Он им пи́шет, что не жела́ет рабо́тать.   He is writing to tell them *or* He says in his letter to them (*lit:* He writes to them) that he doesn't want to work.

Она́ ему́ отвеча́ет, что не игра́ет на пиани́но.   She answers (to) him that she doesn't play the piano.

Не говори́ли ли вы нам, что не понима́ете по-ру́сски?   Didn't you tell (to) us that you didn't understand Russian?

Or the part of the direct object can be taken by an infinitive:

Она́ запреща́ет ему́ She forbids (to) him to read
чита́ть мою́ кни́гу.   my book.

THE VERBS **СЛУ́ШАТЬ** (I) TO LISTEN and **СЛЫ́-
ШАТЬ** (II) TO HEAR: You must be particularly careful
not to confuse these two verbs. **слу́шать** *to listen* is a verb
of the 1st conjugation: **слу́шаю, слу́шаешь, слу́шает,
слу́шаем, слу́шаете, слу́шают ;** and **слы́шать** *to hear*
of the 2nd: **слы́шу, слы́шишь, слы́шит, слы́шим,
слы́шите, слы́шат.**

Both verbs take a direct object in the accusative:
    Я слы́шу вас. I hear you *or* I can hear you.
    Я слу́шаю вас. I'm listening *to* you.

CONSTRUCTION WITH **КАК :** In English we say *"I'm
listening to him playing the piano"* or *"She is watching her aunt
buy the hat"*, but in Russian one must say *"I'm listening (to)
HOW he is playing the piano"* and *"She is watching HOW her
aunt buys the hat"* :
    Я слу́шаю, как он игра́ет на пиани́но.
    Она́ смо́трит, как тётя покупа́ет шля́пу.

УПРАЖНЕНИЯ

Ли́дия Ива́новна смо́трит, как америка́нец пи́шет ва́шей
тёте письмо́. Я люблю́ слу́шать, как они́ говоря́т по-
ру́сски. Я ча́сто слы́шу, как Влади́мир Петро́вич игра́ет
на пиани́но. Вы э́то говори́те наро́чно. Она́ замеча́ет,
что вы наро́чно э́то де́лаете. Что она́ вам писа́ла? Она́
мне пи́шет, что ей о́чень жаль моего́ бра́та. Почему́
жаль? Потому́ что он без рабо́ты. Она́ у вас рабо́тает,
не так ли? По-мо́ему они́ вас никогда́ не замеча́ют, не
так ли? По-мо́ему э́то ва́ша зубна́я щётка. Как по-
ва́шему, она́ свобо́дно говори́т по-ру́сски? Я никогда́ не
слы́шал, как она́ говори́т, поэ́тому не зна́ю. Да́йте мне
ва́шу кни́гу! Да́йте ему́ соло́нку! Да́йте мое́й тёте
маслёнку! Да́йте ва́шему бра́ту мою́ щётку!

LESSON No. 15   УРОК № ПЯТНА́ДЦАТЬ (15)

дава́ть (I): даю́, даёшь ; они́ даю́т. *Ex:* Она́ даёт мне каранда́ш.	to give (*NOTE that* -ва- *is dropped in conjugation*)
спра́шивать (I): спра́шиваю, спра́шиваешь. *Ex:* Он спра́шивает тётю, когда́ уро́к.	to ask (*a question*)
проси́ть (II): прошу́, про́сишь ; про́сят. *Ex:* Он проси́л у меня́ кни́гу. Я прошу́ вас не чита́ть газе́ты.	to ask (*for something or for something to be done*)
отвеча́ть (I): отвеча́ю, отвеча́ешь. *Ex:* Он мне отвеча́ет на вопро́с. Он ей отвеча́ет, что нет у него́ её кни́ги.	to answer (*a question*)
гото́вить (II): гото́влю, гото́вишь ; они́ гото́вят. *Ex:* Она́ гото́вит ему́ обе́д.	to prepare (*see note on* л, *Lesson* 13)
ждать (I): жду, ждёшь ; они́ ждут. *Ex:* Я вас жду. Она́ ждёт по́езда.	to wait for (+*gen*)

всегда́ (*adv*) always   всё everything, all
почти́ (*adv*) almost

БЫТЬ *TO BE:* From Lesson 6 you will remember that Russian verbs have only one conjugated tense. The only exception to this is the verb **быть** "to be" which has two conjugated tenses, one present and the other future. But in modern Russian only one form of the present tense of **быть** is commonly used, the 3rd person singular (also used for the 3rd person plural)—**есть** (see Lessons 7 and 8). The *future tense of* **быть** is as follows:

я бу́ду I shall be		**мы бу́дем**	we shall be
ты бу́дешь you (*sing*) will be		**вы бу́дете**	you will be
он **она́** } **бу́дет** he, she, it **оно́** will be		**они́ бу́дут**	they will be

The Russian future is a true future always, unlike the English *shall* and *will*, which at times have in them a sense of desire or wish.

With the future of **быть** you can now express the verb "*to have*" in the future (see Lesson 8).

Positive	*Negative*
У меня́ бу́дет автомоби́ль.	**У него́ не бу́дет автомоби́ля.**
I shall have a car.	He won't have a car.
У неё бу́дет уро́к сего́дня.	**У них не бу́дет сего́дня уро́ка.**
She'll have a lesson to-day.	They won't be having a lesson to-day.

БЫТЬ "to be" *AS AN AUXILIARY VERB:* An auxiliary verb is one which can be used to form a compound tense of another verb, or of itself. We have six important auxiliary verbs in English: *have, be, shall, will, may* and *do*. In Russian the only verb used as an auxiliary is **быть**. It is used to form a compound future of all verbs of the "imperfective aspect", i.e. of verbs in Part I of this book.

Imperfective and perfective aspects of verbs: The imperfective aspect of a Russian verb is used to indicate an *uncompleted action*, the perfective to indicate a *completed action*. That is the important thing to remember until the subject is more fully treated in Part II (from Lesson 33 onwards). Verbs in Part I are nearly all imperfectives. The diagram on page 192 may be glanced at; it need not be carefully studied just yet. The conjugated tense of imperfective verbs is *present* in meaning.

COMPOUND FUTURE OF IMPERFECTIVE
VERBS : The future tense of all the verbs that you have met up to this point is formed quite simply by adding the infinitive to the appropriate person and number of the future of **быть :**

я бу́ду чита́ть	I shall read
ты бу́дешь чита́ть	you (*fam*) will read
он, она́ бу́дет чита́ть	he, she will read
мы бу́дем чита́ть	we shall read
вы бу́дете чита́ть	you will read
они́ бу́дут чита́ть	they will read

Past tense of быть : This is formed quite regularly (see Lesson 9): singular—**был** (masculine), **была́** (feminine), **бы́ло** (neuter); plural—**бы́ли** (all genders). Note the difference in stress between the feminine and neuter. *To be* may be implied in the present tense but *must* be used in all other tenses.

"*TO HAVE*" **IN THE PAST TENSE :** Compare the following examples with the future examples given above:

Positive	*Negative*
У меня́ был автомоби́ль.	У него́ не́ было автомоби́ля.
I had a car.	He didn't have a car.
У неё была́ ло́шадь.	У них не́ было ло́шади.
She had a horse.	They didn't have a horse.

Note that in the negative the neuter form of the verb must always be used, and that the stress is thrown back on to **не**.

VERBS IN -АВАТЬ : These verbs (*see above* **дава́ть**) always drop the suffix **-ва-** in conjugation, but not in the past tense (*past tense of* **дава́ть : дава́л, дава́ла, дава́ло, дава́ли**). These verbs are always 1st conjugation and always take the stress on the conjugation endings throughout.

2nd CONJUGATION VERBS IN **-СИТЬ :** 2nd conjugation verbs with a stem ending in **-с** change **-с** to **-ш** *in the 1st person singular only* (*see above* **проси́ть**).

УПРАЖНЕНИЯ

Кого́ вы ждёте? Я вас спра́шиваю, кого́ вы ждёте. Она́ не жела́ет мне отвеча́ть на вопро́с. Вы наро́чно не отвеча́ете на мой вопро́с. Па́вел Петро́вич про́сит жену́ не игра́ть на пиани́но. Прошу́ вас не говори́ть так гро́мко! Вы слы́шали, что э́та америка́нка даёт на́шей тёте но́вый автомоби́ль? Он всегда́ ей всё даёт. Серге́й Влади́мирович про́сит у нас автомоби́ль. Мы вас спра́шиваем, когда́ обе́д. Когда́ мы бу́дем обе́дать? Гото́вили ли вы нам сего́дня обе́д? Бу́дете ли вы обе́дать у нас сего́дня? Мы у них пло́хо обе́дали, у них не́ было мя́са. Ве́ра не зна́ла, как нам гото́вить обе́д; у неё не́ было ры́бы. Она́ спра́шивает его́, лю́бит ли он смотре́ть, как она́ гото́вит ему́ обе́д. Он всегда́ про́сит меня́ чита́ть ему́ ва́шу кни́гу.

LESSON No. 16   УРОК № ШЕСТНА́ДЦАТЬ (16)

жи́тель (*m*) inhabitant
пло́щадь (*f*) town square
ку́ртка man's, boy's jacket
ку́рточка woman's jacket
карма́н pocket
ла́вка shop (small)
ла́вочник shopkeeper
шу́тка joke, jest
пото́м afterwards, then, later on

обы́чно usually
ре́дко rarely, seldom
иногда́ occasionally
вчера́ yesterday
за́втра to-morrow
сейча́с now (*lit.* at this hour)
че́рез ча́с in an hour's time

помога́ть (I): помога́ю, помога́ешь to help ⎫
меша́ть (I): меша́ю, меша́ешь to hinder ⎬ + dative
обеща́ть (I): обеща́ю, обеща́ешь to promise ⎭
скуча́ть (I): скуча́ю, скуча́ешь to be bored
злить (II): злю, злишь; они́ злят to anger, annoy
быва́ть (I): быва́ю, быва́ешь to frequent; to happen from time to time
шути́ть (II): шучу́, шу́тишь; они́ шу́тят to joke

IMPERATIVE OF VERBS: That form of a verb which expresses a command is called the imperative. Thus: *Do* this. *Drink* that. *Come* here. *Go* there. The words *do*, *drink*, *come*, and *go* are imperatives.

Russian imperatives: The commonest form in use is that of the 2nd person plural, but the 2nd person singular is frequently heard, or met in Russian texts, and you should be familiar with it.

Formation of the Russian Imperative: To form the imperative in the 2nd person singular, drop the ending of the 2nd person singular of the conjugated tense and add:

   (*a*) **-й** if the stem ends in a vowel.

   (*b*) **-и** if the stem ends in a consonant and the stress in the 1st person singular is on the ending.

   (*c*) **-ь** if the stem ends in a consonant and the stress in the 1st person singular is on the stem.

Examples:

читáть (I): читáю, читáешь: 2nd pers *imp sing* читáй!
говорúть (II): говорю́, говорúшь: ,,   говорú!
писáть (I): пишу́, пúшешь: ,,   пишú!
любúть (II): люблю́, лю́бишь: ,,   любú!
быть (I): бу́ду, бу́дешь: ,,   будь!

To form the 2nd person imperative, plural, add **-те** to the singular form of the imperative:

   читáйте! говорúте! пишúте! любúте! бу́дьте!

Note the stressed syllable in these imperatives and that in Russian an exclamation mark is usually placed after an imperative.

These simple rules apply to the formation of imperatives of most Russian verbs irrespective of whether they belong to conjugation I or II. Exceptions will be noted as they occur.

Note that verbs in **-авать** form their imperative from the infinitive:

   давáть (I): даю́, даёшь imperative давáй! давáйте!

The imperative form дáйте! which you have already met, comes from the perfective form дать, an irregular verb (see pages 74, 310). One uses **дайте!**, rather than **давайте!**, when one wants to convey a greater sense of urgency.

2nd CONJUGATION VERBS IN **-ТИТЬ** : 2nd conjugation verbs with a stem ending in **-т** change **-т** to **-ч** in the *1st person singular only.* (See above **шутить**)

УПРАЖНЕНИЯ

Говори́те по-ру́сски, пожа́луйста! Пожа́луйста отвеча́йте мне на вопро́с! Гото́вьте обе́д! Жди́те его́ там! Всегда́ помога́йте подру́ге! Не меша́йте ему́ рабо́тать! Не скуча́йте без меня́! Не зли́те соба́ку! Смотри́те на их автомоби́ль! Учи́те ру́сский язы́к! Держи́те мою́ ча́шку! Благодари́те её за обе́д! Иди́те в шко́лу!

Он всегда́ меша́ет на́шему бра́ту, когда́ говори́т так гро́мко. Вчера́ у нас был ла́вочник. Э́тот америка́нец иногда́ у них быва́ет. Вы так ре́дко быва́ете у нас! Обы́чно я о́чень скуча́ю без вас. За́втра бу́ду вам помога́ть. Вчера́ она́ обеща́ла, что бу́дет здесь. Че́рез ча́с бу́ду покупа́ть вам ку́ртку. Она́ покупа́ет у ла́вочника ку́рточку.

LESSON No. 17   УРОК № СЕМНА́ДЦАТЬ (17)

Nominatives	*Instrumental case*
весна́ (*f*) spring	**весно́й** during, in (the) spring
ле́то (*n*) summer	**ле́том** during, in (the) summer
о́сень (*f*) autumn, fall	**о́сенью** during, in the autumn, fall
зима́ (*f*) winter	**зимо́й** during, in (the) winter
день (*m*) day	**днём** during, in (the) (by) day
ночь (*f*) night	**но́чью** during, in (the) (by) night
у́тро (*n*) morning	**у́тром** during, in (the) morning
ве́чер (*m*) evening	**ве́чером** during, in (the) evening

Note: In these words the instrumental indicates *during.*

INSTRUMENTAL CASE: This will be dealt with more fully later, but it is convenient to know one of its functions at this stage. The instrumental, as its name implies, is used without a preposition to indicate the instrument or agent with which something is done: *I write with a pen* = **я пишу́ перо́м.** The last word is the instrumental of **перо́** *pen.* This case is also commonly used to indicate *a period of time,* and implies the equivalent to our *during, in, by* in such phrases as those at the head of this Lesson. These words must be memorized and their instrumental case known.

INSTRUMENTAL CASE-ENDINGS OF NOUNS: From the above list it will be seen that the characteristic endings of the instrumental singular for masculine and neuter nouns is **-м** and for feminines **-й** and **-ю.** Full endings are:

	masc	*fem*	*neut*
Instrumental:	-ом, -ем, -ём	-ой, -ей, -ью	-ом, -ем

See also Lesson 2 and page 150 in the Appendix for TABLE. The *stress* of the instrumental singular is always the same as that of the genitive singular.

INSTRUMENTAL OF POSSESSIVE PRONOUNS: The same form serves as instrumental singular for both masculine and neuter:

мой, моё	instrumental =	мои́м (*m & n*)
твой, твоё	,,	твои́м (*m & n*)
моя́	,,	мое́й (*f*)
твоя́	,,	твое́й (*f*)
наш, на́ше	,,	на́шим (*m & n*)
ваш, ва́ше	,,	ва́шим (*m & n*)
на́ша	,,	на́шей (*f*)
ва́ша	,,	ва́шей (*f*)

САМ: СВОЙ: СА́МЫЙ: These are highly important words which must not be confused. One must distinguish their respective meanings carefully.

(I) **сам, сама́, само́; са́ми** = *-self* (*-selves*) in the pronouns *myself, yourself, yourselves, himself, herself, itself, our-*

selves, themselves. It strengthens or emphasizes the personal pronoun and usually follows or is near to it:

Я сам читáю кнѝги. I read books myself.

Он сам говорѝл, что . . . He himself said that . . .

Вы сáми виновáты. You yourself are at fault (=You have only yourself to blame).

DECLENSION

	masc	*fem*
Nom:	сам	самá
Gen:	самогó	самóй
Dat:	самомý	самóй
Acc:	Nom or Gen	самоё or самý
Ins:	самѝм	самóй (-ю)
Prp:	о самóм	о самóй

	neut	*plur*
Nom:	самó	сáми
Gen:	самогó	самѝх
Dat:	самомý	самѝм
Acc:	самó	Nom or Gen
Ins:	самѝм	самѝми
Prp:	о самóм	о самѝх

(2) **свой, своя́, своё ; свой** = one's own. It is declined like **мой** and translates our pronouns *my, your, his, her, its, our, their* when they refer to the subject of the clause (Latin *suus*). Compare the following examples:

Он читáет своѝ кнѝгу.	He is reading his (own) book.
Он читáет егó кнѝгу.	He is reading his (another's) book.
Скажѝте (*pf*) **емý послáть телегрáмму своемý брáту.**	Tell him to send a telegram to his (own) brother.
Скажѝте емý послáть телегрáмму егó брáту.	Tell him to send a telegram to his (another's) brother.
Скажѝте емý послáть телегрáмму вáшему брáту.	Tell him to send a telegram to your brother.

Consequently **свой** almost invariably occurs in oblique cases only. Note, however, such expressions as **э́то свои́ лю́ди,** *they are very close relations or friends of ours* and **он свой** (**челове́к**), *he is one of us.*

(3) **са́мый, са́мая, са́мое ; са́мые** = *the very, the most,* is declined like a hard attributive adjective. *It can never be used by itself.* It is used either with another adjective to express the superlative degree of comparison: **са́мый большо́й ма́льчик,** *the biggest boy,* **са́мая дорога́я кни́га,** *the most expensive book;* or in the expression **тот (же) са́мый, та (же) са́мая, то (же) са́мое ; те (же) са́мые** *the same, the very same,* **тот** and **са́мый** both being declined to agree with the noun qualified.

УПРАЖНЕНИЯ

Не пиши́те карандашо́м, пожа́луйста! Мой това́рищ, Ива́н, всегда́ пи́шет перо́м. Смотри́те, она́ пи́шет ва́шим карандашо́м! Смотри́те, как она́ пи́шет его́ перо́м! У́тром он всегда́ чита́ет газе́ту, а ве́чером игра́ет на пиани́но. Зимо́й мы игра́ем в футбо́л, а ле́том в те́ннис. Алекса́ндр Петро́вич всегда́ рабо́тает но́чью; днём он никогда́ ничего́ не де́лает. Прошу́ вас не писа́ть им письмо́ карандашо́м. Не отвеча́йте им на э́то письмо́! Алекса́ндра Ива́новна не жела́ет отвеча́ть на тако́е письмо́. Сего́дня у́тром я смотре́л, как они́ игра́ют в футбо́л. Сего́дня ве́чером я бу́ду слу́шать, как он игра́ет на пиани́но. Вчера́ у́тром у ла́вочника не́ было мя́са. Я по́мню, как вчера́ ве́чером вы помога́ли ей гото́вить обе́д. За́втра у́тром мы бу́дем гото́вить но́вый уро́к. Мы бу́дем вас ждать за́втра ве́чером.

LESSON No. 18   УРО́К № ВОСЕМНА́ДЦАТЬ (18)

о(об) preposition + prepositional case = *about, concerning.*
    (**об** before a vowel, **обо** before certain consonants)

в(во) preposition + prepositional case = *in, at* (place, location)
    (**во** before certain combinations of consonants)

на preposition + prepositional case = *on, in* (place, location)

дом (*m*) house	в доме in the house
шко́ла (*f*) school	в шко́ле in, at school
го́род (*m*) city	в го́роде in the city, in town
уро́к (*m*) lesson	об уро́ке about the lesson
кни́га (*f*) book	о кни́ге about the book
письмо́ (*n*) letter	о письме́ about the letter
столи́ца (*f*) capital city	в столи́це in the capital
Ло́ндон (*m*) London	в Ло́ндоне in London
Москва́ (*f*) Moscow	в Москве́ in Moscow
кино́ (*n*)★ cinema	в кино́★ in, at the cinema
стена́ (*f*) wall	на стене́ on the wall
земля́ (*f*) earth	на земле́ on (the) earth
река́ (*f*) river	на реке́ on the river

★*indeclinable* (*see pages* 30 *and* 316)

PREPOSITIONAL CASE: The prepositional case answers such questions as *Where?*—где? *About whom?*—о ком? *About what?*—о чём? (ком is the prepositional of кто and чём is the prepositional of что). It is so called because it is *always* used with a preposition and, in fact, by itself it has no meaning at all. For this reason, tables of declension are always given with the preposition о—*about, concerning*. It is important to remember this since the other cases, except the nominative, can be used either after a given preposition, or, without any preposition, directly after a verb which happens to govern that particular case. The prepositional is sometimes called the "locative" case, since one of its chief functions is to indicate *location* (see examples above).

FORMATION OF THE PREPOSITIONAL SINGULAR OF NOUNS: The prepositional singular ending of most nouns of all three genders is -e. There are three types of nouns that take their prepositional in -и: feminine nouns in -ь (ло́шадь, *horse*—на ло́шади, *on a horse*), feminine nouns in -ия (а́рмия, *army*—в а́рмии, *in the army*) and neuter nouns in -ие (зда́ние, building—в зда́нии, *in the building*).

PREPOSITIONAL OF PERSONAL PRONOUNS:
(*See also Lessons* 8, 9 *and* 14)

Nom:	я	ты	он	она́	оно́
Prp:	обо мне	о тебе́	о нём	о ней	о нём

Nom:	мы	вы	они́
Prp:	о нас	о вас	о них

PREPOSITIONAL OF POSSESSIVE PRONOUNS:
The same form serves for both masculine and neuter. Thus:
мой, моё: о моём ; твой, твоё: о твоём ; наш, на́ше:
о на́шем ; ваш, ва́ше: о ва́шем.

For the feminine the prepositional has the same form as the
genitive and dative: о мое́й, о твое́й, о на́шей, о ва́шей.

В and НА with accusative and prepositional: When
used with the accusative, в and на indicate *motion*, в being
used of *motion into* and на of *motion onto*. When used with
the prepositional в and на indicate *location only* without any
sense of motion. Thus:

Он идёт в шко́лу. (*acc*)   He is going to school. (*motion*)
Он рабо́тает в шко́ле. (*prp*)   He works at school. (*loca-
tion*)
Э́тот по́езд идёт в Москву́. (*acc*)   This train is going to
Moscow. (*motion*)
Она́ чита́ет в ва́шей ко́мнате. (*prp*)   She is reading in
your room. (*location*)

The idiomatic use of **на**, rather than **в**, with certain nouns
should be carefully noted. Thus in Russian one says **на
вокза́л, на ста́нцию** *to the railway station*, **на вокза́ле, на
ста́нции** *at the railway station*. The same applies to **у́лица**
street and **уро́к** *lesson*. Other instances will be pointed out
as they occur.

FLEETING -E- AND -O-: Masculine nouns with **-e-** or
-o- in the last syllable of the nominative may drop these
vowels in all other cases of singular and plural. Thus:

Nom:	отéц *father*	нéмец *a German*	кусóк *piece*.
Gen:	отцá	нéмца	кускá
Dat:	отцý	нéмцу	кускý
Acc:	отцá	нéмца	кусóк
Ins:	отцóм	нéмцем	кускóм
Prp:	об отцé	о нéмце	о кускé

BUT

Nom:	урóк *lesson*
Gen:	урóка
Dat:	урóку
Acc:	урóк
Ins:	урóком
Prp:	об урóке

The stress in such nouns remains constant. When the "fleeting" -e- or -o- is stressed in the nominative, the stress is on the ending in the other cases.

Note the difference in the instrumentals of отéц and нéмец: отцÓM and нéмцEM. Masculine nouns with a stem ending in ж, ч, ш, щ or ц take -ом in the instrumental if the ending is stressed, and -ем if the stress is on the stem.

ЖИТЬ (I) *to live:* This verb deviates slightly from the regular in that it has a separate stem for the present (conjugated) tense:

живý, живёшь, живёт, живём, живёте, живýт.

Imperative: живй!, живйте! The past tense is formed in the regular manner from the infinitive: жил, жилá, жйло ; жйли.

IRREGULAR VERBS БЕЖÁТЬ *to run*, ЕСТЬ *to eat* and ХОТÉТЬ *to want:* There are very few truly irregular verbs in Russian. They must, however, be learnt carefully because they are all in very common use. From the following examples you will see that these verbs combine elements of both the first and second conjugations:

бежáть to run: бегý, бежйшь, бежйт, бежйм, бежйте, бегýт. *Imp:* бегй! бегйте! *Past:* бежáл, -а, -о ; -и.

есть   to eat: **ем, ешь, ест, еди́м, еди́те, едя́т**

Imperative: **ешь! е́шьте!**

Past: **ел, -а, -о ; -и**

хоте́ть   to want: **хочу́, хо́чешь, хо́чет, хоти́м, хоти́те, хотя́т**

Past: **хоте́л, -а, -о ; -и**

УПРАЖНЕНИЯ

Где они́ живу́т?   Оте́ц живёт в Ло́ндоне, а брат в Москве́.   У него́ в Ло́ндоне но́вый дом.   Где вы бу́дете обе́дать, до́ма и́ли в рестора́не?   Вчера́ на уро́ке мы говори́ли о ва́шей кни́ге.   Э́тот авто́бус идёт на вокза́л. Они́ ждут по́езда на вокза́ле.   Зимо́й она́ живёт в столи́це, а ле́том в дере́вне.   Весно́й я иногда́ быва́ю в Ло́ндоне, а иногда́ в Москве́.   В шко́ле он скуча́ет, а до́ма никогда́ не рабо́тает.   Вчера́ у́тром мы вас жда́ли на пло́щади, но вас не́ было.   О чём вы говори́ли вчера́ на уро́ке?   О ком вы говори́те, обо мне?

— Что ты там притих?

Хотите ли вы жить в столице или в деревне? Она не хочет его ждать на площади. Я рыбы не ем. Куда вы бежите? Бегите сюда! Мы бежим на урок, а они бегут в кино. Не хотите ли есть мясо сегодня? Вы мяса не едите?

LESSON No. 19   УРОК № ДЕВЯТНАДЦАТЬ (19)

рука	arm, hand	земля	land, earth
голова	head	вода	water
ум	mind, intellect	муж	husband
наука	science	жена	wife
жизнь (f)	life	мужчина	man
терпение	patience	женщина	woman

куда   where to (=*whither*)
сюда   (to) here (=*hither*)
туда   (to) there (=*thither*)
раз   once, one time
разговор   talk, conversation

разговаривать (I)
разговариваю,
разговариваешь } *to talk with, converse with*, followed by the preposition **c** (**co**) governing the instrumental. **c**+*ins*=*with*.

CARDINAL NUMBERS: Numbers such as "*one*", "*two*", "*thirty*", "*a hundred*" are called *cardinals*, whereas such forms as "*first*", "*second*", "*thirtieth*", "*hundredth*" are known as *ordinals*. The cardinal numbers in Russian are declined more or less like nouns.

The cardinal number **один** *one* is the only one to be declined in all three genders. It must always agree with the noun to which it refers in gender and case.

	masc	*fem*	*neut*
Nom:	один	одна	одно
Gen:	одного	одной	одного
Dat:	одному	одной	одному
Acc:	Nom or Gen	одну	одно
Ins:	одним	одной (-ою)	одним
Prp:	об одном	об одной	об одном

The form of the masculine accusative depends on the noun.

Agreement of оди́н with noun:

masc

Nom:	оди́н брат	оди́н уро́к
Gen:	одного́ бра́та	одного́ уро́ка
Dat:	одному́ бра́ту	одному́ уро́ку
Acc:	одного́ бра́та	оди́н уро́к
Ins:	одни́м бра́том	одни́м уро́ком
Prp:	об одно́м бра́те	об одно́м уро́ке

	fem	*neut*
Nom:	одна́ кни́га	одно́ по́ле
Gen:	одно́й кни́ги	одного́ по́ля
Dat:	одно́й кни́ге	одному́ по́лю
Acc:	одну́ кни́гу	одно́ по́ле
Ins:	одно́й кни́гой	одни́м по́лем
Prp:	об одно́й кни́ге	об одно́м по́ле

оди́н has many uses apart from the strictly numerical sense. It can also have the meaning of *same*, *alone*, *only* and *certain*:

Они́ живу́т в одно́м до́ме.   They live in the same house.

Она́ одна́ меня́ понима́ет.   She alone understands me.

Он оди́н здесь понима́ет по-ру́сски.   He is the only one here who understands Russian.

Там была́ одна́ вода́.   There was nothing but water there. ("Water only was there")

Я знал одну́ же́нщину.   I knew (*or* used to know) a certain woman.

НЕТ НИ . . .   When this phrase is followed by оди́н in the genitive, it is equivalent to our *not one*, *not a*, *not a single*. Thus:

Нет ни одного́ до́ма.   There isn't a single house.

У нас нет ни одно́й кни́ги.   We haven't a single book.

Нет ни is a strong phrase and usually our "*even*" is implied in it.   In translating the above examples one could equally say: "*There isn't even a single house*" or "*We haven't even a single book*".

INSTRUMENTAL OF PERSONAL PRONOUNS:
(*See also Lessons* 2, 4, 8, 9, 10 *and* 18)

Nom:	я	ты	он	онá	онó	мы	вы	онú
Ins:	мной	тобóй	им	ей	им	нáми	вáми	úми
	(-óю)	(-óю)		(éю)				

INSTRUMENTAL OF POSSESSIVE PRONOUNS:
The same form serves for both masculine and neuter: **мой, моё: мойм; твой, твоё: твойм; наш, нáше: нáшим; ваш, вáше: вáшим.** These should not be confused with the forms of the prepositional (see Lesson 18). The feminine has the same form as the genitive, dative and prepositional.

FULL DECLENSION SINGULAR OF ÉТОТ, ÉТА, ÉТО:

	masc	*fem*	*neut*
Nom:	éтот	éта	éто
Gen:	éтого	éтой	éтого
Dat:	éтому	éтой	éтому
Acc:	Nom or Gen	éту	éто
Ins:	éтим	éтой (-ою)	éтим
Prp:	об éтом	об éтой	об éтом

Note that **éтот** has the same declension as **одúн** the only difference being the stress.

тот is declined in exactly the same way as **éтот**.

КУДÁ, СЮДÁ, ТУДÁ: Note that Russian has two sets
of words meaning *where*, *here* and *there*. **где, здесь, (вот),** and **там** which you already know, are purely locative in meaning and are linked with the use of **в** and **на** with the prepositional (see Lesson 18). **Кудá, сюдá, тудá** always imply *motion* and correspond to **в** and **на** with accusative:

Кудá вы идёте? Where are you going?
Я идý в шкóлу. I am going to school.
Где вы рабóтаете? Where do you work?
Я рабóтаю в éго лáвке. I work in his shop.
Идúте сюдá, в éту кóмнату! Come here into this room.

Пишúте письмó здесь, в э́той кóмнате! Write your letter here in this room.

Идúте туда́, в тот дом! Go over there to that house.

Мы там рабóтаем, в том зда́нии. We work there, in that building. (= *That's where we work, in that building.*)

STRESS OF FEMININE NOUNS IN -Á, -Я́: Many feminine nouns with their nominative in **a** or **я** stressed, move the stress back to the stem for the accusative singular, while retaining the stress on the ending for the other cases. Thus:

Nom:	**рука́**	arm, hand	**голова́**	head
Gen:	**рукú**		**головы́**	
Dat:	**руке́**		**голове́**	
Acc:	**ру́ку**		**гóлову**	
Ins:	**рукóй (-óю)**		**головóй (-óю)**	
Prp:	**о руке́**		**о голове́**	

Nom:	**земля́**	earth	**вода́**	water
Gen:	**землú**		**воды́**	
Dat:	**земле́**		**воде́**	
Acc:	**зе́млю**		**вóду**	
Ins:	**землёй (-ёю)**		**водóй (-óю)**	
Prp:	**о земле́**		**о воде́**	

река́, *river,* **стена́,** *wall,* **зима́,** *winter,* **доска́,** *board,* *blackboard* follow a similar stress pattern. However, there are other nouns such as **жена́,** *wife,* **весна́,** *spring,* **госпожа́,** *Mrs,* **Москва́,** *Moscow* in which the stress remains on the ending for the accusative. Further examples will be pointed out as they occur. **с** + *ins* = *with, along with.*

УПРАЖНЕНИЯ

Мы с ним всегда́ обéдаем в однóм рестора́не. Он всегда́ ку́шает однó мя́со. У них дóма одúн хлеб. Почему́ у вас сегóдня тóлько одна́ кнúга? В ва́шей ку́ртке тóлько одúн карма́н. У негó нет ни однóй ку́ртки. У отца́ ни однóго карандаша́ нет. Сегóдня у тебя́ нет ни однóго урóка. Я не понима́ю ни однóго слóва в ва́шем

письме́. Она́ ни одного́ сло́ва не понима́ет по-ру́сски. Не
понима́ю, почему́ он всегда́ де́ржит ру́ку в карма́не. В
э́той ко́мнате нет ни одного́ сту́ла. Где Бори́с Ива́нович?
Он в той ко́мнате разгова́ривает с одни́м не́мцем. Я не
жела́ю с ним разгова́ривать. Она́ с ни́ми никогда́ не раз-
гова́ривала. Смотри́те, пожа́луйста, на до́ску!

Look back over the previous practices inserting where
appropriate э́тот and тот in their correct case and gender.

QUERIES:
   (1) Have you mastered the writing alphabet? If not, you
      should do so, and from now use it for writing Russian
      words or phrases which you wish to memorize.
   (2) Have you begun to use the Vocabulary at the end of the
      book? If not, begin to do so now and it will tell you
      what ла́вка means.

LESSON No. 20   УРОК № ДВА́ДЦАТЬ (20)

прекра́сный	beautiful	молодо́й	young
краси́вый	pretty	пусто́й	empty
но́вый	new	больно́й	sick
холо́дный	cold	плохо́й	bad
тёплый	warm	дорого́й	dear, expensive
дешёвый	cheap	большо́й	big

бара́н ram (sheep)
ры́ба fish
поколе́ние generation
дово́льно (*adv*) enough
дёшево (*adv*) cheap(ly)
до́рого (*adv*) dear(ly)
да́же even

весь (*m*) вся (*f*) всё (*n*)—all, the whole (*adj*)

всё (*sing*) everything   все (*pl*) everyone, everybody

Прекра́сно! Splendid! Excellent!

Коне́чно! Of course!

Мо́жет быть   Не мо́жет быть!

it's possible   it's not possible!

(it) may be   it can't be!

perhaps   Impossible!

мо́жно (*adv*)   one may, can (do something)

нельзя́ (*adv*)   one may not = it is forbidden

сто́ить (II)   to cost:

Ско́лько э́то сто́ит? = How much does this cost? How much is this?

Э́то до́рого сто́ит = This costs a lot. This is dear.

Э́то дёшево сто́ит = This is cheap. This doesn't cost much.

Э́тот автомоби́ль ему́ до́рого сто́ил = He had to pay a lot for this car. (*lit.* "This car cost him dearly")

Ско́лько вам сто́ила э́та кни́га? = How much did this book cost you.

Э́то им бу́дет сто́ить оди́н рубль = This will cost them one rouble.

Э́то ничего́ не сто́ит = This doesn't cost anything *or* This isn't worth anything.

Не сто́ит вам рабо́тать сего́дня = You'd better not do any work to-day (= "It's not worth your while . . .")

Не сто́ит!   Don't mention it!

CARDINAL NUMERALS 2, 3 and 4: The cardinal number 2 has two forms, **два** when used with masculine and neuter nouns and **две** when used with feminines. **три**, *three* and **четы́ре**, *four* are the same for all three genders. **два, две, три, четы́ре** represent the nominative form of these numerals and likewise serve as the accusative when used with inanimate nouns.

☞   *Nouns following* **два, две, три, четы́ре** *must always be in the genitive singular.* Thus:

> **два стола́**   two tables
> **две кни́ги**   two books
> **три карандаша́**   three pencils
> **четы́ре бра́та**   four brothers

This is a most important rule and you should try to memorize it *exactly* as given above. It is misleading simply to think that *two*, *three* and *four* take the genitive singular, because, as you will see later, this is not so with cases other than the nominative and accusative inanimate.

DECLENSION OF FULL FORM ADJECTIVES: Attributive adjectives (see Lesson 13) are fully declined. Their declension is regular and is determined by the ending of the nominative singular masculine, depending upon whether this ending is hard or soft. Adjectives with the hard endings **-ый** and **-ой** are the commonest, so they will be taken first. It is important to remember the four following points which apply to *all* adjectives:

1. (*a*) Adjectives qualifying masculine animate nouns have the same ending for the accusative as for the genitive; (*b*) when qualifying masculine inanimate nouns, they have the same ending for the accusative as for the nominative. In other words, the same principle is followed as with *masc* nouns.

2. In the feminine, adjectives have the same ending **-ой** for four cases: genitive, dative, instrumental and prepositional.

3. The neuter form of adjectives is the same as the masculine except in the nominative and accusative.

4. The stress is *always* fixed as in the nominative.

MODEL DECLENSIONS

1. *Full form singular declension of hard adjectives in* **-ый** *and* **-ой**:

	masc	fem	neut
N:	но́вый	но́вая	но́вое
G:	но́вого	но́вой	но́вого
D:	но́вому	но́вой	но́вому
A:	N or G	но́вую	но́вое
I:	но́вым	но́вой(-ою)	но́вым
P:	о но́вом	о но́вой	о но́вом

	masc	*fem*	*neut*
N:	молодо́й	молода́я	молодо́е
G:	молодо́го	молодо́й	молодо́го
D:	молодо́му	молодо́й	молодо́му
A:	N or G	молоду́ю	молодо́е
I:	молоды́м	молодо́й(-о́ю)	молоды́м
P:	о молодо́м	о молодо́й	о молодо́м

2. *Full form singular of* **-ый** *and* **-ой** *adjectives* + *noun:*

	masc	*fem*
N:	молодо́й бара́н	молода́я ры́ба
G:	молодо́го бара́на	молодо́й ры́бы
D:	молодо́му бара́ну	молодо́й ры́бе
A:	молодо́го бара́на	молоду́ю ры́бу
I:	молоды́м бара́ном	молодо́й ры́бой
P:	о молодо́м бара́не	о молодо́й ры́бе

N:	но́вый стол	но́вая газе́та
G:	но́вого стола́	но́вой газе́ты
D:	но́вому столу́	но́вой газе́те
A:	но́вый стол	но́вую газе́ту
I:	но́вым столо́м	но́вой газе́той
P:	о но́вом столе́	о но́вой газе́те

neut

N:	молодо́е поколе́ние
G:	молодо́го поколе́ния
D:	молодо́му поколе́нию
A:	молодо́е поколе́ние
I:	молоды́м поколе́нием
P:	о молодо́м поколе́нии

N:	но́вое сло́во
G:	но́вого сло́ва
D:	но́вому сло́ву
A:	но́вое сло́во
I:	но́вым сло́вом
P:	о но́вом сло́ве

These model declensions exemplify the three principal features of the declension of all full form adjectives. (See also TABLE on page 154.)

Note that when the stem of an adjective ends in **г, к, х, ж, ч, ш, щ** or **ц** the Orthographical Rule (see Lesson 3) must, as always, be observed. Consequently **плохóй, дорогóй, большóй** in the instrumental case are **плохи́м, дороги́м, больши́м.** Remember, however, that **и** after **ш** is always pronounced as **ы.**

Stress: The stress of full form adjectives remains the same throughout as that of the nominative singular masculine. *There are no exceptions to this rule.*

Pronunciation: The **г** of the genitive ending **-ого** is pronounced as **в.** Thus **нóвого** is pronounced as if written **"нóвава", молодóго** as if **"маладóва".**

In adjectives with the stress on the stem, such as **нóвый,** there is no difference in the sound of the feminine and neuter nominatives, **-ая** and **-ое.** The unstressed **о** of the neuter is pronounced as **а** and the final unstressed **я** and **е** have the same indeterminate sound.

PRACTICE: **УПРАЖНЕНИЯ**

Take this PRACTICE carefully and, first covering the English, try to work out the meaning of the Russian. Write out the translation of everything that you find difficult. Then look at the English and correct what you have done. Finally go over it all at least twice, or more often if necessary, until you have assimilated all the words and grammar in the Lesson. This method should be applied *from now until the end of the Lessons in Part I.* If you find words that you do not remember or have not yet met, look them up in the Vocabulary at the end of the book.

He does not have the patience to learn Russian.	У негó нет терпéния учи́ть рýсский язы́к.
This young German does not understand Russian.	Этот молодóй нéмец рýсского языкá не понимáет.

The younger generation likes to study science.	Молодо́е поколе́ние лю́бит изуча́ть нау́ку.
How much did his new jacket cost our young neighbour?	Ско́лько сто́ила на́шему молодо́му сосе́ду его́ но́вая ку́ртка?
She isn't allowed to have any wine.	Ей вина́ нельзя́.
This sick student isn't allowed to eat meat.	Э́тому больно́му студе́нту нельзя́ ку́шать мя́са.
One (you) mustn't stroll about this town alone (by one-, yourself).	Одному́ нельзя́ гуля́ть в э́том го́роде.
May I play the piano? No, you may (can) not!	Мо́жно (мне) игра́ть на пиани́но? Нет, нельзя́!
One can never find him! (lit. "It's never possible to know where he might be").	Никогда́ нельзя́ знать, где он мо́жет быть.
Everyone knows that this is very expensive wine.	Все зна́ют, что э́то о́чень дорого́е вино́.
Everything is dear in this shop.	В э́той ла́вке всё до́рого сто́ит.
Perhaps you know how much this pretty dress costs.	Мо́жет быть вы зна́ете, ско́лько сто́ит э́то краси́вое пла́тье?
Everyone says that the whole house cost him only 4 roubles.	Все говоря́т, что весь дом ему́ сто́ил то́лько четы́ре рубля́.
Impossible! That's too cheap!	Не мо́жет быть! Это сли́шком дёшево!
They say that the whole of Moscow listened to him speaking about the new satellite.	Говоря́т, что вся Москва́ слу́шала, как он говори́т о но́вом спу́тнике.
May I have two pieces of bread, please? Is that enough?	Мо́жно мне два куска́ хле́ба, пожа́луйста? Дово́льно?
I'm going off to buy two books and two pencils.	Я иду́ покупа́ть две кни́ги и два карандаша́.

СОБИРАТЕЛЬ АВТОГРАФОВ

LESSON No. 21 УРОК № ДВА́ДЦАТЬ ОДИ́Н (21)

си́ний dark blue	**по́здний** late
зде́шний local	**ни́жний** lower
после́дний last	**ве́рхний** upper
вне́шний external	**пре́жний** previous,
вече́рний (*adj*) evening	former
у́тренний (*adj*) morning	**ле́тний** (*adj*) summer
пере́дний (*adj*) front	**осе́нний** (*adj*) autumn
да́льний distant	**зи́мний** (*adj*) winter
сре́дний middle, central	**весе́нний** (*adj*) spring
сосе́дний adjoining,	**хоро́ший** good
neighbouring	**о́бщий** general, common
ра́нний early	

не́бо sky: **си́нее не́бо** ; **вече́рнее не́бо.**

вид appearance, aspect: **вне́шний вид** outward appearance.

поли́тика politics, policy: **вне́шняя поли́тика** foreign policy.

торго́вля trade: **вне́шняя торго́вля** foreign trade.

звезда́ star: **у́тренняя звезда́** ; **вече́рняя звезда́.**

часть (*f*) part: **пере́дняя часть** ; **ни́жняя часть** ; **ве́рхняя часть.**

восто́к east: **Да́льний Восто́к** Far East.

А́зия Asia: **Сре́дняя А́зия** Central Asia.

эта́ж storey, floor { **пе́рвый эта́ж** ground floor. **второ́й эта́ж** 1st floor. **ни́жний эта́ж** lower storey. **ве́рхний эта́ж** upper storey.

Note that many attributive adjectives are used by themselves as nouns. For example, **передняя** (**ко́мната** is understood)=*lobby, entrance hall;* **больно́й** (**челове́к** understood)=*an invalid;* **ру́сский** (**мужчи́на** understood) —*a Russian (m);* **ру́сская** (**же́нщина** understood)—*a Russian (f).*

SINGULAR DECLENSION OF SOFT ENDING ADJECTIVES: Soft ending attributive adjectives are those with nominative endings in **-ий, -яя, -ее.** As you will see below, the endings correspond completely with the endings of the hard adjectival declension (see Lesson 20), the only difference being that the first vowel of the ending is softened.

Declension of soft ending adjective **си́ний** (*dark*) *blue:*

	masc	fem	neut
Nom:	си́ний	си́няя	си́нее
Gen:	си́него	си́ней	си́него
Dat:	си́нему	си́ней	си́нему
Acc:	*Nom* or *Gen*	си́нюю	си́нее
Ins:	си́ним	си́ней (-ею)	си́ним
Prp:	о си́нем	о си́ней	о си́нем

STRESS: Soft ending adjectives are always stressed on the stem, never on the ending.

PRONUNCIATION: The same principles of pronunciation apply as given in Lesson 20. **си́него** is pronounced as if written **"си́нива".** The feminine and neuter nominative endings both have the same sound: **"ие".**

DECLENSION OF ADJECTIVES WITH STEM ENDING IN **Ж, Ч, Ш, Щ:** Because of the requirements of the Rules of Orthography (see Lesson 3), these adjectives appear to have "mixed" endings, some hard, some soft. Here the position of the stress is of utmost importance—as you will see below by comparing the declension of **хоро́ший** and of **большо́й.** Endings in **-е** when unstressed change **-е** to **-о** when stressed.

Declension of хоро́ший, большо́й:

masc

			fem	
Nom:	хоро́ший	большо́й	хоро́шая	больша́я
Gen:	хоро́шего	большо́го	хоро́шей	большо́й
Dat:	хоро́шему	большо́му	хоро́шей	большо́й
Acc:	Nom or Gen		хоро́шую	большу́ю
Ins:	хоро́шим	больши́м	хоро́шей	большо́й
Prp:	о хоро́шем	о большо́м	о хоро́шей	о большо́й

neut

Nom:	хоро́шее	большо́е
Gen:	хоро́шего	большо́го
Dat:	хоро́шему	большо́му
Acc:	хоро́шее	большо́е
Ins:	хоро́шим	больши́м
Prp:	о хоро́шем	о большо́м

DECLENSION OF ADJECTIVES WITH STEM ENDING IN **Г, К, Х**: These adjectives follow the hard declension, but, because of the Orthographical Rule, change **ы** to **и** in the masculine nominative and the masculine/neuter instrumental.

Declension of ру́сский, плохо́й:

masc

			fem	
Nom:	ру́сский	плохо́й	ру́сская	плоха́я
Gen:	ру́сского	плохо́го	ру́сской	плохо́й
Dat:	ру́сскому	плохо́му	ру́сской	плохо́й
Acc:	Nom or Gen		ру́сскую	плоху́ю
Ins:	ру́сским	плохи́м	ру́сской	плохо́й
Prp:	о ру́сском	о плохо́м	о ру́сской	о плохо́й

neut

Nom:	ру́сское	плохо́е
Gen:	ру́сского	плохо́го
Dat:	ру́сскому	плохо́му
Acc:	ру́сское	плохо́е
Ins:	ру́сским	плохи́м
Prp:	о ру́сском	о плохо́м

DECLENSION OF ВЕСЬ "ALL":

	masc	*fem*	*neut*
Nom:	весь	вся	всё
Gen:	всего	всей	всего
Dat:	всему	всей	всему
Acc:	*Nom* or *Gen*	всю	всё
Ins:	всем	всей (-ею)	всем
Prp:	обо всём	обо всей	обо всём

Prepositions governing the instrumental

за = behind; beyond; after; for

между = between, among

над (надо) = over, above

перед (-о) = before (*place* or *time*)

под (подо) = under (*place*)

с (со) = along with, with

Prepositions governing the prepositional

в (во) = in, at (*place* or *time*)

на = on, in, at (*place* or *time*)

о (об, обо) = concerning, about

при = in the presence *or* time of; at, on (*an occasion*)

KINDS OF PREPOSITIONS: It is convenient to regard Russian prepositions in general as falling into two categories:

(1) **Primary prepositions:** Those words which are proper prepositions and no other part of speech. Examples are all those given above (also see the Summary on page 157).

(2) **Derivative prepositions:** These are either other parts of speech used as prepositions, or words derived from other parts of speech. For example **насчёт** is in fact the noun **счёт** (*account*) prefixed by the primary preposition **на**. Thus, as a preposition, this combination means *about, concerning* and governs the genitive: **Он говорил насчёт меня** = *He spoke about me.*

The primary prepositions are used not only as such, but, as you will learn, very many of them play an important part as prefixes to verbs. (See pages 221–4).

Every preposition governs one or two cases (**по** can govern three) and any case but the nominative can be governed by a preposition. But note **за** in the idiomatic expression **что за . . .** followed by the nominative:

Что э́то за стол? What table is this? What kind of a table is this?

Что за кни́га! What a book!

Action or place: You will find that the prepositions which govern more than one case, govern each case in accordance with whether there is *motion* (=action) or *no motion* (= when the preposition indicates only the locality or place where something happens). This important principle will be explained more fully in the next Lesson.

When certain prepositions add -**o**: When a preposition is either a single consonant (**в, с**) or ends in a consonant (**над**) and the word it governs begins with more than one consonant, then the letter **o** is usually added to the preposition. Thus:

> **во вто́рник** *on Tuesday.* **на́до мно́й** *above me.*

Pronunciation: The Russian preposition has no stress of its own and is pronounced with the noun (or pronoun, or adjective) as if the two words were one:

> **во вто́рник** pronounce as "**вафто́рник**"
> **надо мно́й** pronounce as "**надамно́й**"

However, occasionally the stress of the noun is thrown back on to the preposition:

> **с го́да на́ год**=*from year to year* ("**зго́да на́гат**")
> **на́ день**=*for the day, just for one day* ("**на́динь**")

Such stress will always be marked in this book.

Remember also the principles governing the correct pronunciation of voiced and voiceless consonants (see page 12): thus **в** before **п, ф, к, х, ш, щ, ч, с,** is pronounced as **ф**:

> **в карма́не** as "**фкарма́ни**"
> **в сад** as "**фсат**"
> **в шкаф** as "**фшкаф**"

с before **б, г, д, ж, з** (not **в**) is pronounced as **з**:

> **с дру́гом** as "**здру́гам**"
> **с бра́том** as "**збра́там**"
> **с зубно́й щёткой** as "**ззубно́й щётка**й"

PRACTICE: **УПРАЖНЕНИЯ**

There isn't a single cloud in the sky.	На небе нет ни одной тучи.
Look at the evening star over there!	Смотрите туда, на вечернюю звезду!
Where do you live, on the ground floor or the first floor? I live on the fifth floor.	Вы где живёте, на первом этаже или на втором? Я живу на шестом.
She was talking yesterday to our mutual friend.	Она вчера разговаривала с нашим общим знакомым.
You're not allowed to sit on the front seat.	Вам нельзя сидеть на переднем месте.
We often visit (*lit:* We are often in) the Far East.	Мы часто бываем на Дальнем Востоке.
Don't interrupt the invalid when he's speaking (*lit:* Don't hinder . . .)	Не мешайте больному говорить!
You mustn't say that in front of the (an) invalid.	Нельзя при больном этого говорить!
Have you spoken with the former owner of this shop (store)?	Говорили ли вы с прежним владельцем этого магазина?
There's a large, dark blue car in front of the house next door.	Перед соседним домом большой автомобиль синего цвета.
There's not much difference between foreign policy and foreign trade.	Между внешней торговлей и внешней политикой нет большой разницы.
On top of (above) the cupboard is a bust of Pushkin.	Над шкафом бюст Пушкина.
Under the ground floor there's a small cellar.	Под первым этажом маленький погреб.
He's waiting for the local schoolmaster in the lobby (hall).	Он ждёт здешнего учителя в передней.
There isn't one good restaurant in this town.	В здешнем городе нет ни одного хорошего ресторана.

LESSON No. 22   УРОК № ДВАДЦАТЬ ДВА (22)

погóда weather
чемодáн suitcase
сундýк trunk
  (*gen* сундукá)
пансиóн boarding house
тамóжня custom-house
дождь (*m*) rain
  (*gen* дождя́)
снег snow
дорóга road
сухóй dry
другóй other, another
какóй? what . . .? what
  kind of a . . .?
такóй such a

небольшóй not very big,
  smallish
мáленький small, little
желéзо iron
желéзный (*adj*) iron
желéзная дорóга = rail-
  way
рáно (*adv*) early
пóздно (*adv*) late
чáсто (*adv*) often
жáрко (*adv*) (it's) hot
хóлодно (*adv*) (it's) cold
сы́ро (*adv*) (it's) damp
вéтрено (*adv*) (it's) windy
сýхо (*adv*) (it's) dry
теплó (*adv*) (it's) warm

Idioms:
 Идёт дождь. It's raining. Идёт снег. It's snowing.
дождь is pronounced as "дощ" or "дошть"; снег as
"снек". The д in пóздно is not sounded.

ADVERBS: What the adjective does for a noun or pronoun, an adverb does for any other part of speech. When we
say:

I *much* admire his ability.
He was *greatly* admired in the town.
She sang *beautifully*.
He went out *merely* because he was
  ill.
He drove *remarkably* fast.

} *much, greatly,
beautifully,
merely* and
remarkably are
adverbs.

RUSSIAN ADVERBS: There are several kinds of
adverbs in Russian as in English, but it may help if Russian
adverbs are regarded as being of two kinds: (1) those which

are adverbs proper, "in their own right" so to speak; and (2) those which can be made from other words. Here we shall call (1) *simple adverbs*, and (2) *derivative adverbs*, because they are derived from other parts of speech. Thus:

Simple adverbs	Derivative adverbs
ужé—already	ýтром—in the morning (*from* ýтро)
здесь ⎫ here тут ⎭	хорошó—well (*from* хорóший)
	крáйне—extremely (*from* крáйний *extreme*)
там—there	
óчень—very	наконéц—at last (*from* конéц, *end*)
тепéрь—now	по-рýсски—in Russian (*from* рýсский)
дáже—even	вверх—upwards (*from* верх, top)
	вниз—downwards (*from* низ, bottom)

Formation of adverbs: Simple adverbs have to be memorized in the form in which they are presented, which does not change. Derivative adverbs are formed from various parts of speech, details of which will be given in future lessons. In the examples given above, **ýтром** is the instrumental case of the noun **ýтро**; **хорошó** and **крáйне** derive from adjectives; the particle **по-** is placed before **рýсски** (the adverbial form of the adjective **рýсский**); and **наконéц, вверх, вниз** are, in fact, accusatives governed by the prepositions **в** and **на**, and written as one word. These examples give an indication of the variety of ways in which adverbs are formed. Russian adverbs never change in form.

Adverbs from adjectives: Most hard-ending adjectives form adverbs by adding **-o** to the stem. This form will be explained more fully in Lesson 28. When such a form is used by itself, it should not be forgotten that a verb (usually the verb "*to be*") is often implied. The adverbial form ending in **-o** is much used in impersonal expressions, that is, when there is no actual person or thing as the subject:

Жáрко = (It is) hot	**Пóздно** = (It is) late
Хóлодно = (It is) cold	**Хорошó** = (It is) well
Рáно = (It is) early	**Интерéсно** = (It is) interesting

This impersonal use requires the case for person concerned to be in the dative:

Мне сегодня хо́лодно.   I feel cold to-day.

Это бу́дет вам о́чень интере́сно.   It will be very interesting for you.

Ей о́чень пло́хо.   She doesn't feel at all well.

PREPOSITIONS WHICH GOVERN MORE THAN ONE CASE:

(1) **с (со)**
$\begin{cases} (a) + genitive = \text{from, from off, down from} \\ (b) + instrumental = \text{with, along with, together} \\ \qquad \text{with} \end{cases}$

(2) **по**
$\begin{cases} (a) + dative = \text{along, throughout, by means of,} \\ \qquad \text{according to} \\ (b) + prepositional = \text{on (at the time of), after} \end{cases}$

(3) **в (во)**
$\begin{cases} (a) + accusative = \text{motion to, into; on, at (\textit{of time})} \\ (b) + prepositional = \text{in, at (\textit{static location}); on,} \\ \qquad \text{at (\textit{of time})} \end{cases}$

(4) **за**
$\begin{cases} (a) + accusative = \text{behind, beyond (\textit{direction,}} \\ \qquad \textit{motion}); \text{ for (\textit{behalf of})} \\ (b) + instrumental = \text{behind, beyond (\textit{static}} \\ \qquad \textit{location}); \text{ for (\textit{purpose}); at (\textit{location})} \end{cases}$

(5) **на**
$\begin{cases} (a) + accusative = \text{on, onto, to (\textit{motion towards});} \\ \qquad \text{to (\textit{event}); for (\textit{time})} \\ (b) + prepositional = \text{on, at (\textit{static location}); on,} \\ \qquad \text{at (\textit{time})} \end{cases}$

The primary prepositions given above govern more than one case. In general, the instrumental and prepositional cases after these prepositions usually represent the *static* or *motionless*; the other cases (genitive, dative, accusative) usually represent *motion (towards)* or *in the direction (of or from)*. The examples given below illustrate the use of these two-case prepositions. Other examples will be found in future Lessons.

Examples:

(1) (a) **Я иду́ с по́чты** = I am coming from the post office.

Он с утра́ начина́ет игра́ть = He starts playing first thing in the morning (from morning).

Она́ с пе́рвого дня рабо́тала = She worked right from the first day.

со стола́ = from the table (= from off the table).

(b) **Она́ разгова́ривает с ним** = She is conversing with him.

Она́ с бра́том там была́ = She was there with her brother.

с ка́ждым ча́сом = with every hour.

С пра́здником! = (With) good wishes. (**пра́здник** = festival day).

(2) (a) **по у́лице** = along the street. **гуля́ть по го́роду** = to stroll about the city. **по по́чте** = by post. **по желе́зной доро́ге** = by rail. **слу́шать му́зыку по ра́дио** = to listen to music on the wireless (**ра́дио** *indec*). **по его́ кни́ге** = according to his book. **по мо́ему** = in my opinion. **по ва́шему** = in your opinion, according to you.

(b) **по прибы́тии** = on arriving, (immediately) after arrival. (**прибы́тие** = *arrival*).

(3) (a) **Я иду́ в шко́лу** = I'm going (in) to school. **смотре́ть в окно́** = to look through (*into*) a window. **в тот день** = on that day.

(b) **Он тепе́рь в Москве́** = He is now in Moscow.

Я э́то чита́л в газе́те = I read it (this) in a newspaper.

в январе́ = in January. **янва́рь** (*m*) = January.

в э́том году́ = this year. (**году́** = prepositional of **год** *year*).

(4) (a) **Я иду́ за сто́л** = I am going to take my place at (the) table (= behind it). **держа́ть за́ руку** = to hold by the hand. **За Царя́, за ро́дину, за ве́ру!** = For Tsar, native land and Faith! (**ро́дина** = native country. **ве́ра** = faith).

(b) **Он за столо́м** = He (is sitting) at the table (= behind it). **Они́ за обе́дом** = They (are) at dinner. **жить за́ городом** = to live out of the city. **идти́ за мя́сом** = to fetch the meat.

(5) (a) **Я иду́ на по́чту, на рабо́ту, на конце́рт** = I'm going to the post office, to work, to a concert. **смотре́ть на** = to look *at*. **на́ день** = for the day. **на ме́сяц** = for a month.

(b) **Я был на Восто́ке** = I was in the East. **на у́лице** = in the street. **на по́чте** = at the post office. **на рабо́те** = at work. **на конце́рте** = at a concert. **на той неде́ле** = last week. **на э́той неде́ле** = this week (**неде́ля** = *week*).

Note: You will probably have to review this part about prepositions. Try to memorize as many of these examples as possible. The prepositional phrases recur frequently.

PRACTICE: **УПРАЖНЕНИЯ**

What nasty weather it is to-day!	Кака́я сего́дня плоха́я пого́да!
What do you think, will it rain to-day or not?	Как вы ду́маете, бу́дет сего́дня дождь и́ли нет?
It didn't rain yesterday, but I think it will to-day.	Вчера́ дождя́ не́ было, но сего́дня по мо́ему бу́дет.
How windy and cold it is to-day!	Как ве́трено и хо́лодно сего́дня!
Look, it's snowing already!	Смотри́те, уже́ снег идёт!
How interesting it (this) all is!	Как э́то всё интере́сно!
(While we were) at dinner he promised to show me all her pictures.	За обе́дом он обеща́л показа́ть мне все её карти́ны.
We're having an early dinner to-day because we're going to a concert in the evening.	Мы сего́дня ра́но обе́даем, потому́ что ве́чером идём на конце́рт.
She lives just outside the town (in the outer suburbs) in a small boarding house.	Она́ живёт за́ городом в небольшо́м пансио́не.
He wasn't at (didn't go to) work last week.	На той неде́ле его́ не́ было на рабо́те.
Uncle is very fond of telling jokes at meal times.	Дя́дя о́чень лю́бит шути́ть за столо́м.
What he had to say about his trip to France was most interesting. (*lit:* How interestingly he related . . .)	Как интере́сно он расска́зывал о пое́здке во Фра́нцию!
At last you've come home from work!	Наконе́ц вы с рабо́ты!
Give her that letter on (from off) the table.	Да́йте ей со стола́ то письмо́!
From the very first day I (*f*) knew that you would speak Russian well.	С пе́рвого дня я зна́ла, что вы бу́дете хорошо́ говори́ть по-ру́сски.

| It's difficult (hard) for an invalid to live in such a damp house. | Больно́му тру́дно жить в тако́м сыро́м до́ме. |

ДОЖДЬ ИДЁТ

LESSON No. 23   УРОК № ДВАДЦАТЬ ТРИ (23)

теа́тр theatre

перево́д translation

пра́здник feast day, holiday

писа́тель (*m*) writer, author (*m*)

мета́лл metal

мост bridge

двор court (yard)

зал hall; reception-room

ме́сяц month

год year

Но́вый год New Year

врач doctor, physician

ма́ло+*gen* a little, not much of

мно́го+*gen* a lot, much, many

ско́лько+*gen* how much? how many?

сто́лько+*gen* so much, so many

по́сле (*prep*)+*gen* after

везде́ (*adv*) everywhere

ва́жно(*adv*) it is important

нева́жно (*adv*) 1 = it's unimportant, never mind! 2 = poorly, badly

переводи́ть (II)
перевожу́, перево́дишь
to translate
сиде́ть (II) сижу́, сиди́шь
to sit, to be sitting
задава́ть (I) like дава́ть
to set (a task)

задава́ть вопро́с to put a
question
быва́ть (I) to happen (*from
time to time*), to be present
быва́ет it happens (*sometimes* or *often*)

PLURAL OF NOUNS: The system of declension in the plural is, on the whole, simple. Basically there is one set of endings which serves for all three genders. The *genitive* varies according to gender and presents some difficulty; it will be dealt with more fully later. There are also some variations in the nominative.

Plural endings of nouns

Nom: Masc and *fem* endings are **-ы** and **-и**.
Neut endings are **-а** and **-я**.
Gen: Masc endings are **-ов, -ев** and **-ей**.
Hard *fem* and *neut* have no ending.
Dat: All genders in **-ам, -ям**.
Acc: Like *nom* or *gen* according to animation.
Ins: All genders in **-ами, -ями**.
Prp: All genders in **-ах, -ях**.

MODEL DECLENSIONS: Masculine nouns plural

Nom:	столы́	бара́ны	словари́	цари́
Gen:	столо́в	бара́нов	словаре́й	царе́й
Dat:	стола́м	бара́нам	словаря́м	царя́м
Acc:	столы́	бара́нов	словари́	царе́й
Ins:	стола́ми	бара́нами	словаря́ми	царя́ми
Prp:	о стола́х	о бара́нах	о словаря́х	о царя́х

Nom:	музе́и	геро́и	врачи́
Gen:	музе́ев	геро́ев	враче́й
Dat:	музе́ям	геро́ям	врача́м
Acc:	музе́и	геро́ев	враче́й
Ins:	музе́ями	геро́ями	врача́ми
Prp:	о музе́ях	о геро́ях	о врача́х

When the Rule of Orthography applies: the **ы** of *nom pl* becomes **и**. *Examples:* уро́к—уро́ки. каранда́ш—каран-

даши́. това́рищ—това́рищи. Masculine nouns in
-ь and -й have *nom pl* in и: автомоби́ль—автомоби́ли.
трамва́й—трамва́и.

**FULL DECLENSION OF CARDINAL NUMERALS
ДВА, ДВЕ, ТРИ, ЧЕТЫ́РЕ**: As you saw in Lesson 20,
the forms **два, две, три, четы́ре,** which always take their
noun in the genitive singular, represent the nominative and
the accusative when qualifying an inanimate noun. In the
declensions given below note that gender is not taken into
consideration apart from the number *two*, and then only in the
nominative if the noun is feminine or in the accusative if it is
a feminine inanimate noun.

	masc and *neut*	*fem*	*all genders*	
Nom:	два	две	три	четы́ре
Gen:	двух	} *all*	трёх	четырёх
Dat:	двум	} *genders*	трём	четырём
Acc:	same as nominative or genitive			
Ins:	двумя́	} *all*	тремя́	четырьмя́
Prp:	о двух	} *genders*	о трёх	о четырёх

Case of nouns following 2, 3, 4 in oblique cases: You
have already seen that **два, две, три, четы́ре** (in the
nominative and inanimate accusative forms) always take the
noun in the genitive singular. However, after the genitive,
dative, instrumental, prepositional and accusative animate
(the so-called "oblique cases") of 2, 3 and 4, and in fact of all
cardinal numerals except **оди́н,** *the noun goes into the plural
and is in the same case as the numeral.* Thus:

Она́ покупа́ла два стола́. = She was buying two tables.

Он идёт на четы́ре конце́рта. = He is going to four concerts.

Он смо́трит на двух враче́й. = He is looking at two doctors.

Они́ перево́дят с трёх языко́в. = They (can) translate
from three languages.

Мы разгова́ривали с двумя́ америка́нцами. = We were
chatting to two Americans.

Он бу́дет на конце́рте с четырьмя́ това́рищами. = He'll be at the concert together with four friends.

Она́ дава́ла уро́ки трём студе́нтам. = She used to give lessons to three students.

Он помога́л двум ла́вочникам. = He was helping two shopkeepers.

Я был в трёх музе́ях. = I visited three museums.

Вы говори́ли о четырёх писа́телях. = You were talking about four writers.

2nd CONJUGATION VERBS WITH STEM ENDING IN -Д: These verbs change д to ж in the 1st *person singular only:*

переводи́ть (II) *to translate* **перевожу́, перево́дишь; перево́дят. сиде́ть** (II) *to be sitting* **сижу́, сиди́шь; сидя́т.**

Examples:

Я перевожу́ с ру́сского на англи́йский, а они́ перево́дят на италья́нский. I translate Russian into English, whereas they translate (it) into Italian.

Я сижу́ на сту́ле. I'm sitting on a chair.

Сиди́те! (*imperative*) Remain seated! Don't get up!

Нельзя́ вам сиде́ть на земле́! You mustn't sit on the ground!

PRACTICE: УПРАЖНЕНИЯ

Last week I went to (was in) three theatres.	На той неде́ле я был в трёх теа́трах.
The noise of cars from the street is very distracting for pupils in school.	Шум автомоби́лей с у́лицы о́чень меша́ет ученика́м в шко́ле.
One (you) mustn't annoy doctors!	Враче́й злить нельзя́!
There are no dictionaries at all in their library.	У них в библиоте́ке совсе́м нет словаре́й.
He is sitting out in the yard talking to four friends (mates) of his.	Он сиди́т на дворе́ и разгова́ривает с четырьмя́ това́рищами.

Yesterday she dined with three writers (authors) in a certain little restaurant on Gorki Street.

Онá вчерá обéдала с тремя писáтелями в однóм небольшóм ресторáне на ýлице Гóрького.

After four days it was already too late.

Пóсле четырёх дней ужé бы́ло пóздно.

I do a lot of translation from Russian into English.

Я óчень мнóго перевожý с рýсского на англи́йский.

She's busy translating two books from French into German.

Она рабóтает над перевóдом двух книг с францýзского на немéцкий.

Pyotr Pavlovich always asks us a lot of questions.

Пётр Пáвлович всегдá задаёт нам мнóго вопрóсов.

I spent a good number of days over this translation.

Я мнóго дней рабóтал над э́тим перевóдом.

It's very important for them to know who you were talking to yesterday.

Им óчень вáжно знать, с кем вы вчерá говори́ли.

I didn't tell her that you were having dinner with us to-day. It doesn't matter!

Я не говори́л ей, что вы с нáми сегóдня обéдаете. Невáжно!

Her translations (translation work) from Russian is poor.

С рýсского онá перевóдит невáжно!

LESSON No. 24   УРОК № ДВÁДЦАТЬ ЧЕТЫ́РЕ (24)

тéло body
блю́до dish, course (of a meal)
колесó wheel
селó village
óзеро lake
яйцó egg
черни́ла ink (*neut* plural only)

усéрдный zealous
учи́лище school, college
чудóвище monster
извéстный well-known
извéстие news, information
учéние studies, teaching, doctrine
содержáние content(s)

вложение enclosure
известно, что... it is
well-known that...
чудовищно! monstrous!
мнение opinion
усердие zeal

брать (I): беру, берёшь
to take, pick up
жалеть (I): жалею, жа-
леешь sorry for (+gen)
срочно (adv) urgently
срочное дело an urgent
matter, affair

Что нового? = What news?
things? How's business?
Fine (= excellent), thanks.

Как дела? = How are
Спасибо, отлично! =

NEUTER NOUNS: PLURAL DECLENSION; Compare with that of masculine nouns, which it resembles. Endings of *nom pl* are: **-a, -я.**

Neuters in **-o** form their nominative plural in **-a** and have no ending in genitive plural.

Neuters in **-e** preceded by **ж, ч, ш, щ** form their nominative plural in **-a** and have no ending in genitive plural.

Neuters ending in **-e** or **-ё** preceded by **и, ь,** or consonants **л, р,** form their nominative plural in **-я.**

Neuters in **-e** preceded by **л** or **р** take a genitive plural in **-ей.**

Neuters in **-ие** take a genitive plural in **-ий.**

MODEL DECLENSIONS: Neuter nouns plural

Nom:	слова	письма	моря
Gen:	слов	писем	морей
Dat:	словам	письмам	морям
Acc:	слова	письма	моря
Ins:	словами	письмами	морями
Prp:	о словах	о письмах	о морях

Nom:	поля	упражнения]	училища
Gen:	полей	упражнений	училищ
Dat:	полям	упражнениям	училищам
Acc:	поля	упражнения	училища
In:	полями	упражнениями	училищами
Prp:	о полях	об упражнениях	об училищах

Fleeting -o- or -e-: A few neuter nouns with stems ending in two consonants insert **-o-** or **-e-** between them in the "no ending" genitive plural; thus: окно́, *gen pl* о́кон, письмо́, *gen pl* пи́сем, кре́сло, *gen pl* кре́сел. Other examples will be noted in future Lessons.

Change of stress in neuter plural: Many neuter nouns change their stress in the plural. Note the following: те́ло, *pl* тела́. колесо́, *pl* колёса. село́, *pl* сёла. о́зеро, *pl* озёра. яйцо́ (pronounced "ийцо́"), *pl* я́йца, (*gen pl* яи́ц). ме́сто, *pl* места́. письмо́, *pl* пи́сьма. сло́во, *pl* слова́. де́ло, *pl* дела́. мо́ре, *pl* моря́. по́ле, *pl* поля́.

CARDINAL NUMERALS 5 to 10:

five	six	seven	eight	nine	ten
пять	шесть	семь	во́семь	де́вять	де́сять

Note: the -ь at the end of семь and во́семь is not usually pronounced.

The forms given above represent the nominative and accusative of these numerals. *These forms always take their noun in the genitive* **plural.**

Note that the principle of "animation" for determining the form of the accusative, which is of such importance when dealing with cardinals *one, two, three* and *four,* ceases to affect numerals from *five* onwards. From *five* onwards the accusative of a cardinal numeral is *always* the same as its nominative, no matter whether the noun concerned is animate or not.

These and all other numerals ending in -ь are declined exactly like feminine nouns in -ь. The only difference is that the stress varies somewhat. *Five* to *ten* all follow the pattern of:

Nom:	пять		во́семь
Gen:	пяти́	but in *eight*	восьми́
Dat:	пяти́	e contracts to ь	восьми́
Acc:	пять	in *gen, dat*	во́семь
Ins:	пятью́	and *prp*	восемью́
Prp:	о пяти́		о восьми́

Pronunciation: As numerals are in such common everyday use, a great deal of slurring inevitably occurs. You will find that many numerals as commonly pronounced by Russians bear little relation to the way in which they are spelt. Thus:

пяти́ is pronounced "пити́" and is commonly sounded "птй"
девяти́ ,, ,, "дивити́" ,, ,, ,, ,, "дьфти́"
десяти́ ,, ,, "дисити́" ,, ,, ,, ,, "дьсти́"

Nouns following oblique cases of numerals: Nouns following an oblique case (a case with a form other than that of the nominative) of *any numeral* from *two* onwards, go into the plural and take the same case as the numeral (see Lesson 23). Thus:

Он люби́л пять же́нщин. He loved five women.
У шести́ америка́нцев не́ было автомоби́лей. Six Americans didn't have cars.
Мы гуля́ли по семи́ у́лицам. We strolled along seven streets.
Он сиди́т с восемью́ студе́нтами. He is sitting with eight students.
Я пишу́ кни́гу о девяти́ геро́ях. I'm writing a book about nine heroes.

CARDINAL NUMERAL О́БА, О́БЕ: BOTH: The same rules apply to о́ба, о́бе as to два, две, три, четы́ре (see Lesson 20) that is, the forms о́ба, о́бе always take the noun in the genitive singular, while the oblique cases take the noun in the plural and in the same case as о́ба which is declined as follows:

	Masculine and neuter	Feminine
Nom:	о́ба	о́бе
Gen:	обо́их	обе́их
Dat:	обо́им	обе́им
Acc:	As nominative or genitive	
Ins:	обо́ими	обе́ими
Prp:	об обо́их	об обе́их

1st CONJUGATION VERB БРАТЬ *to take:* This verb inserts **e** between **б** and **p** and is conjugated: **беру́, берёшь ;**

беру́т ; imperative бери́! бери́те! *Past tense:* брал, брала́, бра́ло ; бра́ли.

1st CONJUGATION VERBS IN -ЕТЬ : These verbs are mostly derived from nouns or adjectives and are conjugated like **жале́ть** *to pity:* **жале́ю, жале́ешь ; жале́ют.** *Imp:* **жале́й! жале́йте!** *Past:* **жале́л, -а, -о ; -и.** (**жа́лость** (*f*)=*pity*.)

PRACTICE: **УПРАЖНЕНИЯ**

I (*f*) always used to give him two courses for dinner. The dinner consisted of two courses.	На обе́д я всегда́ дава́ла ему́ два блю́да. Обе́д состоя́л из двух блюд.
How many wheels are there on your car? Four wheels of course!	Ско́лько колёс на ва́шем автомоби́ле? Четы́ре колеса́, коне́чно!
Write in ink, please! I haven't any ink.	Пиши́те черни́лами, пожа́луйста! Нет у меня́ черни́л.
What would you like (to be prepared) for dinner? Eggs. Give me three eggs. She is making him an omelette of three eggs.	Что вам пригото́вить на обе́д? Я́йца. Да́йте мне три яйца́! Она́ ему́ гото́вит омле́т из трёх яйц.
Russian is studied in nine schools in this town.	В девяти́ учили́щах зде́шнего го́рода изуча́ют ру́сский язы́к.
It's monstrous! She doesn't know at all what my book is about (i.e. the contents of the book).	Чудо́вищно! Она́ совсе́м не зна́ет содержа́ния мое́й кни́ги!
Do you remember what her letters were about?	По́мните ли вы содержа́ние её пи́сем?
These are letters with enclosures.	Э́то пи́сьма со вложе́ниями.

She was asking him what he knew about the teachings of Marx and Lenin.	Она спрашивала его, что он знает об учениях Маркса и Ленина.
Why do you write so little? Do you begrudge (*lit*: are you sorry for) the ink, or what?	Что это вы так мало пишете? Жалеете чернил, что ли?
I'm very sorry that you don't do the exercises at all.	Я очень жалею, что вы упражнений совсем не делаете.
He takes six textbooks from the table and goes off to school.	Он берёт со стола шесть учебников и идёт в школу.
How much does she charge (take) for such work?	Сколько она берёт за такую работу?
This evening a very well known play is going to be presented. They're going to the theatre to get tickets. They're booking seats at the theatre.	Сегодня вечером идёт очень известная пьеса. Они идут в театр за билетами. Они берут места в театр.
Are there many lakes in your region (province)?	Много ли озёр в вашей области?
In the region (district) of our town there are eight villages and one very deep lake.	В районе нашего города восемь сёл и одно очень глубокое озеро.
Yesterday morning we viewed all the villages and lakes of this district from a very high tower.	Вчера утром мы смотрели с высокой башни на все сёла и озёра этого района.

LESSON No. 25   УРОК № ДВАДЦАТЬ ПЯТЬ (25)

свеча	candle	**жизнь** (*f*)	life
открытка	post card	**степь** (*f*)	steppe
шутка	joke	**подушка**	pillow

ма́рка postage stamp
посте́ль (*f*) bed, bedding
о́чередь (*f*) turn, queue
дверь (*f*) door
ум mind, intellect
у́мный clever, intelligent
откры́тый open
закры́тый shut, closed
на́до it is necessary

быть без ума́ от + *gen* to be mad (*about something*)
уме́ть (I) : **уме́ю, уме́ешь** to know how to (*do something*)
рисова́ть (I) : **рису́ю, рису́ешь** to draw, sketch
е́сли if

на́до is used impersonally with the dative, thus:

Мне на́до идти́ = I must go.

Вам на́до бу́дет мно́го писа́ть = You will have to do a lot of writing.

Ему́ на́до бы́ло помога́ть ей. = He had to help her.

FEMININE NOUNS PLURAL: An important characteristic of feminine nouns in the plural is that the accusative is the same as the nominative of inanimates, and the same as the genitive of animates. This does *not* apply to feminine nouns in the singular.

MODEL DECLENSIONS : Feminine nouns plural

inanimate

Nom:	ко́мнаты	ве́щи	а́рмии
Gen:	комнат	веще́й	а́рмий
Dat:	ко́мнатам	веща́м	а́рмиям
Acc:	ко́мнаты	ве́щи	а́рмии
Ins:	ко́мнатами	веща́ми	а́рмиями
Prp:	о ко́мнатах	о веща́х	об а́рмиях

animate

Nom:	ры́бы	ло́шади	ня́ни
Gen:	рыб	лошаде́й	нянь
Dat:	ры́бам	лошадя́м	ня́ням
Acc:	рыб	лошаде́й	нянь
Ins:	ры́бами	лошадя́ми	ня́нями
Prp:	о ры́бах	о лошадя́х	о ня́нях

Note that feminine singulars ending in **-а** preceded by a consonant other than **г, к, х, ж, ч, ш, щ** form *nom pl* in **-ы**. Where **-а** is preceded by **г, к, х, ж, ч, ш, щ** *nom pl* is in **-и**.

Feminine singulars in **-ь, -я, -ия** have **-и** in *nom pl*. Feminine singular nominatives in **-a** have genitive plural with *no ending*. Those ending in **-ь** form *gen pl* in **-ей**. Those in **-ия** form *gen pl* in **-ий**.

Fleeting -o- or -e-: Feminine nouns with stems ending in two consonants usually insert **-o-** or **-e-** between them in the "no ending" genitive plural. Examples: **таре́лка— таре́лок ; салфе́тка — салфе́ток ; ча́шка — ча́шек ; щётка — щёток ; ла́вка — ла́вок ; ку́ртка — ку́рток ; откры́тка — откры́ток ; поду́шка — поду́шек ; ма́рка — ма́рок ; земля́ — земе́ль.** *See* p. 319.

Stress: The feminine nouns mentioned in Lesson 19, which move the stress back to the stem in the accusative singular, have the same stress for the *nom pl* as for *acc sing*. Note also plural of **жена́ : жёны.**

Regular declension of nouns: With this Lesson you have completed the regular declension of nouns. From this point onwards all nouns may be assumed to follow the regular declensions unless your attention is drawn to some irregularity or deviation from the regular patterns which you have learnt.

SUMMARY OF DECLENSION OF NOUNS: A summary of the regular endings of nouns will be found on pages 150–2 at the end of Part I. Refer to this constantly until you are confident that you know them. Deviations from the regular will be noted in the Lessons as you proceed.

1st CONJUGATION VERBS IN -ОВАТЬ: These verbs change the verbal suffix **-ов-** to **-y-** in conjugation. Thus **рисова́ть,** *to draw, sketch* is conjugated:

> *Present:* **рису́ю, рису́ешь ; рису́ют**
> *Imperative:* **рису́й! рису́йте!**
> *Past:* **рисова́л, -a, -o ; -и**

CONDITIONAL-SUBJUNCTIVE: The English verb has a tense formed with *should* or *would* which is used in statements in which a condition is expressed or implied. For example: *If I should be there, I'll speak to him.* or *He would do it if he could.* In English we can use this "conditional" (*a*) in the past, (*b*) present, (*c*) future or "future in the past", as in:

Past: (*a*) I should have done it.
Present: (*b*) If the boy is good, I'll give him a dime.
Future in
the past: (*c*) I should be helping him on Tuesday next.

In English we also have a "subjunctive mood" which is much used in subordinate or secondary clauses. For example: *I'm telling you so that you may understand.* and *My wish is that he be helped.* Here *you may understand* and *he be helped* are in the subjunctive.

In Russian there is neither a conditional tense, nor a subjunctive mood, to correspond with our English forms. The "conditional-subjunctive" construction used in Russian is of great simplicity and will no doubt be viewed with gratitude by those who have had to struggle with the more complex conditionals and subjunctives of some other languages.

The Russian conditional-subjunctive consists simply of the past tense of the verb used together with the particle **бы** (sometimes contracted to **б**). This compound is used where in English we use *either* the conditional *or* the subjunctive. Thus:

он читáл бы
or } can mean {
он бы читáл

{
he would have read = English *Past.*
he would be reading = *Present.*
he would read = *Future.*
}

Note: Whatever the tense or mood may be in English, in Russian *only the past tense* is used with **бы**. In fact, once **бы** is used with the past tense (and note that it may not be used with any other tense), the verb ceases to refer to any specific tense and can be used of all three, as shown above. **бы** may be placed almost anywhere in a sentence, *but never at the beginning.*

ЧТÓБЫ: **бы** combined with **что** as **чтóбы** (or **чтоб**) means *in order that, that* and is used with the past tense to express a conditional-subjunctive meaning. It is used particularly after verbs of *wishing*. Thus:

Я не жела́ю, что́бы вы сего́дня игра́ли.   I don't want you to play to-day.

Он жела́ет, что́бы вы учи́ли ру́сский язы́к.   He wants you to learn Russian.

When the subject of the subordinate clause is the same as that of the principle clause, **что́бы** is followed by an infinitive just as in English:

Она́ идёт в шко́лу, что́бы рабо́тать.   She is going to school (in order) to work.

Е́СЛИ = IF : The use of "*if*" necessarily implies a condition. Thus: "*If I can, I shall do this.*" or "*If I could, I would do this*". Thus the subject promises to perform a certain action, given the *condition* that he is able to do it. Note, however, that in the first example there seems to be a possibility that the condition will be *fulfilled*, whereas in the second example it is implied that the condition will remain *unfulfilled*. A condition which implies that fulfilment is possible necessarily refers to the future, whereas a condition which is likely to remain unfulfilled can refer to past, present or future.

In Russian a condition that is likely to be fulfilled is expressed by **е́сли**, *if*, with both the principal and subordinate verbs in the future tense:

Е́сли вы бу́дете мно́го чита́ть, вы ско́ро бу́дете понима́ть Пу́шкина.   If you read a lot, you will soon be understanding Pushkin.

Е́сли вы не бу́дете меня́ злить, за́втра я бу́ду помога́ть вам с упражне́ниями.   If you don't annoy me, I'll help you with your practice to-morrow.

But, if it is implied that the condition will remain unfulfilled, both verbs are given in the conditional-subjunctive (*past tense* + **бы**):

Éсли бы вы мно́го чита́ли, вы бы тепе́рь понима́ли Пу́шкина. If you had read a lot, you would have been understanding Pushkin by now.

Éсли бы вы меня́ не зли́ли, я бы помога́л вам за́втра с упражне́ниями. If you hadn't annoyed me, I would have helped you with your practice to-morrow.

Note carefully that *the Russian conditional subjunctive verb can refer to any tense, past, present or future.* The context of the sentence together with the use of adverbs of *time* shows you to which time the condition refers, and what tense of the English verb should be used in translation.

Further examples of the use of the conditional-subjunctive will be found in the PRACTICE for this Lesson.

CARDINAL NUMERALS ; THE "TEENS" : For these refer to the Summary of Cardinal Numerals at the head of Lesson 32 (page 183). They are declined exactly like feminine nouns in **-ь** and, unlike the numerals **пять** to **де́сять,** do not shift the stress to the ending in the oblique cases.

PRACTICE: **УПРАЖНЕНИЯ**

If you're going to prevent me from working now, I shan't go to watch you playing tennis to-morrow.

Éсли сейча́с вы бу́дете меша́ть мне рабо́тать, я не бу́ду смотре́ть, как вы игра́ете в те́ннис за́втра.

If he had wanted to have dinner with us, he wouldn't have said such things to our aunts.

Éсли бы он жела́л обе́дать у нас, он не говори́л бы тётям таки́х веще́й.

There are twelve doors and seventeen windows in our house.

В на́шем до́ме двена́дцать двере́й и семна́дцать о́кон.

How many squares are there in this town?

Ско́лько площаде́й в э́том го́роде?

I do dislike queues. We always have to wait in a queue.

Я о́чень не люблю́ очереде́й. Всегда́ нам на́до ждать в о́череди.

Can you draw? She's excellent at pencil drawing.	Уме́ете ли вы рисова́ть? Она́ отли́чно рису́ет карандашо́м.
I very much want you to be able to draw well.	Я о́чень жела́ю, что́бы вы уме́ли хорошо́ рисова́ть.
You'd be bored, if I weren't here.	Вы бы скуча́ли, е́сли бы меня́ здесь не́ было.
You'll be bored if I'm not here.	Вы бу́дете скуча́ть, е́сли меня́ здесь не бу́дет.
Don't forget that I lived in France for seventeen months and I understand French very well.	Не забыва́йте, что я семна́дцать ме́сяцев жил во Фра́нции и хорошо́ понима́ю по-францу́зски.
Don't you want to live with us?	Вы не жела́ете жить у нас?
Wouldn't you like to live in Russia?	Не жела́ли бы вы жить в Росси́и?
They told me a lot about the steppes of Southern Russia and Central Asia.	Они́ мне мно́го расска́зывали о степя́х ю́жной Росси́и и Сре́дней А́зии.
We have to go now to the shop and to the post office. We're going to buy 16 postcards and 18 stamps.	Нам сейча́с на́до идти́ в ла́вку и на по́чту. Мы бу́дем покупа́ть шестна́дцать откры́ток и восемна́дцать ма́рок.

LESSON No. 26   УРО́К № ДВА́ДЦАТЬ ШЕСТЬ (26)

чёрный	black	живо́й	alive, lively
зелёный	green	ми́лый	kind, lovable
бе́лый	white	мать	mother
кра́сный	red	дочь	daughter
голубо́й	light blue	вре́мя	time
кори́чневый	brown	и́мя	first name
жёлтый	yellow	дед	grandfather
тёмный	dark	ба́бушка	grandmother, granny
се́рый	grey		
больно́й	sick, unhealthy	пе́рвый	first

второй	second	**седьмой**	seventh
третий	third	**восьмой**	eighth
четвёртый	fourth	**девятый**	ninth
пятый	fifth	**десятый**	tenth
шестой	sixth		

PLURAL DECLENSION OF ADJECTIVES: Adjectives are declined in all six cases of the plural, but one form serves for all three genders.

Endings of adjectives in the nominative:

Singular:	*hard*	*soft*	Plural:	*all genders*
Masc:	**-ый, -ой**	**-ий**	*hard:*	**-ые, (-ые)**
Fem:	**-ая**	**-яя**	*soft:*	**-ие**
Neut:	**-ое**	**-ее**		

Plural of новый and молодой—hard form attributives:

Nom:	**новые**	**молоды́е**
Gen:	**новых**	**молоды́х**
Dat:	**новым**	**молоды́м**
Acc:	*as nominative or genitive*	
Ins:	**новыми**	**молоды́ми**
Prp:	**о новых**	**о молоды́х**

Since the principle of "animation" in determining the form of the accusative applies to both masculine and feminine nouns in the plural (see Lessons 23 and 25), the principle applies likewise to the plural form of adjectives.

As you will see, there is a resemblance between plural nouns and adjectives in the oblique cases (genitive, dative, instrumental, prepositional). Be particularly careful not to confuse the plural endings of nouns and adjectives.

ADJECTIVES FOLLOWING CARDINAL NUMERALS: In Lessons 20, 23 and 24 you learnt the behaviour of nouns coupled with numerals. You shall now see what happens when a noun following a cardinal numeral is qualified by an adjective.

The first important thing to remember when this combination of words occurs is that the noun is not in any way affected by the presence of the adjective; it must *always* take the number and case required by the cardinal numeral.

(1) **After два, две, три, четыре :** the noun must remain in the genitive singular, BUT the qualifying adjective is put in the *genitive plural*. If the noun is feminine, the adjective is often put in the Nominative plural. Thus:

два зелёных стола́ two green tables

две краси́вые англича́нки two pretty Englishwomen

три молоды́х студе́нта three young students

четы́ре дороги́х пансио́на four expensive boarding houses

(2) **In all other instances :** the adjective agrees fully with the noun in the normal way:

Он ждал трёх молоды́х студе́нтов. He was waiting for three young students.

на двух зелёных стола́х on two green tables

Да́йте э́то двум краси́вым англича́нкам! Give this to the two pretty Englishwomen.

Она́ игра́ет с пятью́ се́рыми соба́ками. She is playing with five grey dogs.

ORDINAL NUMERALS : These are simply numerical adjectives. They are declined and they behave exactly like all other adjectives. All ordinals have the form of hard ending adjectives, with one exception, **тре́тий**, *third*, which is soft, but belongs to a declension that you have not met up to this point:

Declension of **тре́тий,** *third:*

	masc	*fem*	*neut*
Nom:	тре́тий	тре́тья	тре́тье
Gen:	тре́тьего	тре́тьей	тре́тьего
Dat:	тре́тьему	тре́тьей	тре́тьему
Acc:	*Nom* or *Gen*	тре́тью	тре́тье
Ins:	тре́тьим	тре́тьей (-ею)	тре́тьим
Prp:	о тре́тьем	о тре́тьей	о тре́тьем

SLIGHTLY IRREGULAR NOUNS : There are four small groups of nouns, in everyday use, which are slightly irregular. The first two groups will be dealt with in this lesson.

(1) Declension of мать, *mother,* **and** дочь, *daughter* :

	sing	pl	sing	pl
N:	мать	ма́тери	дочь	до́чери
G:	ма́тери	матере́й	до́чери	дочере́й
D:	ма́тери	матеря́м	до́чери	дочеря́м
A:	мать	матере́й	дочь	дочере́й
I:	ма́терью	матеря́ми	до́черью	дочерьми́
P:	о ма́тери	о матеря́х	о до́чери	о дочеря́х

(2) Neuter nouns ending in -мя : There are ten of these altogether and their declension follows that of вре́мя *time* :

	Singular	Plural
Nom:	вре́мя	времена́
Gen:	вре́мени	времён
Dat:	вре́мени	времена́м
Acc:	вре́мя	времена́
Ins:	вре́менем	времена́ми
Prp:	о вре́мени	о времена́х

Note that the genitive, dative and prepositional singular are the same. Other common nouns of the same declension are: зна́мя, *banner, flag* (this noun is stressed -ён- throughout in the plural). и́мя, *first, Christian name.* пла́мя, *flame, flames* (no plural). пле́мя, *tribe, race.* се́мя, *seed* (this noun has семя́н in the genitive plural).

DECLENSION OF SURNAMES IN **-ОВ, -ЕВ** AND **-ИН :** These follow the pattern of **Ива́нов, Ива́нова, Ива́новы** :

	masc	fem	plur
Nom:	Ива́нов	Ива́нова	Ива́новы
Gen:	Ива́нова	Ива́новой	Ива́новых
Dat:	Ива́нову	Ива́новой	Ива́новым
Acc:	Ива́нова	Ива́нову	Ива́новых
Ins:	Ива́новым	Ива́новой	Ива́новыми
Prp:	об Ива́нове	об Ива́новой	об Ива́новых

Surnames in **-ов, ев** and **-ин** are in fact a peculiar form of possessive adjective indicating possession by a particular person. **Ива́нов** therefore simply means "belonging to Ivan". Apart from the numerous surnames formed from Christian names, there are also many formed on an "occupational" basis: **Попо́в** (поп = *priest*), **Кузнецо́в** (кузне́ц = *blacksmith*), **Филосо́фов** (фило́соф = *philosopher*) and others of far stranger derivation: **Абрико́сов** (абрико́с = *apricot*), **Амфитеа́тров** (амфитеа́тр = *amphitheatre*), **Грибое́дов** (= *mushroom-eater*), **Щёпкин** (ще́пка = *chip*).

Masculine nouns and names usually form this type of possessive adjective in **-ов** and **-ев,** while feminine names and nouns are in **-ин:** **Алекса́ндр** forms **Алекса́ндров** while **Алекса́ндра** forms **Алекса́ндрин.**

It is important to note that when these possessive adjectives are used in their strictly literal sense and not as surnames, the masculine prepositional is in **-ом** instead of **-е.**

PRACTICE: **УПРАЖНЕНИЯ**

Our neighbour has five pretty daughters.	У на́шего сосе́да пять краси́вых дочере́й.
What is her grandfather called? (What are his 1st name and patronymic?) Mikhail Vasilievich.	Как и́мя и о́тчество её де́да? Михаи́л Васи́лиевич. ("Миха́л Васи́льч").
Do you know how many Christian names King George VI had?	Зна́ете ли вы ско́лько имён бы́ло у короля́ Гео́ргия Шесто́го?
I haven't the time to talk to him to-day.	У меня́ нет вре́мени разгова́ривать с ним сего́дня.
In our spare time we always draw from life (do nature drawing).	В свобо́дное вре́мя мы всегда́ рису́ем с нату́ры.
Up to that time granny hadn't known that they had seven invalids in their house (home).	До того́ вре́мени ба́бушка не знала́, что у них в до́ме семь больны́х.
From that time on (since that time) he has had a strong dislike for black cats.	С того́ вре́мени он о́чень не лю́бит чёрных ко́шек.

Lately he has been mad about your daughter.	В после́днее вре́мя он без ума́ от ва́шей до́чери.
Now is not the time for joking, my good woman!*	Тепе́рь не вре́мя шути́ть, мать моя́!
Time is short (is running out), my dear fellow!	Вре́мя не ждёт, ми́лый мой!
Why do you keep on looking at me? or Why do you look at me all the time?	Почему́ вы всё вре́мя смо́трите на меня́?
She is staying with them only for a (short) while.	Она́ у них то́лько на (коро́ткое) вре́мя.
From time to time granny tells us that we should eat white, rather than black bread.	От вре́мени до вре́мени ба́бушка нам говори́т, что нам на́до ку́шать бе́лый хлеб, а не чёрный.
Don't forget what I told you at the second lesson.	Не забыва́йте, что я вам говори́л на второ́м уро́ке!
To-morrow she will have to go and buy three red pencils.	За́втра ей на́до бу́дет идти́ покупа́ть три кра́сных карандаша́.

*Russians use **ма́тушка** or **ма́ма** when speaking to their mother. The expression **мать моя́** is used for "*my good woman*".

LESSON No. 27   УРОК № ДВА́ДЦАТЬ СЕМЬ (27)

ва́нна bath	**звони́ть** (II): звоню́, зво- ни́шь; звоня́т to ring
ва́нная bathroom	**звони́ть по телефо́ну** to telephone
ку́хня kitchen	**ребёнок** child
столо́вая dining room	**ками́н** fireplace
ключ key	**сын** son
замо́к lock	**у́голь** (*m*) (*gen* угля́) coal
час hour	**за́ново** again, anew
часы́ (*pl*) watch, clock	**зате́м** then, after that
дым smoke	
звоно́к hand bell, door bell	

Plurals

друзья́ friends	**сту́лья** chairs

пе́рья	pens, feathers	но́жницы	scissors
дере́вья	trees	де́ти	children
де́ньги	money	бра́тья	brothers
лю́ди	people	сыновья́	sons
очки́	spectacles	мужья́	husbands

SOFT FORM ADJECTIVES PLURAL:

One form serves for all three genders—as with hard form attributes. Because of the Orthographical rule, the so-called "mixed endings" adjectives have exactly the same endings in the plural as the soft form adjectives. The characteristic nominative plural ending for soft form adjectives is **-е**.

SOFT FORM ADJECTIVES PLURAL DECLENSION:

N:	си́ние	хоро́шие	ру́сские	больши́е
G:	си́них	хоро́ших	ру́сских	больши́х
D:	си́ним	хоро́шим	ру́сским	больши́м
A:	As *nominative*	or *genitive*		
I:	си́ними	хоро́шими	ру́сскими	больши́ми
P:	о си́них	о хоро́ших	о ру́сских	о больши́х

SUMMARY OF DECLENSION OF ADJECTIVES: What has been given completes the declension of adjectives, which do *not* deviate from the rules. The stress of an attributive adjective is fixed throughout as in the *masc nom singular*. A Summary of adjectival inflexions will be found on page 154 at the end of Part I. To this you should refer constantly until you are confident that you know them all.

PLURAL DECLENSIONS OF Э́ТОТ, ТОТ, ОДИ́Н:

Like the adjectives, these have only one set of endings in the plural, serving for all three genders. The plural form of *one* **одни́** can be used in several ways: in a purely numerical sense it is used with those nouns which have no singular form, such as **часы́**, *clock*, *watch* and **но́жницы,** *scissors*. Like the singular form, it is also often used in the sense of *same, alone, only, certain* (see Lesson 19).

Plurals

of	этот, эта, это	тот, та, то	один, одна, одно:
Nom:	эти	те	одни́
Gen:	э́тих	тех	одни́х
Dat:	э́тим	тем	одни́м
Acc:	same as nominative or genitive		
Ins:	э́тими	те́ми	одни́ми
Prp:	об э́тих	о тех	об одни́х

PLURALS OF POSSESSIVE PRONOUNS:

Nom:	мой	твой	на́ши	ва́ши
Gen:	мои́х	твои́х	на́ших	ва́ших
Dat:	мои́м	твои́м	на́шим	ва́шим
Acc:	as nominative or genitive			
Ins:	мои́ми	твои́ми	на́шими	ва́шими
Prp:	о мои́х	о твои́х	о на́ших	о ва́ших

PLURAL OF ORDINAL NUMERAL ТРЕТИЙ

Nom:	тре́тьи
Gen:	тре́тьих
Dat:	тре́тьим
Acc:	Nom or Gen
Ins:	тре́тьими
Prp:	о тре́тьих

SLIGHTLY IRREGULAR NOUNS (contd)

Nouns used in the plural only: These five very common nouns exist only in the plural. They are declined as follows:

	money	glasses	children
Nom:	де́ньги	очки́	де́ти
Gen:	де́нег	очко́в	дете́й
Dat:	деньга́м	очка́м	де́тям
Acc:	де́ньги	очки́	дете́й
Ins:	деньга́ми	очка́ми	детьми́
Prp:	о деньга́х	об очка́х	о де́тях

	people	scissors
Nom:	лю́ди	но́жницы
Gen:	людéй	но́жниц
Dat:	лю́дям	но́жницам
Acc:	людéй	но́жницы
Ins:	людьми́	но́жницами
Prp:	о лю́дях	о но́жницах

Note: **дéти** is the plural of **ребёнок** (*gen sing* **ребёнка**), *a child.* **лю́ди** is used for the plural of **человéк,** *man, person, human being.*

Plurals in **-ья:**

Nom:	сту́лья chairs	**брáтья** brothers
Gen:	сту́льев	**пéрья** pens
Dat:	сту́льям	**дерéвья** trees, wood
Acc:	сту́лья	*follow this*
Ins:	сту́льями	*pattern*
Prp:	о сту́льях	

Nom:	друзья́ friends	
Gen:	друзéй	**сыновья́** sons
Dat:	друзья́м	**мужья́** husbands
Acc:	друзéй	*follow this*
Ins:	друзья́ми	*pattern*
Prp:	о друзья́х	

Note: In this type of declension, when the stress is on the stem, the genitive *pl* is in **-ьев;** when it is on the ending the genitive *pl* is in **-ей.** Remember that a genitive plural in **-ей** can *never* be preceded by soft sign **-ь.**

CARDINAL NUMERALS 20 TO 40: двáдцать, *twenty,* and **три́дцать,** *thirty,* are both declined exactly like **пять** with the stress on the ending in the oblique cases. **со́рок,** *forty,* has only two forms: **со́рок,** for nominative and accusative; and **сорокá,** for all the other cases.

COMPOUND CARDINAL NUMERALS: A compound cardinal numeral is one that is made up of two or more parts: twenty-one, forty-four, a hundred and twenty-five. The two important points to remember about Russian compound cardinals are:

(1) All parts of a compound cardinal numeral must be declined. Thus: *nom* **двáдцать три,** *gen* **двадцатú трёх,** *dat* **двадцатú трём** and so on.

(2) The case and number of the noun are dictated by the *last* component part of a compound cardinal numeral. Thus: *twenty-one tables* = **двáдцать одúн стол: стол,** singular to agree with **одúн.** *thirty-two books* = **трúдцать две кнúги: кнúги,** genitive singular, because of **две.** *forty-five trees* = **сóрок пять дерéвьев: дерéвьев,** genitive plural after **пять.**

Compound cardinal numerals + noun:

	animate	inanimate
N:	двáдцать одúн студéнт	двáдцать одúн стол
G:	двадцатú одногó студéнта	двадцатú одногó столá
D:	двадцатú одномý студéнту	двадцатú одномý столý
A:	двáдцать одногó студéнта	двáдцать одúн стол
I:	двадцатью однúм студéнтом	двадцатью однúм столóм
P:	о двадцатú однóм студéнте	о двадцатú однóм столé
N:	трúдцать три лóшади	трúдцать две рекú
G:	тридцатú трёх лошадéй	тридцатú двух рек
D:	тридцатú трём лошадя́м	тридцатú двум рéкам
A:	трúдцать трёх лошадéй	трúдцать две рекú
I:	тридцатью тремя́ лошадьмú	тридцатью двумя́ рéками
P:	о тридцатú трёх лошадя́х	о тридцатú двух рéках
N:	сóрок шесть друзéй	сóрок вóсемь дерéвьев
G:	сорокá шестú друзéй	сорокá восьмú дерéвьев
D:	сорокá шестú друзья́м	сорокá восьмú дерéвьям
A:	сóрок шесть друзéй	сóрок вóсемь дерéвьев
I:	сорокá шестью друзья́ми	сорокá восемью дерéвьями
P:	о сорокá шестú друзья́х	о сорокá восьмú дерéвьях

Examples of the use of compound cardinal numerals will be found in the PRACTICE below.

PRACTICE: **УПРАЖНЕНИЯ**

Are you alone here?	Вы здесь одни?
We've only got one clock in the whole house.	У нас на весь дом одни часы́.
There's nothing but cats in granny's room.	У ба́бушки в ко́мнате одни́ ко́шки.
These (those) people have no money at all.	У э́тих люде́й совсе́м нет де́нег.
Yesterday the Ivanov brothers were playing with our children.	Вчера́ бра́тья Ива́новы игра́ли с на́шими детьми́.
She had never heard of Dostoyevsky's "Brothers Karamazov".	Она́ никогда́ не слы́шала о "Бра́тьях Карама́зовых" Достое́вского.
How many sons have you?	Ско́лько у вас сынове́й?
He and I are great friends.	Мы с ним (*idiom*) больши́е друзья́.
Can you hear the bell (ringing)? Who is it ringing?	Вы слы́шите звоно́к? Кто э́то звони́т?
Wives always ask their husbands how much money they have.	Жёны всегда́ спра́шивают муже́й, ско́лько у них де́нег.
Where is the key to this cupboard?	Где ключ от э́того шка́фа?
Why is there so much smoke in the kitchen?	Почему́ на ку́хне сто́лько ды́ма?
Go to the kitchen and take the milk.	Иди́те на ку́хню и бери́те молоко́!
Do you like Russian cooking?	Лю́бите ли вы ру́сскую ку́хню?
They always dine in the kitchen and not in the dining room.	Они́ всегда́ обе́дают не в столо́вой, а на ку́хне.
Do you know that Russian (over there) wearing spectacles?	Зна́ете ли вы того́ ру́сского в очка́х?

Look, there's no coal at all in the fireplace.	Смотри́те, в ками́не совсе́м нет угля́!
I'm going to ring up our friends now.	Я сейча́с бу́ду звони́ть по телефо́ну на́шим друзья́м.
In my pocket I have 21 roubles and 43 copecks.	У меня́ в карма́не два́дцать оди́н ру́бль и со́рок три копе́йки.

LESSON No. 28   УРОК № ДВА́ДЦАТЬ ВО́СЕМЬ (28)

Attributive ("*full*") *form*:	*Predicative* ("*short*") *form*	*Related words*
ма́лый, -ая, -ое ; -ые small	мал, мала́, мало́ ; малы́	
вели́кий, -ая, -ое ; -ие big, large, great	вели́к, -а́, -о́ ; -и́	
ста́рый, -ая, -ое ; -ые old	стар, -а́, -о́ ; -ы	стари́к old man, стару́ха old woman
молодо́й, -а́я, -о́е ; -ы́е young	мо́лод, -а́, -о ; -ы	молоде́ц! fine fellow! well done!
краси́вый, -ая, -ое ; -ые beautiful	краси́в, -а, -о ; -ы	краса́вец handsome man; краса́вица beautiful woman
некраси́вый, -ая, -ое ; -ые plain, ugly	некраси́в, -а, -о ; -ы	
плохо́й, -а́я, -о́е ; -и́е bad	плох, -а́, -о ; -и́	
за́нятый, -ая, -ое ; -ые engaged, busy	за́нят, -а́, -о ; -ы	заня́тие occupation

пра́вый, -ая, -ое ; -ые right	прав, -а́, -о ; -ы in the right	непра́в in the wrong; пра́вая сторона́ right side напра́во to the right
живо́й, -а́я, -о́е ; -ые alive, lively	жив, -а́, -о ; -ы	Жи́во! Quickly!
здоро́вый, -ая, -ое ; -ые healthy	здоро́в, -а, -о ; -ы	Здоро́во! Hello! Здо́рово! Well done! Жив, здоро́в. = Alive and well.

PREDICATIVE ("Short form") ADJECTIVES: In Lesson 13 you were told of the important distinction made in Russian between *attributive* and *predicative* adjectives. The "full form" adjectives that we have been dealing with so far, are, in most instances, used attributively. However, when an adjective is predicative, it can in Russian have a short form distinct from the full form. This predicative, short form can exist only in the nominative, since it is always the predicate implied or expressed of the verb *to be*. There are three forms, one for each gender, in the singular and one common form for all three genders in the plural.

Formation of predicative adjectives: The adjectival ending of the full form nominative singular is dropped and replaced with the following endings:

masc sing	*fem sing*	*neut sing*	*plural: all genders*
No ending	**-a**	**-o**	**-ы**
			(и *after* г, к, х, ж, ч, ш, щ)

Examples:

молодо́й молода́я молодо́е молоды́е ⎫ Full
краси́вый краси́вая краси́вое краси́вые ⎭ forms

мо́лод молода́ мо́лодо мо́лоды   } Short

краси́в краси́ва краси́во краси́вы   } forms

attributive adj + noun:

молодо́й брат   (a, the) young brother

здоро́вый ма́льчик   (a, the) healthy boy

краси́вый го́род   (a, the) beautiful city

noun + predicative adj:

брат мо́лод   the brother is young

ма́льчик здоро́в   the boy is well (healthy)

го́род краси́в   the city is beautiful

Note: In modern Russian *only hard-ending adjectives can have a short form.* Soft-ending short forms are mostly archaic and found in poetry. Adjectives in **-ский** never have a short form. Where an adjective does not have a short form, the full form is also used predicatively. There are also other adjectives where the short form is not idiomatic. For instance, **вели́к** and **мал** (short forms of **вели́кий** and **ма́лый**) are always used as the predicatives of **большо́й** and **ма́ленький,** which do not have short forms. On the other hand, **рад, -а ; -ы** *happy, glad,* have no full forms and can be used only predicatively. *Use only those short forms that are given to you as such. Experience in Russian usage will show you which ones are commonly used.*

Fleeting -e- and -o- : When a full form adjective has two consonants together before its adjectival ending (**-ый, -ой**), **-o-** or **-e-** is inserted between these consonants in the masculine short form. The following are useful examples which should be memorized:

	Full Forms	*Short Forms*
ill, sick, sore	**больно́й** (льн)	**бо́лен, больна́, -о́ ; -ы́**
strong	**си́льный** (льн)	**си́лен, сильна́, -о ; -ы́**
cold	**холо́дный** (дн)	**хо́лоден, холодна́, -о ; -ы**
warm	**тёплый** (пл)	**тёпел, тепла́, -о́ ; -ы**
free	**свобо́дный** (дн)	**свобо́ден, свобо́дна, -о ; -ы**
poor	**бе́дный** (дн)	**бе́ден, бедна́, -о ; -ы**
difficult	**тру́дный** (дн)	**тру́ден, трудна́, -о ; -ы**
full, complete	**по́лный** (лн)	**по́лон, полна́, -о ; -ы**

| hungry | голóдный (дн) | гóлоден, голоднá, -о ; -ы |
| content, pleased | довóльный (-льн) | { довóлен, довóльна, -о ; -ы
{ довóльно = enough |

ADVERBIAL USE OF NEUTER SHORT FORM ADJECTIVES: In Lesson 22 we saw that in Russian many adverbs are derived from other parts of speech including adjectives. Adverbs derived from adjectives are also very common in English: *slow* (*adj*), *slowly* (*adv*), *correct* (*adj*), *correctly* (*adv*). In Russian, the neuter short form of an adjective can always be used as an adverb. Thus:

Он говори́т по-ру́сски свобóдно. He speaks Russian *fluently*.

Я вас плóхо понимáю. I don't understand you *very well*.

   (*lit:* I understand you *badly*).

Онá краси́во пи́шет. She writes *prettily, nicely*.

Sometimes a change of stress distinguishes between the neuter predicative adjective and the same form used as an adverb. Thus **малó** is the neuter short form used always as a predicate as in **крéсло малó** = *the armchair is* (*too*) *small*, but the adverbial form is **мáло** as in **он мáло говори́т по-ру́сски** = *he doesn't speak much Russian.*

Stress of short form adjectives: Always note stress changes in the short forms. In full form adjectives the stress is always constant, but, as you can see in the examples given above, it can vary greatly in the short forms. When fleeting **-е-** or **-о-** is inserted in the short form, the stress tends to move back (**хóлоден, гóлоден**), but in general the masculine short form tends to retain the stress of the full form adjective, whereas the feminine often has it on the final syllable. Exceptions, however, are numerous and *the stress pattern of each individual short form adjective should be noted carefully*.

SHORT FORM NEUTER ADJECTIVES + DATIVE: Predicative neuter adjectives are often used with the meaning *I am, you are, he, she, it is* in such expressions as:

Мне хóлодно. = I am cold.   **Мне теплó.** = I feel warm.

Вам легко́. = It's easy for you.   **Ему́ тру́дно.** = It's difficult for him.

Мне бо́льно. = It hurts (me).   **Ей пло́хо.** = She is (feeling) ill, sick.

НУ́ЖЕН and ДО́ЛЖЕН: **ну́жен, нужна́, ну́жно, нужны́** the short forms of the adjective **ну́жный** *necessary* are commonly used to express *need for something or somebody*. The object in English (*as in "I need a book"*) becomes the subject in Russian (*book*) and the English subject (*I*) goes into the dative:

Мне нужна́ кни́га = I need a book.

Нужны́ ли вам де́ньги? = Do you need money?

Ей ну́жно перо́ = She wants a pen.

Мне ну́жен бу́дет ключ. = I shall need a key.

Ему́ не нужна́ была́ на́ша по́мощь. = He had no need for our help.

Вы мне о́чень нужны́. = I need you very much *or* I want to see you very much.

This type of expression is closely connected with the noun **нужда́**, *need, want, necessity.*

до́лжен, должна́, должно́, должны́, the short forms of the adjective **до́лжный**, *due, owing*, are used to express the need or obligation *to do something.* This is equivalent to the English expressions *need to, ought to, should, must.* This type of expression is closely connected with the noun **долг**, *debt, obligation.* Examples:

Я до́лжен идти́ сейча́с в ла́вку = I must go to the shop now.

Она́ должна́ вам помога́ть. = She ought to help you.

Они́ должны́ бу́дут нас ждать. = They will have to wait for us.

Note that the same form is used for expressions of owing debts, but in the past and future the verb **быть** is placed before the adjective:

Он мне до́лжен три рубля́ = He owes me three roubles.

Она́ была́ должна́ нам семна́дцать рубле́й = She owed us seventeen roubles.

Я бу́ду до́лжен вам три́дцать два рубля́ = I shall owe you thirty-two roubles.

The neuter form **ну́жно** can also be used impersonally like **на́до** to express the *need* to do something. Here, however, there is no sense of obligation or duty as with **до́лжен**:

Мне $\left\{\begin{array}{l} \text{ну́жно} \\ \text{на́до} \end{array}\right\}$ **идти́ сейча́с в ла́вку** = I must go to the shop now.

Им $\left\{\begin{array}{l} \text{ну́жно} \\ \text{на́до} \end{array}\right\}$ **бу́дет нас ждать** = They will have to wait for us.

PRACTICE: **УПРАЖНЕНИЯ**

Your jacket is (too) small for you and your shoes are (too) big.	Эта ку́ртка вам мала́, а боти́нки велики́.
He's (too) old to play football.	Он сли́шком ста́р, что́бы игра́ть в футбо́л.
You're still young!	Вы ещё мо́лоды!
Is the doctor free to-day, or is he busy?	Врач свобо́ден сего́дня, и́ли за́нят?
Have you any rooms vacant? (*lit:* Do you not have . . . ?)	Нет ли у вас свобо́дных ко́мнат?
No, all our rooms are occupied.	Нет, все ко́мнаты у нас за́няты.
You're right. To go (get, reach) there, one should go to the right.	Вы пра́вы. Идти́ туда́ на́до напра́во.
When are we having dinner? I'm very hungry.	Когда́ бу́дем обе́дать? Я о́чень го́лоден.
She is very pleased with your work.	Она́ о́чень дово́льна ва́шей рабо́той.
I am very pleased with you.	Я ва́ми о́чень дово́лен.
She doesn't know her lesson at all well.	Она́ о́чень пло́хо зна́ет уро́к.
Is this church open?	Откры́та ли э́та це́рковь?
This door is locked.	Э́та дверь закры́та на замо́к.

He was feeling very sick yesterday.	Ему́ вчера́ бы́ло о́чень пло́хо.
It's difficult to work when there's such a noise out on the street.	Тру́дно рабо́тать, когда́ на у́лице сто́лько шу́ма. (сто́лько = *so much, so many*.)
I'm very ill to-day. What is the matter with you?	Я о́чень бо́лен сего́дня. А что с ва́ми?
It hurts! Where does it hurt?	(Мне) бо́льно! Где вам бо́льно?

LESSON No. 29   УРО́К № ДВА́ДЦАТЬ ДЕ́ВЯТЬ (29)

ви́деть (II): ви́жу, ви́дишь; ви́дят.   to see (д *changes to* ж *in* 1st *pers sing only.*   See *Lesson* 23) +*acc.*

встреча́ть (I): встреча́ю, встреча́ешь.   to meet +*acc.*
Я всегда́ встреча́ю её в э́той ла́вке.

знако́мить (II): знако́млю, знако́мишь.   to acquaint (*transitive*): " . . . *someone with someone else*"; (л *inserted in* 1st *pers sing only.*   See Lesson 13) +с +*instr.*
Она́ ча́сто знако́мит меня́ с америка́нцами.
Знако́мьте их с ру́сскими людьми́!

находи́ть (II): нахожу́, нахо́дишь.   to find (д *changes to* ж *as in* ви́деть) +*acc.*
Он всегда́ нахо́дит де́ньги на у́лице.
Я нахожу́, что вы пло́хо пи́шете.

ста́вить (II): ста́влю, ста́вишь.   to put, place (*in a standing position;* л *inserted as in* знако́мить) +*acc.*
Иногда́ я ста́влю ла́мпу на э́тот стол.
Ста́вьте шкаф сюда́!

пока́зывать (I): пока́зываю, пока́зываешь.   to show +*acc* ("*something*") +*dat* ("*to someone*").
Он пока́зывал мне ва́ше письмо́.

боле́ть (I): боле́ю, боле́ешь.   to be sick, ill.
Я ча́сто боле́ю.
Зимо́й она́ всегда́ боле́ет.

Not to be confused with:

болéть (II) : **болúт, боля́т.**   to ache (used only in 3*rd pers*).

   У меня́ голова́ болúт.

   У него́ зу́бы боля́т.

петь (I) : **пою́, поёшь ; пою́т.**   **пой/-те! пел, -а, -о ; -и.**
   to sing (*conjugation stem:* **по-**)+*acc* (*"something"*),+
   dat (*"to someone"*).

   Она́ поёт им а́рию.

Not to be confused with:

пить (I) : **пью, пьёшь ; пьют.**   **пей/-те! пил, -а, -о ; -и.**
   to drink (**и** *contracts to* **ь** *in conjugation*) +*acc*.

   Она́ никогда́ не пьёт вина́.

   Пéйте чай!

Like **пить** are **бить**, (I) *to strike, beat,* **лить**, (I) *to pour* and
шить, (I) *to sew*.

SUMMARY OF PRIMARY PREPOSITIONS AND THE CASES THEY GOVERN :

Genitive	*Dative*	*Accusative*
без without	**к (ко)** towards	**в (во)** into, to
для for	**по** along; in	**за** behind (direction)
до up to, until	accordance with	**на** onto, to, for
из (изо) out of, from		**о (об, обо)** against
ра́ди for the sake of		**под(о)** under
с (со) down from, of		**про** about
у at		**чéрез** across, through
от (ото) out of, from		**по** each; up to
		сквозь through

Instrumental	*Prepositional*
за behind, after, at, for	**в (во)** in
мéжду among	**о (об, обо)** about, concerning
над(о) over, above	**на** on
пéред before, in front of	**при** in time *or* presence of
под(о) under	**до** after
с (со) with	

With **в, на, под, за, о, чéрез, сквозь** the accusative
always indicates *motion*, never rest (location, place).

Instrumental or prepositional indicate *rest*, not motion:

$$\left.\begin{array}{l}\text{with } ins\text{: } \text{под, за}\\ \text{with } prp\text{: } \text{на, в (во)}\end{array}\right\} = \text{place } (static)$$

Prepositions ending in a consonant may have **-о** before a combination of consonants such as **мн-, вр-, вс-**:

во мне, ко мне, вовремя = in time

EXAMPLES OF USE OF PREPOSITIONS: **УПРАЖНЕНИЯ**

Beginners often find it difficult in practice to use Russian prepositions correctly.   It is a tricky part of the language which is best taken seriously from the outset.   Hence, instead of the normal PRACTICE, we give many examples of the ways prepositions will appear in reading matter or be heard in everyday life.   These examples must be known.   Practise them in this way: (1) Take each case separately.   (2) On one piece of paper write out the Russian phrase.   (3) On another write out the corresponding English phrase.   (4) When you have finished a case, test yourself: first see whether you know the English for the Russian, and afterwards see whether you can *write* the Russian for the English phrases. Do this exercise thoroughly, memorizing as you do it.   If well done, you should not have great trouble with these common prepositions in the future.

(1) **With the genitive: я без денег.** = I haven't any money.   **Она это делает для вас.** = She's doing this for you.   **До станции пять километров.** = It's five kilometres to the station.   **Дети до пяти лет** = Children under five years of age.   **Он работает с утра до вечера** = He works from morning till evening.   **Мы пьём чай из стаканов.** = We drink tea out of glasses.   **Один из его товарищей** = One of his friends.   **Из чего это?** = What is this made of?   **Он ходит из одной комнаты в другую.** = He walks about from one room into another.   **от начала до конца** = from beginning to end.   **От города до станции два километра.** = From the town to the station is two kilometres.   **У меня письмо от дочери.** = I have a letter from my daughter.   **на восток от города** = east of the town. **ключ от этой комнаты** = the key to this room.   **Он без ума от неё.** = He's mad about her.   **Я без ума от вашей книги** = I'm mad about your book.   **Он это говорит ради шутки.** = He's saying this just for a joke.   **Я это делаю**

ра́ди вас. = I'm doing this for your sake. Ра́ди Бо́га! = For Heaven's (*lit* God's) sake! Ча́шка упа́ла со стола́. = The cup fell from the table. с ва́шего разреше́ния = with your permission.

(2) **With the dative :** Иди́те сюда́ ко мне! = Come over here to me. Иди́те к тому́ зда́нию! = Go over to that building (*without necessarily entering it*). Это письмо́ к нему́. = This letter is for him.

(3) **With the accusative :** Они́ ста́вят стол в пере́днюю. = They're putting the table into the lobby. в го́ру = uphill. Иди́те за́ реку! = Cross over the river (*lit* "Go beyond the river"). Он всегда́ ста́вит э́тот стул за шкаф. = He always puts this chair behind the cupboard. рабо́тать за свобо́ду = to work for freedom. Ста́вьте стака́ны на стол! = Put the glasses on the table. На что э́то ему́? = What does he want this for? Вы гото́вили уро́к на э́ту неде́лю? = Have you prepared the lesson for this week (this week's lesson)? ста́вить на ме́сто = to put something in its proper place, to replace. бок о́ бок = side by side. Он идёт на рабо́ту рука́ о́б руку с ней. = He is going to work hand in hand (arm in arm) with her. Я уда́рил го́лову о сте́ну. = I hit my head against the wall. Он ста́вит стака́н под стул. = He is putting the glass under the chair. Я иду́ под де́рево. = I'm going under the tree. под ве́чер, у́тро = towards evening, morning. под Но́вый год = New Year's Eve. петь под му́зыку = to sing to the music of. под го́ру = uphill. Он уже́ слы́шал про э́то. = He has already heard about this. Она́ ему́ говори́ла про меня́. = She spoke to him about me. идти́ че́рез у́лицу = to cross the street. Он идёт туда́ че́рез по́ле. = He's going there through the field, he's crossing the field to get there. по́ два я́блока на челове́ка = two apples apiece. с ма́я по сентя́брь = from May to September. Вы ви́дите сквозь тума́н? = Can you see through the fog? говори́ть сквозь зу́бы = to talk with teeth clenched.

(4) **With the instrumental :** дом за реко́й = the house beyond, on the other side of the river. стул за шка́фом =

the chair, behind the cupboard.   **между о́кнами** = between
the windows.   **между на́ми** = between ourselves, between
you and me.   **между про́чим** = by the way, incidentally.
Ла́мпа виси́т над столо́м. = The lamp is hanging above
the table.   **Он рабо́тает над тру́дной пробле́мой.** = He
is working at a difficult problem.   **Пе́ред до́мом был сад.**
= In front of the house was a garden.   **перед обе́дом** =
(immediately) before dinner.   **Стака́н под столо́м.** = The
glass is under the table.   **Он под аре́стом.** = He's under
arrest.   **под дождём** = in the rain.   **Он игра́ет с детьми́.**
= He's playing with the children.   **чай с молоко́м,**
лимо́ном = tea with milk, lemon.   **хлеб с ма́слом** = bread
and butter.   **С удово́льствием!** = With pleasure!   **Мы с**
ва́ми = You and I.   **Что с ва́ми?** = What's the matter with
you?   **с после́дним по́ездом** = by the last train.

(5) **With the prepositional: Стол в пере́дней.** = The
table is in the lobby.   **Что она́ ду́мает о них?** = What does
she think of them?   **на заво́де** = at the factory.   **на уро́ке**
= at the lesson.   **на о́пере** = at the opera.   **на бале́те** = at
the ballet.   **на пье́се** = at the play.   **Э́та кни́га на ру́с-**
ском языке́. = This book is in Russian.   **Не говори́те**
э́того при де́тях! = Don't say that in front of the children.
Докуме́нты при вас? = Have you your papers (documents)
with you?   **при дворе́** = at court.   **при Петре́ Вели́ком** =
under, in the reign of Peter the Great.

DERIVATIVE PREPOSITIONS (see Lesson 21):
Governing the genitive:

близ near	**из-за** from behind; because of
вме́сто instead of	**насчёт** about, concerning, as re-
вне outside of	gards
во́зле near, beside	**о́коло** near, about, approximately
вокру́г round, around	**по́сле** after
	среди́ among, amidst

Governing the dative: **благодаря́** thanks to

Examples: **близ Москвы́** = near Moscow.   **вме́сто него́**
= instead of him.   **вне шко́лы** = outside of, out of school.

ла́вка во́зле до́ма = the shop (is) near, beside the house. вокру́г све́та = around the world. из-за до́ма = from behind the house. из-за ва́с = because of you. о́коло теа́тра = near the theatre. о́коло четырёх = about four. по́сле конце́рта = after the concert. среди́ друзе́й = amongst friends. благодаря́ вам = thanks to you. вне о́череди = out of turn. благодаря́ его́ рабо́те = thanks to his work.

LESSON No. 30 УРОК № ТРИДЦАТЬ (30)

ви́деться* (II) + c + *instr*
  to meet, see one another

встреча́ться (I) + c + *instr*
  to meet (prearranged)

гото́виться (II) to prepare oneself (for . . . к + *dat*)

смея́ться (I): смею́сь, смеёшься to laugh (at . . . над + *instr*)

знако́миться (II) to become acquainted (with . . . c + *instr*)

купа́ться (I) to bathe (*intransitive*)

наде́яться (I): наде́юсь, наде́ешься to hope

находи́ться (II): нахожу́сь, нахо́дишься to be found, situated (French *se trouver*)

появля́ться (I) to appear

случа́ться (I) to happen, occur

конча́ться (I) to finish, end (*intransitive*)

зли́ться (II) to become angry

СЕБЯ́ = -self (*reflexive pronoun*)

пора́ = it's time

давно́ пора́ = it's high time

Pronunciation:* The verbal reflexive particles **-ться, **-тся** are pronounced **-цца**.

REFLEXIVE VERBS: When we say "*I wash myself*", "*he shaves himself*", the action of the verb is "reflected" back on the doer, who in this sense becomes the object of the verb. Such verbs are said to be "reflexive": -*self* is the ending of our reflexive pronouns. In Russian the reflexive pronoun corresponding to *self* is **себя́** and this word is used with the verb when nominative and accusative refer to the same person. Thus:

я зна́ю себя́ = *I know myself.*   **Мы зна́ем себя́** = *we know ourselves,* etc.

Reflexive pronoun себя́: This has no nominative but has *gen* **себя́,** *dat* **себе́,** *acc* **себя́,** *ins* **собо́й,** *prp* **о себе́.** It is used as a reflexive to replace inflected forms of all personal pronouns when they refer back to the subject of the sentence or clause in which they are.   For example, subject pronoun **я** has **себя́** and not **меня́** as its object in such sentences as **я ви́дел себя́** = *I saw myself.* **себя́** can be preceded by prepositions as in **Он де́лает э́то для себя́** = *He does it for himself.* **Он говори́л с собо́й** = *He talked to himself.*

Себя́ is of great importance in its shortened forms **-ся** and **-сь,** which become reflexive particles added as suffixes to make verbs reflexive.   (Be careful not to confuse **себя́** with **сам, свой, са́мый** = *the very, the most,* particularly **свой.** See page 80–1.)

Russian verbs ending in **-ся (-сь): себя́** is shortened to **-ся** (**-сь** after a vowel) and is added to the verbal form in Russian to make it a reflexive verb, which generally has the effect of making a transitive verb intransitive.   For example:

умыва́ть (I) = *to wash something* or *somebody* (*transitive*).

умыва́ться (I) = *to wash oneself* (*intransitive:* action remains with the doer).

After a vowel **ся** becomes **сь.**   So,

я умыва́юсь = *I wash myself*

Conjugation of Russian reflexive verbs: These are conjugated in exactly the same way as non-reflexive verbs of the same type, except that the reflexive pronoun (**ся** or **сь**) becomes a suffix.   So,

ты умыва́ешься.   он, она́ умыва́ется.

мы умыва́емся.   вы умыва́етесь.   они́ умыва́ются.

☞   Note that the reflexive suffix is always pronounced *hard.* Thus **ся** is pronounced as **са,** and **сь** as hard **с.**

True reflexive verbs and others with -ся (-сь): *to wash one-self* is a true reflexive verb in both English and Russian. But in Russian there are many verbs with this suffix which are not true reflexives.   For example:

собира́ть (I)   to collect *or* gather something.

But: собира́ться (I)=to assemble, (*also*+infinitive=to intend, prepare to).

слу́шать (I *tr*) *to listen to* in the reflexive слу́шаться means *to obey*.   Such verbs are sometimes called "neutral verbs".

Reciprocal verbs : The particle suffix -ся, -сь is also used to form what are called "reciprocal" verbs, because they represent mutual or reciprocal action rather than the truly reflexive.   Thus:

обнима́ть *trs* (I)=to embrace (*somebody*).
обнима́ться *intr*=to embrace one another.
мы обнима́емся=*we embrace one another*.
Past: мы обнима́лись=*we embraced one another*.

THE PASSIVE: When we say "*The clothes are being washed*" or "*it is being done*", then "*being washed*" and "*being done*" are said to be in the passive (*or* passive voice): in contrast to "*They washed the clothes*" and "*They did it*", which are said to be in the active (*or* active voice) of the verbs *to wash* or *to do*.

To express the passive in Russian : There are two ways: (1) by using the reflexive form of the verb; and (2) by using the 3rd person plural of the active+noun or pronoun in the accusative.   Thus:

(1) стро́ится теа́тр=*a theatre is being built*.
(2) говоря́т, что . . .=*they say that* which also means *it is said that* . . .

The English phrase *his, my, your*, etc., *name is* . . . can be expressed in the manner of (2), using the verb звать (I) *to call:* я зову́, ты зовёшь ; -у́т.   Thus:

What is your name ? (*lit:* What do they call you ?)=**как вас зову́т ?**

My name is Ivan Ivanovich=**Меня́ зову́т Ива́ном Ива́новичем.**★

His name is . . .=**Его́ зову́т . . .**

★ Note the predicate in the instrumental. Some verbs are normally followed by the instrumental.

When naming objects the verb **называ́ть** (I) is used transitively, and **называ́ться** intransitively or as an impersonal verb.   Thus:

Как э́то называ́ется ? *or* **Как э́то называ́ют ?**   *What is this (thing) called ?   How do they call this ?*

IMPERSONAL VERBS : Some verbs are used impersonally, that is only in the third person, mostly in the singular and with implied *"it"* as their subject. For example **ка́жется**, *3rd pers sing* of **каза́ться** (I) *to seem.* Thus: **Ка́жется, что его́ нет здесь** *it seems, (it appears) that he is not here.*   *"It seems"* is the equivalent for *I think, I fancy* and so **ка́жется** is a useful form.   Note the use of the dative with impersonal verbs:

Мне ка́жется, что они́ его́ пло́хо понима́ют.=It seems to me that they don't understand him very well.

Ему́ ду́мается, что вы не писа́ли ему́ э́того письма́= He thinks (seems to think) that you didn't write him this letter.

Мне по́мнится, что она́ здесь жила́=I seem to remember that she used to live here.

Note the impersonal verb **нездоро́виться** (II), *to be, feel unwell:*

Мне сего́дня нездоро́вится=I don't feel well to-day.

Do not confuse this verb with the reciprocal verb **здоро́ваться** (I)=*to greet, say how do you do:*
Я с ни́ми всегда́ здоро́ваюсь=I always say hello to them.

PRACTICE: **УПРАЖНЕНИЯ**

Why do you keep on being angry with him?	Почему́ вы всё вре́мя зли́тесь на него́?
Where is the post office here?	Где тут нахо́дится по́чта?
At that time the American embassy was situated near the university building.	В то вре́мя америка́нское посо́льство находи́лось во́зле зда́ния университе́та.
They always used to laugh at our sons.	Они́ всегда́ смея́лись над на́шими сыновья́ми.
You shouldn't laugh at me! (*Do not confuse impersonal* на́до *with preposition* над +o).	Не на́до смея́ться на́до мно́й!
I often meet (see) her at work.	Я ча́сто ви́жусь с ней на рабо́те.
I meet him once a week near the post office.	Мы с ним встреча́емся раз в неде́лю во́зле по́чты.
They're going to the station to meet their friends.	Они́ иду́т на вокза́л встреча́ть това́рищей.
Do you see how healthy he is? He is never sick and that is because he bathes in the sea every day.	Вы ви́дите, како́й он здоро́вый? Он никогда́ не боле́ет, а э́то потому́, что он ка́ждый день купа́ется в мо́ре.
What is this thing called in Russian?	Как э́та вещь называ́ется по-ру́сски?
We often meet (become acquainted with) Russians in that club.	Мы ча́сто знако́мимся с ру́сскими в э́том клу́бе.
Sometimes it so happens that I have to (sit up) working till late at night.	Иногда́ случа́ется (быва́ет) так, что мне ну́жно рабо́тать до по́здней но́чи.
I think you were hoping to meet her at their place.	Вы, ка́жется, наде́ялись встре́титься с ней у них.
I think their house is on this street.	Ка́жется, их дом нахо́дится на э́той у́лице.

Рисунок Л. и Ю. Черепановых

APPENDIX

INFLEXIONS OF NOUNS: SUMMARY

Masculines:

Rule of declension { Animates are identical in *acc* and *gen* } *In*
{ Inanimates in *acc* and *nom* } *sing and pl*

Ending			Nom	Gen	Dat	Acc	Ins	Prp
Con-sonant	[1]	*Sing:* бара́н|	-а	-у	-а	-ом	-е
		Pl: |ы	-ов	-ам	-ов	-ами	-ах
	[2]	журна́л|	-а	-у	*Nom*	-ом	-е
		|ы	-ов	-ам	-ы	-ами	-ах
-ь	[3]	писа́тел|ь	-я	-ю	-я	-ем	-е
		|и	-ей	-ям	-ей	-ями	-ях
	[4]	автомоби́л|ь	-я	-ю	-ь	-ем	-е
		|и	-ей	-ям	-и	-ями	-ях
-й	[5]	геро́|й	-я	-ю	-я	-ем	-е
		|и	-ев	-ям	-ев	-ями	-ях
	[6]	музе́|й	-я	-ю	-й	-ем	-е
		|и	-ев	-ям	-и	-ями	-ях
-ий	[7]	жре́б|ий	-ия	-ию	-ий	-ием	-ии
		|ии	-нев	-иям	-ии	-иями	-иях
-ёнок	[8]	реб|ёнок	-ёнка	-ёнку	-ёнка	-ёнком	-ёнке
		|я́та	-я́т	-я́там	-я́т	-я́тами	-я́тах

Names of males in -ин	[9]	англича́нин*	-а	-у	-а	-ом	-ка́
		англича́н|е	англи--ам чан		Gen	-ами	-ах

*These nouns drop -ин in the plural.

Noun with fleeting -о-	[10]	кус|о́к	-ка́	-ку́	-о́к	-ко́м	-ке́
		|ки́	-ко́в	-ка́м	-ки́	-ка́ми	-ка́х

Feminines:

Rule of declension { Animates identical in *gen* and *acc* } *pl*
{ Inanimates in *nom* and *acc* } *only*

Ending		Nom	Gen	Dat	Acc	Ins	Prp
-а	[11]	*Sing:* ры́б|а	-ы	-е	-у	-ой (ою)	-е
		Pl: |ы	(ры́б)	-ам	Gen	-ами	-ах
	[12]	газе́т|а	-ы	-е	-у	-ой (ою)	-е
		|ы	(газет)	-ам	-ы	-ами	-ах
-я	[13]	неде́л|я	-и	-е	-ю	-ей (ею)	-е
		|и	-ь	-ям	-и	-ями	-ях
-ия	[14]	а́рми|я	-и	-и	-ю	-ей (ею)	-и
		|и	-й	-ям	-и	-ями	-ях
-ь	[15]	тетра́д|ь	-и	-и	-ь	-ью	-и
		|и	-ей	-ям	-и	-ями	-ях
-чка -чек	[16]	де́воч|ка	-ки	-ке	-ку	-кой	-ке
		|ки	-ек	-кам	-ек	-ками	-ках

with fleeting e in *gen* and *acc pl*

Neuters:

Rule of declension: Nom and acc of *sing* are identical, as are *nom* and *acc* of *pl* of all neuters.

Ending		Nom	Gen	Dat	Acc	Ins	Prp
-о	[17]	сло́в|о	-а	-у	-о	-ом	-е
		|а́	слов	-а́м	-а́	-а́ми	-а́х
-е	[18]	мо́р|е	-я	-ю	-е	-ем	-е
		|я́	-е́й	-я́м	-я́	-я́ми	-я́х
-ье	[19]	воскресе́н|ье	-ья	-ью	-ье	-ьем	-ье
		|ья	-ий	-ьям	-ья	-ьями	-ьях
-ие	[20]	упражне́н|ие	-ия	-ию	-ие	-нем	-ии
		|ия	-ий	-иям	-ия	-иями	-иях
-ще	[21]	учи́лищ|е	-а	-у	-е	-ем	-е
		|а	(учи́-лищ)	-ам	-а	-ами	-ах

-ен- declen- sion	**[22]** {	врём|я |ена́	-ени -ён	-ени -ена́м	-я -ена́	-енем -ена́ми	-ени -ена́х

Fleeting vowels -о, -е, -ё

Nom	Gen	Pl		Nom	Gen	Pl	
оте́ц	отца́	отцы́	father	кусо́к	куска́	куски́	piece
осёл	осла́	ослы́	donkey	песо́к	песка́	пески́	sand
козёл	козла́	козлы́	goat	огóнь(m)	огня́	огни́	fire
у́гол	угла́	углы́	corner	ве́тер	ве́тра	ве́тры	wind
коне́ц	конца́	концы́	end	заём	за́йма	за́ймы	loan
купе́ц	купца́	купцы́	merchant	у́голь(m)	угля́	у́гли	coal
замо́к	замка́	замки́	lock	молото́к	-ка́	-ки́	hammer
за́мок	за́мка	за́мки	castle				

Animate

Nom:	оте́ц	отцы́
Gen:	отца́	отцо́в
Dat:	отцу́	отца́м
Acc:	отца́	отцо́в
Ins:	отцо́м	отца́ми
Prp:	об отце́	об отца́х

Inanimate

Nom:	кусо́к	куски́	день (m) day	дни
Gen:	куска́	куско́в	дня	дней
Dat:	куску́	куска́м	дню	дням
Acc:	кусо́к	куски́	день	дни
Ins:	куско́м	куска́ми	днём	дня́ми
Prp:	о куске́	о куска́х	о дне	о днях

Fleeting **-о-, -е-, -ё-** : Most masculine nouns with stressed **-о-, -е-** or **-ё-** in the final syllable of *nom sing* drop these vowels in all other cases of *sing* and *pl*. The stress is then usually passed on to the case-ending as in the examples given above of the declension of these nouns. Other examples of these nouns are given in the lists on pages 114, 119. The declension of **день** should be memorized, as this is a very common word. Note also **сон,** *gen sing* **сна,** *pl* **сны** = *sleep;* also *dream.*

STRESSED SYLLABLE OF NOUNS: SUMMARY

The stressed syllable of nouns varies considerably and there are few reliable rules. Most nouns of foreign origin have stress fixed by that of the nominative singular: **ваго́н. пассажи́р.**

Most nouns of more than two syllables also have stress fixed by their nominative singular: **америка́нец. автомоби́ль.**

Masculine nouns:

(a) Many frequently recurring *masc* nouns of one syllable and some of two syllables have stress on the case-ending throughout.   These have to be memorized as they occur.

    Examples: **стол, столá.   карандáш, -á,** etc.

(b) Stress on the *gen sing* ending of *masc* nouns indicates stress on dative, instrumental and prepositional singular ending.

    Examples: **стол, столá** ; and *pl:* **столы́.**

(c) When the stressed syllable is *not* the genitive singular ending, that stress remains throughout the singular.

    Examples: **мáльчик, мáльчика, -у, -а, -ом, -е.   Мéсяц, -а,** etc.

Feminine nouns:

(a) Feminine nouns with *nom sing* in unstressed **-а, -я**, retain the *nom sing* stress throughout, *sing* and *pl.*

    Examples: **шля́па, -ы, -е, -у, -ой, -е** ; *pl:* **шля́пы,** etc.

(b) Many feminine nouns with *nom sing* in **á, я́** stressed move the stress back to the stem in the *acc sing* while retaining it on the ending in the other cases.   In the plural such nouns take the stress on the stem throughout.   Some keep the stress on the ending of *acc sing*, but have it on the stem throughout the plural.

    Examples: **сестрá,** *acc* **сестрý,** *gen* **сестры́,** *pl* **сёстры** ; **рукá,** *acc* **рýку,** *gen* **руки́,** *pl* **рýки.**

(c) Feminine nouns ending in soft sign **-ь** follow the rules for masculine nouns (c) given above.

Neuter nouns:

(a) Those unstressed in the *nom sing* ending in **-о, -е** have fixed stress throughout the *sing.*

(b) Neuter nouns stressed in the *nom sing* in **-ó, -ё** retain that stress throughout the *sing.*

(c) In the plural, *neut* nouns of two syllables usually have the stress of the plural on the syllable *other than* the stressed syllable of the singular.

    Example: Nom sing: **мóре.   *Nom pl:*** **моря́** and so on.

In this book, nouns in which attention is not drawn to some irregularity or deviation from regularity may be assumed to be regular.   Attention will be drawn to irregularities, or to deviations from expected stress.

By learning the nominative and genitive singular and the nominative plural of each noun, you have the key to all other cases in the singular and plural, and also to stressed syllable.

Thus: **стол** as above.   And: **брат** brother, *gen* **-а** ; *pl.* **-ья.**

INFLEXIONS OF ADJECTIVES: SUMMARY

	HARD Endings		SOFT Endings	MIXED Endings (unstressed after ж, ч, ш, щ)
	1 но́вый, -ая, -ое	**2** второ́й, -ая, -ое	**3** си́ний, -яя, -ее	**4** хоро́ший, -ая, -ее

Singular

	HARD masc	HARD fem	HARD neut	SOFT masc	SOFT fem	SOFT neut	MIXED masc	MIXED fem	MIXED neut
Nom	-ый, -ой	-ая	-ое	-ий	-яя	-ее	-ий	-ая	-ее
Gen	-ого	-ой	-ого	-его	-ей	-его	-его	-ей	-его
Dat	-ому	-ой	-ому	-ему	-ей	-ему	-ему	-ей	-ему
Acc	-ый, -ой, -ого	-ую	-ое	-ий, -его	-юю	-ее	-ий, -его	-ую	-ее
Ins	-ым	-ой, -ою	-ым	-им	-ей, -ею	-им	-им	-ей, -ею	-им
Prp	-ом	-ой	-ом	-ем	-ей	-ем	-ем	-ей	-ем

Plural: all genders

	HARD	SOFT	MIXED
Nom	-ые	-ие	-ие
Gen	-ых	-их	-их
Dat	-ым	-им	-им
Acc	-ые, -ых	-ие, -их	-ие, -их
Ins	-ыми	-ими	-ими
Prp	-ых	-их	-их

Rule: With animate and inanimate nouns: Masculine and neuter adjectives in the singular and of all genders in the plural have the same endings for accusative and nominative when they refer to inanimates. Those of masculine gender have the same endings for genitive and accusative in both singular and plural when they refer to animates. Adjectival ending **-ого**, **-его** *pr* **г** as **в**.

DECLENSION OF PRONOUNS: TABLE

	Nom	Gen	Dat	Acc	Ins	Prp
Sing:	я	меня	мне	меня	мной(-ою)	мне
Pl.:	мы	нас	нам	нас	нами	нас
Sing:	ты	тебя	тебе	тебя	тобой(-ою)	тебе
Pl.:	вы	вас	вам	вас	вами	вас
Masc.:	он	его	ему	его	им	нём*
Fem.:	она	её	ей	её	ею(ей)	ней
Neut.:	оно	его	ему	его	им	нём
Pl.:	они	их	им	их	ими	них
						*See page 51
who:	кто	кого	кому	кого	кем	ком
what:	что	чего	чему	что	чем	чём
	Like кто and что are declined никто and ничто					
Masc.:	мой	моего	моему	N or G	моим	моём
Fem.:	моя	моей	моей	мою	моей(-ею)	моей
Neut.:	моё	моего	моему	моё	моим	моём
Pl.:	мои	моих	моим	N or G	моими	моих
Masc.:	наш	нашего	нашему	N or G	нашим	нашем
Fem.:	наша	нашей	нашей	нашу	нашей(-ею)	нашей
Neut.:	наше	нашего	нашему	наше	нашим	нашем
Pl.:	наши	наших	нашим	N or G	нашими	наших
	—	себя	себе	себя	собой	себе

Part II page 254

	Nom	Gen	Dat	Acc	Ins	Prp
Masc:	чей whose	чьегó	чьемý	чей*	чьим	чьём
Fem:	чья	чьей	чьей	чью	чьей	чьей
Neut:	чьё	чьегó	чьемý	чьё	чьим	чьём
Pl:	чьи	чьих	чьим	чьи*	чьими	чьих
Masc:	этот	этого	этому	этот*	этим	этом
Fem:	эта	этой	этой	эту	этой	этой
Neut:	это	этого	этому	это	этим	этом
Pl:	эти	этих	этим	эти*	этими	этих
Masc:	тот	тогó	томý	тот*	тем	том
Fem:	та	той	той	ту	той	той
Neut:	то	тогó	томý	то	тем	том
Pl:	те	тех	тем	те*	тéми	тех
Masc:	сей this	сегó	семý	сей*	сим	сём
Fem:	сия	сей	сей	сию	сей(сéю)	сей
Neut:	сиé	сегó	семý	сиé	сим	сём
Pl:	сии	сих	сим	сии*	сими	сих
Masc:	сам -self	самогó	самомý	самогó*	самúм	самóм
Fem:	самá	самóй	самóй	самоё	самóй	самóй
Neut:	самó	самогó	самомý	самó	самúм	самóм
Pl:	сáми	самúх	самúм	самúх*	самúми	самúх
Masc:	весь all	всегó	всемý	весь*	всем	всём
Fem:	вся	всей	всей	всю	всей(всéю)	всей
Neut:	всё	всегó	всемý	всё	всем	всём
Pl:	все	всех	всем	все*	всéми	всех
	нéсколько	нéскольких	нéскольким	нéсколько*	нéсколькими	нéскольких

* Note that the principles of animation apply to *masc sing acc* and to all *pl acc.*

PRIMARY PREPOSITIONS
and the cases they govern

Summary

gen	*instr*	*acc*	*prepl*	*dat*
без, для, до, из,	**над** **пéред**	**про**	**при**	
от, рáди, у		**сквозь**		
		чéрез		
(*rare*)←**мéжду**→				
	place ←**ЗА**→	motion		
	place ←**ПОД**→	motion		**К**
		motion ←**В**→	place	
		motion ←**НА**→	place	
		against ←**О**→	*of, about*	
			←**ПО**	→
←**С**	→			

***без** (**безо**) + *gen* = without

***в** (**во**) + *acc* = in, to. + *prp* = in (place)

для + *gen* = for

до + *gen* = up, to, till

мéжду (**меж**) + *ins* = between + *gen* (rare)

на + *acc* = onto (motion) + *prp* = on (place)

над + *ins* = over, above

***о** (**об, обо**) + *prp* = of, about. + *acc* = against

***под** (**пóдо**) + *ins* = under. + *acc* = motion

при + *prp* = presence, time of

про + *acc* = about, concerning

рáди + *gen* = for the sake of

за + *acc* = behind, beyond. + *ins* = for, behind (place)

*от (ото) + *gen* = out of, from

*с (со) + *gen* = down from, out of. + *ins* = with. + *acc* = about

*из (изо) + *gen* = out of

*к (ко) + *dat* = towards, to

перед(-о) + *ins* = in front of, before

по + *dat* = along, by. + *acc* = up to, each. + *prp* = on account of, after

сквозь + *acc* = through

у + *gen* = near, at, at the house of

через (чрез) + *acc* = across

*Prepositions ending in a consonant add **о** before certain combinations of consonants.

Stress: nearly always on the noun or pronoun, not on the preposition.

The idiomatic phrase **что за** meaning *what kind (of)* is followed by the *nominative*. For example: **Это ещё что за выдумки?** What kind of nonsense is this, that?

CONJUGATION OF быть = *to be, to be present; to exist.*

Present tense: Only two forms of this tense are likely to be met:

3rd pers sing: **есть**, *is, there is* — in current use.

3rd pers pl: **суть**, *are, there are* — may be met in classical literature; little used to-day, except in exact science.

Past tense: я, ты был, была. он был, она была. оно было. мы, вы, они были.

Conditional/subjunctive: я был бы etc.

Future tense: я буду, ты будешь, он, она, оно будет, мы будем, вы будете, они будут.

Imperative: будь! будьте!

не есть = *is not.* нет = *there is not* (emphatic) + *gen.*

POSSESSION: *to have, possess* is expressed by the present, past or future of **быть.** See pages 50–2, 75.

Present	Past	Future
у меня	у меня был, -а, -о ; -и	у меня { будет будут
у тебя		
у него		
у неё } есть		
у нас		
у вас		
у них		

Negative: у меня нет + *gen.* у меня не было + *gen.* у меня не будет + *gen.*

Interrogative: Есть ли у вас?

Subject in the genitive: у него есть карандаш.

имѣ́ть (*I tr*) *to have*: This verb is also used for *to have*: (**имѣ́ю, имѣ́ешь**). One finds it mostly with abstract nouns (*to have courage*, etc.). **имѣ́ться** = There is *or* there are.

быть *as auxiliary verb*: It is used to form the compound future of imperfective verbs, and is the only true auxiliary verb in Russian.

REGULAR CONJUGATIONS OF VERBS: RECAPITULATION

Imperfective aspect

Infinitive: **ЧИТА́ТЬ** (I)   *Infinitive:* **ГОВОРИ́ТЬ** (II)

Conjugated tense, present in meaning

1st form	2nd form	1st form	2nd form
я чита́-ю	-у	я говор-ю́	-у
ты чита́-ешь	-ешь	ты говор-и́шь	-ишь
он чита́-ет	-ет	он говор-и́т	-ит
мы чита́-ем	-ем	мы говор-и́м	-им
вы чита́ете	-ете	вы говор-и́те	-ите
они́ чита́-ют	-ут	они́ говор-я́т	-ат

Past tense

я чита́-л, -а, (-о)   я ты, он говори́-л, -а, (-о)
мы чита́-ли   мы говори́-ли

Conditional/subjunctive

я ⎫
ты ⎬ чита́л бы
он ⎭
мы, вы, они́ чита́ли бы

я ⎫
ты ⎬ говори́л бы
он ⎭
мы, вы, они́ говори́ли бы

Future, compounded with **быть**, *to be*

я бу́ду чита́ть
ты бу́дешь „
он бу́дет „   я бу́ду говори́ть
мы бу́дем „   etc.
вы бу́дете „
они́ бу́дут „

Imperative

чита́-й   говор-и́
чита́-йте   говор-и́те

PART II

THE FUNDAMENTALS OF THE LANGUAGE

> Волко́в боя́ться, в лес не
> ходи́ть.
> Что посе́ешь, то и пожнёшь.
> *Russian proverbs*

HOW TO STUDY PART II

In Part I you have learnt grammar with **упражнёние** *which illustrated it and helped to drive it home. This has covered essential elements sufficiently to enable you to begin reading Russian written for Russians. Part II expands the grammar of Part I far enough for most practical purposes, but, whereas Part I dealt mostly with what is regular and consistent, Part II embraces not only some new and equally important elements but also those deviations and variations from the regular which come up again and again in reading, writing or speaking Russian. What is given of grammar in Part II has to be known. It does not include anything that can be avoided, whether you merely wish to read Russian with some ease, or aim further and be able to use it in speech for finding your way about or for simple but fairly comprehensive everyday purposes, or to write a letter. But, as there are in Part II no set exercises "keyed" to the grammar given, the method of practice has to be different. From now onwards, proceed as follows:*

(1) Study the Preliminary pages carefully before proceeding to the Lessons. You *must know* the essential Mutations and have a fairly clear idea of how Russian words are built up. Refer again and again to these pages: they will save many frustrations.

(2) In general, study grammar as in Part I and memorize everything new. Know the words and how they are used in the examples. Then, but not before, go on to the Reading.

(3) Everything strange in the Reading is explained in the Notes. First go over the Reading and try to make sense of it without looking at the Translation or Notes. Next, with the aid of the Notes, write out your own translation of it. Next, compare and correct this with the aid of the Translation and Notes. Always note the mistakes you have made. Finally, read over the Russian text aloud until you can pronounce it well, knowing the meaning of every word as you go along. This helps you to *think in Russian*: your ultimate goal.

(4) Then go on to the Conversations. These are usually simple and straightforward. They contain much that is highly practical. List new words and memorize them. The words in these **Разговоры** are mostly everyday practical vocabulary. If you have a friend who speaks Russian, enlist his or her help from time to time, though you should be able to get along fairly well without such help.

(5) Finally go over the whole of each Lesson at least once more before proceeding. *Do not leave a Lesson until you know it fairly well.*

(6) Constant review of all that has gone before is essential: say, after every fifth Lesson.

NEVER MIND SLOW PROGRESS SO LONG AS YOU KEEP GOING.

These notes are intended to give you some general idea of the way Russian words are made up, including the formal elements of which they are made. But first you must know the various *kinds* of words of which the parts of speech consist. The object in stating these things now is not at all pedantic. It is essentially practical in that it will help you very much in the acquisition of vocabulary, for it explains factors in word-formation which otherwise would baffle and possibly frustrate the learner. To be conscious of these factors saves time in learning the language.

Kinds of Russian words

(1) *Invariable words:* These are words which never change in form. They may be indeclinable nouns such as **кófe, кинó,** which you have already met. Or they may be particles such as the interrogative **ли.** Or conjunctions such as **и** and **йли.** Or prepositions such as **для** (+*gen*), **на** (+*acc* and *prp*) or **по** (+*dat* and *prp*). All these are quite simple but, as you will have to know what nouns are indeclinable, a list for reference is given on page 316.

(2) *Primary words:* These are words which cannot be split into simpler elements. They are therefore often called "elemental words". They can be nouns, pronouns, adjectives, simple numbers or verbs. For example:

$$\text{брат — наш — сам — жить — пять}$$

(3) *Derivative words:* These spring (or derive) from primary words and are clearly related to the words from which they derive. Examples are:

$$\text{обéд-ать. перéд-няя. рабóт-ник.}$$

(4) *Compound words:* These are words made by joining together any of the words already mentioned in (1), (2) and (3). Examples are:

пóсле + зáвтра = послезáвтра = the day after tomorrow
гром + о + отвóд = громоотвóд = lightning conductor.

(5) *Compound abbreviated words:* These are modern words formed by joining together parts of longer words which, if used as they are, would be cumbersome. There are three kinds of these words in common use in the Soviet Union:

   (i) words consisting of a syllable of one word prefixed to another word: **ветврáч** from **ветеринáрный врач** = *veterinary surgeon.* We often say "vet" for this in English.

   (ii) the full parts of an expression reduced to syllables as in **колхóз** from **коллектúвное хозяйство** = *collective farm.*

   (iii) initials only used to form a short word to take the place of a whole expression, as in **вуз** from **вы́сшее учéбное заведéние** = *institute of higher education.*

The last method is much used for official abbreviations of Soviet institutions and organizations. An example is **ВОКС** for "All-Union Society for Cultural Relations".

Formal elements in the composition of Russian words

(1) *The root:* This is the ultimate base or element from which words are made with the aid of additions placed before the root (*prefixes*), or after the root (*suffixes*). The root always contains a "*lexical meaning*", which may be described as the meaning that is common to all members of a group or family of related words. For example **УЧ** is the root common to:

> **уч-и́ть. уч-и́тель. уч-е́ние. уч-ени́к. из-уч-а́ть.**

(2) *The stem:* This is the part of a word which remains when the grammatical inflexion (ending) is struck off. When a word has no inflexional ending—as in **дом** for example—the word itself is the stem. The stems of the following words are in large letters: **РУССК-ий, -ая, -ое ; -ие. У́МН-ый. БЕЗУ́М-ие. УМЕ́-ть. РАЗ-У́МН-ый. УМ** *noun*=mind, intellect.

(3) *The inflexion:* This is the grammatical ending added to a stem to indicate number, gender, case, person or the part of a verb. Examples:

Noun: студе́нт, -а, -у, -а, -ом, -е ; -ы . . .
Adjective: но́в-ый, -ого, -ому, -ый (-ого), -ым, -ом ; -ые . . .
Numeral: оди́н, одн-а́, одн-о́ ; одн-и́.
Verb: чита́-ть : чита́-ю, -ешь, -ет ; -ем, -ете, -ют.

(4) *The prefix:* This is an addition placed *before* a root to add to or modify its meaning. All primary prepositions except **к (ко)** and **для** are used as prefixes. A list of prefixes is given on page 222. Examples:

> **род** *birth.* **на-ро́д** *people.* **у-ро́д** *monster, freak.*

(5) *The suffix:* This is a particle placed *after* the root. Suffixes are added to nouns, adjectives, verbs, adverbs and participles. Examples:

Noun: **постро́й-ка ; стро́й-тель**
Adjective: **строй-тельный ; стро́й-ный**
Verb: **стро́и-ть**
Adverb: **стро́й-но**
Participles: **стро́-ящий**
            строй-вший } To be dealt with on pages 279–289.

Note on vocabulary: When you meet a new Russian word and the meaning is not given, look it up in the Vocabulary at the end of the book and make a note of the meaning. Memorize all such words, if not immediately, then at your leisure.

MUTATIONS

A mutation is a change in a vowel or consonant. Mutations occur frequently in Russian but they follow regular patterns that are governed by certain rules which can be learnt. These mutations are an important part of the phonetic system of the language.

Vowels: See page 16 for BASIC RULES OF SPELLING. The only exceptions to these rules are in some words of foreign origin.

Mutations of consonants: After the labials (lip sounds) **б, в, м, п,** and **ф** (rare), in the stem of a conjugation II verb, the letter **л** is inserted in the 1*st pers sing* only of the present tense. Thus:

	1st pers sing	2nd pers sing
люб/**и́ть** *to love*	я люб**Лю́**	ты лю́бишь
лов/**и́ть** *to catch*	лов**Лю́**	ло́вишь
куп/**и́ть** *to buy*	куп**Лю́**	ку́пишь

TABLE OF MUTATIONS: For reference

Gutturals	*Dentals*	*Sibilants*	*Hissing sounds*
Г	Д	З	mutate to Ж
К	Т	Ц	mutate to Ч
Х	—	С	mutate to Ш
СК	СТ	—	mutate to Щ

Gutturals are throat sounds. Dentals are sounds made with the tip of the tongue against the back of the front teeth. Sibilants are *ss* sounds including Russian **з** or **ц**. Hissing sounds are **ж, ч, ш, щ**. You will see from the Table above that ten sounds mutate to hissing sounds, which always demand observance of the Rules of Spelling (see page 16).

Such mutations are found in all parts of speech which inflect, but particularly in the present tense of verbs:

д+ю changes to **жу** ⎫
т+ю   „   „ **чу** ⎬ dental to hissing

з+ю   „   „ **жу** ⎫
с+ю   „   „ **шу** ⎬ sibilant to hissing

And similarly with the gutturals and dentals. Note the following:

пах/**а́ть**	*to dig, till*	я паш**у́**	ты па́шешь
иск/**а́ть**	*to seek*	ищ**у́**	и́щешь
ви́д/**еть**	*to see*	ви́жу	ви́дишь
пуст/**и́ть**	*to let (go)*	пущ**у́**	пу́стишь
кра́с/**ить**	*to paint*	кра́шу	кра́сишь
шут/**и́ть**	*to joke*	шучу́	шу́тишь
ход/**и́ть**	*to go on foot*	хожу́	хо́дишь

Mutations in general: Perhaps the most important mutations, after those which occur in verbs, and the vowel-mutations because of the rules of spelling, are in words derived from other words (derivatives). Many examples could be given here and you will find many as you proceed with the study of Russian. What are given at this point merely illustrate the kinds of mutations you may expect to find. Such as:

(a) in the comparative of adjectives:

Positive		Comparative	
дорого́й	dear	доро́же	dearer
молодо́й	young	моло́же	younger
бога́тый	rich	бога́че	richer
просто́й	simple	про́ще	simpler
бли́зкий	near	бли́же	nearer
далёкий	far	да́льше	further, farther

—и т. д. = *and so forth;* etc. See also page 237, Adverbs.

(b) in derivatives:

друг friend: (*pl* друзья́). дру́жба friendship. дру́жеский (*adj*) friendly. лик image. лицо́ face. ли́чность personality.

оте́ц father. оте́чество fatherland, native country.

Occasionally there is a "reverse mutation", as from ж to г:

бежа́ть to run: я бегу́, ты бежи́шь.

And note the mutations in these two verbs:

-чь to г: мочь to be able to: я могу́, ты мо́жешь, etc.
-чь to к: течь to flow: теку́, течёшь, etc.

You will also find mutations in some diminutives. See pages 266–7. A knowledge of how mutations work should help in memorizing words as your vocabulary expands.

Verbal suffixes and conjugation

When you come to the treatment of verbs which deviate from regular conjugation (pages 296–309) you will find how very important suffixes can be, and how much time can be saved by paying attention to them. Just to make sure that you are clear about suffixes, look carefully at the following:

Roots	Roots + suffix(es)	Nouns and verbs
ИГР-, game, play	игр-а noun suffix -а	игра́ *a game, play*
	игр-а-ть verb suffix -а- + ending	игра́ть *to play*
	игр-ушка noun suffix	игру́шка *plaything, toy*
СМЕ(х)-, laugh		смех *laughter*
	сме-я́-ть-ся: -я́ = verb suffix	смея́ться *to laugh*
	сме-(ш)-ной adjective suffix	смешно́й *funny*

-ВЕТ-, say, speak	со-вет prefix со-	совет *council*
	со-вет-ова-ть prefix + root + suffix	советовать *to advise*
БОЛ(ь)-, ill, pain, ache		боль *pain*
	бол-е-ть verb suffix -e-	болеть *to be ill*
	боль-ной adjective suffix	больной *sick, ill*
ЗВ-, call	зв-ание noun suffix	звание *calling*
	зв-а-ть verb suffix -a-	звать *to call*

Suffixes in the above words are: **-а, -ушка, -я-, -ова-, -е-, -ание, -а-, -ной.**

WORD FAMILIES

A group of words which have a root in common is, for convenience, called a "word family". An example is given below, based on the related roots **-куп-** and **-коп-** which both have the dictionary meaning of *buy, save, heap (up)*:

> **купить** (*pf* II) to buy. **копить** (II *ipf*) to save, hoard.

These two verbs start the word family. Now consider the following:

Verbs: **покупать** (*ipf* I) to buy
выкупать (*ipf* I) to buy off, to redeem, ransom
подкупать (*ipf* I) to bribe, "grease the palm"
закупать (*ipf* I) to buy up, to lay in a stock

Nouns: **подкуп** bribery, graft (**под** *prp* = under)
копна stack, rick
копейка copeck
выкуп ransom
закупщик buyer
скупщик buyer up, one who "scoops" or "corners" something
купец dealer, merchant
купечество merchant class
покупка purchase
скуповатость (*f*) stinginess (*a mild word*)
скупость (*f*) greed, avarice (*a strong word*)

Adjectives: **скуповатый** parsimonious (*mild*)
скупой miserly, tight-fisted (*strong*)
купеческий merchant's, pertaining to the merchant class

One more example will be given of the many word families in Russian. Incidentally, you do not have to learn all these words now, but you should know most of them by the time you have finished the course. Consider the following rich list of words from two related roots:

ГРАД, ГО́РОД : These related root-words, now meaning *town, city*, originally meant "enclosure", and in some of their offspring this last meaning still survives. Not all words in the **град-го́род** family need be given here; some of them are now rare or quite archaic. We give some not uncommon as well as some very common formations from these two essentially similar roots: both by way of example of Russian word-formation and to be memorized (not just yet, but later) as of practical value. In these, and in all compounded or derivative words, allow for mutations.

Root words ГРАД-ГОРОД and their derivatives

1 гражд-ани́н	4 город-о́к	10 город-и́ть
2 ,, -а́нка	5 город-ово́й	11 город-и́шко
3 гражд-а́нство	6 город-ско́й	12 город-ни́чий
	7 горож-а́нин	
	8 ,, -а́нка	
	9 горож-а́не	

13 о-горо́д	22 при́-город
14 о-горо́д-и́ть	23 при́-город-ный
15 о-горо́д-ник	24 пре-гра́д-а
16 о-горо́д-ница	25 пере-горо́д-ка
17 о-горо́д-ничество	
18 о-горо́д-нический	
19 о-горо́д-ничать	
20 о-горо́д-ный	
21 о-гра́д-а	

Compound words : сло́жные слова́

26 Ленин-гра́д	28 градо-нача́ль-ник	30 го́род-геро́й
27 Сталин-гра́д	29 градо-нача́ль-ство	31 градо-строи́тель-ство

Compound abbreviated words : сло́жно-сокращённые слова́

32 гор-сове́т : городско́й сове́т *оги́з : объедине́ние госуда́р-ственных изда́тельств.

*сель-сове́т : се́льский сове́т *госизда́т : госуда́рственное изда́тельство.

Meanings and explanation : 1. *citizen.* 2. *citizeness.* 3. *citizenship.* 4. *little town.* 5. (*town*) *policeman.* 6. *urban* (*adj*). 7. *town-dweller* (*m*). 8. *town-dweller* (*f*). 9. *town(s) folk.* 10. *to make a fuss, talk nonsense.* 11. *godforsaken village.* 12. *mayor* (*of*) *a city* or *town governor* (*adj*). 13. *kitchen or market garden.* 14. *to fence in* (II *pf*). 15. *market gardener* (*m*). 16. *market gardener* (*f*). 17. *market gardening.* 18. (*of*) *market gardening* (*adj*). 19. *to do market gardening* (I). 20. (*of*) *market gardening* (*adj*). 21. *fence.* 22. *suburb.* 23. *suburban, local* (*adj*). 24. *barrier, obstacle.* 25. *partition.* 26. *Leningrad.* 27. *Stalingrad.* 28.

town governor. 29. *borough.* 30. *hero-city or -town* (one notable for some (war) achievement, such as Leningrad, Stalingrad *or* London). 31. *urban construction, building.* 32. *town Soviet (council).* **Village Soviet; Central Publishing House; State Publishing House.*

Note: The words in the Russian list are divided by hyphens to show their parts.

*These three are unrelated to the **град-го́род** groups, but are given here as examples of a logical development of word-formation in Russian, especially since 1917. The full names of many Soviet institutions are often very long, and this method of "telescoping" is used to shorten them for everyday use. There are dozens of such words. New words are constantly being added to Russian; others fall into disuse. The examples given above—of words made by adding prefixes or suffixes or by compounding—explain why you often see some very long words in Russian. If you know the meaning of their elements, you can generally make out the full meaning of such long words. You need never be very frightened of long words in Russian for this reason.

BUT YOU *MUST* KNOW YOUR MUTATIONS!

NOUN-FORMING SUFFIXES

Apart from the diminutive suffixes (for which see pages 266–7), Russian uses many suffixes to make nouns from nouns and other parts of speech. Here you may glance at some of the most productive of these suffixes, of which those marked with an asterisk are the most important and should be carefully noted now:

I Suffixes denoting doer of action or agent

masc suffix	corresponding feminine suffix	NOTES
*-**тель**	*-**ница**	These derive mostly from verbs. If the verbal stem is -**a**-, the noun has stressed -**а́**-.
чита́тель (*m*) reader	**чита́тельница** (*f*) reader	
руководи́тель (*m*) guide	**руководи́тельница** (*f*) guide	
*-**чик**	*-**чица**	Stress varies
лётчик airman	**лётчица** airwoman	
перево́дчик (*m*) translator, interpreter	**перево́дчица** (*f*) translator, interpreter	
*-**ник**	*-**ница**	Stress varies
рабо́тник workman	**рабо́тница** workman	
учени́к pupil	**учени́ца** (*f*) pupil	
-**ик**	No corresponding *fem*	
фи́зик physicist		
хи́мик chemist		

-ец	-ка	
комсомо́лец	комсомо́лка Komsomol member	Denotes member- ship of an organiza-
ленингра́дец Leningrader	ленингра́дка а woman of Leningrad	tion, *or* nationality, *or* citizenship of.
испа́нец Spaniard	испа́нка Spanish woman	

-ин	-ка	
грузи́н Georgian	грузи́нка Georgian woman	Denotes nationality
тата́рин Tartar	тата́рка Tartar woman	or place of residence

*-анин	*-ка	
граждани́н citizen	гражда́нка citizen- ess	Denotes city *or* town
горожа́нин city dweller	горожа́нка (*f*) city dweller	of residence; *or* local status. The stress
харьковча́нин a man of Kharkoff	харьковча́нка a woman of Kharkoff	varies.

*-ич	*-ка	
москви́ч Moscovite	москви́чка Moscow woman	Denotes one's city or township. Final syllable stressed.

-ак, -як	-ка, -чка	
сибиря́к a Siberian	сибиря́чка Siberian woman	
земля́к fellow- countryman, fellow- villager	земля́чка woman from the same countryside or village	

Foreign suffixes: **-ист** (= *ist*), **-ионе́р** (= *-ary*), **-е́нт** (= *-ent*), **-а́нт** (= *-ant*, *-ent*, *-ate*) usually have feminine forms in **-ка**: **тракори́ст**, **-ка** tractor-driver (*m* and *f*). Suffixes in **-тор** (= *tor*), **-тарь** (= *tary*) have feminine forms in **-ша**. Thus: **до́кторша, дире́кторша, секрета́рша**.

Suffixes which form feminine abstract nouns

*-ОСТЬ	го́рдость	pride	These derive from *adjs*
	мо́лодость	youth	and retain stress of their
	реши́тельность	resolution	*adj. Final syllable is never stressed.*

-ота	краснота́	redness	
-ета	нищета́	misery	Stress on last syllable.
-ина	глубина́	depth	

-изна	дороговизна	dearness.	
-ка	стро́йка	building, construction	Stress varies.

-ба	молотьба́	threshing	Stress on final syllable.

Suffixes which form neuter nouns

*-**анпе** (-**ия**): **собра́ние** assembly *from* **собра́ть** (I *pf*) to gather: (соберу́, -рёшь)

-**ение** (-**ия**): **чте́ние** reading *from* **чита́ть**

*-**СТВО**   **произво́дство** production *from* **производи́ть** to produce, manufacture.

        мастерство́ skill, craftsmanship *from* **ма́стер** skilled artisan.

        чу́вство feeling *from* **чу́вствовать** to feel.

*-**изм** (=*ism*) **материали́зм** materialism. Fixed stress on final syllable.

LESSON No. 31   УРОК № ТРИ́ДЦАТЬ ОДИ́Н

Indeterminate verb:	*Determinate verb:*
indet **ходи́ть** (II)=to go, come (*on foot*)=**идти́** (I) *det*	
хожу́, хо́дишь, хо́дит	иду́, идёшь, идёт,
хо́дим, хо́дите, хо́дят	идём, идёте, иду́т
Past: ходи́л, -а, -о ; -и	*Past:* шёл, шла, шло ; шли
Imp: ходи́! ходи́те!	*Imp:* иди́! иди́те!

е́здить (II)=to go, come (*otherwise than on foot*)=**е́хать** (I)	
е́зжу, е́здишь, е́здит,	е́ду, е́дешь, е́дет,
е́здим, е́здите, е́здят	е́дем, е́дете, е́дут
Past: е́здил, -а, -о ; -и	*Past:* е́хал, -а, -о ; -и
Imp: е́зди! е́здите!	*Imp:* езжа́й! езжа́йте!

RUSSIAN VERBS OF MOVEMENT: These are a very important group of verbs which demand special attention, because, where we would use one verbal form in English, it has to be expressed in Russian by *one* of *two* Russian verbal forms known as either "indeterminate" or "determinate". All Russian verbs of this nature express some kind of *movement*. They are of two kinds, both *ipf* in aspect (see p. 75).

An *indeterminate verb* expresses movement that occurs *more than once*; movement that is frequentative, repetitive or habitual. There need not be any particular destination or precise direction of the movement expressed by an indeterminate verb.

A *determinate* verb expresses *one single movement* that is taking place (but not yet completed) on *one definite occasion* and in *one specific direction*. First study the SUMMARY on page 173 and then go on. Compare the following examples:

Indeterminate	*Determinate*
Дети ходят в школу. *Children go to school.*	Смотрите, как эти дети идут в школу! *Look at those children going to school.*
Она часто ездит в Москву. *She often goes to Moscow.*	Сегодня она едет в Москву. *She's going to Moscow to-day.*
Он никогда не ходил в театр. *He never went (used to go) to the theatre.*	Куда это вы вчера шли? В театр. *Where was it that you were going yesterday? To the theatre.*
Мы часто ездили заграницу. *We often used to go abroad.*	Мы его видели на улице когда мы ехали на вокзал. *We saw him in the street yesterday when we were on the way to the railway station.*
Вы каждый день будете к нам ходить? *Are you going to come and see us every day?*	Скажите мне, когда вы будете идти гулять. *Tell me when you are going out for a walk.*
Он всё время ходит по комнате. *He keeps on walking up and down the room.*	
Они ездят по всей Европе. *They travel about all over Europe.*	

ходить and идти are also used of trains and other vehicles:
Поезда на Ленинград часто ходят с этого вокзала.
Trains for Leningrad leave this station frequently.

Их автомобиль шёл óчень мéдленно. *Their car was moving along very slowly.*

идти is used both determinately and indeterminately in such purely figurative expressions as **дождь идёт** = *it rains* (frequentative) or *it is raining*; **снег идёт** = *it snows* (frequentative) or *it is snowing*. **ходить** must not be used in such phrases.

☞ **Learn these two verbs thoroughly.** You *must* know how to use these and other verbs of movement: the essence of the difference between indeterminate and determinate is contained in **ходить/идти, éздить/éхать.**

SUMMARY

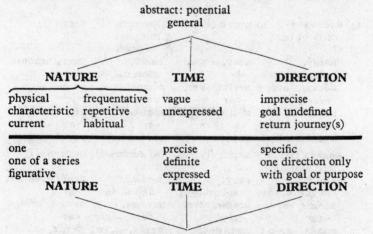

INDETERMINATE VERB = SIMPLE FACT OF MOVEMENT

abstract: potential
general

NATURE		TIME	DIRECTION
physical	frequentative	vague	imprecise
characteristic	repetitive	unexpressed	goal undefined
current	habitual		return journey(s)
one		precise	specific
one of a series		definite	one direction only
figurative		expressed	with goal or purpose
NATURE		**TIME**	**DIRECTION**

DETERMINATE VERB = PRECISION OF MOVEMENT

concrete: actual
particular

IN NEGATIVE SENTENCES: Indeterminate imperfectives express simple and permanent *absence of movement or action.* Negative imperatives are *prohibitions.*

Determinate imperfectives express absence of movement or action *on one occasion.* Negative determinate imperatives are *warnings* rather than prohibitions.

I. COMMON IMPERFECTIVE VERBS OF MOVEMENT CONJUGATED IN THEIR INDETERMINATE AND DETERMINATE FORMS

(1) *going* or *coming on foot*. (2) *riding* or *driving*. (3) *carrying by hand*.
(4) *carrying by vehicle*. (5) *leading* or *conducting*. (6) *flying*.
(7) *running*. (8) *swimming* or *floating*.

Indeterminate	*Determinate*	*Indeterminate*	*Determinate*
(1) ходи́ть (II) to go or come *on foot*	идти́ (I)	(2) е́здить (II) to ride or drive	е́хать (I)
pres хожу́, хо́дишь, -ит хо́дим, -ите хо́дят	иду́, идёшь, -ёт идём, -ёте, -у́т	е́зжу, е́здишь, -ит е́здим, -ите, е́здят	е́ду, е́дешь, -ет е́дем, -ете, -ут
pa ходи́л, ходи́ла, -о ; -и	шёл, шла, шло ; шли	е́здил, -а, -о ; -и	е́хал, -а, -о ; -и
imp ходи́! ходи́те!	иди́! иди́те!	е́зди! е́здите	*езжа́й! езжа́йте!
(3) носи́ть (II) to carry by hand	нести́ (I)	(4) вози́ть (II) to convey, transport	везти́ (I)
ношу́, но́сишь, -ит но́сим, -ите, но́сят	несу́, -ёшь, -ёт несём, -ёте, -су́т	вожу́, во́зишь, -ит во́зим, -ите, во́зят	везу́, везёшь, -ёт везём, -ёте, -у́т
носи́л, -а, -о ; -и	нёс, несла́, -ло ; -ли	вози́л, -а, -о ; -и	вёз, везла́, -ло́ ; -ли́
носи́! носи́те!	неси́! неси́те!	вози́! вози́те!	вези́! вези́те!
(5) води́ть (II) to lead (on foot)	вести́ (I)	(6) лета́ть (I) to fly	лете́ть (II)
вожу́, во́дишь, -ит во́дим, -ите, -дят	веду́, ведёшь, -ёт ведём, -ёте, -ду́т	лета́ю, -а́ешь, а́ет лета́ем, -а́ете, -а́ют	лечу́, лети́шь, -и́т лети́м, -и́те, -я́т
води́л, -а, -о ; -и	вёл, вела́, -о́ ; -и	лета́л, -а, -о ; -и	лете́л, -а, -о ; -и
води́! води́те!	веди́! веди́те!	лета́й! лета́йте!	лети́! лети́те
(7) бе́гать (I) to run	бежа́ть (*irr*)	(8) пла́вать (I) to swim *or* float	плыть (I)
бе́гаю, -аешь, -ает бе́гаем, -аете, -ают	бегу́, бежи́шь, -и́т бежи́м, -и́те, бегу́т	пла́ваю, -аешь, -ает пла́ваем, -аете, -ают	плыву́, -вёшь, -ёт плывём, -ёте, -у́т

бе́гал, -а, -о ;	бежа́л, -а, -о ;	пла́вал, -а,	плы́л, -а́, -о́ ;
-и	-и	-о ; -и	-и
бе́гай!	беги́!	пла́вай!	плыви́!
бе́гайте!	беги́те!	пла́вайте!	плыви́те!

Notes: **езжа́й! езжа́йте!**—from the verb **езжа́ть** (I) which is seldom used without a prefix. It means *to go frequently.* The *pf* forms of its imperative (**поезжа́й! поезжа́йте!**) are also used as imperatives of **е́хать.**

The eight pairs of verbs given above are very common and, as they make compounds with prefixes, it is important to know their conjugation thoroughly. Pairs 1–5 are *2nd conj* for indeterminates (*indet*) and *1st conj* for determinates (*det*). Pairs 6–8 reverse this and are *1st conj* for *indet*, and *2nd conj* for *det*, except **плыть** (I), and **бежа́ть** (*irr*).

Refer to page 165 MUTATIONS and you will see that these verbs follow expected patterns. Distinguish between **иду́, идёшь, идёт** and **е́ду, е́дешь, е́дет.**

Stress: Indet 1–5 have a shifting stress from *1st pers sing* to stem; and *det* (except **е́хать**) have fixed stress on final syllable. *Indet* 6–8 are *reg* like **де́лать** but have stress on the final syllable.

Memorizing these conjugations: Before starting to memorize these "double" imperfective verbs, make absolutely sure that you have mastered **ходи́ть** and **идти́** with the examples on pages 171–4. The forms of these verbs are repeated above to complete the picture of the commonest and most *essential* Russian verbs of movement. (See page 182 for completion of the list).

Many students will find that the Summary on page 173 will help them to make their minds perfectly clear about the basic differences between an indeterminate and a determinate imperfective Russian verb of movement. You will appreciate later how highly important this is.

EXAMPLES OF THE USE OF THE COMMON IMPERFECTIVE VERBS OF MOVEMENT

Note that **носи́ть-нести́, вози́ть-везти́, води́ть-вести́** can all be translated into English as "take".

1. **носи́ть-нести́** to take, carry by hand *or* on one's person. *indet* **носи́ть**

Она́ всегда́ носи́ла ребёнка на рука́х. She always carried (used to carry) the child in her arms.

Кни́ги на́до носи́ть в портфе́ле. One should carry books in a briefcase.

This verb is also used for *to wear* habitually (clothes, glasses, etc.).

Она́ тогда́ носи́ла тёмные очки́. At that time she used to wear dark glasses.

Зимо́й я всегда́ ношу́ шерстяны́е носки́. I always wear woollen socks in winter.

det **нести́**

Куда́ вы идёте? Я несу́ э́ти кни́ги в библиоте́ку. Where are you going? I am taking these books to the library.

Неси́те чемода́н сюда́, а сунду́к неси́те в спа́льню! Bring the suitcase here and take the trunk into the bedroom.

Note that **нести́** can *never* be used for *to wear*. In the determinate sense this verb must be expressed by **быть** and the prepositions **в** or **на** with the prepositional case:

Она́ в кра́сном пла́тье. She is wearing a red dress.

На нём была́ ста́рая шля́па. He was wearing an old hat.

2. **вози́ть-везти́** to take, carry, convey or transport *by vehicle*:

indet **вози́ть**

Он нас всегда́ вози́л в теа́тр на своём автомоби́ле. He always used to take us to the theatre in his car.

Ка́ждый день я бу́ду вози́ть о́вощи на ры́нок. I shall take (transport) the vegetables to market every day.

det **везти́**

Куда́ вы е́дете? Я везу́ сы́на в шко́лу. Where are you going? I am driving my son to school.

Вези́те меня́ пря́мо на вокза́л! Take (drive) me straight to the station.

везти́ is also used impersonally in the sense of *to have good luck*:

Ему́ всегда́ везёт. He is always lucky.

Вам сего́дня везёт. Your luck is in to-day.

Мне не везло́. I was unlucky.

3. **водить-вести** to take, lead, conduct *on foot*:

indet **водить**

Она водит собаку гулять пять раз в день. She takes her dog out for a walk five times a day.

Он водил нас по музею. He took (showed) us round the museum.

Больного надо водить за руку. The invalid has to be led by the hand.

det **вести**

Куда вы ведёте больного? Where are you taking the invalid?

Ведите меня к заведующему! Take me to the manager.

4. **летать-лететь** to fly

indet **летать**

Он часто летает в Париж. He often flies to Paris.

Птицы летают Birds fly.

det **лететь**

Он сегодня в Париж летит. He is flying to Paris to-day.

Казалось, что птица летит прямо на солнце. It seemed as if the bird was flying straight for the sun.

5. **бегать-бежать** to run

indet **бегать**

Каждый день я бегаю за покупками. Every day I run off to do the shopping.

Дети бегают по саду. The children are running about in the garden.

det **бежать** also *to escape, flee*

Я бегу за покупками. I'm rushing off to do the shopping.

Уже поздно! Бегите скорей на работу! Бегу! It's late! Hurry off to work now! I'm off!

Они бежали из тюрьмы They escaped from prison.

6. **плавать-плыть** to swim, float

indet **плавать**

Летом мы каждый день ходим плавать. In summer we go swimming every day.

Вы плаваете? Can you swim?

det плыть

Я плыл из Гáмбурга в Лóндон на небольшóм парохóде. I was travelling from Hamburg to London on board a small ship.

Motion to:	*Motion from:*
(*a*) куда́? = (to) where? Whither?	(*b*) отку́да? = from where?
сюда́ = (to) here, hither.	отсю́да = from here.
туда́ = (to) there, thither.	отту́да = from there.

Prepositions:

(*a*) **в (во)** + *acc* = motion into, to
    на + *acc* = motion onto, to
    к (ко) + *dat* = motion towards, to

(*b*) **из(о)** + *gen* = out of, from
    с (со) + *gen* = from off, from
    от + *gen* = from, away from (*distance* or *person*)

(*c*) **по** + *dat* = moving along *or* within.
    за + *instr* = for the purpose of (*getting something*)

(*a*) **в Лóндон** = to London.
    на вокзáл = to the station.
    к дóктору = to the doctor

(*b*) **из Лóндона** = from London.
    с вокзáла = from the station.
    от дóктора = from the doctor.
    с комóда = from off the chest of drawers.

(*c*) **по гóроду** = about the city.
    за карандашóм = for (= to get) a pencil.
    за хлéбом = for (= to get) bread.

Some common idiomatic uses: det ipf **идти́** is used for (*a*) rain(ing) and snow(ing):

    шёл дождь = it was raining.   **снег идёт** = it is snowing.

—and for (*b*) passage of time, and seasons, and progress in activity:

    идёт врéмя.   моё дéло идёт хорошó.

идти́ is used (*a*) for time taken in the post by telegrams and letters:

    телегрáмма шла два часá а письмó шло два дня.

—and, together with **ходи́ть,** for (*b*) movement of trains, trams, buses, ships, clocks and watches and machines which "go" by their own power. Often a word other than "*go*" is used to translate such self-movement:

    Э́ти часы́ не иду́т = This watch has stopped (*normally it goes*).
    Э́ти часы́ не хóдят. = This watch doesn't go (*at all*).

Э́тот пóезд хóдит мéжду Лóндоном и Брáйтоном. = This train runs between London and Brighton.

Корáбль шёл мéдленно. = The ship sailed slowly (from) . . .

But for motor-cars **éздить-éхать** are also commonly used: **Автомоби́ль éхал мéдленно по гóроду.** = The car moved slowly about the city.

LIST FOR REFERENCE

II. LESS COMMON IMPERFECTIVE VERBS OF MOVEMENT CONJUGATED IN THEIR INDETERMINATE AND DETERMINATE FORMS (*continues and completes List on page* 174)

(9) *wandering* or *roaming*. (10) *chasing* or *driving*. (11) *rolling* (transitive) or *trundling*. (12) *climbing* or *clambering*. (13) *creeping* or *crawling*. (14) *planting* or *seating* (transitive). (15) *dragging* or *pulling*.

Indeterminate	Determinate	Indeterminate	Determinate
(9) бродить (II) to wander, roam	брести (I)	(10) гонять (I) to chase	гнать (II)
брожу, бродишь, -ит	бреду, -ёшь, -ёт	гоняю, -ешь, -ет	гоню, гонишь, -ит
бродим, -ите, -ят	бредём, -ёте, -ут	гоняем, -ете, -ют	гоним, -ите, -ят
бродил, -а, -о ; -и	брёл, -á, -ó ; -и	гонял, -а, -о ; -и	гнал, -á, -о ; -и
броди! бродите!	бреди! бредите!	гоняй! гоняйте!	гони! гоните!
(11) катать (I) to roll (*transitive*)	катить (II)	(12) лазить (II) to climb, clamber	лезть (I)
катаю, -ешь, -ет	качу, катишь, -ит	лажу, лазишь, -ит	лезу, -ешь, -ет
катаем, -ете, -ют	катим, -ите, -ят	лазим, -ите, -ят	лезем, -ете, -ут
катал, -а, -о ; -и	катил, -а ; -о ; -и	лазил, -а, -о ; -и	лез, лезла, -о ; -и
катай! катайте!	кати! катите!	лазь! лазьте!	лезь! лезьте!
(13) ползать (I) to creep, crawl	ползти (I)	(14) сажать (I) to plant; to make someone sit	*садить (II)
ползаю, -ешь, -ет	ползу, -ёшь, -ёт	сажаю, -ешь, -ет	сажу, садишь, -ит
ползаем, -ете, ют	ползём, -ёте, -ут	сажаем, -ете, -ют	садим, -ите, -ят
ползал, -а, -о ; -и	полз, ползла, -ó ; -и	сажал, -а, -о ; -и	садил, -а, -о ; -и
ползай! ползайте!	ползи! ползите!	сажай! сажайте!	сади! садите!

(15) **таска́ть** (I)   to drag, pull: (16) **тащи́ть** (II)
таска́ю, -ешь, -ет   тащу́, та́щишь, -ит
таска́ем, -ете, -ют   та́щим, -ите, -ат
таска́л, -а, -о ; -и   тащи́л, -а, -о ; -и
таска́й! таска́йте!   тащи́! тащи́те!

Frequency of verbs of movement: The first sixteen verbs given on page 175 are of frequent occurrence in both speech and the written language. They must all be mastered for active vocabulary.   Of first importance are **ходи́ть/идти́** and **éхать.**   The second list of sixteen verbs given above may be regarded as for "passive" vocabulary and as verbs which, with prefixes make other verbs.   You should be able to recognize these, and know their basic meaning.   The determinate forms of all the simple verbs occur more frequently than their indeterminate forms.

*****сади́ться** has several meanings, the commonest being *to sit down* (*intr*), and should be memorized.   It also means *to mount a horse*, *to shrink* (of material), *to settle* (of dust); and *to set* or *sink* (of the sun).

лета́ть to fly about
aimlessly.

(*See page* 174)

(*Illustration by Frederick Carter*)

(6) **лете́ть** to fly with definite aim(s).

READING   БÉЛКА И ВОЛК   ЧТÉНИЕ
The Squirrel and the Wolf

Бéлка пры́гала с вéтки на вéтку и упáла прямо на
A squirrel was jumping from branch to branch and fell
сóнного вóлка. Волк вскочи́л и хотéл её съесть.
straight onto a sleepy wolf.   The wolf jumped up and was
Бéлка стáла проси́ть: ,,Пусти́ меня!"   Волк сказáл:
about to (*lit:* wanted to) eat her up.   The squirrel began to

„Хорошо́, я пущу́ тебя́, то́лько ты скажи́ мне,
beg: "Let me go!" The wolf said: "All right, I'll let you
отчего́ вы, бе́лки, так ве́селы. Мне всегда́ ску́чно, а
go, only you tell me why you squirrels (are) so gay. I'm
на вас смо́тришь, вы там вверху́ всё игра́ете и
always bored, but one looks at you (and) you're up there
пры́гаете.'' Волк пусти́л, а бе́лка ушла́ на де́рево и
always playing and jumping about. The wolf let her go, and
отту́да сказа́ла: „Тебе́ оттого́ ску́чно, что ты зол.
the squirrel went away into the tree and from there said:
Тебе́ злость се́рдце жжёт. А мы ве́селы оттого́, что
"(The reason) why you're bored is that you're angry.
мы до́бры и никому́ зла не де́лаем.''
Malice burns your heart. But we are gay because we're good
(kind) and we do no evil to anybody.''

Л. Н. Толсто́й
А́збука (1872 г.)

бе́лка = squirrel. пры́гать (I) = to jump. волк = wolf. ве́тка (gen
-и, gen pl ве́ток) = branch. па́дать (I)/упа́сть (I упаду́, -ёшь. pa
упа́л) = to fall. пря́мо = straight. со́нный = sleepy. вска́кивать
(I)/вскочи́ть (II) = to jump up. стать (I ста́ну, -ешь pf) = to begin,
set about. проси́ть (II ipf прошу́, про́сишь)/попроси́ть = to ask,
to beg. пуска́ть (I)/пусти́ть (II пущу́, пу́стишь) = to let go. от-
чего́ = why. ве́сел, -а́, -о ; -ы short form of весёлый = gay. ску́ч-
ный (ску́чно adv) = boring. вверху́ = up above (place where).
пры́гать (I)/пры́гнуть (I) = to jump. пре́жде = first, before.
де́рево = tree. отту́да = from there. сказа́ть (I скажу́, ска́жешь
pf) = to say. а то = otherwise. боя́ться (II бою́сь, бои́шься ipf) =
to fear. уходи́ть (II)/уйти́ (I) (like идти́) = to go away. (past: ушёл,
ушла́, -о́ ; -и́). зол, зла, -о ; -ы short form of злой, зла́я, -ое, -ые
= evil, malicious or angry. злость (f) = malice or fury. се́рдце =
heart. жечь (I ipf жгу, жжёшь, жгут ; past: жёг, жгла, -о ;
-и) = to burn (tr). до́брый = good, kind. никто́ (like кто) =
nobody (dat никому́).

FREE TRANSLATION: *A squirrel was frolicking from branch to branch and
fell off onto a wolf who was dozing. The wolf jumped up and was about to
eat the squirrel up. Whereupon the squirrel set about imploring the wolf to
let her go. The wolf said: "Very well, I'll release you, only first you must
tell me what it is that you squirrels are so merry and gay about. I'm always
bored, but when I take a look at you, you're always playing and jumping
about up there." The wolf let her go, she went up into the tree and from*

there said: "*You're bored because you're so ill-tempered. Your heart is consumed by anger and malice. As for us we're merry and gay because we're kind and we don't do anyone any harm.*"

This passage includes some *pf* verbs (=completed action), of which explanation will be given in Lesson 33.

Note: The free translation is given to show you the difference between "free" and literal translation. Tolstoy writes simple Russian, easy to understand, but very concise and not always easy to render into literal English that is good. But what fine practice! Your PRACTICE in Part II will consist of annotated passages with a *literal* translation intended to help you to make your own free translation. Also, you shall have Conversations with everyday words and phrases which must be mastered.

РАЗГОВÓР : CONVERSATION

Greetings and other useful phrases

Здрáвствуйте! Hello! (*An "all-purposes" greeting.*)

Дóброе ýтро.   Good morning.

Дóбрый день.   Дóбрый вéчер.   Good day.   Good evening.

Как вы поживáете?   How are you?

Рад(-а) вас вѝдеть.   Pleased (glad) to see you.

Я так рад, что встрéтил вас!   Very glad to have met you.

Как делá?   How are things (business)?

Что нóвого?   What's new?

Хорошó.   Отлѝчно.   Well.   Perfectly (fine).

Спасѝбо.   Благодарю̀ вас.   Thanks.   (I) thank you.

Разрешѝте узнáть вáшу фамѝлию?   May I (permit me to) know your (sur-)name.

Я приéхал из Áнглии (Амéрики).   I'm (come) from England (America).

Я приéхал в Совéтский Сою̀з как студéнт; как турѝст; по дéлу.   I've come to the Soviet Union, as a student; as a tourist; on business.

Разрешѝте представить вам . . .   Permit (allow) me to introduce . . . to you.

Представьте меня, пожáлуйста.   Introduce me, please.

Простѝте.   Pardon (forgive) me.

Извинѝте.   Excuse me.

Нé за что. (*idiom*)   Don't mention it.

Ничегó!   Never mind.   It's nothing.

Пожáлуйста, говорѝте мéдленно.   Please speak slowly.

Я всё ещё учу́сь ру́сскому языку́. I'm still only learning Russian.

До свида́ния. Till we meet again. *Au revoir.*

Споко́йной но́чи. Good night (=*peaceful night*).

Проща́йте. Good-bye; Farewell (to be used when not
meeting again).

LESSON No. 32   УРОК № ТРИ́ДЦАТЬ ДВА

0	ну́ль (*m*), но́ль (*m*)	30	три́дцать
1	оди́н, одна́, одно́;	40	со́рок
	одни́. (раз in counting	50	пятьдеся́т
	1, 2, 3, etc.)	60	шестьдеся́т
2	два, две, два	70	се́мьдесят
3	три	80	во́семьдесят
4	четыре	90	девяно́сто
5	пять	100	сто
6	шесть	101	сто оди́н, одна́, одно́,
7	семь		одни́
8	во́семь	102	сто два, две, два
9	де́вять	103	сто три
10	де́сять	110	сто де́сять
11	оди́ннадцать	120	сто два́дцать
12	двена́дцать	200	две́сти
13	трина́дцать	300	три́ста
14	четы́рнадцать	400	четы́реста
15	пятна́дцать	500	пятьсо́т
16	шестна́дцать	600	шестьсо́т
17	семна́дцать	700	семьсо́т
18	восемна́дцать	800	восемьсо́т
19	девятна́дцать	900	девятьсо́т
20	два́дцать	1000	ты́сяча (*f*). 2000
21	два́дцать оди́н, одна́,		две ты́сячи. 5000 пять
	одно́; одни́		ты́сяч.
22	два́дцать два, две,	1000000	миллио́н (*m*)
	два		
23 24	два́дцать три, четы́ре, etc.		

CARDINAL NUMERALS AND THEIR DECLEN-
SION: нуль (ноль) is a masculine noun, ты́сяча is a feminine noun, and миллио́н is a masculine noun. They are declined like their types. Numerals ending in **-ть** are declined like feminine nouns ending in a consonant + **ь**. Compound numerals (that is, consisting of two or more separate numerals) are each one declined: **два́дцать оди́н, двадцати́ одного́,** etc.

оди́н, одна́, одно́ ; одни́: This numeral is declined like a pronoun (**э́тот** *this;* or **сам** *-self*) and agrees in gender, number and case with its noun. The same rule applies when it is used to make a compound number.

		Singular			*Plural:* *all*
	masc	*fem*	*neut*		*genders*
N:	оди́н	одна́	одно́	*All but ins pl stressed on last syllable*	одни́
G:	одного́	одно́й	одного́		одни́х
D:	одному́	одно́й	одному́		одни́м
A:	N or G	одну́	одно́		N or G
I:	одни́м	одно́й (-о́ю)	одни́м		одни́ми
P: (об) одно́м	одно́й	одно́м		одни́х

In addition to the ordinary meaning—*one*—**оди́н** is used as an emphatic to mean *only one, alone, one thing, nothing but.* The plural form **одни́** is used with plural pronouns and nouns, including those nouns used in the plural form only. *Are you alone at home ?* = **Вы одни́ до́ма ?** and **одни́ часы́** = *one watch or clock.*

Learning the numerals: First learn one to twenty, and then the declensions of these words, also **о́ба, о́бе.** The remainder should similarly be learnt in groups. You should know *all* cardinals before finishing Part II.

	2		**3**	**4**
	masc and n.	*fem*		
Nom:	два	две	три	четы́ре
Gen:	двух	двух	трёх	четырёх
Dat:	двум	двум	трём	четырём
Acc:	N or G	N or G	N or G	N or G
Ins:	двумя́	двумя́	тремя́	четырьмя́
Prp:	о двух	о двух	о трёх	о четырёх

	5, 6, 7, 9, 10	8	11-19	20, 30
Nom:	пять	восемь	одиннадцать	двадцать
Gen:	пяти́	восьми́	одиннадцати	двадцати́
Dat:	пяти́	восьми́	одиннадцати	двадцати́
Acc:	пять	восемь	одиннадцать	двадцать
Ins:	пятью	восемью	одиннадцатью	двадцатью
Prp:	о пяти́	о восьми́	об одиннадцати	о двадцати́

	40	50-70	80	100
Nom:	сорок	пятьдеся́т	восемьдесят	сто
Gen:	сорока́	пяти́десяти	восьми́десяти	ста
Dat:	сорока́	пяти́десяти	восьми́десяти	ста
Acc:	сорок	пятьдеся́т	восемьдесят	сто
Ins:	сорока́	пятью́десятью	восемью́десятью	ста
Prp:	о сорока́	о пяти́десяти	о восьми́десяти	о ста

	200	300	400	500-900
N:	двести	триста	четыреста	пятьсо́т
G:	двухсо́т	трёхсо́т	четырёхсо́т	пятисо́т
D:	двумста́м	трёмста́м	четырёмста́м	пятиста́м
A:	двести	триста	четыреста	пятьсо́т
I:	двумяста́ми	тремяста́ми	четырьмяста́ми	пятьюста́ми
P:	о двухста́х	о трёхста́х	о четырёхста́х	о пятиста́х

	800	1000	1000000
Nom:	восемьсо́т	ты́сяча (f noun)	миллио́н (m noun)
Gen:	восьмисо́т	ты́сячи	миллио́на
Dat:	восьмиста́м	ты́сяче	миллио́ну
Acc:	восемьсо́т	ты́сячу	миллио́н
Ins:	восемьюста́ми	ты́сячей (-ею)	миллио́ном
Prp:	о восьмиста́х	о ты́сяче	о миллио́не

	о́ба (m and n)	о́бе (f) = both (num)
Nom:	о́ба	о́бе
Gen:	обо́их	обе́их
Dat:	обо́им	обе́им
Acc:	Nom or Gen	Nom or Gen
Ins:	обо́ими	обе́ими
Prp:	об обо́их	об обе́их

Stress: Numerals 2, 3, 4, 5–10, 20 and 30 are stressed on the *endings*. 11–19 are stressed on the *stem*.

40, 90, 100: *Nom and acc:* сорок девяно́сто сто
All other cases: сорока́ девяно́ста ста

о́ба, о́бе: these words, meaning *both*, are treated as a numeral in Russian, although *both* can be either an *adj*, a *pron* or an *adv* in English. See page 115.

Position of numeral word: When placed before a noun it expresses the exact figure. But when placed *after* a noun, it expresses "*about*", "*approximately*". Generally, cardinals precede the word referred to.

Before the noun

де́сять рубле́й = ten roubles
четы́ре го́да = four years

After the noun

рубле́й де́сять = about 10 roubles
го́да четы́ре = four years or so

CASES GOVERNED BY CARDINAL NUMERALS:

Rules:

(1) When **два, две, три, четы́ре, о́ба, о́бе** are in the *nominative* or *accusative with an inanimate noun* they govern (are followed by) the genitive *singular* of the noun governed.

(2) All numerals from **пять** upwards either in the *nominative* or the *accusative* case govern the genitive plural. (Remember that with the cardinal numerals the "animation principle" applies only to **два, две, три, четы́ре, о́ба, о́бе**).

(3) A long form (attributive) adjective following **два, две, три, четы́ре, о́ба, о́бе** is sometimes put in the nominative plural, but is generally in the genitive plural.

(4) In the oblique cases (that is, all but the *nom* or the *acc* when this is similar to the *nom*), of *all* numerals, the case of the numeral decides the case of the noun which will always be in the plural except, of course, after **оди́н, одна́, одно́** when the noun must be singular.

(5) In all compound numerals the case and number of the noun is decided by the *last* numeral.

(6) **ты́сяча** and **миллио́н** no matter what their case, always take the noun in the *genitive plural* (= *a thousand* of, *a million* of).

Раз, *pl* **ра́за,** *gen pl* **раз** : **раз** is a noun meaning *time*. It is used in counting and alone means "*one time, once*". Note the following:

Ско́лько раз? = How many times? (**раз**—*gen pl*)
Мно́го раз = many times. (**раз**—*gen pl*)

два ра́за twice. три ра́за three times. четы́ре ра́за four times.
(ра́за—*gen sing*)

пять, шесть, де́сять, сто ра́з = five, six, ten, a hundred times.

Idiom:

не раз = more than once. Я не раз чита́л э́ту кни́гу. = I have read
this book more than once.

ни ра́зу + не = not even once, never. Я ни ра́зу не чита́л э́той
кни́ги = I have never read this book.

Note that the words ско́лько and мно́го govern the genitive.

Translation of years: Our word *year(s)* is expressed in Russian by two
words—год the ordinary word for "year" and лет (genitive plural of
ле́то = *summer*). The following rules must be known:

(1) After оди́н whether by itself or in a compound numeral, use год
for *year* or *years*.

(2) After два, две, три, четы́ре, о́ба, обе or compound numerals
ending with any of these, го́да, the *gen sing*, must be used.

(3) From пять upwards лет must be used.

(4) After ско́лько = how much *or* how many? ⎫
     не́сколько = a few   ⎬ лет = years
     мно́го = much, many   ⎪
     ма́ло = a little, few   ⎭

To express age: Remember the rules for год and лет, and then the
name, noun or pronoun is put in the dative. Thus:

Ско́лько вам лет? = (*lit:* "How many to you of summers) = How old
are you?

Мне три́дцать оди́н год. = I am thirty-one years of age. (*lit:* to me
are . . .)

Ему́ два́дцать два го́да. = He is twenty-two years of age. (= to him
are 22 years)

Ей пять лет. = She is five years old (of·age).

Ива́ну Ива́новичу Ива́нову со́рок лет. = Ivan Ivanovich Ivanov(-*ff*)
is forty years of age.

Note: -в at the end of Russian surnames is pronounced -*ff*, and often
written -ff in English transliteration.

СЧИТА́ЛКА: A COUNTING RHYME

Помоги́те! Help (me)!

Не могу́ оди́н реши́ть и прошу́ сове́та: I can't decide myself and I ask (your) advice:

Ско́лько пу́говиц приши́ть? How many buttons (should I)
sew on?

И како́го цве́та? And of what colour?

СОРÓКИ БРАНЯ́ТСЯ: MAGPIES SQUABBLE

Раз, два — голова́!   One, two—a head!

Три, четы́ре — пла́тье!   Three, four—a dress!

Пять, шесть — ка́шу есть!   Five, six—(let's) eat the porridge!

Семь, во́семь — се́но ко́сим!   Seven, eight—we mow the hay!

Де́вять, де́сять — муку́ ве́сить!   Nine, ten—weigh the flour!

Оди́ннадцать, двена́дцать — соро́ки браня́тся!   Eleven, twelve—magpies are squabbling!

Что они́ браня́тся?   Why are they squabbling?

Грош потеря́ли.   They've lost half a copeck.

Грош потеря́ли — копе́ечку нашли́!   They lost half a copeck—(now) they've found a (dear little) copeck.

Копе́ечку нашли́ — в ла́вочку пошли́!   They've found a copeck—now they've gone to the (little) shop!

Что они́ купи́ли?   What have they bought?

Кра́сный сарафа́н.   A red sarafan.

Как раздели́ли?   How did they divide it?

Кому́ клин,   For one the gusset,

кому́ стан,   for another the bodice,

кому́ весь сарафа́н,   for another, the whole sarafan,

кому́ пу́говки литы́е,   for another the moulded buttons

кому́ пе́тли золоты́е,   for another, the golden loops,

а соро́чьим дочеря́м по кисе́йным рукава́м!   and for the magpies' daughters   a muslin sleeve each!

From **Весёлые карти́нки, сентя́брь 1959.**

Compare the above rhyme with the English "One, two, buckle my shoe," etc.

NOTES

помога́ть (I)+*dat*=to help.   **реши́ть** (II)=to solve *or* decide. **проси́ть** (II)=to ask.   **я прошу́, ты про́сишь.   сове́т**=advice. **пу́говица**=button.   **приши́ть**= (I *pf*)=to sew (on): **пришью́, -пьёшь.   голова́**=head.   **цвет** (*pl* **цвета́**)=colour.   **счита́лка** *is in the same word-family as* **счита́ть**=to count, reckon.   **раз**=*one* (in counting).   **ка́ша**=buckwheat porridge, a popular dish.   **есть**=to eat.   *Pres* **ем, ешь, ест, еди́м, еди́те, едя́т**—see page 86.   **коси́ть**

(II) = to mow: **я кошу́, ты ко́сишь.** **се́но** = hay. **ве́сить** (II) = to weigh. **соро́ка** = magpie. **брани́ть** (II) = to squabble, scold. **что** = *here* what about? **грош** = a small coin. **потеря́ть** (*pf*) = to lose. **копе́йка** (*gen pl* **-е́ек**) = copeck. *dim* **копе́ечка** (*gen pl* **-чек**). **нашли́** past of **найти́** (I *pf*) = to find. **ла́вка** = shop, *dim* **ла́вочка** = little shop. **пошли́** *past of* **пойти́** (*pf of* **идти́**). See pages 171 & 219. **купи́ть** (II *pf*) = to buy, *pa* купи́л, -а ; -и. **сарафа́н** = sarafan: a national dress worn by women. **раздели́ть** (II *pf*) = to divide. **клин** = gusset. **стан** = bodice. **пу́говка** = small button. **золото́й** = golden. **пе́тля** (*pl* **-и**) = loop. **кисея́** = muslin, **кисе́йный** (*adj*). **рука́в** = sleeve (*also* arm of the sea, estuary, firth).

Learning by heart: Work out every word and line carefully until you can read the rhyme through and understand it all. But unless you have a Russian friend to help you with not only the pronunciation but the rhythm, it is better not to attempt learning by heart just yet. You may come back to it later.

РАЗГОВОР : HOTEL, LODGINGS

гости́ница } hotel	**столо́вая** dining-room
оте́ль (*m*) }	**рестора́н** restaurant
пансио́н boarding house	**буфе́т** refreshment room
общежи́тие hostel	**дежу́рная** maid (on duty)
спра́вочное бюро́ Inquiry office	**ве́щи** luggage
бюро́ обслу́живания Service Bureau	**умыва́льник** wash basin
лифт lift	**убо́рная** } lavatory
ле́стница stairs	**туале́т** }
ко́мната } room	**мужско́й, -а́я** men's
но́мер }	**же́нский, -ая** women's
ва́нная bathroom	**1-й эта́ж** 1st or ground floor
односпа́льная крова́ть single bed	**2-й эта́ж** 2nd floor
двуспа́льная крова́ть double bed	**3-й эта́ж** 3rd floor
ключ key	

Я жела́ю ко́мнату с двуспа́льной крова́тью и с ва́нной. I want a double room with bath.

Ваш но́мер на тре́тьем этаже́. Хоти́те, я вас провожу́? Your room is on the second floor. Would you like me to take you there?

Это ключи́ от ва́шего но́мера. Уходя́ оставля́йте ключи́ дежу́рной. These are the keys to your room. When going out leave the keys with the maid.

Мо́жете распоряди́ться мои́ми веща́ми? Разреши́те, я вам помогу́. Can you see to my luggage? Permit me to help you.

Разбуди́те меня́, пожа́луйста, в во́семь. Please wake me at eight.

Я хочу́ приня́ть ва́нну (душ). I wish to take a bath (shower).

Горя́чая вода́ у вас есть? Do you have hot water?

Обрати́тесь к дежу́рной, е́сли что вам ну́жно. Вот звоно́к к дежу́рной. Ask the maid if you need any-thing. You press this button for the maid.

Е́сли жела́ете, что́бы у́тром принесли́ вам за́втрак в ко́мнату, позвони́те в буфе́т. If you wish breakfast to be brought to your room in the morning, ring (down) to the refreshment room.

Я хочу́ отда́ть ко́е-что в сти́рку (чи́стку, утю́жку). I'd like to have some things laundered (cleaned, pressed).

Вам ну́жно почи́стить о́бувь? Do you want to have your shoes cleaned?

Гото́в ли мой костю́м (моё пла́тье)? Ваш костю́м (ва́ше пла́тье) бу́дет гото́в(о) к шести́ часа́м. Is my suit (dress) ready? Your suit (dress) will be ready by six o'clock.

Я уезжа́ю за́втра. В кото́ром часу́ наме́рены вы уезжа́ть? I'm leaving tomorrow. What time do you intend leaving?

ЗА́ЯЦ И ЛЯГУ́ШКА
Ру́сская ска́зка

Стал за́яц тужи́ть : как на бе́лом све́те жить?

Никто́ его́ не бои́тся, никто́ не убега́ет, все его́ обижа́ют!

Да так заду́мался, так закручи́нился, что и жить не захоте́л, пошёл к ре́чке — топи́ться.

Пришёл на бе́рег, а на берегу́ лягу́шка сиде́ла, ста́рые ко́сти гре́ла.

Услыха́ла лягу́шка, что кто-то идёт, да бух в во́ду!

За́яц так обра́довался, что и топи́ться не стал :

— Ага́! Кой-кому́ и я стра́шен!

ВЕСЁЛЫЕ КАРТИ́НКИ (Де́тский юмористи́ческий Журна́л. № 4, апре́ль 1960.)

заяц = hare. **лягу́шка** = frog. **тужи́ть** (II *ipf*) = to worry, grieve. **бе́лый** = white. **свет** = world, society *also* light. **на бе́лом све́те** = in the wide world. **убега́ть** (I)/**убежа́ть** (like **бежа́ть**) = to run away. **обижа́ть** (I)/**оби́дить** (II) = to insult, offend. **заду́маться** = to be plunged into thought. **закручи́ниться** (II) = to grow sad, sorrowful. **захоте́ть** = to begin to want, to conceive a desire. **ре́чка** = stream. **топи́ться** (II) = to drown oneself. **бе́рег** = shore, riverside. **кость** (*f*) = bone. **греть** (I) to warm (*tr*). **слыха́ть/услыха́ть** (*in pa only*) = to hear. **кто-то** = somebody. **бух!** = splash! plop! **ра́доваться** (I) **ра́дуюсь, -ешься)/об-** = to rejoice. **ага́** = aha! **кой-кто** (**что**) = someone (-thing) or other. **стра́шный** = fearsome, (*short form* **стра́шен, страшна́, -о ; -ы**). **Весёлые карти́нки** = Merry Pictures (USSR children's periodical).

TRANSLATION:　　　　　The Hare and the Frog　　　　A Russian Tale

A hare began to grieve: how was he to go on living in the wide world? Nobody feared him, nobody fled from him, everybody insulted him.

And he began to think so deeply and he grew so sad, that he had no desire to go on living (so) he went to the stream to drown himself.

He came to the bank of the stream and, on the shore, a frog was sitting, warming (its) old bones. The frog heard that somebody was coming and went splash! into the stream.

The hare was so delighted that he did not (decided not to) drown himself.

"Aha!" (he said). "There is someone (after all) to whom I am fearsome!"

LESSON No. 33　　УРОК № ТРИ́ДЦАТЬ ТРИ

Imperfective verbs	**Their perfective aspect**
де́лать (I) to do, make	**сде́лать** to have done, made
ду́мать (I) to think	**поду́мать** to think (for a while)*
знать (I) to know	**узна́ть** to find out, learn
конча́ть (I) to finish	**ко́нчить** (II) to finish (quickly)
	ко́нчу, ко́нчишь ; ко́нчат
начина́ть (I) to begin	**нача́ть** (I) to begin (on a specific occasion)
	начну́, начнёшь ; -ну́т
отвеча́ть (I) to answer	**отве́тить** (II) to answer (then)
	отве́чу, -тишь ; -тят

★ *The words in brackets after perfectives are explanatory.*

рабóтать (I)   to work   **порабóтать**   to do a piece of work, work for a while

спрáшивать (I)   to ask   **спросúть** (II)   to ask (once) **спрошý, спрóсишь; -óсят**

слýшать (I)   to listen   **послýшать**   to listen (for a while)

слýшаться (I)   to obey   **послýшаться**   to obey (one command)

игрáть/сыгрáть (I)   to play

ASPECTS OF RUSSIAN VERBS

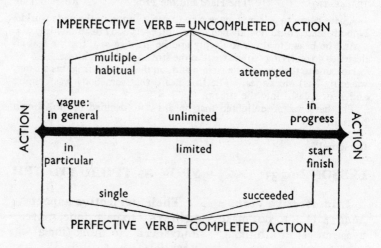

I. THE IDEA OF "ASPECT":

The word "aspect" means the way a thing presents itself to the eye or mind. The definition is important here, for the Russian verbal system is strongly and, to foreigners, peculiarly characterized by an attitude of mind which views an act or state as being either (*a*) *incomplete* (that is, "imperfect") *or* (*b*) *complete* (that is, "perfect"). Russian has forms for each of these "aspects" of nearly every verb. They are called (*a*) the imperfective aspect and (*b*) the perfective aspect. In this book from now they will be marked (*ipf*) and (*pf*).

Now have a good look at the diagram given above which clearly defines the differences between *ipf* and *pf* Russian verbs.   Then study the examples given above, and from now onwards learn verbs in pairs *ipf/pf*.   You will soon realize in the READING MATTER to be given the importance of aspect for *meaning*.

Imperfective and perfective aspects: In Part I you have met few perfective (*pf*) verbs, and then only the parts of them necessary for some particular purpose.   You have been dealing almost entirely with imperfective verbs, which are commoner than perfectives.   Now let us consider both.

Definition I: The imperfective aspect implies uncompleted, prolonged, continuous, recurring or habitual action, laying little stress on progress (past, present or future) but making clear the *process*.

Definition II: The perfective aspect makes clear that the action has been or will be completed and thus lays stress on completion of action, accomplished fact: on *result*.

Take **читáть** (I *ipf*) *to read*.   The present tense of this imperfective verb can be translated *I read* (often, seldom, sometimes, every day, in the evening), or *I do read* (in the morning, when not working, etc.), or *I am reading* (just now, etc.).   In English we achieve—often with words other than the verb—the equivalent of the Russian imperfective aspect. The action is in progress (Definition I), uncompleted, and thus demands an imperfective verb in Russian.

The perfective **прочитáть** (I) (corresponding to the imperfective aspect **читáть**) means *to read through* (and *have finished* reading.)   It can also be translated as *to have read* (and by implication have finished the reading of something). The action has been carried to completion and achieved a clear result.

It is consistent to use qualifying and modifying words such as *always, regularly, constantly* for imperfective verbs.   But it would be quite illogical to use such words with a perfective verb.   With a perfective, one can use only such qualifiers as emphasize or are consistent with the completed action: *I read right through the Lesson one evening last week.*

Russian verbs in pairs : There are a few Russian verbs of only one aspect, and you will meet them. *From now onwards you have to learn your Russian verbs in pairs:* in both imperfective and perfective aspects. This is not so difficult as it may seem, for, even in this matter of aspects, Russian mostly follows definite patterns. The perfective aspect is formed or shown in the following ways:

Imperfective	*Perfective*
(*a*)	(*a*) formed with a prefix:
читáть (*ipf* I) *to read*	**прочитáть** (*pf* I) *to have read*
готóвить (*ipf* II) to *prepare*	**приготóвить** (*pf* II) *to have prepared*
(*b*)	(*b*) shown by difference in the length of the infinitive:
понимáть (*ipf* I) *to understand*	**понять** (*pf* I) *to have understood*
(*c*)	(*c*) by alteration of the vowel between root and infinitive ending:
получáть (*ipf* I) *to receive* (*usually*)	**получить** (*pf* II) *to have received* (*once*)
(*d*)	(*d*) by inserting a suffix between root and *inf* ending:
прыгать (*ipf* I) *to jump, jump about*	**прыгнуть** (*pf* I) *to make, take a jump* (once)

Note: The suffix **-ну-** in perfective verbs usually indicates sudden, abrupt or instantaneous action.

(*e*)	(*e*) by using verbs with different roots (see also p. 196):
говорить (*ipf* II) *to speak, say* or *tell*	**сказáть** (*pf* I) *to say* or *tell on one occasion*

(f)	*(f)*	by dropping a suffix (between root and *inf* ending:
расска́зывать *(ipf* I) to tell, relate at any time	**рассказа́ть** *(pf* I) *to have* told or related *(once)*	
дава́ть *(ipf* I) *to give*	**дать** *(pf irr)* *to have given*	

Note: The suffixes **-ыва-**, **-(и)ва-** usually indicate repetition or prolongation of the action: they make verbs called "iterative".

Conjugation: Verbs in the perfective aspect have a past tense similar to the past tense of imperfectives of similar type. Thus: **я говори́л. я сказа́л.** The form of a perfective verb which corresponds to the *present* tense of an imperfective verb has a *future meaning.* The future of imperfective verbs *only* is a compound tense made with the future form of **быть** *to be* (see page 75).

Imperfective future: **я бу́ду говори́ть.** I shall speak.

Perfective future: **я скажу́.** I shall tell.

If you think over this use of the present tense *form* that has a future meaning in verbs of the perfective aspect, you will realize that it is logical. Uncompleted action (that is, *action in progress*) is consistent only with the imperfective aspect. Completion must occur at a certain moment in time, a moment which becomes fixed in the past or is foreseen in the future. Strictly, there can be *no moment of real completion in the present*, because the present is ever changing. Thus, the perfective aspect of a Russian verb *cannot* have a true present tense. The form of the perfective corresponding to the form of the present tense imperfective *must* have a future meaning. It is as simple as that! When referring to this present tense *form* of a perfective verb, we shall call it in this book the perfective future. Incidentally, it is a much used and convenient form.

Note: Both the present imperfective and the perfective future are the only Russian tenses that are fully conjugated. They are in some grammars both referred to as simply "the conjugated tense".

PRACTICE IN PART II: You must always *pay particular attention to verbs*. In this book you will find a vocabulary of verbs which includes those of the highest frequency and, wherever we give you the conjugated tense with a verb, whether imperfective or perfective, you must memorize it. This is often best done by copying out that tense in full. All this is an important part of your practice.   You should go back over both READING and CONVERSATIONS again and again until you know all the words, but *especially the verbs*.   It is much easier to acquire a vocabulary of nouns, adjectives, adverbs and other Russian parts of speech than it is of verbs: these last demand concentrated attention and effort.

ipf	*pf*
брать (I) to take	**взять** to take
беру́, берёшь; беру́т	**возьму́, возьмёшь ; -му́т** (*See also p.* 225)
дава́ть (I) to give	**дать** to give (*irregular.* See *pp.* 78–79)
даю́, даёшь ; даю́т	**дам, дашь, даст, дади́м, дади́те, даду́т**
жела́ть (I) to wish	**пожела́ть** to wish, desire (*then*)
ку́шать (I) to eat	1. **ску́шать** to eat up
	2. **поку́шать** to taste, to eat
плати́ть (II) to pay **плачу́, пла́тишь ; -а́тят**	**заплати́ть** to pay up (*and, finish with it*)
получа́ть (I) to receive	**получи́ть** (II) to have received
	получу́, полу́чишь ; -у́чат
слы́шать (II) to hear	**услы́шать** to hear (*at that moment*)
*****уме́ть** (I) to know how **уме́ю, уме́ешь ; уме́ют**	**суме́ть** to know how (French *savoir*) (*also* to succeed in)

*****уме́ть** derives from **ум**=*mind* (with **у́мный** (*adj*)=*clever* and **у́мница** (*m* or *f*)=*a clever man* or *woman*.)   Verbs in **-еть** (I) usually denote a gradual process.   The verb used for physical ability to do something (French *pouvoir*) is **мочь** (I) *to be able, can:* **могу́, мо́жешь, мо́гут.**   (The infinitive of this verb is little used.)

II. TENSES OF PERFECTIVE VERBS: In general, the conjugation of *pf* verbs follows the same principles and rules as those for *ipf* verbs.   When a *pf* verb is made by adding a prefix to an *ipf*, then the *pf* forms follow exactly those of the *ipf*, the only difference being the addition of the *pf* prefix.

Verbs given at the head of these Lessons may be regarded as regular, unless (as in such instances as **брать/взять** *to take*) deviations from the regular are given with the infinitives.   Be sure to memorize all the deviations.

Infinitive endings: *All* infinitives—*ipf* and *pf*—end in **-ти** (these are all *conj* I verbs) or **-чь** (also all *conj* I); or **-ть**. The verbs ending in **-ть** may have a vowel before the ending. Thus, you will find the endings: **-ти, -чь** (*not many*) and **-(а)ть, -(я)ть, -(и)ть, -(ы)ть, -(е)ть, -(о)ть, -(у)ть.**

These vowels which come before the **-ть** endings are important.   You will find, as you go along, that they are suffixes added to the root or stem, which in the majority of cases provide a clue to the conjugation of a simple verb.   All compounds of that verb follow exactly the conjugation of the simple verb.

FUTURE TENSE PERFECTIVE: The use of this tense —the conjugated tense of *pf* verbs—tends to cause some difficulty at first.   What you must always remember, as already explained, is that, by its nature, a *pf* verb cannot have a present tense, and that the *form* corresponding to the present *must* have a future meaning.   You thus have two future tenses in Russian, one *ipf* made with **быть,** the other, the *pf,* made by inflexion.   So,

ipf	(1) *ipf*	*pf*	(2) *pf*
infinitives	*futures*	*infinitives*	*futures*
to think **ду́мать**	я бу́ду ду́мать	поду́мать	я поду́маю
to stroll **гуля́ть**	я бу́ду гуля́ть	погуля́ть	я погуля́ю

Both (1) and (2) are usually translated in the same way: *I shall think, I shall stroll,* but their meanings must be different to take account of the difference between the Russian *ipf* and *pf*.   And so, the real meanings are:

(1) *ipf*	(2) *pf*
I shall be thinking.	I shall think a little.
I shall be strolling.	I shall go for a little stroll.

To repeat once more, in (1) the action is not completed, in (2) its completion can be assumed.

The English "future perfect", as in *I shall have written*, demands the future perfective: **я напишу́** (*from* **написа́ть** *pf*).

English present, past, or conditional: We very often use these tenses with a future meaning, and then they are all expressed by the *pf* future in Russian:

You said that you're coming	
You said you were coming	= **Вы сказа́ли, что придёте.**
You said you would be coming	You said you will come.

Note that **что** = *that* must be expressed in Russian and is preceded by a comma in writing.

быва́ло and **стать**: **быва́ло** (*from* **быва́ть**) + *pf* is used to express habitual action and translates "*used to*":

Он, быва́ло, приходи́л к нам по-вечера́м = *He used to come to us in the evening.*

стать (I *pf*) is often used instead of **быть** to make a future *ipf* (**стать**: **ста́ну, -ешь** *to become*). **Я ста́ну рабо́тать** = *I shall work.*

It is more common in the negative, and is more emphatic than **быть**:

Я не ста́ну об э́том говори́ть = *I shall (certainly) not talk about it.*

РАЗГОВО́Р: *Meeting people*

Добро́ пожа́ловать! Welcome!

Мы прие́хали из . . . We come from . . .

Как вы дое́хали (долете́ли)? What sort of journey (flight) did you have? (*lit:* How did you travel, fly?)

Это мой това́рищ (прия́тель, прия́тельница). This is my friend (*m*) (*f*).

Я мно́го слыха́л о вас. I've heard a lot about you.

Она́ у нас одна́ говори́т по-ру́сски. She's the only one (of us) who speaks Russian.

Где вы живёте? Where do you live?

Я живу́ в го́роде, но в посёлке у меня́ есть и да́ча. I live in the city, and have a (small) house in a village.

Мой прия́тель Ива́нов с Да́льнего Восто́ка. My friend Ivanov is (comes) from the Far East.

Прошу́ (про́сим) вас . . . May I (we) ask you . . .

Скажи́те (мне), пожа́луйста . . . Tell me, please . . .

Повтори́те (это), пожа́луйста! Please repeat (that).

Я хочу́ пригласи́ть вас в кино́. I'd like to invite you (to come with me) to the cinema.

Спаси́бо, но мне хо́чется погуля́ть по у́лицам. Thanks, but I'd like to go for a stroll in the streets.

Извини́те, не могу́! Excuse me (Sorry), but I can't.

О́чень вам благода́рен. I'm very grateful to you.

Кака́я у вас профе́ссия? What's your profession, work?

Я изуча́ю ру́сский язы́к. I'm a student of Russian.

Поздравля́ю вас! I congratulate you.

Я ма́ло понима́ю по-ру́сски. I understand little Russian.

Я не по́нял, что вы сказа́ли. I didn't understand what you said.

Хоти́те ли папиро́су? Would you like a cigarette?

Нет, папиро́сы у меня́ есть, но спи́чек нет. No, I have cigarettes, but I haven't any matches.

Да, да́йте мне папиро́су, пожа́луйста! Yes, give me a cigarette, please.

Прекра́сно! Спаси́бо! That's fine. Thanks.

Здесь кури́ть воспреща́ется. Smoking's prohibited here.

Скажи́те, пожа́луйста! (Что вы говори́те?) You don't say so?

Чорт возьми́! Чорт побери́! Чорт подери́! The devil take it!

ЛИСА́ И РАК

Ру́сская ска́зка

Ви́дит Рак, что Лиса́ бе́гать мастери́ца. Ста́ло ему́ зави́дно, и говори́т он ку́мушке:

— А что, Лиса́, ведь я ши́бче тебя́ бе́гать уме́ю.

— Куда́ тебе́, уса́тому-пучегла́зому!

— А пра́во же, скоре́й тебя́. Дава́й перегоня́ться?

— Дава́й!

Вы́шли на по́ле, ста́ли. Лиса́ побежа́ла, а Рак уцепи́лся клешне́ю за её хвост. Бежи́т ку́мушка, торо́пится, не огля́дывается, а Рак — ни гугу́, виси́т на хвосте́, пока́чивается. Добежа́ла Лиса́ до конца́ по́ля, оберну́лась, смо́трит — где же Рак? А он уже́

отцепи́лся, стои́т себе́ посме́ивается, уса́ми по-
шеве́ливает.

— Эх, ку́мушка, — говори́т, — как ты до́лго! Я
уже́ давно́ тебя́ жду!

ВЕСЁЛЫЕ КАРТИНКИ (1960 г.)

рак=crawfish. мастери́ца=clever woman, clever at. зави́дно=
envious. ку́мушка=gossip (person). ведь=of course, after all.
ши́бко (adv)=fast. ши́бче=faster. уме́ть (I уме́ю, уме́ешь)=
to know how. куда́ тебе́! (idiom)=Go on with you! ус=whisker.
уса́тый=bewhiskered. пучегла́зый=goggle-eyed. ско́рый=
quick. дава́й=let us. перегоня́ться=to race each other. стать
=to take up a stand. уцепи́ться (II pf)=to cling. клешня́=claw
(of crustacean). хвост=tail. торопи́ться (II)/по-=to hasten,
hurry. огля́дываться (I)/огляну́ться (I)=to look back. ни гугу́
(idiom)=not a word; висе́ть (II вишу́, виси́шь)=to hang (intransitive), to be hanging. пока́чиваться (I)=to sway about. оберну́ть-
ся (I pf)=to turn back. отцепи́ться (II pf)=to unhook oneself, to
get loose. посме́иваться (I ipf)=to chuckle. пошеве́ливать (I
ipf)=to stir, shake. до́лгий (до́лго)=long (of time). давно́=long
ago. ждать (I жду, ждёшь)=to wait.

*Names of personified animals are often written with a capital letter in such
tales as this.*

TRANSLATION: The Fox and the Crawfish   A Russian Tale

The Crawfish saw that the Fox was a very clever dame at running. He
began to feel envious and he said to his gossip:
   "Now then, Fox, I can run faster than you, can't I ?"
   "Get along with you, you bewhiskered, goggle-eyed thing!"
   "Really now, I'm faster than you. Let's have a race, shall we ?"
   "Let's!"
They went out into a field and took up their positions. The Fox
started to run, while the Crawfish with his claw caught hold of her tail
(brush). The gossip runs*, hurries along, (and) doesn't look round,
while the Crawfish—with never a word—hangs onto her brush swinging
from side to side. The Fox got to the end of the field, turned, looks—
where is the Crawfish ? But he had already let go and is standing there
chuckling and shaking his whiskers.
   "Eh, gossip!" he says, "what a time you've been. I've already been
waiting for you for a long time."

*Note: To heighten dramatic effect, Russian often uses the present
tense where we would use the past.

LESSON No. 34   УРОК № ТРИ́ДЦАТЬ ЧЕТЫ́РЕ

пе́рвый, -ая, -ое ; -ые
first
второ́й, -а́я, -о́е ; -ы́е
second
тре́тий, -тья, -тье ; -тьи
third
четвёртый, -ая, -ое ; -ые
fourth
пя́тый, -ая, -ое ; -ые
fifth
шесто́й, -а́я, -о́е ; -ы́е
sixth
седьмо́й, -а́я, -о́е ; -ы́е
seventh
восьмо́й, -а́я, -о́е ; -ы́е
eighth
девя́тый, -ая, -ое ; -ые
ninth
деся́тый, -ая, -ое ; -ые
tenth
оди́ннадцатый, -ая, -ое ;
-ые eleventh
двена́дцатый, -ая, -ое ;
-ые twelfth
трина́дцатый 13th
четы́рнадцатый 14th

пятна́дцатый 15th
шестна́дцатый 16th
семна́дцатый 17th
восемна́дцатый 18th
девятна́дцатый 19th
двадца́тый 20th
два́дцать пе́рвый twenty
first
тридца́тый 30th
сороково́й, -а́я, -о́е ; -ы́е
40th
пятидеся́тый 50th
шестидеся́тый 60th
семидеся́тый 70th
восьмидеся́тый 80th
девяно́стый 90th
со́тый 100th
двухсо́тый 200th
трёхсо́тый 300th
четырёхсо́тый 400th
пятисо́тый 500th
шестисо́тый 600th...
ты́сячный 1000th
двухты́сячный 2000th
пятиты́сячный 5000th
миллио́нный millionth

ORDINAL NUMERALS: These express the numerical order of persons or things, as in the *first* house, the *second* floor, the *third* man. *First, second, third* are ordinal numerals. In Russian they are treated as long form attributive adjectives: they are declined accordingly, and agree in gender, number and case with their noun. All of them, except пе́рвый (1*st*) and второ́й (2*nd*) are derived from their corresponding cardinals. **седьмóй** (*7th*) has a modified stem.   On the whole their forms and use are straightforward, but note underlining in the above list for some slight peculiarities.

Abridgement: As we write 1*st*, 2*nd*, 3*rd*, etc., to abridge our ordinals, so the Russians write: **1-й, 2-й, 3-й** to abridge theirs.

Declension of ordinals: With the exception of **трéтий** (3*rd*), the ordinals are declined like hard adjectives, 2nd, 6th, 7th and 8th ending in **-óй,** all the remainder in **-ый. трéтий** is declined below.

Russian preference for ordinals: It is correct grammar to say or write **Урóк нóмер пять** = Lesson number five, but **пя́тый урóк** sounds better.   You will find that, more often than not, Russian prefers an ordinal where we use a cardinal. And so:

> **Двадца́тая глава́** = our *Chapter* 20.
> **деся́тая страни́ца** = page 10.

Declension of **трéтий**: The declension of this ordinal numeral is in a class almost by itself, and may be considered a model for some other less common attributive adjectives.   It is therefore given in full:

	masc	*fem*	*neut*	*plural*
N:	трéтий	трéтья	трéтье	трéтьи
G:	трéтьего	трéтьей	трéтьего	трéтьих
D:	трéтьему	трéтьей	трéтьему	трéтьим
A:	N or G	трéтью	трéтье	N or G
I:	трéтьим	трéтьей(-ею)	трéтьим	трéтьими
P:	о трéтьем	о трéтьей	о трéтьем	о трéтьих

See also page 125.

Ordinal compound numerals: These are made with a cardinal number which remains in the nominative throughout + a declined ordinal.

1		2	
	пéрвый стол		втора́я у́лица
Nom:	пéрвого стола́	*Nom:*	вторóй у́лицы
два́дцать +	пéрвому столу́	три́дцать +	вторóй у́лице
	пéрвый стол		вторýю у́лицу
	пéрвым столóм		вторóй у́лицей
	пéрвом столé		вторóй у́лице

(1) (*the*) *twenty-first table*.   (2) (*the*) *thirty-second street*.

Collective numerals:

óба, óбе both. See page 115.

2 **двóе** two of
3 **трóе** three of
4 **чéтверо** four of
5 **пя́теро** five of
6 **шéстеро** six of
7 **сéмеро** seven of
8 **вóсьмеро** ⎱ now un-
10 **дéсятеро** ⎰ common, but found in classical literature

Other collective words:

пáра (+*gen pl*) a pair (of)
деся́ток (+*gen pl*) ten (of)
сóтня (*pl* **сóтни**) a hundred of

Fractions to note:

половúна (+*gen*) (a) half
пол short form ($\frac{1}{2}$)
полторá one and a half ($1\frac{1}{2}$)
чéтверть (*f*) (a) quarter (*gen pl* **четвертéй**)
треть (*f*) a third

The form for 9 is archaic.

COLLECTIVE NUMERALS: The special forms for 2, 3, 4, 5, 6 and 7 given above are used to express a number of (similar) persons or things in a group or collective sense. Thus:

Collective numerals and case: A collective numeral in the nominative governs the *gen pl* of its noun. In oblique cases it agrees with its noun or pronoun.

Declension of collectives: The numerals **двóе** and **трóе** are similarly declined. **Чéтверо** (note **ы** in case endings) is the model for the remainder:

Nom:	двóе	трóе	чéтверо
Gen:	двойх	тройх	четверы́х
Dat:	двойм	тройм	четверы́м
Acc:		N or G	N or G
Ins:	двойми	тройми	четверы́ми
Prp:	о двойх	о тройх	о четверы́х

Nouns used only in the plural: **часы́** *watch, clock.* **очкú** (a pair of) *spectacles.* **нóжницы** (a pair of) *scissors.* **брю́ки** (a pair of) *trousers.* **сýтки**=*day and night.* Such nouns are preceded by collective numerals to express their plurals: **трóе очкóв ; чéтверо нóжниц.**

> **двóе часóв** = two watches or clocks
> **трóе очкóв** = three pairs of spectacles
> **чéтверо нóжниц** = four pairs of scissors

Note that **час** (*sing* of **часы́**) means *hour*, and has *gen sing* **чáса**, *gen pl* **часóв**. It is used for the hour of the day and then the cardinal number is used + case and number which it governs. See page 210 and, for hour of day, pages 211–2.

FRACTIONS : For practical purposes few fractions are necessary, and they will be given here.

половѝна (*no f*), with fixed stress throughout = *a half*, a half of, governs the *gen:* **половѝна недéли** = *half the week.*

пол- is a shortened form of this noun and, combined with the *gen sing* of certain nouns, forms useful compound words. The following must be memorized:

полбутѝлки = half a bottle.	**полвéка** = half a century.
полгóда = half a year; six months.	**полдня́** = half a day.
полнóчи = half a night.	**полфýнта** = half a pound.
получасá = half an hour.	**полдю́жины** = half a dozen.

And note: **пóлдень** midday, noon; **пóлночь** midnight.

When **пол-** is used before a place-name beginning with a capital letter, or a noun beginning with **л-** or a vowel, the resultant compound is written with a hyphen. So we have:

пол-Лóндона = half (of) London.	**пол-Москвы́** = half (of) Moscow.
пол-я́блока = half an apple.	**пол-óсени** = half the autumn.

полторá, полторы́ (*f*) = 1½: This is a useful noun, much used in everyday speech. In Russian it is regarded as a numeral word. It derives from **пол + вторá** (= **вторóго**) and, like **óба, óбе, два, две, три, четы́ре,** is followed by the *gen sing* of the noun which it governs. **полторá** has one form **полýтора** for all oblique cases and genders. Note well the following examples:

> **полторы́ минýты** = 1½ minutes.
> **полторá рубля́** = 1½ roubles.
> **с полýтора рубля́ми** = with 1½ roubles.
> **óколо полýтора ты́сяч** = about 1,500 (= 1½ thousand).
> In **полторы́ недéли** = 1½ weeks, the feminine form is used.

The word **сýтки** (*pl*) meaning "a day and a night", "24 hours", or "round the clock" is used after **полторá** to mean 36 hours.

Adjectives qualifying **полторá** may be in either *nom* or *gen* plural. Thus: **дóбрые (дóбрых) полторá часá** = a good hour and a half.

треть = ⅓ and **чéтверть** = ¼: These are declined like feminine nouns ending in **-ь**. So:

двe трéти = two-thirds.   **три чéтверти** = three-quarters.

See page 211–2 for other fractions.

Declension and use of **óба, óбе:** This is a collective word and is followed by the genitive like 2, 3, 4. For declension see page 185. For nouns following 2, 3, 4—see page 92.

КАЛЕНДÁРЬ

ЯНВÁРЬ	**4**	**5**	**6**
	ПОНЕДÉЛЬНИК	ВТÓРНИК	СРЕДÁ
7	**8**	**9**	**10**
ЧЕТВÉРГ	ПЯ́ТНИЦА	СУББÓТА	ВОСКРЕСÉНЬЕ

*янвáрь (*gen* **января́**) January
феврáль (**-я́**) February
март (**-а**) March
апрéль (**-я**) April
май (**-я**) May
июнь (**-я**) June
июль (**-я**) July
áвгуст (**-а**) August
сентя́брь (**-я́**) September
октя́брь (**-я́**) October
ноя́брь (**-я́**) November
декáбрь (**-я́**) December
век, *gen* **вéка,** *gen pl* **векóв,**
    century; age, epoch

понедéльник Monday
втóрник Tuesday
средá Wednesday
четвéрг Thursday
пя́тница Friday
суббóта Saturday
воскресéнье Sunday
в понедéльник ⎫
во втóрник ⎪
в срéду ⎪
в четвéрг ⎬ **В** + *acc*
в пя́тницу ⎪ = *on*
в суббóту ⎪
в воскресéнье ⎭

день day (**дня,** *pl* **дни**)
недéля (**-и, -и**) week
мéсяц (**-а, -ы**) month
год (**-а ;** *pl* **гóды** *or* **годá**) year
ежегóдно (*adv*) yearly
на э́той недéле = this week

на бу́дущей неде́ле   next week
на про́шлой неде́ле   last week
не́сколько (*adv*)   a few
число́, *gen* числа́, *pl* чи́сла   date, number

Рождество́ Christmas   на Рождество́ for Christmas
Па́сха Easter   на Па́сху for Easter

*Note: Names of months are written with a small letter, except at the beginning of a sentence. These are all masculine nouns.

To express date: The neuter form of the *ordinal* number is used, to agree with число́ (= *date, number, quantity*), which may be expressed but is more often omitted. Thus:

Како́е сего́дня число́? = *What is the date to-day?*

Сего́дня {
пе́рвое января́ =
второ́е февраля́ *To-day is the*
тре́тье ма́рта
} {
1st of January.
2nd of February.
3rd of March, etc.
}

Како́го числа́? = *On what date . . . ?*
Сего́дня 1-е (число́) = *To-day is the 1st.*

Note that when the date is given, the name of the month is in the genitive.

Сего́дня, пе́рвое (1-ое) января́, Но́вый год. = *To-day is the 1st of January, New Year's Day.*

But if the name of the month is not indicated, the ordinal is in the nominative case:

Тепе́рь ты́сяча девятьсо́т шестьдеся́т второ́й год = *It is now* 1962.

Abbreviations: г., гг. are used for год, го́ды ; в., вв. for век, века́. Roman numerals are used for centuries: XIX в., XX в. = (19th), (20th) century.

To express age:

Ско́лько вам лет? = *What age are you?*
Ско́лько ему́ лет? = *What age is he?*
Ему́ оди́н год = *He is one year old.*
Ему́ два, три, четы́ре го́да = *He is two, three, four years of age.*
Ему́ пять лет. = *He is five years of age.*
Ему́ со́рок лет. = *He is forty years of age.*

You see by these examples that **год** is used for *one* year old, that **год** in the *gen* singular is used after **два, три, четы́ре,** and that **лет** (*gen pl* of **ле́то** = *summer*) is used after **пять,** as it is after numbers from five upwards. The *dat* of the noun or pronoun is used in questions. Thus, the question in Russian is *How many to you of years* or *of summers ?* and so forth.

Answer : **Мне четы́ре го́да** = *I am four years old.*
Ей четы́ре го́да. = *She is four years old, of age.*
Past : **Мари́и бы́ло два́дцать лет.** = *Mary was twenty years of age.*
Fut : **Ей бу́дет три́дцать лет в э́том ме́сяце.** = *She'll be thirty years of age this month.*

РАЗГОВО́Р : THE DATE

Кото́рое сего́дня у нас число́ ?   What date are we to-day ?
Сего́дня пя́тое декабря́, день конститу́ции.   To-day's the 5th December, Constitution Day.
Ско́лько вам лет ?   What age are you ?
Мне три́дцать пять лет.   I'm thirty-five years old.
Когда́ вы родили́сь ?   When were you born ?
Я роди́лся тре́тьего ноября́, ты́сяча девятьсо́т два́дцать четвёртого го́да.   I was born on the 3rd November 1924.
Что вы сего́дня хоти́те де́лать ?   What do you want to do to-day ?
Сего́дня ничего́, но за́втра ве́чером я хочу́ пойти́ в теа́тр.   To-day nothing, but I want to go to the theatre to-morrow evening.
Ско́лько лет ва́шей сестре́ Мари́и ?   What age is your sister Mary ?
За́втра ей бу́дет семна́дцать лет.   She'll be seventeen to-morrow.
Вы не рабо́таете в воскресе́нье ?   Don't you work on Sunday ?

Нет, потому́ что я нача́льник а нача́лники не рабо́тают по воскресе́ньям. No, because I'm a boss and bosses don't work on Sundays.

Хорошо́! Сейча́с иду́т репети́ции но́вой пье́сы. That's good. They're now rehearsing a new play.

За́втра интере́сный спекта́кль в теа́тре о́перы и бале́та. To-morrow there's an interesting show at the Theatre of Opera and Ballet.

И что идёт в кино́? And what's on at the cinema?

Я не зна́ю. Мне не нра́вится кино́. I don't know. I don't like the cinema.

Не хоти́те ли пойти́ в цирк? Wouldn't you like to go to the circus?

Спаси́бо, я предпочита́ю бале́т. Thank you, I prefer the ballet.

ЗНАЕТЕ ЛИ ВЫ?

ФА́КТЫ И ЦИФРЫ

1. Сове́тский Сою́з по разме́ру террито́рии — 22,4 миллио́на квадра́тных киломе́тров — са́мое большо́е госуда́рство в ми́ре. На э́той пло́щади могли́ бы размести́ться Соединённые Шта́ты Аме́рики почти́ 3 раза, Индия — 7 раз, Япо́ния — 60, Голла́ндия — 700 раз.

*

2. Протяжённость террито́рии СССР с се́вера на юг составля́ет 5 ты́сяч киломе́тров, то есть бо́лее полови́ны расстоя́ния от эква́тора до по́люса. Расстоя́ние от са́мой за́падной то́чки страны́ до са́мой восто́чной — 10 ты́сяч киломе́тров, то есть приме́рно че́тверть длины́ эква́тора.

FACTS AND FIGURES

The Soviet Union (is) in extent of territory 22.4 million square kilometers—the biggest state in the world. In this area the United States of America could be placed nearly three times, India seven times, Japan 60 times, (and) Holland 700 times.

*

The length of the territory of the USSR from north to south extends for five thousand kilometers, that is more than half the distance from the equator to the Pole. The distance from the most western point to the most eastern (is) 10,000 kilometers, that is roughly a quarter of the length of the equator.

*

3. Жи́тели СССР Но́вый год встреча́ют 11 раз: когда́ в Москве́ 7 часо́в ве́чера то на се́веро-восто́ке страны́, наприме́р на Чуко́тке, — уже́ 5 часо́в утра́ сле́дующего дня.

*

Inhabitants of the USSR meet (greet) the New Year eleven times: when in Moscow it is 7 o'clock in the evening, then in the north-east of the country, for example, in Chukotsk, it is already 5 o'clock in the morning of the next day.

*

4. По рельéфу террито́рию СССР мо́жно подраздели́ть на две почти́ ра́вные ча́сти, разделённые сиби́рской реко́й Енисе́ем. В за́падной полови́не страны́ преоблада́ют равни́ны и ни́зменности, восто́чная полови́на — почти́ сплошь гори́стая.

*

According to the relief (map) of the USSR it is possible to divide it in two almost equal parts, the dividing line (being) the Siberian River Yenisei. In the western half of the country plains and lowlands predominate, the eastern half (is) almost continuously mountainous.

*

5. Вы́сшая то́чка СССР — пик Ста́лина в гора́х Пами́ра — 7495 ме́тров. Ни́зшая то́чка — впа́дина Карагие в Казахста́не — 132 ме́тра ни́же у́ровня мо́ря.

*

The highest point of the USSR (is) Stalin Peak in the Pamir Mountains, 7495 meters. The lowest point is the Karagie depression in Kazakstan, 132 meters below the level of the sea.

Культу́ра и жизнь No. 8, 1960

1: **разме́р** = size, extent. **по разме́ру** = in extent. **госуда́рство** = state. **квадра́тный** = square. **киломе́тр** = kilometer. **пло́щадь** (f) = area; square. **могли́ бы** from **мочь** (I ipf): **могу́, мо́жешь; мо́гут.** Past: **мог, могла́, -о́, -и́. размести́ть** (II pf) = to accommodate; **-ся,** to be accommodated. **почти́** = almost.

2: **протяжённость** (f) = length. **се́вер** = north. **юг** = south. **на юг** = to the south. **составля́ть** (I pf) = to make up (extend). **то есть** = that is. **бо́лее** = more (than). **полови́на** = half. **расстоя́ние** = distance. **эква́тор** = equator. **по́люс** = Pole. **за́пад** = west. **за́падный** = western. **са́мый** = very, most. **то́чка** = point. **страна́** = region. **восто́к** = east. **восто́чный** = eastern. **приме́рно** = roughly. **че́тверть** = quarter. **длина́** = length.

3: **жи́тель** = inhabitant. **Но́вый год** = New Year. **встреча́ть** (I ipf) = to meet, welcome. **наприме́р** = for example. **Чуко́тка** = Chukot. **сле́дующий** = next, following.

4: **рельéф** = relief (map). **подраздели́ть** (II pf) = to (sub-)divide. **ра́вный** = equal. **часть** (f) = part. **разделе́ние** = division. **сиби́рский** = Siberian. **Енисе́й** = Yenisei. **преоблада́ть** (irr pf) = to pre-

dominate. **равнина**=plain. **низменность** (*f*)=lowland. **сплошь**
=continuously. **гора**=mountain. **гористый**=mountainous.
5: **высший**=highest. **пик**=peak. **Памир**=the Pamirs. **низший**
=lowest. **впадина**=depression. **ниже**=below. **уровень** (*m*)=
level.

Note: From this point onwards the stress on a word which is known
will often be omitted. This will help you to become accustomed to unstressed Russian. Stress will be found either in the explanatory notes
or in the Vocabulary at the end of the book. As you know, stress is not
marked in Russian, except in textbooks for learners or in dictionaries.

LESSON No. 35   УРОК № ТРИДЦАТЬ ПЯТЬ

секунда second

минута minute

час hour, (*pl*) **часы**, *gen
sing* **часа** (after 2, 3, 4
otherwise **часа**), *gen pl*
часов

часы (*no sing*) watch, clock

четверть (*f*) quarter

половина half

без+*gen* less; "*to*"

полдень (*m*) noon, *gen*
полудня

полночь (*f*) midnight, *gen*
полуночи

по полуночи after midnight

под утро towards morning

некогда there's no time

когда when

иногда sometimes

уже (**уж**) already

уже не no longer

скорее quickly

поскорее more quickly

долго a long time

давно long since

сейчас now

тотчас immediately

ранний (*adj*) early

рано (*adv*) early

поздний (*adj*) late

поздно (*adv*) late

потом later, afterwards

ровно exactly, punctually

ровно час exactly one hour

ровно в час at 1 sharp,
punctually at one

сутки 24 hours (=day and
night)

ежедневно (*adv*) daily

в одну минуту in 1 minute

каждую минуту every
minute

каждый час every hour

каждые два часа every
two hours

через час in (=*after the
lapse of*) an hour

THE TIME OF DAY

(1) Use cardinals for the full hour

Который час?	*What time is it?*	numbers **two** to **four** govern *gen sing* of nouns
час	*one o'clock*	
два часа́	*two o'clock*	
три часа́	*three o'clock*	
четы́ре часа́	*four o'clock*	

пять часо́в	*five o'clock*	Numbers **from five onwards** govern the *gen pl* of nouns
шесть часо́в	*six o'clock*	
семь часо́в	*seven o'clock*	
во́семь часо́в	*eight o'clock*	
де́вять часо́в	*nine o'clock*	
де́сять часо́в	*ten o'clock*	
оди́ннадцать часо́в	11 *o'clock*	
двена́дцать часо́в	12 *o'clock*	

a.m. and p.m. are expressed by the words:

утра́ (*of the*) morning—from about 6 a.m. to noon.

дня day = *afternoon*—from noon to 6 p.m.   **три часа́ дня** = 3 p.m.

ве́чера evening—from 6 p.m. to midnight.

но́чи night—from midnight to 6 a.m.   **четы́ре часа́ но́чи** = 4 a.m.

в + *acc* is used for *at* when referring to the hour:

в час = *at* 1 *o'clock*.   But note **в** + *prp* in **в полови́не второ́го** = *at half past one* (= *half of the second*)

(2) Use ordinals for fractions of the hour:

12.5 пять мину́т пе́рвого   *five minutes of the first*

12.15 че́тверть пе́рвого   *a quarter of the first*

12.30 полови́на пе́рвого   *a half of the first*

1.10 де́сять мину́т второ́го   *ten minutes of the second*

1.15 че́тверть второ́го   *a quarter of the second*

1.20 два́дцать мину́т второ́го   *twenty minutes of the second*

1.25 два́дцать пять мину́т второ́го   *twenty-five minutes of the second*

(3) From the half hour без is used :

12.45 без че́тверти час   *less a quarter (of) one o'clock*

1.40 без двадцати́ мину́т два.   *less* 20 *minutes of two* (and *not* "of the third hour")

1.50 без десяти́ мину́т два.   *less* 10 (*minutes*) *of two* ("*minutes*" may be omitted)

This is the commonest way of stating fractions of the hour, and it is at first a little awkward for the English-speaking learner.   One *must* make oneself familiar with the Russian use of the "first hour" for 12 o'clock; the "second hour" for 1 o'clock and so on.   Practise by setting the hands of a watch at any time and working out what that would be in Russian. First go over the full hours:

час ; два часа́ ; три часа́ ; четы́ре часа́ ; пять часо́в, etc.

When you can say them with little hesitation, go on to fractions of the hour:

> **пять мину́т пе́рвого ; че́тверть пе́рвого.**
> **11.10 де́сять мину́т двена́дцатого.**
> **10.20 два́дцать мину́т оди́ннадцатого.**

—and use "midnight" or "midday" for 12 midnight and 12 midday:

> **по́лночь.   по́лдень.**

You *have to learn all this*, because the chances are that it will be the way Russians *say* the hour.   But there is another and simpler way which you should also know, and it is similar to our way of telling the time as it is stated in our (and Russian) TIME TABLES:

час пятна́дцать = 1.15

два три́дцать = 2.30

три два́дцать два = 3.22

четы́ре семна́дцать = 4.17, **и так да́лее** (= and so forth).

Prepositions: The following prepositions are used in expressions of time:

без + *gen* = *to*.   **без че́тверти во́семь** = a quarter to eight.

в + *acc* = *at*.   **в час, в два часа́** = at one, two o'clock.   See page 143.

в+*prp*=*at* (with **половина** "half").   **в половине третьего**=at half past two.   See page 215.

до+*gen*=*till*, *up to*.   **до восьми часов**=until, up to eight.

за+*acc*=*before*.   **за час до . . .**=an hour before . . .

к+*dat*=*by*.   **к трём**=by three.

между+*ins*=*between*.   **между двумя и четырьмя**=between two and three.

на+*acc* ⎫ See examples on page 143.   **она опоздала на две минуты**=
  +*prp* ⎭   she was two minutes late.

около+*gen*=*about*.   **около двух часов**=about two o'clock.

по+*dat*=*during*.   **по вечерам**=in the evenings.   **по воскресеньям**
  =on Sundays.

под+*acc*=*towards*.   **под утро**=towards morning.

после+*gen*=*after*.   **после пяти**=after five.

с+*gen* . . . **до**+*gen* . . . =*from . . . to . . .*   **с двух до пяти**=between two and five.

Phrases and idioms relating to time

около часа=*about 1 o'clock*.   **вовремя**=*on time*.

в+*acc* and *prp* is used for *at such a time*: **в котором часу?**=*At what time?*   **в час**=*at 1 o'clock*.   **в пятом часу**=*after 4 o'clock*.   **в полдень**=*at noon*.

до+*gen*=until: **до которого часа открыт сегодня ресторан?**
Up to what time is the restaurant open to-day?

с часу на час=*at any time*.   **ровно в час**=*at one sharp*.

скоро=soon (*adv*): **скоро шесть часов**=(*It will*) *soon be six o'clock*.

через+*acc*=at the end of (a day, etc.): **поезд уходит через четверть часа**=*The train leaves in a quarter of an hour*.

пора=*it is time* (+*inf*).   **один час** ⎫
давно пора=*it is high time*.   **час времени** ⎭ *one hour* (60 *minutes*).

часовой (*adj*)=*hour*, also *one o'clock*.   **часовой поезд**=*the 1 o'clock train*.

частый (*adj*)=*frequent*.   **Он у меня частый гость**=*He's a frequent guest at my house*.

часто (*adv*)=*often*.   **чаще**=*more often*.

сутки: Russian has this special word (*pl* only) to express the period of twenty-four hours (=a day and a night).   *gen* (*pl*) **суток**.   Thus:

целые сутки=the whole day and night.

двое суток=two days and nights (forty-eight hours).

трое суток=three days and nights.

четверо суток=four days and nights.

Чтобы получить пропуск, я простоял в очереди целые сутки.=
In order to get a permit, I stood in a queue all day and night.

Расписа́ние TIME TABLE

АЭРОФЛОТ

ВО ФРАНЦИЮ, ЧЕХОСЛОВАКИЮ, ГЕРМАНИЮ, ПОЛЬШУ и т. д.

Номера рейсов		SU-049	AF-741	SU-III	SU-III	DH-601	DH-603
Типы самолетов		★Ту-104А	Конст.	Ил-14М	Ил-14М	Ил-14	Ил-14
Дни вылета		(1) (4)	(3) (7)	(1)	(2) (3) (4) (5) (6) (7)	(1) (2) (3) (5) (7)	(4) (6)
Москва (Внуково)	о★	10.35	19.50	8.25	8.25	7.40	15.05
Вильнюс .	п★ о			11.00 12.15	11.00 12.15	10.30 11.50	↓
Варшава .	п о			11.50 12.35			17.05 17.55
Прага . .	п о						
Берлин . .	п о			14.15	12.55	12.40	19.45
Париж . .	п	12.30	00.05	—	—	—	—
Время в пути		3.55	6.15	7.50	6.30	7.00	6.40

СХЕМА РАСПОЛОЖЕНИЯ МЕСТ В САМОЛЁТАХ

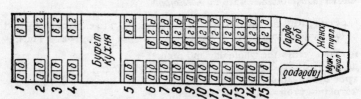

Ту-104А

THE FUNDAMENTALS OF THE LANGUAGE

THE FUNDAMENTALS OF THE LANGUAGE   215

Notes on the TIME TABLE

АЭРОФЛОТ: State air line which serves the whole USSR.
Номера рейсов: Flight numbers.   SU=*Aeroflot*.   AF=*Air France*.
DH=*Deutsche Lufthansa*.
Типы самолётов: Types of aeroplanes.   See below★.
Дни вылета: Days of flights.   (1)=Monday, (7)=Sunday, etc.
★*Abbreviations:*

> **Ту-104А**=Tupolev (50 seats).
> **Конст.**=Constellation.
> **Ил-14М**=Ilyushin (18 seats).
> **Ил-14**=Ilyushin (18 seats).
> **о**=**отправление**   departure.
> **п**=**прибытие**   arrival.
> **Внуково**=Moscow Airport.
> **Время в пути**=Time taken on journey.

Twenty-four hours clock: Note that in the USSR the 24-hour clock is used for time tables for air, sea, river-boat and land travel.

You should now become acquainted with the Russian italic alphabet. See page 21.

FURTHER EXAMPLES OF THE USE OF **В** AND **НА** IN EXPRESSIONS OF TIME

As Russian usage in this field tends to be rather confusing, these examples should be studied carefully:

В and НА with the accusative:

в четверг	on Thursday	на третий день	on the third day
в тот день	on that day	на Новый год	on New Year's day
в прошлую субботу	last Saturday	на Рождество, Пасху	on, for Christmas, Easter
в будущую среду	next Wednesday	на зиму	for the winter
в три дня	in three days' time	на другой день	(on) the next day
		на два дня	for two days
три раза в день	three times a day	план на будущий месяц, на этот год	the plan for next month, this year

В and НА with the prepositional:

в тысяча девятьсот шестидесятом году	} in 1960	на праздниках	during the holiday(s)/feast day(s)
		на каникулах	during the (= in) vacation

в январе́ (ме́сяце)	in (the month of) January	на деся́том году́	in the tenth year (*of one's life*)
в э́том году́	this year	на э́той неде́ле	this week
в про́шлом году́	last year	на про́шлой неде́ле	last week
в бу́дущем году́	next year	на бу́дущей неде́ле	next week

РАЗГОВОР : MONEY, EXCHANGE

рубль (*m*) rouble
копе́йка copeck
де́ньги (*pl, gen* де́нег)
моне́та coin
ме́лочь (*f*) small change
сда́ча one's change (after paying)
бума́жные де́ньги paper money
пятирублёвая бума́жка 5 rouble note
фунт сте́рлингов £ sterling
до́ллар dollar
нали́чные (де́ньги) cash
(ба́нковый) чек cheque

аккредити́в traveller's cheque, letter of credit
касси́р cashier, teller
банк bank
курс валю́ты rate of exchange
валю́та currency
получа́ть де́ньги по че́ку to cash a cheque
вы́писать чек to write out a cheque
разме́нивать(I) / **разменя́ть**(I) to change, exchange
иностра́нная валю́та foreign currency

оди́н рубль = сто (100) копе́ек
пята́к = 5 copeck piece   полти́на = 50 copecks
гри́венник = 10 copecks piece

See also page 366, APPENDIX, MONEY, WEIGHTS, & MEASURES

Я хочу́ разменя́ть два́дцать фу́нтов сте́рлингов на рубли́. I want to change £20 into roubles.

По тури́стскому ку́рсу вы мо́жете получи́ть 29 рубле́й на оди́н фунт.   On the tourist rate of exchange you can get 29 roubles to the pound.

Где мо́жно разменя́ть иностра́нную валю́ту?   Where can one change foreign currency?

Могу́ ли я здесь получи́ть де́ньги по че́ку (аккредити́ву)? Can I cash a (traveller's) cheque here?

Ско́лько у вас иностра́нной валю́ты?   How much foreign currency do you have?

У меня́ 30 фу́нтов сте́рлингов че́ками и 70 до́лларов нали́чными.   I have £30 in cheques and 70 dollars in cash.

По сегодняшнему курсу вам следует пятьсот рублей. By to-day's rate of exchange you should get 500 roubles.

В каком виде желаете получить ваши деньги, крупными или мелкими бумажками? How (in what form) would you like (to receive) your money, large or small notes?

Дайте мне, пожалуйста, семь десятирублёвых, четыре пятирублёвых, а остальное мелочью. Please give me 7 ten rouble notes, 4 five rouble notes and the rest in small change.

Сколько же выходит? How much does that make?

Вот вам перо. Вы можете выписать ваши чеки здесь. Here is a pen. You can write your cheque out here.

Рассчитайте, пожалуйста, сколько мне следует. Please work out (calculate) how much I should get.

Сколько выходит по вашему расчёту? How much do you make that come to? (*lit:* How much does that come to according to your calculation?)

ЗНАЕТЕ ЛИ ВЫ?

ЦИФРЫ И ФАКТЫ

FIGURES AND FACTS

1. В СССР насчитывается более 150 тысяч рек длиной более 10 километров.

In the USSR there numbers more than 150 thousand rivers of more than 10 kilometers (in length).

Самая большая река по площади бассейна — Обь — 2 425 000 квадратных километров.

The very biggest river by the area of (its) basin—the Ob—has 2,425,000 square kilometers.

Самая длинная река — Лёна — 4320 километров.

The longest river—the Lena—is 4320 kilometers.

*

2. В СССР находится самое большое озеро в мире — Каспийское море и самое глубокое озеро в мире — Байкал— Его глубина — 1741 метр.

In the USSR is found the biggest lake in the world—the Caspian Sea, and the deepest lake in the world—Baikal. Its depth: 1741 meters.

*

3. Климат Советского Союза крайне разнообразен. В то время, когда на севере Сибири температура ниже — 50° С, в Западной Грузии цветут розы. Минимальная температура наблюдалась на северо-востоке Сибири: около — 70° С. Максимальная — была отмечена на юге Узбекистана, в Термезе:+50° С.

The climate of the Soviet Union (is) extremely diverse (varied). At the time when in the north of Siberia the temperature is below (zero) — 50° C(entigrade), in Western Georgia roses are blooming. The minimum temperature observed in the north-east of Siberia (was) about — 70° (*i.e. below zero*). The maximum was recorded in the south of Uzbekistan, in Termez: + 50° C.

*

4. СССР граничит с 12 государствами. Более чем на 60 тысяч километров протянулись его границы.

Нет ни одной другой страны, которая имела бы такую длинную границу и граничила бы с таким большим числом государств.

The USSR borders on 12 states (countries). Its frontiers stretch more than 60 thousand kilometers.

There is not one other country which has such a long frontier and borders on such a large number of states.

Культура и жизнь № 3, 1960

1: **насчитывать** (I *ipf*)=to count. **-ся**, to number. **река (реки)**= river. **длина**=length. **площадь** (*f*)=area. **бассейн**=basin (of river).

2: **находить** (II *ipf*)=to come on, find: **нахожу, находишь ; -ят. находиться**=to be situated. **озеро**=lake. **глубокий**=deep. **глубина**=depth.

3: **крайне** (*adv*)=extremely. **разнообразный**=diverse (short form: **разнообразен, -на, -но ;-ны**). **в то время**=at the time. **ниже**= below. **С**=Centigrade. **Западная Грузия**=Western Georgia. **цвести** (I *ipf*)=to. bloom: **цвету, -ёшь ; -ут. минимальный** =minimum. **наблюдать**=(*like*) to observe; **-ся**, to be observed. **около** (*prep*+*gen*)=near, about. **максимальный**=maximum. **отмеченный** (*p.p.pa*)=recorded (*from* **отмечать/отметить**, to note, observe.)

4: **граничить** (II *pf*)=to border on. **протянуть** (II *pf*)=to stretch. **граница**=frontier. **нет ни одного, одной**=not even one. **число** =number.

— Все последние дни я думаю только о вас!
Рисунок Е. Горохова.

LESSON No. 36   УРОК № ТРИ́ДЦАТЬ ШЕСТЬ

PERFECTIVES OF VERBS OF MOVEMENT: Verbs
of movement with two forms of the imperfective, indeterminate and determinate, form their perfectives by adding the
prefix **по-** to the *determinate* imperfective infinitive.   Thus:

Indeterminate ipf	Determinate ipf	Perfective
ходи́ть	идти́	пойти́
е́здить	е́хать	пое́хать
води́ть	вести́	повести́
вози́ть	везти́	повезти́
носи́ть	нести́	понести́
лета́ть	лете́ть	полете́ть

Note that when идти́ has a prefix it is usually spelt **-йти́.**

This method of forming the perfective is perfectly logical, since the
determinate imperfective already refers to a definite action on a definite
occasion which is not yet completed.   It is moving, as it were, towards
the completion which is achieved in the perfective.

In practice, this type of perfective can have a double meaning. As well as indicating a completed movement, it can also simply stress the *commencement* of the movement: "*to set off*". Thus:

Я хочу поéхать в Рим. = I want to go to Rome.
Пóсле обéда он пошёл в теáтр. = After dinner he set off for the theatre.

The indeterminate imperfectives also have perfectives formed with the prefix **по-**, *but* these perfectives are strictly limited to that use of the indeterminate where there is absolutely *no* sense of *direction* or *destination*. Their only function is to limit the time during which the movement takes place. Thus:

> **походúть**   to walk about (up and down) for a while
> **побéгать**   to run about for a while, to have a run
> **поплáвать**   to have a swim

Obviously, this type of usage is strictly limited. It is of the greatest importance not to confuse these comparatively rare forms with the true, direct perfectives of verbs of movement which are formed from the determinate imperfective.

"ILLOGICAL" USE OF VERBS OF MOVEMENT: One of the most surprising features in the whole Russian verbal system is the "illogical" use of the indeterminate imperfectives of verbs of movement. As you have seen (pages 171–192), these are extreme imperfective forms expressing *repeated or habitual movement*, or *movement where there is absolutely no sense of direction or destination at all*. However, these verbs are also very frequently used (in the past tense only) in a purely perfective sense to indicate a "round trip": a single journey to a definite destination with a definite return to the point of departure. Thus:

Сегóдня ýтром я ходúл на пóчту. = This morning I went to the post office. (*and came back*)
Лéтом онú éздили в Дáнию. = They went to Denmark in the summer. (*and have returned*)

The indeterminate imperfective can be used in this way *only in the past tense*.

To enable one to use the same type of construction in the future tense, a "true" perfective is formed by means of the prefix **с-** added to the indeterminate imperfective: **сходúть, съéздить** :

Сегóдня ýтром я схожý на пóчту. = This morning I shall go to the post office. (*and come back*)
Лéтом мы съéздим во Фрáнцию. = We shall go to France in the summer. (*and return*)

Do not confuse the perfective **сходúть** ("*round trip*") with the imperfective compound **сходúть** (*perfective* **сойтú**), *to come down, to descend*.

PREFIXES TO VERBS: The system of adding prefixes to verbs to modify or change their meaning is very important. On pages 194–6 you saw that many verbs form their perfective aspects by adding a prefix to the imperfective. Thus the direct perfective of **писа́ть** *to write* is **написа́ть** which means *to write a definite thing on a particular occasion*. By using other prefixes in place of **на-** one can form a whole series of different verbs each with its own specific shade of meaning. Thus:

вписа́ть *to write in, to insert (in writing)*
вы́писать *to write, copy out, to write for, to order (in writing), to subscribe to (a periodical)*
дописа́ть *to finish writing*
записа́ть *to note down*
описа́ть *to describe*
переписа́ть *to write out again, to copy out*
подписа́ть *to sign*
приписа́ть *to add (in writing), to ascribe, attribute*
прописа́ть *to prescribe*
расписа́ть *to paint*
расписа́ться *to sign one's name*
списа́ть *to copy from*

Note that all these verbs are perfectives each with a specific meaning of its own. Quite obviously the simple imperfective **писать** would be insufficient to express these different shades of meaning in those instances where the use of the imperfective aspect is required. Consequently each of these perfectives has its own imperfective formed by adding the suffix **-ыв-**: **впи́сывать, выпи́сывать, допи́сывать, запи́сывать, опи́сывать, перепи́сывать, подпи́сывать, припи́сывать, пропи́сывать, распи́сывать, распи́сываться, спи́сывать.**

All primary prepositions except **к** and **для** may be used as prefixes.

In the list of prefixes which follows here immediately, all of them important, an indication is given of the new meaning imparted to a simple verb by the addition of a prefix. It is important to know the values for *all* these prefixes; but it is inadvisable to regard them as rigid. Verbs can have their meaning altered so much by the addition of a prefix that the only safe rule is to memorize from the outset a working list of the most useful verbs. Here the keeping of a notebook becomes very helpful.

Prefixes	What they indicate	Examples
БЕЗ- (безо-, бес-)	*without*, lack of	**беспоко́ить** (II *ipf*) /**побеспоко́ить** (II *pf*) to disturb (**поко́й** = *calm*)
В- (во-)	*into*, entrance into	**впуска́ть** (I)/**впусти́ть** (II) to let in, to admit
ВЗ- (вс-, воз-, вос-)	*up*, upward movement	**возника́ть** (I) /**возни́кнуть** (I) to arise, to spring, crop up
ВЫ-	(*a*) *out of*, outward movement	**выраста́ть** (I) /**вы́расти** (I) (**вы́расту, -ешь**) to grow up
	(*b*) achievement, fulfilment	**выпива́ть** (I)/**вы́пить** (I) (**вы́пью, вы́пьешь**) to drink up, drain (a cup)
ДО-	*up to*, reaching a goal	**добива́ться** (I) to strive for/ **доби́ться** (I) to achieve (**добью́сь, добьёшься**)
ЗА-	(*a*) short *or* swift action	**заходи́ть/зайти́** to call, drop in on
	(*b*) beginning of action	**запла́кать** (I *pf*) to burst into tears
ИЗ- (изо-, ис-)	(*a*) outward movement (*figurative*)	**издава́ть/изда́ть** to publish
	(*b*) achievement, fulfilment	**исполня́ть** (I) /**испо́лнить** (II) to fulfil
НА-	*onto*, accumulation, satiety	**наеда́ться** (I) /**нае́сться** (*irr* **есть**) to eat one's fill
О- (об-, обо-)	(*a*) *around, about*	**объясня́ть** (I) /**объясни́ть** (II) to explain **окружа́ть** (I)/**окружи́ть** (II) to surround
	(*b*) abrupt action	**обра́доваться** (I) (**обра́дуюсь, -ешься** *pf*) to be overjoyed

ОТ- (ото-)	*away from*, distance	отдава́ть (I) /отда́ть (*irr* like да́ть) to give away
ПЕРЕ-	(*a*) *across*, through, over, *trans-*	пережива́ть (I) /пережи́ть (I) to live through, experience
	(*b*) *again*, *re-*	переде́лывать (I) /переде́лать (I) to alter (do again)
ПО-	(*a*) completion	посыла́ть (I)/посла́ть (I) (пошлю́, пошлёшь) to have sent
	(*b*) for a (short) while	поигра́ть (I) to play for a while
		поговори́ть (II) to talk for a while, to have a chat
ПОД- (подо-)	(*a*) *under*, *sub-*	поднима́ть (I) /подня́ть (I) (подниму́, подни́мешь) to lift up, raise (i.e. from underneath)
	(*b*) approach	подходи́ть (II) /подойти́ (I) to approach; *also* to suit, to go well with
ПРЕД- (предо-)	*pre-*, before, in front of	представля́ть (I) /предста́вить (II) to present, introduce
ПРИ-	*presence*, joining to, adding to, arrival at	прибыва́ть (I) /прибы́ть (прибу́ду, прибу́дешь) to arrive
		принима́ть (I) /приня́ть (I) (приму́, при́мешь) to receive, to "be at home"
		прибавля́ть (I) /приба́вить (II) to add
ПРО-	*passage* by, through, along	провожа́ть (I) /проводи́ть (II) to accompany, see off
РАЗ- (разо-, рас-)	(*a*) separation	разбива́ть (I) /разби́ть (I) (разобью́, разобьёшь) to break
	(*b*) beginning of an action	рассмея́ться (I) to burst out laughing

С- (со-)	(a) gathering together	**созыва́ть** (I)/**созва́ть** (I) (**созову́, созовёшь**) to summon, call together
	(b) downward motion, *from off*	**сходи́ть** (II) /**сойти́** (I) to come down from, alight
У-	(a) movement *away from*	**удаля́ться** (I)/**удали́ться** (II) to move off, retire
	(b) sudden action	**узнава́ть** (I)/**узна́ть** (I) to recognize, find out

VERBS WITH IMPERFECTIVE IN **-ИМАТЬ** AND PERFECTIVE IN **-ЯТЬ**:

In this class of verbs the **-я- (-а-)** suffix of the perfective stands in place of an Old Slavonic letter which in ancient times had a nasal sound. Consequently, the root **-им-** reappears in the actual conjugation of the perfective. (See page 126 for the interchange of **-я-** and **-ен-** in neuter nouns such as **время**):

Imperfective	*Perfective*	
*занима́ть занима́ю, занима́ешь	*заня́ть займу́, займёшь	to occupy
*занима́ться	*заня́ться	to be occupied; to study (+ *ins*)
нанима́ть	наня́ть найму́, наймёшь	to rent, hire
обнима́ть	*обня́ть обниму́, обни́мешь	to embrace
*понима́ть	*поня́ть пойму́, поймёшь	to understand
*поднима́ть (*or* подыма́ть)	*подня́ть подниму́ (*or* подыму́), подни́мешь (*or* поды́мешь)	to raise, lift up
*поднима́ться (*or* подыма́ться)	*подня́ться	to go (get) up, ascend, rise
*принима́ть	*приня́ть приму́, при́мешь	to receive
*снима́ть	*снять сниму́, сни́мешь	to take off, remove, to photograph
*снима́ться	*сня́ться	to have one's photograph taken
But note:		
вынима́ть	вы́нуть вы́ну, вы́нешь	to take out, extract

Note also the perfectives *стать *to become, to begin:* ста́ну, ста́нешь. *встать *to stand up:* вста́ну, вста́нешь. *нача́ть *to begin:* начну́, начнёшь. *взять (*pf*) *to take:* возьму́, возьмёшь.

* These verbs occur frequently and should be memorized for "active memory". Verbs not so marked may be met in reading.

РАЗГОВОР: THE HAIRDRESSER

парикма́хер hairdresser
парикма́херская hairdresser's
же́нский women's
мужско́й men's
во́лосы (*gen* воло́с) hair
бри́тва razor
компре́сс hot towels
лы́сый bald
се́тка для воло́с hair-net
стричь/по- (I стригу́, стри-жёшь) to cut hair
стри́чься/по- to have a hair-cut
борода́ beard
усы́ moustache, whiskers
ше́я neck
заты́лок back of the head
подборо́док chin
но́жницы (*fem pl*) scissors
шампу́нь (*m* and *f*) shampoo

зави́вка "пермане́нт" permanent wave
причёска hair-do
маши́нка clippers
гребёнка comb
щётка для воло́с hairbrush
масса́ж massage
пробо́р parting
шпи́лька hair-pin
брить (I бре́ю, бре́ешь)/по- to shave (*tr*)
бритьё shaving
бри́твенное мы́ло shaving soap
бри́твенные принадле́жности shaving things
безопа́сная бри́тва safety razor
суши́ть (II)/вы́- to dry
суши́лка dryer
стри́жка haircut

Чья о́чередь? Очередь, ка́жется, за ва́ми. Пожа́луйте. Whose turn? It's your turn, I think. Please.

Я хочу́ постри́чься. I want a haircut.

Не сли́шком ко́ротко сза́ди, пожа́луйста. Not too short at the back, please.

Мо́жете бока́ немно́го подстри́чь. You can trim the sides a little.

Пробо́р у вас сле́ва и́ли спра́ва? Do you have your parting on the right or on the left?

Жела́ете посмотре́ться в зе́ркало? Вы дово́льны? Would you care to look in the mirror. Are you satisfied?

О́чень. Ско́лько я вам до́лжен? Yes, very. How much do I owe you?

Семь, пятьдесят. Вот вам восемь; мы в расчёте. По-
корнейше благодарю́. Seven (roubles), fifty (copecks).
Here's eight. Keep the change. My humble thanks.

Можете дать мне шампу́нь? Только скажи́те, долго ли
ждать придётся. Can you give me a shampoo? Only
tell me if I have to wait long.

Мне надо зави́вку "пермане́нт" сделать. Можно ли
записа́ться на послеза́втра? I need a permanent wave.
Can I make an appointment for the day after to-morrow?

Каку́ю причёску предпочита́ете? What style do you
prefer?

Без пробо́ра, во́лны сза́ди и по бока́м. No parting, waves
back and sides.

Можете мне сделать маникю́р? Can I have a manicure?

Какого цвета лак предпочита́ете, ро́зовый или красный?
What colour lacquer do you prefer, pink or red?

У вас бри́твенные принадле́жности здесь име́ются? Do
you keep shaving gear here?

Мне нужна́ ки́сточка для бритья́. I need a shaving brush.

АКУ́ЛА 1

Л. Н. Толсто́й

Наш кора́бль стоя́л на я́коре у бе́рега А́фрики. День
был прекра́сный. С мо́ря дул све́жий ве́тер, но к ве́черу
пого́да измени́лась: ста́ло ду́шно и то́чно из то́пленной
пе́чки несло́ на нас горя́чим во́здухом с пусты́ни Саха́ры.

Пе́ред зака́том со́лнца капита́н вы́шел на па́лубу,
кри́кнул: "Купа́ться!", и в одну́ мину́ту матро́сы по-
пры́гали в во́ду, опусти́ли в во́ду па́рус, привяза́ли его́ и
в па́русе устро́или купа́льню.

На корабле́ с на́ми бы́ло два ма́льчика. Ма́льчики
пе́рвые попры́гали в во́ду, но им те́сно бы́ло в па́русе, и
они́ взду́мали плавать наперегонки́ в откры́том мо́ре.

Оба, как я́щерицы, вытя́гивались в воде́ и что бы́ло
си́лы поплы́ли к тому́ ме́сту, где был бочо́нок над я́корем.

Оди́н ма́льчик снача́ла перегна́л това́рища, но пото́м
стал отстава́ть. Оте́ц ма́льчика, ста́рый артиллери́ст,

стоя́л на па́лубе и любова́лся на своего́ сыни́шку. Когда́ сын стал отстава́ть, отец кри́кнул ему́:

— Не выдава́й! Понату́жься!

Вдруг с па́лубы кто-то кри́кнул: "Аку́ла!" — и все мы увида́ли в воде́ спи́ну морско́го чудо́вища.

Аку́ла плыла́ пря́мо на ма́льчиков.

— Наза́д! Назад! Верни́тесь! Аку́ла! — закрича́л артиллерист. Но ребя́та не слыха́ли его́, плы́ли да́льше, смея́лись и крича́ли ещё веселе́е и гро́мче пре́жнего.

Артиллери́ст, бле́дный как полотно́, не шевеля́сь, смотре́л на дете́й.

аку́ла = shark. кора́бль = ship. стоя́ть = to stand: стою́, -и́шь. *Past* стоя́л. стоя́ть на я́коре = to lie at anchor. бе́рег = shore. А́фрика = Africa. дуть/поду́ть = to blow: ду́ю, ду́ешь. дул = blew. све́жий ве́тер = cool wind. к ве́черу = towards evening. измени́ться = to change. измени́лась *agrees with* пого́да. станови́ться/стать = to grow, become. (стать : ста́ну. -ешь.) ста́ло ду́шно = it turned sultry. то́чно = as if. то́пленный (то́плёный) = heated. печь, пе́чка (*dim*) = stove. нести́ = to carry. несло́ = carried. горя́чий = hot. во́здух = air. пусты́ня = desert. Саха́ра = Sahara. пе́ред + *ins* = before. зака́т со́лнца = setting of the sun. выходи́ть/вы́йти = to come out. вы́шел, -шла, -шло ; -шли = came out. па́луба = deck. кри́кнуть (*pf*) = to call out. купа́ться = to bathe. (*Inf* as *imp* = categorical command: "*Get bathing!*"). попры́гать = to jump, scamper. опуска́ть/опусти́ть = to pull down, lower. па́рус = sail. привяза́ть = to attach. устро́ить = to arrange. купа́льня = bathing pool. бы́ло два ма́льчика = there were two boys (*gen sing* after два). те́сный = restricted, tight. им бы́ло те́сно (*idiom*) = they were crowded. взду́мать = to take it into one's head. наперего́нки (*adv*) = racing, competing(ly). откры́тый = open. я́щерица = lizard. вытя́гиваться = to stretch (*intr*) си́ла = strength. что бы́ло си́лы (*idiom*) = with all one's force. пла́вать/плыть = to swim. поплы́ть = to strike out swimming. к тому́ ме́сту = towards that place. бочо́нок = barrel. перегна́ть = to overtake. отстава́ть = to lag behind. любова́ться на = to admire. сын, *dim* сыни́шка = son. выдава́ть/вы́дать = to give up, betray. понату́житься = to put one's back into. вдруг = suddenly. ви́деть/уви́деть = to see. уви́деть = to spot, catch sight. спина́ = the back. морско́й (*adj*) = sea. чудо́вище = monster. пря́мо на = straight at. наза́д (*adv*) = backwards (here "*Get back!*"). верну́ть (*pf*) = to return. верну́ться = to come back. закрича́ть = to give a shout. ребя́та = children, youngsters. слыха́ть = to hear. да́льше = further, on. смея́ться = to laugh. весёлый, ве́село (*adv*) = merry. веселе́е =

more merrily. **пре́жний** = previous. **пре́жнего** = than before. **бле́дный** = pale. **полотно́** = linen (sheet). **шевели́ться** = to stir. **смотре́ть на** = to look at.

TRANSLATION   **THE SHARK 1**   L. N. Tolstoy

Our ship lay at anchor off the shore of Africa. It was a beautiful day. A fresh wind was blowing from the sea, but towards evening the weather changed: it became stifling just as if out of a hot stove the baking air from the Sahara Desert drifted to us.

Before sunset the captain came out on deck (and) shouted: "Get bathing!" and in one minute the sailors were scampering overboard, they lowered a sail into the water, made it fast, and in the sail made a swimming pool.

There were two boys with us on the ship. The boys were the first to scamper into the water, but they were restricted (crowded) in the sail and took it into their heads to swim competitively in the open sea.

Like lizards they both stretched themselves in the water and struck out with all their strength towards the place where, above the anchor, there was a barrel.

At first one boy overtook his shipmate, but afterwards began to lag behind. The boy's father, an old artilleryman, was standing on deck admiring his little son. When the son began to lag behind, the father shouted to him:

"Don't let us down! Put your back into it!"

Suddenly from the deck somebody shouted: "Shark!"—and in the water we all caught sight of the sea monster's back.

The shark swam straight at the boys.

"Back! Back! Come back! It's a shark!"—the artilleryman kept shouting. But the children did not hear him (as they) swam on, laughed and called out more merrily and louder than before.

Pale as a sheet, the artilleryman, not stirring, was looking at the children.

Continued on page 235.

LESSON No. 37   УРОК No. ТРИ́ДЦАТЬ СЕМЬ

When you know the prefixes and vocabulary at the beginning of the last Lesson, turn back to the indeterminate and determinate imperfective verbs. These verbs, as you will see, have a perfective form to be used as a normal perfective when completed action is expressed. Note that the conjugation of all these verbs follows the normal principles of conjugation.

PREFIXATION AND ASPECT: Prefixes of direction with verbs of movement do not change the aspect of *in*determinate imperfectives. But the determinate imperfectives become perfectives.

PREFIXES OF DIRECTION

With indeterminate imperfectives	*With determinate imperfectives*
NO CHANGE OF ASPECT	*CHANGE ASPECT TO PERFECTIVE*
ходи́ть = *ipf indet*	**идти́** = *ipf det*
уходи́ть = *ipf*	**уйти́** = *pf*

ALL prefixed *det ipf* verbs are perfective in aspect.

Non-prefixed verbs of movement: These have two *ipf* forms and they are used to distinguish between the *habitual* and the *actual*.   Thus:

Habitual = indeterminate *ipf* as in *I go to the office every day.*
Actual = determinate *ipf* as in *I'm going to the office now.*

Prefixed verbs have only one *ipf* which cannot make this distinction.

Important opposites

в←→вы:	{**входи́ть/войти́** to go *in*}	←→ {**выходи́ть/вы́йти** to go *out*}
при←→у:	{**приходи́ть/прийти́** to come, *arrive*}	←→ {**уходи́ть/уйти́** to go out, *away*}
под←→от:	{**подходи́ть/подойти́** to *approach*}	←→ {**отходи́ть/отойти́** to move away, *leave*}
вз(вс)←→с:	{**всходи́ть/взойти́** to go *up*}	←→ {**сходи́ть/сойти́** to go/come *down*}

Example of Prefixation with y-: Take the series of imperfective indeterminate and determinate verbs on page 174 and, by adding the prefix **y-** to each, sixteen new verbs are created.   They all have in them the meaning of **y** = *away.*

Note: When a prefix is used, **е́здить** is replaced by **-езжа́ть** (I) which form is used *only* in prefixation.   Note also that **идти́** becomes

-йти́ in prefixation: **уйду́, уйдёшь ; уйду́т.**   In general the forms of both *indet* and *det* verbs take prefixes without change of form or conjugation.   The pattern of the parent verb is followed.

indet ipf	*new ipf*	*det ipf*	*new pf verb*
(1) **ходи́ть** (II)	**уходи́ть** (II)	**идти́** (I)	**уйти́** (I) = to go away
(2) **е́здить** (-езжа́ть)	**уезжа́ть** (I)	**е́хать**	**уе́хать** = to drive away
(3) **носи́ть**	**уноси́ть**	**нести́**	**унести́** = to carry away by hand
(4) **вози́ть**	**увози́ть**	**везти́**	**увезти́** = to take away by vehicle
(5) **води́ть**	**уводи́ть**	**вести́**	**увести́** = to lead away
(6) **лета́ть**	**улета́ть**	**лете́ть**	**улете́ть** = to fly away
(7) **бе́гать**	**убега́ть**	**бежа́ть**	**убежа́ть** = to run away
(8) **пла́вать**	**уплыва́ть***	**плыть**	**уплы́ть** = to swim *or* float away

*The *det ipf* + suffix **-ва-** is used instead of **пла́вать** to form the new *ipf*.

FREQUENTLY USED VERBS OF MOTION

indet ipf	*det ipf*	*indet ipf*	*det ipf*
ходи́ть (II)	**идти́** (I)	**е́здить** (II)	**е́хать** (I)
to go *or* come on foot	to go *or* come + prefix, form	to go *or* come by vehicle	

ipf	*pf* = once	*ipf*	*pf* = once
входи́ть	**войти́**	**въезжа́ть**[1]	**въе́хать**
to go in, enter		to drive in	
выходи́ть[6]	**вы́йти**[2]	**выезжа́ть**	**вы́ехать**[2]
to go out, leave		to go out by vehicle	
доходи́ть	**дойти́**	**доезжа́ть**	**дое́хать**
to go *or* come up to, reach		to reach by vehicle	
заходи́ть[3]	**зайти́**	**заезжа́ть**	**зае́хать**
to drop in, call on		to call at on the way	
находи́ть	**найти́**	———	———
to come upon, find			
отходи́ть	**отойти́**	**отъезжа́ть**	**отъе́хать**
to go away, move from		to drive away from	
приходи́ть	**прийти́** *or* **придти́**	**приезжа́ть**	**прие́хать**
to arrive, come		to arrive	

проходи́ть[4]	**пройти́**	**проезжа́ть проéхать**	
to pass by, through		to pass by in a vehicle	
сходи́ть[5]	**сойти́**	———	———
to go *or* come down from[5], off			
уходи́ть	**уйти́**	**уезжа́ть**	**уéхать**
to go off, away		to leave by vehicle	

For **пойти́** and **поéхать** see pages 219–20.

Notes: A verb of motion (**пойти́**) followed by **за** + *instr = to go to, to fetch.* Thus: I shall go to fetch (some) tobacco = **я пойду́ за табако́м.**

[1] **-езжа́ть** with a prefix, and hard sign **ъ** before **е**.

[2] Prefix **вы-** is unstressed in *ipf* and stressed in *pf* verbs.

[3] **заходи́ть** is also used for *to go down*, *set* of the sun.

[4] **проходи́ть** is also used *to cover a distance.*

[5] **сходи́ть-сойти́** + **с** must be used when speaking of *getting off ships*, and may be used for *getting off a vehicle.*

But note: [6] **выходи́т-вы́йти** + **из** + *gen* is generally used for *getting out o* or *off* automobiles, buses and vehicles in general.

Adverbial expressions with these verbs: Be warned that it is incorrect to use adverbial expressions indicating repeated or habitual action with determinate *ipfs*. Such verbs express only a *single* happening. But such expressions are constantly used to strengthen or clarify indeterminate *ipfs* as, for example:

ка́ждое у́тро = every morning. **ка́ждый день** = every day. **ча́сто** = often.

ка́ждый ве́чер = every evening. **ка́ждый год** = every year. **всегда́** = always.

Предприимчивость. Рисунок Э. Змойро.

VERBS OF POSITION : With verbs of *sitting*, *standing* or *lying* it is important in Russian to make a distinction between the actual *position* (state of rest) where there is no actual movement, and the *movement* performed to assume that position.　Important verbs are marked ⋆.

(1) The verbs describing the actual position where there is no movement are:

　　　⋆сиде́ть (II), сижу́, сиди́шь　to sit, to be sitting
　　　⋆лежа́ть (II), лежу́, лежи́шь　to lie, to be lying
　　　⋆стоя́ть (II), стою́, стои́шь　to stand, to be standing

The perfectives of these verbs are **посиде́ть, полежа́ть, постоя́ть.**　The function of these is simply to limit the time during which the particular position is held, **посиде́ть** = to sit *for a while*; and so forth.

(2) The verbs describing the movement performed to assume the position are:

Imperfective	*Perfective*	
⋆сади́ться (II)	⋆сесть (I)	to sit down
сажу́сь, сади́шься	ся́ду, ся́дешь	
Imp: сади́сь! сади́тесь!	*Past:* сел, -а, -о ; -и	
	сядь! ся́дьте!	
⋆ложи́ться (II)	⋆лечь (I)	to lie down
ложу́сь, ложи́шься	ля́гу, ля́жешь ; ля́гут	
Imp: ложи́сь! ложи́тесь!	*Past:* лёг, легла́, -о́ ; -и́	
	ляг! ля́гте!	
⋆встава́ть (I)	⋆встать (I)	to stand up
встаю́, встаёшь	вста́ну, вста́нешь	
Imp: встава́й! встава́йте!	*Past:* встал, -а, -о ; -и	
	встань! вста́ньте!	

The perfective **стать** is also used in the sense *to go and stand*:

　　　Он стал у две́ри. = *He went and stood by the door.*

Verbs "to put": In Russian one makes a distinction between *putting in a lying position* and *placing in a standing position*:

⋆класть (I)	⋆положи́ть (II)	to put in a lying
кладу́, кладёшь	положу́, поло́жишь	position
Past: клал, -а, -о ; -и		
Imp: клади́! клади́те!		
⋆ста́вить (II)	⋆поста́вить (II)	to place in a stand-
ста́влю, ста́вишь		ing position
Imp: ставь! ста́вьте!		

Russian usage of these verbs can at times appear strange:
Она́ ста́вила таре́лки на стол. = *She was putting the plates down on the table.*

Compounds of "putting" verbs : When prefixation occurs класть/положи́ть become -кла́дывать/-ложи́ть, ста́вить/поста́вить become -ставля́ть/-ста́вить.

> скла́дывать/сложи́ть   to put together, to pack
> *составля́ть/соста́вить   to compose
> укла́дывать/*уложи́ть   to put, pack away
> раскла́дывать/разложи́ть   to lay out
> переставля́ть/переста́вить   to move (objects)
> подкла́дывать/подложи́ть   to lay under, to line (clothes)
> подставля́ть/подста́вить   to substitute

IMPERFECTIVE AND PERFECTIVE IMPERATIVES : The imperative of an imperfective verb implies "*continue to do this, go on doing it or continue to repeat this action*". A perfective imperative implies "*do this action once*". That is the basic distinction. In practice, however, it will be found that other distinctions sometimes arise. For instance сади́тесь! ложи́тесь! встава́йте! are considered to be rather more polite than the perfective imperatives ся́дьте! ля́гте! вста́ньте!—which can sound a little peremptory. But in the majority of cases the basic distinction given above should be observed.

Note carefully : With a negative the imperfective imperative *must* be used:

Напиши́те ему́ сего́дня!   Write to him to-day.

but

Не пиши́те ему́ сего́дня!   Don't write to him to-day.

There is one common exception to this rule: the perfective imperative of забы́ть *to forget* (compound of быть "to be") is very often used with a negative: **Не забу́дьте!** = Don't forget.

OTHER FORMS OF THE IMPERATIVE: An infinitive can often be used as an imperative. This can either have the force of a particularly strong and peremptory command as in **Молча́ть!** = *Silence!* **Не сметь кури́ть!** = *Don't you dare smoke!* or it can have a quasi-official character as when giving directions or instructions of a more or less technical nature.

Sometimes the 2nd person (usually singular) of the *pres* is found used as a rather condescending imperative:

Пойдёшь наве́рх и принесёшь мне очки́.   Go upstairs and bring me my spectacles.

Note : The past tense is used as an imperative in these expressions:

> **Пошёл!** = Off you go!   Be off!
> **Пошли́!**
> **Пое́хали!** } = Let's go!   Off we go!

РАЗГОВОР: FINDING THE WAY

тротуа́р pavement, sidewalk
милиционе́р militiaman
у́лица street
переу́лок lane
проспе́кт avenue
шоссе́ highway
ла́вка small shop
магази́н store
универма́г department store
кни́жный магази́н book store
апте́ка chemist's
гастроно́м food shop, delicatessen
часовщи́к watchmaker
портно́й tailor
ко́нсульство consulate
посо́льство embassy
теа́тр theatre
цирк circus
путеводи́тель (*m*) guide book
делега́ция delegation
экску́рсия excursion
зда́ние building
особня́к private house

па́мятник monument
жило́й дом apartment house
высо́тное зда́ние multi-storied building
дворе́ц palace
парк park
парк о́тдыха и культу́ры park of rest and culture
зоопа́рк zoo
ботани́ческий сад botanical garden
собо́р cathedral
це́рковь (*f*) church
монасты́рь (*m*) monastery
музе́й museum
карти́нная галере́я picture gallery
вы́ставка exhibition
вход entrance
гид guide
напра́во to the right
нале́во to the left
пря́мо straight ahead

Скажи́те мне, пожа́луйста, как пройти́ отсю́да на Не́вский проспе́кт. Please tell me how to get from here to the Nevski Prospect.

Далеко́ ли отсю́да? Is it far from here?

Е́сли хоти́те пройти́ пешко́м, то пять мину́т ходьбы́. If you want to go on foot, it's five minute's walk.

Иди́те всё пря́мо, а у тре́тьего перекрёстка сверни́те нале́во. Go straight on and at the third crossing, turn to the left.

Ся́дьте лу́чше на авто́бус. Остано́вка тут же за угло́м. It'd be better if you took a bus. The stop is right here, just round the corner.

Где здесь ближа́йшее метро́? Where is the nearest underground (station) here?

Мне сейча́с надо на Каза́нский вокза́л, а отту́да мне надо
будет к трём часа́м попа́сть на Пло́щадь Маяко́вского.
I have to go to the Kazan Station now and from
there I shall have to get to Mayakovsky Square by three
o'clock.

Мо́жете указа́ть мне, пожа́луйста, где здесь автобусная
остано́вка? Please can you show me where is the
nearest bus stop here?

До́лго ли придётся ждать до сле́дующего по́езда? Will
we (one) have to wait long for the next train?

Мо́жете мне посове́товать хоро́ший путеводи́тель Москвы́
на англи́йском языке́? Can you recommend me a
good guide book of Moscow in English?

АКУ́ЛА 2

Матро́сы спусти́ли ло́дку, бро́сились в неё и, сгиба́я
вёсла, понесли́сь что бы́ло си́лы к ма́льчикам. Но они́
бы́ли ещё далеко́ от них, когда́ аку́ла уже́ была́ не да́льше
двадцати́ шаго́в.

Ма́льчики снача́ла не слыха́ли того́, что им крича́ли, и
не вида́ли аку́лы; но пото́м оди́н из них огляну́лся, и мы
все услыха́ли пронзи́тельный визг, и ма́льчики поплы́ли
в ра́зные сто́роны.

Визг э́тот как бу́дто разбуди́л артиллери́ста. Он со-
рва́лся с ме́ста и побежа́л к пу́шкам. Он поверну́л
хо́бот, прилёг к пу́шке, прице́лился и взял фити́ль.

Мы все, ско́лько нас ни́ было на корабле́, за́мерли от
стра́ха и жда́ли, что бу́дет.

Разда́лся вы́стрел, и мы увида́ли, что артиллери́ст упал
по́дле пу́шки и закры́л лицо́ рука́ми. Что сде́лалось с
аку́лой и с ма́льчиками, мы не вида́ли, потому́ что на
мину́ту дым застла́л нам глаза́.

Но когда́ дым разошёлся над водо́ю, со всех сторо́н по-
слы́шался снача́ла ти́хий ро́пот, пото́м ро́пот э́тот стал
сильне́е, и наконе́ц со всех сторо́н разда́лся гро́мкий,
ра́достный крик.

Ста́рый артиллери́ст откры́л лицо́, подня́лся и посмотре́л на мо́ре.

По волна́м колыха́лось жёлтое брю́хо мёртвой аку́лы. В не́сколько мину́т ло́дка подплыла́ к ма́льчикам и привезла́ их на кора́бль.

Л. Н. ТОЛСТОЙ (1828–1910)

спусти́ть = to lower. **бро́ситься** = to throw oneself. **сгиба́ть** = to bend. **сгиба́я** (*v adv*) = bending. **весло́**, *pl* **вёсла** = oar(s). **(по)нести́сь** (*pf*) = to rush off. **да́льний** = distant. **да́льше** = further. **шаг** = step. **того́, что** = that which, what. **огляну́ться** (*pf*) = to look back. **услы́шать** (*pf*) = to hear. **пронзи́тельный** = piercing. **визг** = shriek. **поплы́ть** (*pf*) = to start swimming. **ра́зный** = different. **сторона́** = side (*pl* **-ы**) *here* directions. **как бу́дто** = as if, as though. **разбуди́ть** (*pf*) = to awaken. **сорва́ться (с)** = to tear oneself away (*from*). **побежа́ть** (II *pf*) = to start running. **пу́шка** = gun, cannon. **поверну́ть** (*pf*) = to turn. **хо́бот (лафе́та)** = trail of gun-carriage. **приле́чь** (*pf*) = to lie, lean (*past* **прилёг, прилегла́, -о ; -й**). **(при)це́литься** = to aim. **брать/взять** = to take (hold of). **фити́ль** (*m*) = wick, tinder. **ско́лько нас ни́ было** (*idiom*) = to the last man. **замира́ть/замере́ть** = to stand stock still. **страх** = fright. **что бу́дет** = *lit* what will be. **раздава́ться/разда́ться** = to resound, boom. **вы́стрел** = shot. **па́дать/(у)па́сть** = to drop, fall. **по́дле** = next to. **закрыва́ть/закры́ть** = to close. **рука́** = arm *or* hand. **сде́латься с** = to happen to. **потому́ что** = because. **на +** *acc* = for (of time). **дым** = smoke. **застила́ть/застла́ть** = to cover (*here* to cloud). **разойти́сь** (I *pf*) = to disperse. *Pa* **разошёлся. над водо́ю** = over the water. **со всех сторо́н** = on all sides. **(по)слы́шаться** = to be heard. **ро́пот** = murmur. **си́льный** = strong, *comp* **сильне́е** = stronger. **наконе́ц** = at last. **ра́достный** = joyful. **откры́ть** (*pf*) = to open, uncover. **подня́ться** = to get up. **волна́** = wave. **по +** *dat* = about. **колыха́ться** = to rock, swing. **жёлтый** = yellow. **брю́хо** = belly. **мёртвый** = dead. **в +** *acc* = in (*time*). **не́сколько** = several, a few. **ло́дка** = boat. **привози́ть/привезти́** = to bring. *Past* **привёз, -везла́, -о ; -везли́**.

TRANSLATION **THE SHARK 2**

The sailors lowered a boat, threw themselves into it and, bending (their) oars, rushed off as fast as they could towards the boys. But they were still far from them when the shark was already not further away than twenty steps (paces = yards).

At first the boys did not hear what (the men) were calling out to them, and (they) did not see the shark; but then one of them looked back, and we all heard a piercing scream, and the boys started swimming in different directions.

This scream was as though it awoke the artilleryman. He tore himself from his place and started running towards the gun. He turned the tail of the gun-carriage, leaned on the gun, aimed and held the slow-match (tinder).

We all, to the last man, on the ship, stopped breathing from fright and awaited what would happen. A shot boomed and we saw that the artilleryman (gunner) had dropped beside the gun and covered his face with his hands. What had happened to the shark and the boys we did not see, because for a minute the smoke clouded (covered) our eyes.

But when the smoke dispersed above the water, on all sides could be heard at first a quiet murmuring, then this murmur became stronger, and finally from all sides arose (resounded) a loud, joyful shout.

The old artilleryman uncovered his face, got up and looked at the sea.

Rocking about on the waves was the yellow belly of the dead shark. In a few minutes the boat rowed up to the boys and brought them to the ship.

LESSON No. 38   УРОК № ТРЙДЦАТЬ ВОСЕМЬ

I. DEGREES OF COMPARISON OF ADJECTIVES: AND ADVERBS: Adjectives and adverbs are said to have three "degrees of comparison": (1) The *positive*, which is the adjective or adverb not making any comparison, as when we say "A *tall* man"; *tall* is positive degree. (2) The *comparative* which expresses comparison between *two* things or persons, as when we say "Jack is *taller* than Jill"; *taller* is comparative degree of the *adj* "tall". (3) The *superlative*, which expresses comparison between *more than two* things or persons, as in "Jill is the *best* pupil in her class"; *best* is the superlative degree of the *adj* "good". These principles apply to the grammar of English, Russian and of most languages.

PREDICATIVE USE OF THE COMPARATIVE DEGREE: In the sentences "Jack is *taller* than Jill", "His house is *bigger* than yours", *taller* and *bigger* are predicative comparatives, that is, they are predicates or objects of the verb "to be".

Russian adjectives have a special short form for the predicative comparative. It is not inflected: the same form serves for all genders and numbers. The predicative comparative is formed by adding -ee (or -ей) to the stem of the adjective, thus: positive **краси́в-ый,** comparative predicative—**краси́в-ее. кра́сный : краснее. до́брый : добрее. си́льный : сильнее. сла́бый : слабее. тру́дный : труднее. бы́стрый : быстрее. ско́рый : скорее. но́вый : новее. прямо́й : прямее. у́мный : умнее.**

There are, however, a number of adjectives with "irregular" predicative comparatives in which the stem is modified according to the principles of mutation (see pages 165–7). Here is a useful list which should be studied carefully:

Positive		Comparative (predicative)	
бли́зкий	near	бли́же	nearer
бога́тый	rich	бога́че	richer
большо́й	big	бо́льше, бо́лее	bigger
высо́кий	high	вы́ше	higher
глубо́кий	deep	глу́бже	deeper
густо́й	thick (of fluids)	гу́ще	thicker
далёкий	remote	да́льше	further away
дешёвый	cheap	деше́вле	cheaper
дорого́й	dear	доро́же	dearer
жа́ркий	hot	жа́рче	hotter
коро́ткий	short	коро́че	shorter
кре́пкий	strong	кре́пче	stronger
ма́ленький, ма́лый	small	ме́ньше, ме́нее	smaller
молодо́й	young	моло́же	younger
мя́гкий	soft	мя́гче	softer.
ни́зкий	low	ни́же	lower
плохо́й	bad	ху́же	worse (from **худо́й** = bad, thin)
по́здний	late	по́зже	later
просто́й	simple	про́ще	simpler
ра́нний	early	ра́ньше	earlier
ре́дкий	rare	ре́же	rarer
сла́дкий	sweet	сла́ще	sweeter
ста́рый	old	ста́рше	older
сухо́й	dry	су́ше	drier
твёрдый	hard	твёрже	harder
ти́хий	quiet	ти́ше	quieter
то́лстый	fat, stout	то́лще	fatter
то́нкий	thin	то́ньше	thinner
у́зкий	narrow	у́же	narrower
хоро́ший	good	лу́чше	better
ча́стый	frequent	ча́ще	more frequent
широ́кий	wide	ши́ре	wider

TRANSLATION OF "THAN" AFTER A COMPARATIVE: A comparative predicative can be followed either by the genitive ("than" not being translated), or by **чем** followed by the nominative or the case in the first part of the comparison. Thus the sentence "My house is bigger than yours" can read either:

Мой дом бо́льше ва́шего.

or: **Мой дом бо́льше, чем ваш.**

The genitive after the comparative cannot be used if the first element of the comparison is in any other case than the nominative. Thus:

В моём до́ме бо́льше карти́н, чем в ва́шем. There are more pictures in my house than in yours.

Similarly **чем** must be used if the comparison is being made between verbs or adverbial phrases:

Лу́чше рабо́тать, чем игра́ть. It is better to work than to play.

чем *must* be used if the object of the comparison is **его́, её, их.**

Ваш автомоби́ль ста́рше, чем его́. Your car is older than his.

In these constructions **чем** can always be replaced by **не́жели.** Note that in comparisons these forms must always be preceded by a comma.

Prefix **по-** *with predicative comparatives:* This is equivalent to adding the English "*somewhat*" or "*rather*" to the comparative: **поста́рше** = somewhat older, **поме́ньше** = rather less, a little less.

Adverbial use of predicative comparatives: The predicative comparative can always be used as an adverb:

Она́ рабо́тает быстре́е, чем вы. She works quicker than you.

Он понима́ет по-ру́сски лу́чше, чем я. He understands Russian better than I.

Note also the exclamations:

Ти́ше! = Quiet! Sh-sh! **Скоре́й!** (**скоре́е!**) = Quickly!

Use of **чем . . . тем . . .:**

Чем до́льше я живу́, тем бо́льше жизнь меня́ интересу́ет. The longer I live, the more life interests me.

Чем по́зже вы придёте, тем ху́же для вас. The later you come, the worse for you.

как мо́жно + *predicative comparative* = *as . . . as possible:*

как мо́жно скоре́е = as quickly as possible
как мо́жно лу́чше = as well as possible

"*As*" *in comparisons: as . . . as . . . :* This is expressed either by **так** (**же**) **. . . как . . .** when the short (predicative) form of the adjective is used or by **тако́й . . . как . . .** when followed by the long (attributive) form:

Она так же краси́ва, как сестра́. She is as beautiful as her sister.
Я никогда́ не чита́л тако́й интере́сной кни́ги, как ва́шей. I've never read a book as interesting as yours.

ATTRIBUTIVE USE OF THE COMPARATIVE DEGREE : Examples of attributive comparatives in English

are: *the poorer son, the bigger house, the elder daughter.* The majority of Russian adjectives form the attributive comparative by using **бо́лее** (=*more*) together with the positive degree of the adjective:

> **бо́лее бе́дный ла́вочник** = the poorer shopkeeper
> **бо́лее бога́тый дом** = the richer house
> **бо́лее здоро́вый ма́льчик** = the healthier boy

ме́нее instead of **бо́лее** is used in a similar construction to express *less*:

> **ме́нее бога́тый сын** = the less rich son
> **ме́нее здоро́вая дочь** = the less healthy daughter

A few adjectives have a special long form for the attributive comparative in **-ший** (declined like **хоро́ший**):

Positive		*Attributive comparative*	
большо́й	big	**бо́льший**	bigger
высо́кий	high	**вы́сший**	higher
ма́ленький, ма́лый	small	**ме́ньший**	smaller, less
молодо́й	young	**мла́дший**	younger
ни́зкий	low	**ни́зший**	lower, inferior
ста́рый	old	**ста́рший**	older, elder
хоро́ший	good	**лу́чший**	better
плохо́й	bad	**ху́дший**	worse

Examples of the use of attributive comparatives:

Вчера́ я ви́дел бо́лее бога́тый дом. Yesterday I saw a richer house.
Они́ вы́брали бо́лее здоро́вого ма́льчика. They chose a healthier boy.
У мла́дшего бра́та нет де́нег. The younger brother has no money.
Мы хоти́м жить в бо́льшем до́ме. We want to live in a bigger house.

Some adjectives, notably those in **-ский** and those with stems longer than three syllables, do not have a special predicative comparative form. Such adjectives express the predicative comparative by means of the short form with **бо́лее**:

Их де́ти бо́лее образо́ванны, не́жели на́ши. Their children are more (better) educated than ours.

THE SUPERLATIVE DEGREE: All adjectives without exception can form the superlative degree by using the pronominal adjective **са́мый** (*most*) before the positive attributive adjective. So,

> **са́мый но́вый стол** = the newest table
> **са́мая но́вая кни́га** = the newest book
> **са́мое но́вое перо́** = the newest pen
> **са́мые но́вые сту́лья** = the newest chairs

са́мый agrees with the adjective that follows in gender, number and case.

This simple way of forming the superlative should be used until the learner has become fairly familiar with Russian.

Superlatives with **всего́** *and* **всех**: The *gen sing* and *gen pl* of **весь** placed after a predicative comparative forms the equivalent of a superlative

лу́чше всего́ = best of all (everything)
лу́чше всех = best of all (everybody)
ста́рше всех = the oldest of all
Ча́ще всего́ я говорю́ по-англи́йски. = Most of all (most frequently) I speak English.

Other forms of the superlative: Although the superlative with **са́мый** is much the commonest form in use, you should eventually become familiar with the following:

(*a*) The attributive comparatives given above (**бо́льший, вы́сший, ме́ньший, мла́дший, ни́зший, ста́рший, лу́чший, ху́дший**) can also be used as superlatives, either by themselves or together with **самый**:

Это (са́мая) лу́чшая кни́га в библиоте́ке. = This is the best book in the library.

(*b*) Note the use of the superlative prefix **наи-** (also **пре-, раз-**). These forms tend to be rather archaic, but the two forms **наилу́чший** = *best*, **наиху́дший** = *worst* are still commonly found.

(*c*) Attributive superlatives are also formed with suffixes: **-е́йший** or, after one of the four "hissing" consonants, **-а́йший**. These are declined like **хоро́ший**:

Positive		*Superlative*	
бли́зкий	near	**ближа́йший**	nearest, very near
бога́тый	rich	**богате́йший**	richest, very rich
высо́кий	high	**высоча́йший**	highest, supreme

дорогóй dear	дражáйший dearest, very dear
корóткий short	кратчáйший shortest, very short
дóбрый kind	добрéйший kindest, very kind
нѝзкий low	нижáйший lowest, very low
мáленький, мáлый small	малéйший smallest, least
пóздний late	позднéйший latest
трýдный hard, difficult	труднéйший hardest, very hard

You should note further examples of this type of superlative as they occur in your reading.

II. VERBS IN -НУТЬ : All verbs with an infinitive in -нуть belong to the first conjugation and are conjugated: -ну, -нешь, -нет, -нем, -нете, -нут.

These verbs present some difficulty in the formation of the past tense since some of them drop the suffix -ну- for the past tense (мёрзнуть *to freeze*, past: мёрз, -ла, -ло ; -ли) and others keep it (толкнýть *to push*, past: толкнýл, -а, -о ; -и). In fact, verbs in -нуть can be divided into two categories:

(1) *Perfectives in* -нуть *denoting a more or less instantaneous or momentary action* (*so-called "semelfactive" verbs*): These verbs always keep the suffix -ну- in the past tense:

Imperfective	Perfective		Past of perfective
мелкáть (I) (мелкáю, -ешь)	мелкнýть	to flash	мелкнýл, -а, -о, -и
*махáть (I) (мáшу, мáшешь)	махнýть	to wave	махнýл, -а, -о ; -и

Note that this last verb takes the object waved in the instrumental: махáть/махнýть рукóй, платкóм = *to wave one's hand, handkerchief.*

*кричáть (II) (кричý, кричѝшь)	*крѝкнуть	to cry out	крѝкнул, -а, -о ; -и
*толкáть (I) (толкáю, -ешь)	*толкнýть	to push	толкнýл, -а, -о ; -и
*двѝгать (I) (двѝгаю, -ешь or двѝжу, двѝжешь)	*двѝнуть	to move	двѝнул, -а, -о ; -и
áхать (I) (áхаю, -ешь)	áхнуть	to exclaim "ah", to gasp	áхнул, -а, -о ; -и
совáть (I) (сую́, суёшь)	*сýнуть	to thrust	сýнул, -а, -о ; -и

N.B. сýнуть рýку в кармáн   to put one's hand into one's pocket.

чиха́ть (I) (чиха́ю, -ешь)	чихну́ть	to sneeze	чихну́л, -а, -о ; -и
*вздыха́ть (I) (вздыха́ю, -ешь)	*вздохну́ть	to sigh	вздохну́л, -а, -о ; -и

(2) *Verbs in* **-нуть** *denoting a process (so-called "inchoative" verbs):* In these verbs the imperfective is usually in **-нуть** and the perfective is a compound formed by prefixation. The imperfective denotes the process taking place; the perfective, the process carried through to its completion. These verbs usually drop the suffix **-ну-** in the past tense of both imperfective and perfective:

Imperfective	*Perfective*		*Past*
вя́нуть	завя́нуть	to fade	(за)вял, -а, -о ; -и
со́хнуть	засо́хнуть	to dry (*intr*)	(за)сох, -ла, -ло ; -ли
мо́кнуть	промо́кнуть	to grow wet, to soak (*intr*)	(про)мок, -ла, -ло ; -ли
ги́бнуть	*поги́бнуть	to perish	(по)гиб, -ла, -ло ; -ли
до́хнуть	подо́хнуть	to die (of animals, derogative if used of humans)	(по)дох, -ла, -ло ; -ли
кре́пнуть	окре́пнуть	to grow strong	(о)креп, -ла, -ло ; -ли
мёрзнуть	замёрзнуть	to freeze (*intr*)	(за)мёрз, -ла, -ло ; -ли
зя́бнуть	прозя́бнуть	to shiver with cold	(про)зяб, -ла, -ло ; -ли
гло́хнуть	огло́хнуть	to grow deaf	(о)глох, -ла, -ло ; -ли
ки́снуть	ски́снуть	to turn sour	(с)кис, -ла, -ло ; -ли
сты́нуть	осты́нуть	to cool (*intr*)	(о)стыл, -а, -о ; -и
*па́хнуть	запа́хнуть to begin to smell of	to smell of (+ ins)	(за)пах, -ла, -ло ; -ли

Note also the following verbs which have **-нуть** only in the perfective, but drop **-ну-** in the past tense as the perfective denotes the culmination of a process:

Imperfective	*Perfective*		*Past of perfective*
*привыка́ть	*привы́кнуть	to become, grow accustomed	привы́к, -ла, -ло ; -ли
отвыка́ть	отвы́кнуть	to become, grow unaccustomed	отвы́к, -ла, -ло ; -ли
*исчеза́ть	*исче́знуть	to disappear	исче́з, -ла, -ло ; -ли

There are, however, two "process" verbs which keep **-ну-** in the past:
*тяну́ть/*потяну́ть   *to pull, drag*, past: (по)тяну́л, -а, -о; -и
*тону́ть/потону́ть   *to drown* (*intr*), past: (по)тону́л, -а, -о; -и

РАЗГОВОР : Passports, Visas and Permits

па́спорт passport
ви́за visa
про́пуск pass, permit
вре́менный про́пуск temporary permit
разреше́ние permission
пребыва́ние stay, residence
анке́та questionnaire (form)

продли́ть (II *pf*) to extend (a visa)
получа́ть (I *ipf*), **получи́ть** (II *pf*) to get, obtain
ка́рточка (small) card
фотографи́ческий photograph(ic), passport photograph
отде́л department section

Где (как) мне получи́ть па́спорт ?   Where do I get my passport ?

Когда́ у вас выходно́й день ?   When's your day off ? (= closed).

Каки́е у вас приёмные часы́ (часы́ заня́тий) ?   What are your (working) hours ?

Где мо́жно получи́ть анке́ту ?   Where do I get a form ?

Ско́лько (фотографи́ческих) ка́рточек нужно вам ?   How many photos do you require ?

Ско́лько сто́ит регистра́ция ?   How much does registration cost ?

Где мне подписа́ться ?   Where must I sign ?

Где иностра́нный отде́л ?   Where's the foreign department ?

Где мо́жно получи́ть выездну́ю ви́зу ?   Where can one get an exit visa ?

Как (мо́жно) продли́ть ви́зу ?   How can one extend a visa ?

Пригото́вьте ваши паспорта́!   Get ready your passports.

Вот мой па́спорт (про́пуск).   Here's my passport (permit).

Предъяви́те ва́ши про́пуски!   Show your permits (passes).

Чтобы фотографи́ровать, вы должны́ иметь разреше́ние.   You must have permission to take photographs.

Я хотел бы продли́ть ви́зу на ме́сяц.   I'd like to extend my visa for a month.

Как мне попа́сть отсю́да в . . . (на . . .) ?   How do I get from here to . . . ?

Это на какой у́лице?   On what street is it?

Авто́бус (такси́) ждёт вас у подъе́зда.   The bus (taxi) is waiting for you at the entrance.

Мо́жно е́хать? Пое́хали? Пошли́? Can one go? Ready to go?

Note: Although entrance to museums, exhibitions, art galleries etc. is often free, it may still be necessary to obtain a про́пуск.   If you do not get it you may be refused entrance.

Для безопасности перехода.

— Скажи, где лежит эта книга об уходе за младенцами?

Useful verbal adverbs :

чита́я (*while*) reading

говоря́ saying, speaking

по́мня remembering

купа́ясь having a bath, bathing

живя́ living

танцу́я dancing

одева́ясь dressing

слы́ша hearing

неся́ carrying, bearing

сто́я standing

бе́гая running (around)

ви́дя seeing

*прочита́в, прочита́вши having read

*поговори́в(ши) having said, told

*сев, се́вши having sat down

вспо́мнивши having remembered, recalled

уви́дев having caught sight of

услы́шав having heard

* See next page.

замёрзши having got **одéвшись** having dressed
frozen (oneself)

Note these forms:

бýдучи (*from* **быть**) while **читáючи** (*poet* and *folk*)
being (*in current use*) while reading

идýчи (*from* **идтú**) while
going (*poetical* and *folk
form only*)

*The forms in **-в** are literary, those in **-вши** may be heard
in speech. *Used as idioms are:* **мóлча** (*adv*) silently.
благодаря (*prep*) thanks to (+*dat*). **хотя** (*conj*) although.
смотря (**на**) looking (at). **смотря** (**по**) according to (+
dat). **нéхотя** unwillingly. **немнóго погодя** (*from* **по-
годúть**) after a little time.

VERBAL ADVERBS : Russian has a form of the *verb* which is by
nature *adverbial in function* and is therefore called the "verbal adverb".
It indicates the state or condition, the time, or the cause of the action of
the subject, and can be formed from both imperfective and perfective
verbs. It can be present or past, and reflexive as well as non-reflexive.

The verbal adverb, being adverbial in function, is not
inflected (that is, there is only one form for the present, and
one form for the past, but neither takes on inflexions for
gender or number). The verbal adverb form is seldom
heard in everyday speech, but it is often used in the written
language. Apart from the examples of fairly frequent use
given at the head of this Lesson, which should be memorized,
it should be recognizable and its general implications understood.

Imperfective verbal adverbs : These are formed from the third
person plural present tense of imperfective verbs by dropping the final
inflexion **-ют, -ут, -ят, -ат** and adding the following suffixes:

(1) **-я** when following vowels, or consonants except hissing **ж, ч, ш,
щ,** which demand the rule of spelling.

(2) **-а** after **ж, ч, ш, щ.**

Thus: (1) **читáя.** (2) **слы́ша.**

(3) *Reflexives:* The particle **-сь** is added after **я** or **а.** Thus:
купáться (I) to bathe: **купá-я-сь** = *who (is, are) bathing*.

(4) *Suffixes* -**ючи** and -**учи**: These are found, but only in folk tales or poetry, except **бу́дучи** (*while being* from **быть**), which is still in general use.

Note: Many monosyllabic imperfective verbs do not form verbal adverbs, nor do verbs ending in -**оть**, nor **писа́ть, спать** nor *ipfs* in -**ну**- and some others.   Note that **бить, вить, пить, шить, ждать, бежа́ть, ре́зать** do not form verbal adverbs.

Imperfectives with infinitive in -**авать**: These drop final **ть** and add -**я** to form *ipf v advs*: **дава́(ть), дава́я**; also all compounds of **дава́ть** (**продава́ть, продава́я**, etc.).

Use and translation: The action of the imperfective verbal adverb is *simultaneous* with that of the verb in the principal clause:

Example:

Купа́ясь сего́дня у́тром я слы́шал, как сосе́дка игра́ет на роя́ле.   While I was taking a bath this morning, I heard the woman next door playing on the grand piano.

IMPORTANT: Remember that a verbal adverb can only refer to the *subject* of the principal clause.

не + *verbal adverb*: This **не** may be translated as *without*:
Не говоря́ ни сло́ва он вы́шел из ко́мнаты.   *Without saying a word, he went out of the room.*

Past verbal adverbs

Formation: (1) By dropping the -**л** of the past tense and adding either suffix -**в** or -**вши**:

прочита́(л), прочита́вши.   поговори́(л), поговори́вши.

(2) When the past tense has no **л**, by adding **я** to the stem:
принести́ *to bring.*   **принеся́** (*or* **принёсши**) *having brought.*
Note: Both forms are met, also **принёсши**.

(3) When the present stem ends in -**д** or -**т** which are dropped in the past tense, the -**д**- or -**т**- are restored and the suffix -**ши** added:

идти́: *past* **шёл.** *v adv* = **ше́дши**   *having gone.*
провести́: **провёл.** *v adv* = **прове́дши**   *having spent time.*

Reflexives: Add -**сь** to the verbal adverb (*not* -**ся**).

Use and translation: The past verbal adverb expresses an action which has happened *before* that expressed by the verb in the principal clause, irrespective of the tense of this last verb.

Example:
Прочита́в кни́гу, она́ верну́лась домо́й.   Having read the book, she returned home.

SUMMARY OF VERBAL ADVERBS

Imperfective verbal *advs* (present)

Suffixes: **-я, -а**

Formed from *third pers pl pres* of *ipf* verbs by dropping **-ют, -ут, -ят, -ат** and adding suffix

Some common *ipfs* do not make *v advs*, nor do *ipfs* in **-ну-**.

Reflexives: take **-сь** after **-я, -а**.

Action *simultaneous* with that of main verb.

Verbal adverb is indeclinable.

Past verbal *advs*

Suffixes: **-в, -вши, -ши**

Formed: (1) by dropping **-л** of past tense and adding suffix **-в** or **-вши**.

(2) In a few verbs with no **-л** in past tense by adding **-я** or **-а** to stem.

(3) Some *pfs* restore stem of *pres* tense and add suffix **-ши**.

Reflexives: take **-сь** after **-вши, -ши**.

Action of *pf v adv precedes* that of main verb.

Verbal adverb is indeclinable.

РАЗГОВОР: POST, TELEPHONE

по́чта, почто́вая конто́ра *or* **почто́вое отделе́ние** post office

телегра́ф telegram office

посы́лка parcel

ма́рка (*gen pl* **ма́рок**) stamp

междунаро́дное письмо́ letter for abroad

заказно́е письмо́ registered letter

де́нежный перево́д postal order

до востре́бования "poste restante"

откры́тка post card

авиапо́чта air mail

авиапо́чтой by air mail

отправи́тель (*m*) sender

для переда́чи c/o

телегра́мма telegram

телегра́фный а́дрес telegraphic address

бланк form

(по)звони́ть по телефо́ну to ring up

тру́бка telephone receiver

содержи́мое contents

адресова́ть *or* **направля́ть** to address

а́дрес address

адреса́т addressee

доста́вка delivery

разно́ска пи́сем delivery of letters

про́сьба пересла́ть please forward to

франкиро́ванный prepaid

конве́рт envelope

распи́ска в получе́нии receipt

накле́ить to stick on

по́дпись (*f*) signature

пове́стка notification

телеграфи́ровать to telegram, wire

телефо́н telephone

телефо́н-автома́т public telephone

телефони́ст(ка) telephone operator

телефо́нная кни́га telephone directory

Проведи́те меня́, пожа́луйста, на по́чту (телегра́ф)! Please take me to the post (telegram) office.

Ма́рки продаю́тся в окне́ *№*. . . . Stamps are sold at Position No. . . .

Ско́лько сто́ит ма́рка для просто́го (заказно́го, междунаро́дного) письма́? How much is a stamp for ordinary (registered, foreign) mail?

Для э́того письма́ вам на́до купи́ть ма́рку на оди́н рубль и два́дцать пять копе́ек. For this letter you will have to buy a stamp for one rouble and 25 copecks.

Мне ну́жно посла́ть просту́ю (сро́чную) телегра́мму. I have to send an ordinary (express) telegram.

В како́м окне́ мо́жно получи́ть бла́нки для телегра́мм? At which position can I get telegram forms?

Вас про́сят к телефо́ну. There's a telephone call for you.

Позвони́те мне по телефо́ну *№*. . . . Give me a ring. My number is . . .

Алло́! Попроси́те к телефо́ну . . . Говори́т . . . Hello! Ask . . . to come to the telephone. This is . . . speaking.

Я хочу́ заказа́ть (телефо́нный) разгово́р с Ло́ндоном. I want to book a long-distance call to London.

Яви́тесь на перегово́рный пункт в . . . Come to the trunk-call office at . . .

Снима́йте тру́бку и набира́йте но́мер! Lift the receiver and dial the number.

Вы нас разъедини́ли. You have cut us off.

За́нято. Пове́сьте тру́бку! It's engaged. Replace the receiver.

Чрезвыча́йно Стра́нные Приключе́ния в Ко́смосе

Не́сколько лет наза́д в моско́вской сту́дии мультипликацио́нных фи́льмов роди́лся заба́вный геро́й — вездесу́щий, энерги́чный фотокорреспонде́нт Мурзи́лка. Его́ удиви́тельные путеше́ствия и приключе́ния пока́заны во мно́гих весёлых фи́льмах. Неда́вно он отпра́вился в но́вый воя́ж. Значи́тельно превыша́я втору́ю косми́ческую ско́рость, неугомо́нный корреспонде́нт помча́лся в свое́й раке́те к Ма́рсу, но вдруг . . . вдруг на Земле́ случи́лось чрезвыча́йное собы́тие: разда́лся плач! Э́то каза́лось невероя́тным: ведь де́ло происходи́ло в XXI ве́ке, когда́ на плане́те все позабы́ли о том, что тако́е слёзы. Мурзи́лка неме́дленно поверну́л ракетопла́н: тре́бовалось вы́яснить, в чём де́ло . . .

Так начина́ется но́вый мультипликацио́нный фильм «Мурзилка на спу́тнике». Для безграни́чных просто́ров Вселе́нной оказа́лись те́сными ра́мки обы́чного экра́на; поэ́тому но́вый фильм рассчи́тан на широ́кий экра́н и бу́дет пе́рвым в СССР мультипликацио́нным фи́льмом тако́го ро́да.

Extraordinary Adventures in the Cosmos

Several years ago in the Moscow animated film studios an amusing hero was born—the ubiquitous, energetic news-photographer Murzilka. His astonishing journeyings and adventures have been shown in many jolly films. Recently he set out on a new trip. Considerably surpassing the second cosmic speed, the indefatigable newsman was dashing his rocket towards Mars, but suddenly . . . suddenly on (from) the Earth sounded a most unusual event: weeping was heard! This seemed incredible. Why, all this was taking place in the 21st century, when on the planet all was forgotten about such things as tears.   Murzilka immediately turned back his rocket-plane: he had to clear up what the matter was . . .

So begins the new animated film: *Murzilka on a Sputnik*.   For the boundless space(s) of the Universe, the usual screen proved (too) narrow; therefore the new film is to be for wide screen and will be the first USSR animated film of such a kind.

Сове́тский Сою́з No. 119, 1960

Не́сколько лет = several years. наза́д = back, ago. сту́дия = studio. мультипликацио́нный фильм = animated film (= cartoon). роди́ться = to be born. заба́вный = amusing, entertaining. вездесу́щий = ubiquitous. энерги́чный = energetic. фотокорреспонде́нт = press correspondent who sends photos. удиви́тельный = amazing.

путеше́ствие = journey(ing). приключе́ние = adventure. по-
ка́заны = shown. отпра́виться *pf* = to set out. воя́ж = voyage,
trip. значи́тельный = considerable. превыша́ть = to exceed, sur-
pass. превыша́я = surpassing. косми́ческий = cosmic. ско́рость
(*f*) = speed. неугомо́нный = tireless. (по)мча́ться = to dart, dash.
раке́та = rocket (*also* tennis racket). Марс = Mars. вдруг = suddenly.
Земля́ = the Earth. случи́ться *pf* = to happen. собы́тие = event.
чрезвыча́йный = extraordinary. раздава́ться/разда́ться = to
resound, echo. плач = weeping. каза́ться = to seem. невероя́тный
= incredible. происходи́ть/произойти́ = to take place. век = century, era. плане́та = planet. позабыва́ть/позабы́ть = to forget
about. о том, что = the thing that. слеза́ = tear. поверну́ть *pf* =
to turn. ракетопла́н = rocket-plane. тре́боваться = to need to.
выясня́ть/вы́яснить = to elucidate, clear up. в чём де́ло = what
(was) the matter. спу́тник = satellite; *also* travelling companion.
(без)грани́чный = (un)bounded. просто́р = space. вселе́нная =
the Universe. оказа́ться = to prove to be. те́сный = narrow,
cramped. ра́мка = frame, limit. обы́чный = usual, ordinary.
экра́н = screen. рассчи́танный = arranged for. широ́кий = wide.
род = kind; *also* family, kin, stock, origin.

Note: From the point of view of vocabulary, this is an interesting piece
of Soviet journalism. It contains many modern words in everyday use.

LESSON No. 39   УРОК № ТРИ́ДЦАТЬ ДЕ́ВЯТЬ

Interrogatives and relatives.

Nom:	кто	*who? who*	что	*what? that, which*
Gen:	кого́		чего́	
Dat:	кому́		чему́	
Acc:	кого́		что	
Ins:	кем		чем	
Prp:	о ком		о чём	

Negative pronouns

Nom:	никто́	*nobody*	ничто́	*nothing*
Gen:	никого́		ничего́	
Dat:	никому́		ничему́	
Acc:	никого́		ничто́	
Ins:	нике́м		ниче́м	
Prp:	ни (о) ко́м		ни (о) чём	

кото́рый, -ая, -ое ; -ые=*who, which.* Declined like **но́вый**, see page 93.

како́й, кака́я, како́е ; каки́е=what, which (kind of). Declined like **ру́сский**.

тако́й, -а́я, -о́е ; -и́е=such (kind of) a. Declined like **ру́сский**, see pages 99, 129.

тако́й . . . како́й . . .=Such . . . as . . . *or* As . . . as . . .

RELATIVE PRONOUNS: A relative pronoun is one which takes the place of a noun previously stated, and joins two parts of a sentence. Thus: I know the man who lives here=**Я зна́ю челове́ка, кото́рый тут живёт.** *who* is a relative pronoun, translated by **кото́рый.** The other relative pronouns used in Russian are **кто** and **что**, also **како́й.** **Кото́рый** and **како́й** are also used as interrogatives. You have already met these common words, which present no great difficulties if one constantly bears in mind the functions of declension and the fact that *a Russian relative pronoun goes in the case demanded by its particular function in the sentence in which it is required.*

кото́рый=*who, which, that* is nearly always used when the antecedent is a noun, and then takes the gender of that noun:

Де́вочка, о кото́рой я говорю́=*The little girl of whom I speak.*

Письмо́, о кото́ром я говорю́=*The letter of which I'm talking.*

кто is used for animates and **что** for inanimates, when the antecedent is a pronoun, expressed or implied.

Thus:

(Тот), кто не рабо́тает, не ест.=(*He who, whoever*) *doesn't work, doesn't eat.*

Все, кто её знал, её люби́ли=*All who knew her loved her.*

Я не по́нял, о чём вы говори́ли.=*I didn't understand what you said.*

Note that the demonstrative pronoun **тот** is commonly used as an antecedent of both **кто, что** and **кото́рый** and then means *he who, the person who, whoever*: **тот, кто . . . тот, кото́рый.**

что *as relative/interrogative and as conjunction:* When **что** = *that* is used as a conjunction and as a relative pronoun (it has both functions) a distinction can be made by stress. Take these sentences:

(1) *He told me that he speaks Russian* = **Он мне сказа́л, что он говори́т по-ру́сски.** (**что**)

(2) *He told me what* (= that which) *he wanted* = **Он мне сказа́л, что он хоте́л.** (**что́**)

In (2) the **что́** is stressed. (In neither instance is it omitted.)

Rule of punctuation: A comma always precedes a relative pronoun in Russian, as exemplified in the above sentences.

Compounds of **что:** Some common compounds are made with prepositions + **что** in its oblique cases:

отчего́? = *from what* (*cause*) = why? *Answer:* **оттого́, что** = *because* . . .

почему́? = *on what* (*ground*) = why? *Answer:* **потому́, что** = *because* . . .

заче́м = *to what* (*object*) = why? *Answer:* **зате́м, что́бы** *or* **что́** = *in order that*

Place of preposition: Note that with the negative pronouns **никто́** *nobody, no one* and **ничто́** *nothing*, a preposition is placed between the particle **ни** and the pronominal part. Thus:

ни о ком. ни о чём. ни у кого́. ни с кем.

The only distinction between interrogatives and relatives is that the former demand the sign of interrogation (?).

The phrase "EACH OTHER": This is expressed idiomatically in Russian by **друг дру́га.**
Thus:

Они́ боя́тся друг дру́га = *They fear each other.*

Они́ ненави́дят друг дру́га. = *They* (*persons*) *hate each other.*

Они́ говори́ли друг с дру́гом. = *They were speaking to each other.*

INTERROGATIVE PRONOUN чей? чья? чьё? WHOSE? OF WHICH?: The interrogative pronoun чей? чья? чьё? whose? of which? always agrees with the noun it qualifies. Its declension is similar to третий (see page 202).

	masc	fem	neut	Plural (all genders)
Nom:	чей	чья	чьё	чьи
Gen:	чьего́	чьей	чьего́	чьих
Dat:	чьему́	чьей	чьему́	чьим
Acc:	Nom or Gen	чью	чьё	Nom or Gen
Ins:	чьим	чьей (чье́ю)	чьим	чьи́ми
Prp:	о чьём	о чьей	о чьём	о чьих

Examples:

Чья э́та кни́га? Whose book is this?

Чьи э́ти часы́? Whose watch is this?

У чьего́ до́ма останови́лись вы? By whose house did you stop?

На чьём автомоби́ле прие́хали вы? In (by) whose car did you come?

Formerly чей was also frequently used as a relative pronoun, thus:

Америка́нец, чью карти́ну вы хоте́ли купи́ть . . . The American, whose picture you wanted to buy . . .

But in modern Russia it is much more usual to use the appropriate genitive form of кото́рый; кото́рого, кото́рой or кото́рых, so that the example given above would read:

Америка́нец, карти́ну кото́рого вы хоте́ли купи́ть . . .

POSSESSIVE ADJECTIVES IN -ИЙ: These adjectives refer to qualities or attributes pertaining to a certain species (usually of animals) and are declined like третий (see page 202). Example: пти́чий = bird's:

	masc	fem	neut	Plural (all genders)
Nom:	пти́чий	пти́чья	пти́чье	пти́чьи
Gen:	пти́чьего	пти́чьей	пти́чьего	пти́чьих
Dat:	пти́чьему	пти́чьей	пти́чьему	пти́чьим
Acc:	Nom or Gen	пти́чью	пти́чье	Nom or Gen
Ins:	пти́чьим	пти́чьей (-ею)	пти́чьим	пти́чьими
Prp:	о пти́чьем	о пти́чьей	о пти́чьем	о пти́чьих

Similar adjectives are во́лчий = wolf's (волк = wolf), ли́сий = fox's (лиса́ = fox), ры́бий = fish's, соба́чий = dog's, коша́чий = cat's, медве́жий = bear's (медве́дь = bear: мёд = honey, ве́дать = to know). Бо́жий = God's, челове́чий = man's, human.

RUSSIAN NAMES OF PERSONS: This is continued from Lesson 5, Part I, page 38.

Russians have only one first name (**имя**) and this is used in addressing only those with whom one is on fairly intimate terms, but even then the plural pronoun **вы** must be used unless the relationship is very intimate.   Among themselves Russians use diminutive forms, but of these the foreigner should be wary (for Diminutives see pages 266-7).   The normal and formal way of addressing a Russian is to use the first name and patronymic.   By accepting this as a general rule, the foreigner can hardly go wrong.   The alternative is to use **гражданин** or **гражданка** with the surname, which is also safe.   Then there is the word **товарищ** (*pl* **-щи**) which foreigners tend to regard as a political word, which it is—and much more.

ТОВАРИЩ, (*pl*) **-ЩИ : USE OF :** You should remember that, in addition to meaning *comrade* in the party political sense, it is an old word with many connotations in literature and still used in everyday life.   It is always a friendly word, and translates

colleague,	*fellow-,* as in school-fellow, fellow-work-
companion,	man, fellow-sufferer, fellow-victim.
friend, as in	*mate,* as in schoolmate, shipmate, class-
school-friend.	mate.

The same form is used for *masc* and *fem*.   Men and women of the same profession or occupation use it in addressing one another.   A fuller appreciation of the scope of this word is gained from others in the same word-family:

товарищеский (*adj*) means *comradely*, also *friendly* as in **товарищеское состязание**=friendly competition, *or* match.   **-ая встреча**=friendly meeting.

товарищество=(1) *comradeship*, also *fellowship;* (2) *association*, also *company*, as in: **на паях**=joint stock company.

Russian doctors address their medical colleagues from abroad as **товарищи,** and there is no reason why foreign doctors and others should not address their Russian counterparts in the same way.

DECLENSION OF NAMES: Masculine first names (**и́мя**) are declined like masculine nouns with the same endings. The stress is normally on the stem. Feminine first names are declined like feminine nouns with the same endings, but in these the stress is always fixed as in the nominative. First, you *must* know these declensions:

	sing	pl
Nom:	това́рищ	това́рищи
Gen:	това́рища	това́рищей
Dat:	това́рищу	това́рищам
Acc:	това́рища	това́рищей
Ins:	това́рищем	това́рищами
Prp:	о това́рище	о това́рищах

	sing	pl	irregular pl
Nom:	граждани́н	гра́ждане	господа́*
Gen:	граждани́на	гра́ждан	госпо́д
Dat:	граждани́ну	гра́жданам	господа́м
Acc:	граждани́на	гра́ждан	госпо́д
Ins:	граждани́ном	гра́жданами	господа́ми
Prp:	о граждани́не	о гра́жданах	о господа́х

*The singular **господи́н** is declined regularly, as is the *fem* **госпожа́** (*gen* **-и́**, *pl* **-и́**).

All masculine names—whether first names, patronymics or surnames —in both singular and plural, have the same forms for genitive as accusative. (But some *masc* surnames of famous men now used as names of places follow the rule for inanimates and then the *acc* is the same as the *nom*): **Го́рький** (=*former* **Ни́жний Но́вгород**).

Patronymics have a masculine and a feminine form, deriving from the father's first name:

	(1)	(2)
Masculine endings of patronymics:	-ович	-евич
Feminine endings of patronymics:	-овна	-евна

(1) are added to first names ending with a *hard* consonant. (2) are added to first names ending with a *soft* consonant or **-и**.

Surnames have a *masc* and *fem* form:

	(1)	(2)	(3)
Masculine forms:	-ов	-ев	-ин
Feminine forms:	-ова	-ева	-ина

Other surnames are like regular attributive adjectives: **Толсто́й, Толста́я**: **Достое́вский, Достое́вская**: **Го́рький, -ая**. See page 67–69.

NAMES OF PERSONS: MODEL DECLENSIONS

Males

	-ович	-ов
Nom:	Ива́н Ива́нович Петро́в	
Gen:	Ива́на Ива́новича Петро́ва	
Dat:	Ива́ну Ива́новичу Петро́ву	
Acc:	Ива́на Ива́новича Петро́ва	
Ins:	Ива́ном Ива́новичем Петро́вым	
Prp:	об Ива́не Ива́новиче Петро́ве	

	-евич	-ев
Nom:	Пётр Никола́евич Андре́ев	
Gen:	Петра́ Никола́евича Андре́ева	
Dat:	Петру́ Никола́евичу Андре́еву	
Acc:	Петра́ Никола́евича Андре́ева	
Ins:	Петро́м Никола́евичем Андре́евым	
Prp:	о Петре́ Никола́евиче Андре́еве	

	-ин (*m*)	-ина (*f*)
Nom:	Буха́рин	Буха́рина
Gen:	Буха́рина	Буха́риной
Dat:	Буха́рину	Буха́риной
Acc:	Буха́рина	Буха́рину
Ins:	Буха́риным	Буха́риной
Prp:	о Буха́рине	о Буха́риной

Females

	-овна	-ова
Nom:	Ни́на Ива́новна Петро́ва	
Gen:	Ни́ны Ива́новны Петро́вой	
Dat:	Ни́не Ива́новне Петро́вой	
Acc:	Ни́ну Ива́новну Петро́ву	
Ins:	Ни́ной Ива́новной Петро́вой	
Prp:	о Ни́не Ива́новне Петро́вой	

	-евна	-ева
Nom:	О́льга Никола́евна Андре́ева	
Gen:	*О́льги Никола́евны Андре́евой	
Dat:	О́льге Никола́евне Андре́евой	
Acc:	О́льгу Никола́евну Андре́еву	
Ins:	О́льгой Никола́евной Андре́евой	
Prp:	об О́льге Никола́евне Андре́евой	

Like attributive adjectives

Nom:	Достоéвский	Толстóй
Gen:	Достоéвского	Толстóго
Dat:	Достоéвскому	Толстóму
Acc:	Достоéвского	Толстóго
Ins:	Достоéвским	Толсты́м
Prp	о Достоéвском	о Толстóм

Note that the Rules of Orthography apply to names of persons as to other words.

РАЗГОВОР : STATIONERY, NEWSPAPERS, BOOKS : SHOPPING

писчебумáжный магазѝн stationer's

кнѝжный магазѝн bookstore

газéта newspaper

журнáл magazine

еженедéльник weekly

ежемéсячный журнáл monthly magazine

газéтный киóск newspaper stand

журналѝст journalist

корреспондéнт correspondent

редáктор editor

издáтельство publishing house

иллюстрѝрованный журнáл pictorial magazine

печáтать (I) to print

печáть (*f*) print (type), the Press

статья́ article (in newspaper)

экземпля́р (a) copy

том volume

писáтель (*m*) writer

драматýрг playwright

ромáн novel

беллетрѝстика fiction

универмáг department store

гастронóм food store

бýлочная baker's

кондѝтерская confectioner's, pastrycook's

парфюмéрный магазѝн shop for cosmetics and toilet requisites

переплёт binding

облóжка paper jacket

фельетóн satire (in newspaper)

юмористѝческое произведéние humorous work

пѝсьменные принадлéжности writing materials

почтóвая, пѝсчая бумáга writing paper

блокнóт writing pad

чернѝла (*neut pl*) ink

промокáтельная бумáга blotting paper

конвéрт envelope

автоматѝческая рýчка fountain pen

записнáя кнѝжка note book

словáрь (*m*) dictionary

рýсско-англѝйский Russian-English

áнгло-рýсский English-Russian

букинѝст second hand bookseller

план гóрода plan (map) of city

путеводѝтель (*m*) guidebook

галантерéйный магазѝн fancy goods store, haberdasher's

магазѝн óбуви shoe shop

магазѝн готóвых вещéй ready made clothes shop

комиссиóнный магазѝн second hand shop

Мне надо идти за покупками. I must go and do some shopping.

Мы найдём все эти вещи в универмаге. We shall find all these things in the department store.

Что вам показать? Пожалуйста, выбирайте. What can I show you? Please take your pick.

Можете мне взвесить 500 грамм гречневой крупы? Отрежьте мне также небольшой кусок ливерной колбасы. Can you give (weigh) for me 500 grammes of buckwheat? And cut me a small piece of liver sausage.

Сколько стоит эта вещь? Я вас плохо понимаю; напишите мне цену, пожалуйста. How much is this? I don't understand you very well; write down the price for me please.

Получите сдачу. Сколько сдачи мне следует? Here's your change. How much change should I get?

Я хотел бы примерить этот однобортный (двубортный) костюм. I should like to try on this single-breasted (double-breasted) suit.

Хорошо ли сидит на мне это пальто? Is this coat a good fit?

Идёт ли мне фасон этого платья? Does the style of this dress suit me?

Какой размер обуви вы носите? What size shoe do you take?

Можно отдать вам мои туфли на починку? Can I give you my shoes to be repaired?

А теперь пойдём в парфюмерный магазин покупать зубную пасту, зубную щётку и лезвия. And now let's go to the perfumer's and buy tooth paste, a tooth brush and razor blades.

РАЗГОВОР: TOBACCO, CIGARETTES, SMOKING

лавка табачных изделий tobacconist's
табак tobacco
папироса cigarette (Russian type with holder attached)

спички matches
зажигалка lighter
фитиль (m) wick
кремни (pl) flints
бензин fuel

сигаре́та	cigarette (without holder)	**кисе́т**	tobacco pouch
тру́бка	pipe	**па́чка**	packet
мундшту́к	cigarette holder	**портсига́р**	cigarette case
		кури́ть (II)/**закури́ть**	to smoke

Вы ку́рите? Do you smoke?

Не хоти́те ли закури́ть? Would you care for a smoke?

Разреши́те предложи́ть вам папиросу (сигаре́ту). Let me offer you a cigarette.

Это лёгкий или кре́пкий таба́к? Is this mild or strong tobacco?

Мне ну́жно бу́дет сегодня купи́ть немно́го табаку́ для тру́бки. I shall have to buy a little pipe tobacco to-day.

Это о́чень арома́тный таба́к, ка́жется. Да́йте мне поню́хать его. This is highly scented tobacco, I think. Let me smell it.

Что вы предпочита́ете, папиро́сы или сигаре́ты? What do you prefer, cigarettes with or without a holder?

Да́йте мне коро́бку спи́чек, пожа́луйста. Give me a box of matches please.

А я нахожу́, что кури́ть — вре́дно. Now, I consider that smoking is harmful.

Здесь кури́ть разреша́ется? Is smoking permitted here?

Нет, кури́ть здесь воспреща́ется. No, smoking is forbidden here.

Проходи́те в кури́тельную; там мо́жете кури́ть ско́лько вам уго́дно. Go through to the smoking room; there you can smoke as much as you like.

АНГЛИ́ЙСКИЕ ЗАМЕ́ТКИ

Мои́ пе́рвые английские впечатле́ния свя́заны с ощуще́нием трево́ги. Я просну́лся в но́мере гости́ницы от во́я сире́н и беспреста́нных сигна́лов автомоби́лей. Вы́глянув в окно́, ничего́ за ним не уви́дел: всё бы́ло заби́то невесо́мой се́рой ва́той. Так вот что тако́е знамени́тый ло́ндонский тума́н!

NOTES ON ENGLAND

My first impressions of England are linked with a sensation of alarm. I woke up in my hotel room because of the wailing of sirens and the incessant hooting of cars. Having looked out of the window, I could see nothing through it: everything was (as it were) choked up with a weightless, grey cotton wool. So this was

Утренние газеты вышли с мрачными заголовками: «Туман-убийца», «Туман парализовал жизнь Лондона», «В катастрофах разбито 100 автомобилей». Действительно, это — настоящее бедствие. Днём ничего не видно в нескольких шагах. На перекрёстках, в центре города, зажигаются и гаснут огни специальных маяков. Автомобили и автобусы идут ощупью, пригородные поезда стоят. Не ходят паромы и пароходы через Ламанш. Самолёты остаются на аэродромах. Связь со всем миром прекращается. В такие дни начинаешь чувствовать, что Англия — это остров. И сразу же поднимаются цены на продукты. Каждый день тумана приносит стране миллионные убытки.

С. М. Навашин.
Наука и жизнь. No. 8, 1960

what the famous London fog was like! The morning papers came out with gloomy headlines: "Killer fog", "Fog paralyses London life", "100 cars smashed in accidents". And in fact this is a real calamity. During the day nothing can be seen at a distance of more than a few paces. At crossings in the centre of the city the lights of special beacons (keep on) lighting up and going out. Cars and buses grope along, the suburban trains are at a standstill. Ferries and steamers do not cross the English Channel. Aeroplanes are grounded at their aerodromes.

Communication with the whole world ceases. On such days you (really) begin to feel that England is an island. And immediately prices of foodstuffs rise. Each day of fog brings the country losses of millions (of pounds).

заметка = note. впечатление = impression. связан(ный) = past participle passive of связывать (I)/связать (I свяжу, свяжешь) = to bind, link. ощущение = sensation. тревога = alarm. просыпаться (I)/проснуться (I) = to wake up. номер = room (in hotel). вой = wailing. сирена = siren. беспрестанный = incessant. сигнал = signal, warning. выглядывать (I)/выглянуть (I) = to look out. забивать (I)/забить (I забью, -ёшь) = to stuff up. невесомый = weightless. серый = grey. вата = cotton wool. знаменитый = famous. туман = fog. утренний = morning (adj). мрачный = gloomy. заголовок (gen -овка) = heading, headline. убийца (m) = murderer. парализовать (I) = to paralyse. катастрофа = catastrophe. разбит(ый) past participle passive of разбивать (I)/разбить (I разобью, разобьёшь) = to smash. настоящий = real. бедствие = calamity. шаг = step, pace. перекрёсток (gen -стка) = crossroads. центр = centre. зажигать(ся) (I)/зажечь(ся) (I like жечь) = to (be) light(ed) up. гаснуть (I)/по-

(*past* гас, га́сла) = to be extinguished.   специа́льный = special. ма́як = beacon, lighthouse.   о́щупью (*adv*) = groping(ly).   при́-город(ный) = suburb(an).   паро́м = ferry.   Ла-Ма́нш = English Channel.   самолёт = aeroplane.   остава́ться (I остаю́сь, остаёшься)/оста́ться (I оста́нусь, оста́нешься) = to remain behind. аэродро́м = aerodrome.   связь (*f*) = connection, link.   мир = world. прекраща́ться (I)/прекрати́ться (II) = to cease (*intrans*). о́стров = island.   сра́зу (же) = immediately.   цена́ (*pl* це́ны) = price.   проду́кты (*pl*) = produce, foodstuffs.   приноси́ть (II)/принести́ (I) = to bring.   миллио́нный = worth millions.   убы́ток (*gen* убы́тка) = loss.

СНЕЖО́К И ЗВЁЗДОЧКА

1. Это́ было́ в А́рктике, на Земле́ Фра́нца-Ио́сифа. Как-то раз мы уви́дели двух ма́леньких медвежа́т, резви́вшихся о́коло ма́тери. Огро́мная медве́дица сиде́ла на верши́не то́роса и неторопли́во, по-хозя́йски огля́дывалась вокру́г. Иногда́ она́ наклоня́ла го́лову к малыша́м, бу́дто нашёптывала им что-то. Э́ту сце́нку удало́сь засня́ть с по́мощью длиннофо́кусного объекти́ва.

2. Пото́м пого́да разбуше-ва́лась, и не́сколько дней мы не покида́ли зимо́вки. То́лько беспоко́йные метеоро́логи, пре-одолева́я сумасше́дший ве́тер, раз в три часа́ ползко́м добира́лись до метеоплоща́дки, что́бы записа́ть показа́ния при-бо́ров. Когда́ бура́н ко́нчился, зимо́вщики сно́ва встре́тили медвежа́т. Ма́ленькие, беспо́мощные, они́ сиде́ли в снегу́ недалеко́ от на́шего жилья́, уткну́вшись друг в дру́га но-са́ми. Должно́ быть, в пургу́

1 It was in the Arctic, in Franz Joseph Land. One day we caught sight of two little bear cubs frisking about near the(ir) mother. The huge she-bear was sitting on top of an ice-block and looking around her in a leisurely, bossy way. Occasionally she lowered her head towards the little ones as if she was whispering something to them. This little scene was successfully photographed with a long-focus lens.

2. Then the weather began to rage and for several days we did not leave the winter hut. Only our restless meteorologists, sur-mounting the mad wind once every three hours, crawling, reached the meteorological platform (= post) to note down the evidence (readings) of the instruments. When the snowstorm ended, the winterers once again met the cubs. Helpless, the little ones sat in the snow not far away from our quarters, huddled together with their noses against one another. It must have been (that) the cubs got separated from their mother in the

детёныши отби́лись от ма́тери. Во вся́ком слу́чае, нигде́ вокру́г мы не нашли́ её следо́в.

storm. At any rate, nowhere around did we find her tracks.

3. Пришло́сь посади́ть незада́чливых малыше́й в мешо́к и доста́вить на зимо́вку. Их встре́тили с прису́щим поля́рникам раду́шием, обласка́ли, накорми́ли. Осо́бенно понра́вилось медвежа́там сла́дкое сгущённое молоко́, и со́ски, неизве́стно почему́ оказа́вшиеся у врача́ зимо́вки, бы́ли неме́дленно разо́драны в кло́чья.

3. One (=we) had to put the hapless mites in a sack and deliver (=convey) them to the winter hut. They were welcomed with innate polar cordiality and were petted and fed. The cubs were particularly pleased with the sugary condensed milk, and the feeding teats (which) it turned out the winter quarter's doctor had, why, no one knew, were immediately torn to shreds.

4. Звере́та бы́стро осво́ились. Ла́сковые, поте́шные, они́ пу́тались под нога́ми, сова́ли чёрные носы́ во все ще́ли, загля́дывали то в одну́, то в другу́ю ко́мнату, всю́ду получа́ли ла́комства и засыпа́ли где попа́ло, те́сно прижа́вшись друг к дру́гу.

4. The little beasts soon settled down. Friendly, amusing, they twisted about under our legs, poked their black muzzles (=noses) into every chink, looked now into one room, and now into another, everywhere they received delicacies, and they fell asleep in any old place, intimately clasped to one another.

5. Пото́м начали́сь ша́лости. Пе́рвый трево́жный сигна́л поступи́л из ку́хни. Зарва́вшиеся го́сти стащи́ли огро́мный кусо́к бара́нины. Мя́гкое наказа́ние не поде́йствовало, и вско́ре, верну́вшись домо́й, зимо́вщики уви́дели по́лный разгро́м. Всё, что могло́ упа́сть, лежа́ло на полу́; от книг и журна́лов оста́лись кло́чья; разби́тые часы́ останови́лись. Среди́ э́того ха́оса два мохна́тых хулига́на боро́лись за пра́во облада́ния уче́бником англи́йского языка́.

5. Later they began to be mischievous. The first alert signal came from the kitchen. The guests, going too far, pinched a huge piece of mutton. The slight punishment did not have any effect, and soon after, the winters, on returning home, beheld complete havoc. Everything that could fall was lying on the floor; tatters were all that was left of the books and magazines; the broken clock had stopped. Amid this chaos the two shaggy hooligans were wrestling (struggling) for the right of possession of a textbook of (on) the English language.

6. Медвежа́та быстро росли́ и день ото дня доставля́ли всё бо́льше хлопо́т. Пришло́сь поду́мать о бу́дущем.

6. The little bears were growing quickly and day by day were causing greater trouble. It was necessary to think of their future.

7. — Подари́м их моско́вским ребя́там! — сказал кто-то.

7. "Let's give them to the kids of Moscow," somebody said.

8. Остальны́е поддержа́ли, и вско́ре наши геро́и уже́ лете́ли над холо́дным океа́ном, а пото́м е́хали в легково́м автомоби́ле по Москве́. Им повезло́: не мно́гие бе́лые медве́ди мо́гут похва́статься, что ви́дели э́тот го́род! . .

8. The others supported (the idea), and soon our heroes were (already) flying over the freezing ocean and later drove in a car through Moscow. They were lucky: not many polar bears can boast that they have seen this city! . . .

9. Здоро́вье у «поля́рников» отли́чное, — сказал ветерина́рный врач зоопа́рка. — Мо́жно посели́ть их на площа́дке молодняка́.

9. "The health of these 'workers of the Arctic' is excellent," said the veterinary surgeon of the Zoological Gardens. "They can be settled (put) in the enclosure (=area) for young animals."

10. Общи́тельные медвежа́та отли́чно чу́вствуют себя́ на но́вом ме́сте. Их назва́ли Снежо́к и Звёздочка.

10. The sociable cubs are feeling fine in their new place. They are called Snowball and Starlet.

CC. 120, 1960   В. КОПАЛИН   V. Kopalin.

А́рктика=the Arctic.   **Земля́ Фра́нца-Ио́сифа**=Franz Joseph Land.   **медвежёнок** (*n pl* **медвежа́та**, *gen pl* **медвежа́т**)=bear cub. **резви́ться** (II)=to frisk, gambol.   **медве́дица**=she-bear.   **верши́на** =top, summit.   **то́рос**=(ice-)hummock.   **(не)торопли́вый**=(un)- hurried.   **по-хозя́йски**=in an authoritative way.   **наклоня́ть** (I)/ **наклони́ть** (II)=to bend down (*trans*).   **малы́ш**=small child, mite. **нашёптывать** (I *ipf*)=to whisper.   **сце́нка**=little scene.   **удава́ть- ся** (I)/**уда́ться** (*like* **дать**: **уда́стся**) *used impersonally*=to succeed. **засня́ть** (I *pf* **засниму́, -ешь**)=to photograph.   **по́мощь** (*f*)=help. **длиннофо́кусный**=long-focus.   **объекти́в**=objective.   **раз- буше́ваться** (I *ipf*)=to rage, bluster (*of weather*).   **покида́ть** (I)/**по- ки́нуть** (I)=to leave, abandon.   **зимо́вка**=winter quarters.   **беспо- ко́йный**=restless.   **метеоро́лог**=meteorologist.   **преодолева́ть** (I **-ева́ю, -ева́ешь**)/**преодоле́ть** (I **-е́ю, -е́ешь**)=to overcome, to sur- mount.   **ползко́м** (*adv*)=crawling (*on all fours*).   **добира́ться** (I)/ **добра́ться** (I **доберу́сь, -ёшься**)=to get to, to reach.   **метеопло- ща́дка** (**метеорологи́ческая площа́дка**)=meteorological post.

запи́сывать (I)/записа́ть (I) = to note down. ноказа́ние = evidence, reading. прибо́р = apparatus. бура́н = snowstorm. зимо́вщик = winterer. сно́ва = once again, anew. беспо́мощный = helpless. жильё = living quarters. утыка́ться (I)/уткну́ться (I) = to bury oneself, hide one's face. пурга́ = blizzard. детёныш = young/little one. отбива́ться (I)/отби́ться (I отобью́сь, отобьёшься) от = to become separated from. во вся́ком слу́чае = at any rate. след = trace. приходи́ться (II)/прийти́сь (I придётся, пришло́сь) *used impersonally* = to be obliged to. посади́ть (II *pf*) = to make to sit, to put sitting. незада́чливый = hapless. мешо́к = sack. прису́щий = inherent. поля́рник = worker of the Arctic. раду́шие = cordiality. ласка́ть (I)/об- = to pet, caress. корми́ть (II)/на- = to feed (*tr*). осо́бенно = particularly. сгущённый = thickened. сгущённое молоко́ = condensed milk. со́ска = rubber teat. неме́дленно = immediately. разо́дран(ный) *past participle passive of* раздира́ть (*I*)/ разодра́ть (I раздеру́, раздерёшь *past* разодра́л) = to tear up, apart. клок (*n pl* кло́чья, *gen pl* кло́чьев) = rag, shred. зверёнок (*n pl* звероя́та, *gen pl* зверя́т) = young beast. осва́иваться (I)/ осво́иться (II) = to fit in, be assimilated. ла́сковый = affectionate. поте́шный = amusing. пу́таться (I) = to get entangled. щель (*f*) = chink. загля́дывать (I)/загляну́ть (I) = to peep in. получа́ть (I)/ получи́ть (II) = to receive. ла́комство = a dainty, tit bit. засыпа́ть (I)/засну́ть (I) = to fall asleep. где попа́ло = in any place at all, any old place. те́сно = closely. прижа́вшись *past verbal adverb of* прижима́ться (I)/прижа́ться (I *like* жать) = to snuggle, cuddle together. ша́лость (*f*) = prank. трево́жный = alert, alarm (*adj*). поступа́ть (I)/поступи́ть (II) = to be forthcoming, to come in. зарва́вшийся = having gone too far, to extremes, overdone things. стащи́ть (II *pf*) = to steal, "pinch". бара́нина = mutton, lamb (meat). мя́гкий (г pronounced as х) = soft. наказа́ние = punishment. де́йствовать (I)/по- = to act, to have an effect. вско́ре = soon after. верну́вшись *past verbal adverb of* возвраща́ться (I)/верну́ться (I) = to return. разгро́м = havoc. разби́тый = broken. хао́с = chaos. мохна́тый = shaggy. хулига́н = hooligan. боро́ться (I *ipf* борю́сь, бо́решься) = to wrestle. пра́во = (one's) right. облада́ние = possession. доставля́ть (I)/доста́вить (II) = to bring, cause. хлопо́ты (*pl*) = troubles, cares. бу́дущее = the future. дари́ть (II)/ по- = to present. подде́рживать (I)/поддержа́ть (II) = to support легково́й автомоби́ль = ordinary car (*as opposed to lorry*). везти́/по- *used impersonally with dat* = to be in luck. бе́лый медве́дь = polar bear. хва́статься (I)/по- = to boast. отли́чный = excellent. ветерина́рный = veterinary. врач = surgeon, doctor. зооша́рк (зоологи́ческий парк) = zoological gardens. сели́ть (II)/по- = to settle (*tr*). молодня́к = young animals. общи́тельный = sociable. снежо́к (*gen* снежка́) = snowball. звёздочка = little star, (звезда́ = star, *pl* звёзды).

LESSON No. 40   УРОК № СОРОК

платок ; платочек handkerchief; small handkerchief

стакан ; стаканчик* tumbler;
small glass

друг (дружок, дружочек)
dear friend

собака ; собачка ; собачёнка
dog; doggie; little cur

сестра ; сестрица* sister;
little sister

лошадь ; лошадка ; лоша-
дёнка horse; small horse;
wretched nag

дева maid; virgin. старая
дева old maid

*девица maiden, spinster

конь, конёк horse, steed;
hobby horse

брат ; братец* brother; dear
brother

мальчик ; мальчишка boy;
urchin

*девушка young girl

*девочка little girl

девчонка slattern

письмо ; письмецо letter;
short letter

яблоко ; яблочко apple; little
apple

село ; селишко village; dirty
little village

*Group:

бáтюшка	dear father	мáтушка	dear (little) mother
бáбушка	granny	дéдушка	grandad, grandpapa
дядюшка	dear uncle	тётушка, тётенька	dear auntie

DIMINUTIVES : A diminutive ending added to the stem of a Russian noun (animate or inanimate) gives it a form which may denote only smallness, but to smallness there is very often added the idea of intimacy, familiarity, affection or—and this is important—some kind of depreciation such as contempt, disdain, irony or sarcasm.   A diminutive suffix can be simple or complex: simple, when it is a single suffix, complex when two or more simple suffixes are joined together, thus blending their primary meanings in such a way as to convey a different and, usually, subtle new meaning.   For the foreigner this quality of Russian presents so many difficulties and pitfalls that, until great familiarity with the language has been achieved, he should avoid using all but the few diminutives such as **дéвушка** and **дéвочка** which have fixed meanings and are part of everyday life.   The diminutive words listed above marked with an asterisk should be known.   The others are given by way of examples.

General rule: Be able to *recognize* a diminutive but, in general, *avoid the active use* of any but those that are part of everyday speech.

Diminutive suffixes: These are masculine, feminine or neuter. *Masculine are:* -ек, -ик, -ок, -ец, -чек, -чик, -очек, -ичек, -онок and -ёнок are used for "dear little" animals, and note -ишка, -ишко which imply some disdain.   *Feminine are:* -ка, -ца, -ичка, -енька,

-очка, -ечка. And -учка, -юшка for some masculines. Also -ёнка, -онка which are usually depreciatory. *Neuter are:* -цо, -це, -ко, -чко. Affectionate are -ечко, -ышко ; and, depreciatory -ишко.

PUBLIC NOTICES : GENERAL
List for reference

аптека pharmacy, chemist's shop

билетная касса ticket window; box office

буфет buffet

вагон для курящих smoking car

ванная bath

Внимание! Attention

вокзал railway station

вход entrance

вход воспрещён entrance forbidden

выход exit

гастроном food shop, store

для мужчин } men } conveni-
для женщин } ences women }

закрыто closed

открыто open

звонок bell. Ring

закусочная snack bar; snack shop

зал hall, big room

зал ожидания waiting room

занято occupied, reserved

свободно unoccupied, free

касса cash desk; pay desk

кафе cafe

к поездам to the train(s)

курительная комната smoking room

для курящих smokers

для некурящих non-smoking room

лифт lift, elevator

метро underground railway

медпункт first aid post

мужская комната men's room

дамская комната ladies' room

опасность (*f*) danger

остановка stopping place, halt

— автобуса bus stop

— троллейбуса trolleybus stop

— трамвая car stop

парикмахерская hairdresser

подъёмник lift, elevator

переход pedestrian crossing

почта *or* почтамт post office

раздева́льня cloak-room

рестора́н restaurant

спра́вки information

спра́вочное бюро́ information bureau

столо́вая dining room

Стоп! Stop!

стоя́нка 1. stopping place; 2. car park

— такси́ taxi rank

— воспреща́ется parking forbidden

телегра́ф telegraph (office)

телефо́н telephone

т = тепло́ warm, hot (water)

х = хо́лодно cold (water)

толка́ть push (bell-push)

тяну́ть pull

туале́т м men's toilet, lavatory

— ж women's toilet, lavatory

убо́рная м, убо́рная ж men's and women's toilet, lavatory

эскала́тор escalator

эта́ж floor, storey

пе́рвый эта́ж ground floor

второ́й эта́ж first floor

тре́тий эта́ж second floor

Note: In the USSR (as in the US) the ground floor is the *first,* the English first floor is the *second,* etc.

For Road Signs and Motoring words and phrases, see pages 309–10.

НЕМНОГО ИСТОРИИ И ГЕОГРАФИИ

Влия́ние ве́чных льдо́в Аркти́ческого бассе́йна осложня́ет жизнь люде́й во мно́гих стра́нах. Значи́тельная часть террито́рии Кана́ды — это райо́ны камени́стой или покры́той мхом и лиша́йником ту́ндры. Холо́дные ма́ссы во́здуха, надвига́ясь со стороны́ Ледови́того океа́на, ча́сто меша́ют созрева́нию ри́са в Се́верной Япо́нии. Не то́лько вся Скандина́вия, но и Герма́ния, По́льша, Ита́лия подве́ржены возде́йствию кли́мата А́рктики.

Осо́бенно больши́е неприя́тности доставля́ют льды Аркти́ческого бассе́йна сове́тским лю́дям и америка́нцам. На трёх четвертя́х террито́рии СССР сре́дняя температу́ра в январе́ достига́ет 40° моро́за по Це́льсию. Са́мый кру́пный штат США — Аля́ска — край жесто́кой сту́жи. Ве́чная мерзлота́ цари́т на семи́ деся́тых её террито́рии.

Хо́лод — изве́чный и непримири́мый враг строи́телей. По подсчётам экономи́стов, он пожира́ет ми́нимум 10 проце́нтов всех капиталовложе́ний.

Учёные ра́зных стран давно́ заду́мываются над тем, как обогре́ть

нашу планéту. Эта мечтá зародилáсь и у П. М. Борúсова, осуще-
ствлéнию инженéрных проéктов которого так часто мешáли вéчная
мерзлотá и жестóкие морóзы.

Гóрный_инженéр и стрóитель постепéнно становúлся также
климатóлогом, геóграфом, океанóграфом, истóриком, палеонтóло-
гом. Около 5 000 статéй и книг по всем этим вопрóсам чúслится в
картотéке П. М. Борúсова. Пытлúвая мысль породúла идéю
увелúчить притóк тёплых вод Гольфстрúма в Поля́рный бассéйн и
пропустúть их через Бéрингов пролúв в Тúхий океáн. В этом
слýчае Гольфстрúм смóжет растопúть дрейфýющие льды Áрктики
и на огрóмных простáнствах отеплúть óбласт сéверных широ́т.
Но для этого надо постро́ить в Бéринговом пролúве плотúну. —
Советский Союз. 1960 г.

TRANSLATION: **SOME HISTORY AND GEOGRAPHY**

The influence of the eternal ice of the Arctic basin complicates the life
of people in many lands. A considerable part of the territory of Canada
(is) tundra region, very stony or covered with moss and lichen. Cold
masses of air moving down from the direction of the Arctic Ocean often
prevent the ripening of rice in Northern Japan. Not only Scandinavia,
but also Germany, Poland and Italy are exposed to the influence of the
Arctic climate.

The ice(s) of the Arctic basin transmit(s) particularly great troubles to
the people of the Soviet Union and to the Americans. In three-quarters
of the territory of the USSR the mean temperature in January reaches
40° centigrade of frost. The largest state of the USA—Alaska—is a
region of brutal cold. Everlasting frost reigns in seven-tenths of its
territory.

Cold is the traditional and unappeasable enemy of builders. According to the calculation of economists, it devours (consumes) ten per cent
of all capital investment.

Scientists of various countries have long been meditating over how to
warm our planet. This dream was conceived in the mind of P. M.
Borisov, the accomplishment of whose engineering projects was so often
impeded by eternal frost and rigorous cold.

A mining engineer and builder, he has step by step also become a
climatologist, geographer, oceanographer, historian (and) palaeontologist. About 5,000 articles and books relating to all these questions are
numbered in the card indexes of P. M. Borisov. His keen mind has
conceived the idea of increasing the flow of warm water from the Gulf
Stream to the Polar Basin and letting it (go) through Bering Strait into
the Pacific Ocean. In this event the Gulf Stream (would) melt the
drifting ice-floes of the Arctic and warm up vast expanses of territory
in northern latitudes. But for this enterprise it is necessary to build a
dam in Bering Strait.

влия́ние = influence ве́чный = eternal. аркти́ческий = Arctic (*adj*). осложня́ть (I)/осложни́ть (II) = to complicate (*tr*). значи́тельный = considerable, significant. райо́н = region. камени́стый = stony. покры́тый = covered (+ *ins*, with). мох (*gen* мха) = moss. лиша́йник or лиша́й = lichen. ту́ндра = tundra. Note carefully the word order used here: "regions of tundra" with all the various adjectival expressions agreeing with "tundra" placed before it. This type of word-order is common in Russian. ма́сса = mass. во́здух = air. надвига́ясь verbal adverb from надвига́ться (I)/надви́нуться (I) = to move upon, to approach (menacingly), to be immanent. Ледови́тый океа́н = Arctic Ocean. меша́ть/по- (I) (+ *dat*) = to hinder. созрева́ние = ripening (*no*). рис = rice. Япо́ния = Japan. Скандина́вия = Scandinavia. Герма́ния = Germany. По́льша = Poland. Ита́лия = Italy. подве́ржен, -а, -о ; -ы = subject to, exposed to (short form past participle passive of подверга́ть (I)/подве́ргнуть (I) = to subject). возде́йствие = influence. кли́мат = climate. неприя́тность (*f*) = unpleasantness, nuisance, trouble. доставля́ть (I)/доста́вить (II) = to cause, *also* to deliver. лёд (*gen* льда) = ice. сре́дний = middle (*adj*), mean. достига́ть (I)/дости́гнуть (I) (*past* дости́г, -ла, -ло ; -ли) = to attain, to achieve, to reach. моро́з = frost. Це́льсий = Celsius. по -ю = centigrade. кру́пный = large. штат = State. США (Соединённые Шта́ты Аме́рики) = USA. Аля́ска = Alaska. край = edge, border *or* country, region. жесто́кий = cruel. сту́жа = cold, hard frost. мерзлота́ = frozen ground. цари́ть (II) = to reign, rule. деся́тая (часть) = a tenth (part). изве́чный = traditional, from of old. (не)примири́мый = (ir)reconcilable. враг = enemy. строи́тель (*m*) = builder. расчёт = calculation. эконо́мист = economist. пожира́ть (I)/пожра́ть (I пожру́, пожрёшь) = to devour. ми́нимум = minimum. проце́нт = per cent, percentage. капиталовложе́ние = capital investment. учёный = scientist, scholar. ра́зный = various, different. заду́мываться (I)/заду́маться (I) = to be plunged into thought, to meditate (над + *ins* = about). обогрева́ть (I)/обогре́ть (I обогре́ю, обогре́ешь) = to warm, heat. плане́та = planet. мечта́ = day-dream, reverie. зарожда́ться (I)/зароди́ться (II) = to (be) engender(ed), to (be) conceive(d). осуществле́ние = realization. инжене́рный = engineering (*adj*). прое́кт = project. го́рный = mining (*adj*). инжене́р = engineer. постепе́нно = gradually. станови́ться (II)/стать (I ста́ну, ста́нешь) = to become (+ *ins*). климато́лог = climatologist. гео́граф = geographer. океано́граф = oceanographer. исто́рик = historian. палеонто́лог = palaeontologist. статья́ = article, item, clause. чи́слиться (II) (*ipf* only) = to be numbered, reckoned. картоте́ка = card index. пытли́вый = inquisitive, searching, keen. мысль (*f*) = thought, idea. иде́я = idea. увели́чивать (I)/увели́чить (I) = to increase. прито́к = flow, influx. Гольфстри́м = the

Gulf Stream. поля́рный = polar. пропуска́ть (I пропуска́ю, -ешь)/пропусти́ть (II пропущу́, пропу́стишь) = to let through. (Бе́рингов) проли́в = (Bering) Strait. Ти́хий океа́н = Pacific Ocean. слу́чай = event, happening. смочь (I смогу́, смо́жешь) *pf* of мочь = to be able. раста́пливать (I)/растопи́ть (II) = to melt (*tr*). дрейфу́ющий *present participle active of* дрейфова́ть (I дрейфу́ю, -ешь) both *ipf* and *pf* = to drift. огро́мный = enormous. простра́нство = space, expanse. отепля́ть (I)/отепли́ть (II) = to warm (up). о́бласть (*f*) = region. широта́ = width, breadth, latitude. плоти́на = dam.

Vocabulary I

Simple conjunctions

*a *and, but, while.* See page 41, Pt. I

*но *but.* See page 41, Pt. I

да (I) *and;* (2) *as an emphatic;* (3) + imperative = a wish

*же (ж) *but, then, and, really*

*и *and*

*и ... и ... *both ... and ...*

и не ... и не ... *neither ... nor ...*

*ни .. ни ... *neither ... nor ...*

-ка as suffix meaning *but* or *just;* emphatic request

Derivative conjunctions

(*a*) From pronouns

*то *then*

*то ... то ... *sometimes ... sometimes ...*

*не то ... но ... *not that, but that*

не то ... не то ... *either ... or ...*

*а не то́ *or else, otherwise*

*да и то *even so*

*-то suffix to express *indefiniteness*

то́-то emphatic *just, precisely*

*что *what*

*чем *than*

*чем ... тем ... *the ... the ...* See page 239

(*b*) Derived from adverbs

*как *as, like, how*

*как не *but, only*

*так *then, so*

лишь *only*

лишь то́лько *as soon as*

лишь бы *provided that*

*когда́ *when*

*где *where*

(*c*) Derived from verbs

ведь *but surely, really, after all*

*пуска́й ; *пусть See page 295.

-мол suffix added to words and means *then* or *it is said*

*хотя́ ; хоть (*v-adv*) *though, although*

впро́чем *however*

Others

*пока́ *while, as long as*

пока́ не *before*

*чтобы ; чтоб *in order that.* See pages 120-1.

Compound conjunctions

*бу́дто *as though, as if*

да́бы *so that, in order that*

*да́же *even*

е́жели ; *е́сли ; е́слибы *if, in case*

*е́сли не unless

и́бо *as, for, because*

ли́бо *or*

ли́бо ... ли́бо ... *either ... or ...*

*и́ли (и́ль) *or*

*и́ли ... и́ли ... *either ... or ...*

зато́ *but then*

не́жели *than*

оттого́ (г = в) *why, therefore*

*потому́ *therefore*

*потому́ что *because*

*поэ́тому *therefore, consequently*

*почему́ *how, why*

*почём *how much*

*почему́-то *for some reason*

сколь *how* as in: **Сколь ча́сто?** = *How often?*

*та́кже ; *тоже́ *too, also*

*так как *as, since, because*

таки́ *well then, and so*

всё-таки *for all that*

так-таки́ *in fact; so, in fact*

ста́ло-быть *as a consequence, hence*

*Words marked with an asterisk occur frequently in speech and in the written language.

Note: Do not be surprised to find many of these words dealt with under other parts of speech. See also page 275–6, among the PARTICLES.

CONJUNCTIONS : A conjunction is a particle which connects, in a sentence or phrase, similar things or ideas; or introduces a clause that is subordinate to a main clause. You have already met in Part I many of these words.

Refer to Lesson 25 in Part I for the use of the Russian conditional/ subjunctive. Always remember that a subordinate clause is preceded by a comma in Russian. (This comma does not necessarily indicate a pause in reading: it is merely a grammatical device.)

It is advisable to memorize the conjunctions in the list given here. Those marked with an asterisk are used in everyday speech; the others may be met in reading. Some are rather confusing, so their meaning and significance should be carefully noted.

KINDS OF CONJUNCTIONS: For convenience these little words are classified in various ways which we shall avoid and consider them merely as: (1) *Simple* conjunctions; (2) *Derivative* conjunctions and (3) *Compound* conjunctions. The vocabulary which you need is listed under these headings. Derivative conjunctions originate from other words: pronouns, adverbs and even verbs. Compound conjunctions are made by joining together either two conjunctions or two other words. The lists provide examples of all these.

Note: The use of conjunctions in Russian, and especially of those which, in English, we would call "subordinating conjunctions"— words such as *if, that, though*, etc.—is perfectly straightforward: when the Russian conditional/subjunctive is not involved, they do not demand any special construction of the sentence.

и has several commonly extended meanings which are better translated than by *and*: by *at all*, *as much as*, *just*, *exactly (as)* or *indeed*.

PUNCTUATION: In Russian a comma is *always* inserted between a main and a subordinate clause—in contrast to English usage which may omit a punctuation mark.

The conjunction **что** is *always* preceded by a comma, and before the whole conjugation when it is a compound such as **потому́ что**.

A comma is placed before all the following conjunctions: **а, но, одна́ко, зато́, что́бы, хотя́, отчего́, когда́, куда́, как.**

АНЕКДО́ТЫ

Шко́льница:

— Не зна́ю, как быть! Мне на́до написа́ть, како́е мое люби́мое произведе́ние и кто мой люби́мый геро́й. Я о́чень люблю́ «Мёртвые ду́ши» Го́голя. А кто там мой люби́мый геро́й, никак не могу́ сказа́ть. Все они нехоро́шие.

Schoolgirl:

"I don't know what to do about it! I have to write what is my favourite literary work and who is my favourite hero. I like very much 'Dead Souls' by Gogol. But who there (in it) is my favourite hero, I can't tell by any means. They are all bad."

*

Семиле́тний ма́льчик у́чит свою́ ма́му игре́ в ша́хматы:

— Зна́ешь, ма́ма, хо́дам и фигу́рам я тебя́ как-нибудь научу́, но ду́мать я тебя́ научи́ть не могу́.

A seven-year-old boy is teaching his mother to play chess:

"You (*fam*) know, mama, I can (shall) teach you the moves and chessmen, but I can't teach you to think."

*

Шестиле́тний ма́льчик:

— Де́душка, я приду́маю тако́е лека́рство, что́бы ты стал молоды́м. Тебе́ бу́дет двена́дцать лет.

— А ско́лько бу́дет твоему́ отцу́?

— Он ещё не роди́тся.

A six-year-old boy:

"Granddad, I'll invent a kind of medicine so that you become young. You'll be twelve years old."

"But how old will your father be?"

"He won't yet be born."

Огонёк 1960

шко́льница = schoolgirl. как быть? = What can be done? What about it? люби́мый = favourite. произведе́ние = work (*of literature, art*). мёртвый = dead. семиле́тний = seven year old. ша́хматы = chess (игра́ть, игра́ в ша́хматы). ход = move. (ваш

ход = your move). **фигу́ра** = figure, chess-man, piece. **шестиле́т-ний** = six year old. **приду́мывать** (I)/**приду́мать** (I) = to think up, to invent. **лека́рство** = medicine. **рожда́ться** (I)/**роди́ться** (II) = to be born.

* * *

+ **genitive**:
***ввиду́** in view of
***вдоль** along
впереди́ in front of
***вро́де** of the kind of, like
всле́дствие because of
***внутри́** within, inside of
***вокру́г** round, around
***кро́ме** besides, except
***ми́мо** by, past
относи́тельно regarding
***пре́жде** before
***про́тив** opposite to

+ **accusative**:
***несмотря́ на** in spite of
спустя́ after
+ **dative**:
***вслед** after
***благодаря́** thanks to
***навстре́чу** to, towards
подо́бно like
+ **instrumental**:
согла́сно according to
***вслед за** after, following
+ **prepositional**:
не говоря́ о not to mention

**The asterisk indicates that the word is in frequent use. It must be memorized.*

DERIVATIVE PREPOSITIONS: See Part I, Lessons 21 and 29. Many words not by nature prepositions have taken on the function of a preposition and, like the primary prepositions, then govern cases. The list given above contains all such derivative prepositions as are likely to be required for everyday speaking, and some others that may be met in reading.

Derivative prepositions may arise from nouns, adjectives, verbs, verbal adverbs or adverbs, and sometimes by compounding two words that are primary prepositions (**из-под** = *from under*), or a primary + another word (**встре́ча** = *meeting*. **навстре́чу** = *to*, *towards*). Much latitude is permitted in Russian in making up such compounds. Note the following:

From verbal adverbs
$$\begin{cases} \text{благодаря́} + dat = \text{thanks to} \\ \text{смотря́ па} + dat = \text{depending on} \\ \text{несмотря́ на} + acc = \text{in spite of} \end{cases}$$

The majority of derivative and compound prepositions govern the genitive. As regards compounds which consist of a word followed by a primary preposition, the general rule is that such a compound will govern the case governed by its primary preposition:

вслед (*adv*) + за + *ins* = after, following, behind
не говоря́ о + *prp* = not to mention

Note: On the whole, derivative and compound prepositions present no special difficulties. Their meaning can be worked out from their constituent elements, but one must note well the case they govern.

There is a tendency in Russian towards using prepositionally more and more words that are not strictly prepositions.   One also finds such words and compounds used adverbially.   From the noun **круг** *circle* we sometimes find **круго́м** as either *adv* or *prp*, and as a *prp* it governs the *gen* to mean *round, around* (less common than **вокру́г**).

PARTICLES : You have already met some of these words but, as particles play an important part in Russian, you must know more about them than has been given up to this point.

Russian particles are unchangeable in form: they are never inflected. Some of them have no meaning of their own when they stand alone: but, when used with other words, they impart a particular meaning to those words.   The commonest examples of such particles are the interrogative **ли** and the conditional/subjunctive **бы**, for which see pages 119–22.

Particles, in effect, are very useful auxiliary words which, quite apart from their particular meaning in a phrase or sentence, often help to make conversation more natural, more colloquial.   For example: **по мо́ему, пожа́луй**. **пожа́луй**=*be it so, if you like* or *I dare say*.   The sentence can be translated: *As far as I'm concerned, I dare say . . .*   Now let us consider some particles in common use, noting to begin with that various parts of speech may be used as particles.

Interrogatives: **ли** you know (see page 46).   **ра́зве** (*adv*)=*really?*— when "Yes" is expected for an answer.   Thus: **Ра́зве я говори́л э́то ?** =*Did I really say that?*   **неуже́ли** (*adv*) is used when hoping for the answer "no", as in **Неуже́ли э́то пра́вда ?**=*Is it really possible?* **Неуже́ли э́то так ?**=*Is it possibly so?*   (=*It can't really be possible?*) **бишь** expresses impatience: **Как бишь его́ зову́т ?**=*What's his name, then?*   Or "Heavens, what *is* his name ?"—indicating that the speaker cannot remember.

Emphatics: **же, ж** (*conj*)=*but, however*, and as a particle for *even, very, also*, to emphasize the word to which it is attached.   Thus: **он же, она́ же**=*the very man, woman*.   **Где ж ?**=*Where then?*   **да́же** (*adv*) =*even*, also used as an emphatic: **Я да́же и не слыха́л об э́том.**= *I didn't even hear about it.*   **уже́, уж**=*already*: **Мы уж отобе́дали**= *We've already dined.*   **ведь**=*after all*: **Ведь э́то так.**=*After all, it is so.*   **Ведь я вам говори́л.**=*Well now, I told you so.*

-то, when attached by a hyphen to a word, emphasizes that word. Thus: **Де́нег-то у меня́ дово́льно.**=*As for* money, *I've enough.* The word *money* is emphasized by **-то**.

Agreement or appreciation: **пожа́луй**=*maybe, I suppose so*.   **Я, пожа́луй, пойду́.**=*I suppose I'll go.*   **мо́жет быть**=*maybe, it may be so*: **Мо́жет быть э́то ве́рно.**=*It may be true.*   **знать***=*inf ipf* for *to know*, but as a particle means *obviously* or *one knows that*: **Знать, он мно́го го́ря вида́л**=*He has obviously seen much grief.*   **чай***=*apparently*, *it seems as if, probably*: **Чай я пойду́ туда́.**   **аво́сь***=*perhaps* and **небо́сь***=*no doubt*.   Those marked with an asterisk are colloquial.

Introductory to or *association with:* Very useful are **например**=*for example.* **значит**=*so then, it means that.* **то-есть** (often abbreviated to **т.е.**)=*that is.* **стало-быть**=*consequently, thus.* **словом** (*adv*)= *in a word, in short.* **к тому же**=*besides, moreover.*

Comparison, likeness to: **словно** (*adv*)=*as if; like.* **словно он знал** =*as if he knew.* **точно** (*adv*)=*exactly, just* (as if). **как-будто**=*as if, as though.*

РАЗГОВОР: AMUSEMENTS, THEATRES, FILMS

театр оперы и балета opera house

драматический театр dramatic theatre (=*straight plays*)

театр эстрады vaudeville theatre

кукольный театр puppet theatre

зелёный театр open-air theatre

балкон balcony

галёрка gallery (gods)

фойе foyer

спектакль (*m*) theatre show

пьеса play

драма (a) drama

комедия comedy

трагедия tragedy

представление presentation

актёр, актриса actor, actress

певец, певица singer

балерина ballerina

танцор male dancer

цирк circus

кинотеатр cinema

экран screen

широкоэкранный фильм wide-screen film

стереофонический звук stereophonic sound

говор sound track

немой фильм silent film

кресло stall seat

партёр the stalls

бенуар 1st tier (stalls level)

ложа box

бельэтаж grand tier, dress circle

1-й ярус 1st tier above grand tier

2-й ярус 2nd tier above grand tier

киножурнал newsreel

документальный фильм documentary

концертный зал concert hall

симфонический концерт symphony concert

камерная музыка chamber music

оркестр orchestra

дирижёр conductor

солист soloist

скрипач violinist

скрипичный концерт violin concerto

капелла choir

композитор composer

касса box office

билет ticket

(за)бронировать to book

забронированный booked

постановка production

режиссёр director (producer)

Какой спектакль вы советуете мне посмотреть сегодня ?
What show do you advise me to see this evening ?

Если у вас ме́сто не заброни́ровано, сомнева́юсь, попадёте ли вы куда-либо. If you haven't booked a seat, I doubt if you'll get in anywhere.

Пойдёмте вме́сте в гла́вную ка́ссу. Let's go together to the main theatre booking office.

Наши места́ на пе́рвом я́русе сбо́ку. Our seats are in the 1st (i.e. 3rd) tier to the side.

Отда́йте пальто́ ваше в гардеро́б; там же мо́жете получи́ть бино́кль. Leave your coat in the cloakroom, there you can get opera glasses.

Эта пье́са в четырёх де́йствиях (а́ктах). This is a four-act play.

Вам хорошо́ видно отсю́да? Can you see well from here?

Нева́жно. В пе́рвом ряду́ было бы лу́чше. Not very well. The first row would have been better.

Сейчас антра́кт — пойдёмте в фойе́. There's an interval now. Let's go to the foyer.

Кури́ть в фойе́ нельзя́ — пойдёмте лу́чше в буфе́т; там кури́ть мо́жно. You can't smoke in the foyer. Let's go to the refreshment room; you can smoke there.

Как вам нра́вится игра́ этого актёра? Беспоцо́бно, не пра́вда ли? How do you like his acting? Incomparable, don't you think?

Декора́ции чьи? По-мо́ему беднова́ты. Who did the scenery? Rather poor (meagre), I think.

Оркестр игра́ет как нельзя́ лу́чше. The orchestra couldn't be playing better.

Вы ча́сто быва́ете на конце́ртах ка́мерной му́зыки? Do you often go to chamber music concerts?

Я ли́чно предпочита́ю цирк. Personally I prefer the circus.

В на́шем ци́рке теперь выступа́ют са́мые тала́нтливые арти́сты. The most talented performers are now appearing in our circus here.

Завтра пойдём смотреть знамени́тый немо́й фильм Эйзенште́йна: "Бронено́сец Потёмкин." To-morrow we shall go and see Eisenstein's famous silent film, "The Battleship Potemkin".

ЧАСТУ́ШКА

Хорошо́ в лесу́ гуля́ть,
То́лько о́чень бо́язно,
Хорошо́ с па́рнем сиде́ть,
То́лько о́чень со́вестно.

часту́шка a two or four-line folk verse or song, mostly humorous, often topical.

па́рень *fellow, lad, chap.*

со́вестный *conscientious, fair; honourable.*

мне со́вестно *It's a matter of conscience to me.* Also *I'm ashamed.*

со́весть (*f*) *conscience.*

Note: The **часту́шка** is a popular verse form in Russian, with a long tradition. It can deal with any subject under the sun, but probably the biggest category comes under the heading **часту́шки о любви́**, from which the above is taken: **Ру́сские часту́шки** (**Москва** 1956). These short items, with their popular and humorous appeal, are good material for memorizing.

TRANSLATION: It's good to stroll in the forest,/Only it's very dangerous,/It's good to be sitting with a fellow,/Only one (is) very ashamed.

Marriage :

(*a*) ***жени́ться** is used of a man marrying.

(*b*) **выходи́ть/вы́йти за́муж :** *lit:* "to go out behind a man" is used of a woman.

жени́ть (*ipf* and *pf*) to marry off (a man to a woman **на**+*acc*).

венча́ться/повенча́ться to be married in church. (**венча́ть**=to crown).

жени́тьба, брак marriage. **жена́тый** (*m*) married. **заму́жняя** (*f*) married.

сва́дьба=wedding. **состоя́ть в бра́ке**=to be married.

Verbs easily confused

буди́ть (II) *to awaken:* бужу́, бу́дишь. *Past:* буди́л.

быть (I) (*irr*) *to be:* есть ; суть. я был. *Fut:* бу́ду, бу́дешь.

бить (I) *to hit:* бью, бьёшь. бил. (*pf* поби́ть).

везти́ (I)   *to convey:* везу́, везёшь. вёз.
вести́ (I)   *to lead:* веду́, ведёшь. вёл.
выть (I)   *to howl:* во́ю, во́ешь. выл.
вить (I)   *to twist:* вью, вьёшь. вил. (*pf* свить).
гла́дить (II) *to stroke, to iron, press* (*clothes*): гла́жу, гла́дьшш.
гляде́ть (II)   *to look:* гляжу́, гляди́шь. гляде́л.
дава́ть (I)   *to give:* даю, даёшь. дава́л.
дави́ть (II)   *to squeeze:* давлю́, да́вишь. дави́л.
дари́ть (II)   *to give:* дарю́, да́ришь. дари́л. (подари́ть (*pf*)
   to make a present of).
*уда́рить (*pf* II)   *to hit once:* уда́рю, уда́ришь. уда́рил.
де́лать (I)   *to do:* де́лаю, де́лаешь. де́лал.
дели́ть (II)   *to divide:* делю́, де́лишь. дели́л.
жать (I)   *to squeeze:* жму, жмёшь. жал ⎱ N.B. Past may have
жать (I)   *to reap:* жну, жнёшь. жал ⎰ two meanings.
сто́ить (II)   *to cost:* сто́ю, сто́ишь. сто́ил.
стоя́ть (II)   *to stand:* стою́, стои́шь. стоя́л.

*These are all *ipf* verbs except уда́рить *to hit*, which is used for *to strike a blow*.

LESSON No. 41   # УРОК № СО́РОК ОДИ́Н

Present participles active
бегу́щий running
гуля́ющий strolling
зна́ющий knowing
живу́щий living
интересу́ющий interesting (*trs*)
куря́щий smoking
иду́щий going
лежа́щий lying (horizontal)
понима́ющий understanding
подходя́щий suiting (suitable)
пла́чущий crying, weeping

подаю́щий giving, presenting, serving (*of food*, etc.)
летя́щий flying
спя́щий sleeping
уча́щийся learning, one who learns
уча́щий teaching, one who teaches
As independent adjectives
путеше́ствующий travelling
сле́дующий following, next
As nouns
куря́щий smoker
некуря́щий non-smoker
бу́дущее the future

PARTICIPLES: Russian participles are verbal forms with adjectival endings, and may be called "verbal adjectives" since they agree with their noun in gender, case and number. The participle, a part of the verb, does the work of an attributive adjective.

In Russian there are:

> ACTIVE participles—present and past.
> PASSIVE participles—present and past

Present participle active: This represents a simultaneous action, and indicates that the person or thing to which it refers is him-, her- or itself doing the action, as when we say in English *the speaking actor, the flying aeroplane*. Here, *speaking* and *flying* are present participles active and would be translated accordingly in Russian. Note that, as the action is continuous or indefinite, the Russian present participle active is formed *only* from *imperfective* verbs. Note also that the present participle active is equivalent to a verb + a relative pronoun. So that such a sentence as *the smoking traveller* (*smoking* is present participle active) is equivalent to saying *the traveller who smokes* or *is smoking* (the last being the English present continuous tense).

Formation of present participle active: Take the third person plural of the imperfective verb, drop the **-т,** and add the suffix **-щ-.**
This suffix is followed by the attributive adjectival endings: **(-щ-) + -ий, -ая, -ее ; -ие.**

Examples:

Conjugation I verbs:
(1) **игра́ть : игра́ю-(т)**
ИГРА́Ю-Щ-ИЙ, -ая, -ее ; -ие
playing
(2) **писа́ть : пишу́-(т)**
пи́шущий, -ая, -ее ; -ие
= writing

Conjugation II verbs:
(1) **говори́ть : говоря́-(т)**
ГОВОРЯ́-Щ-ИЙ, -ая, -ее ; -ие
= speaking
(2) **стуча́ть : стуча́щий, -ая, -ее ; -ие** = knocking, banging

Reflexive present participles active: The particle **-ся** can be added to these participles, making them reflexive. This **-ся** *never* changes to **-сь** after a vowel, as in reflexive verbs.

учи́ть *to teach*
уча́щий *teaching, one who teaches* = *teacher*

учи́ться *to study, learn*
уча́щийся *learning, one who learns* = *learner*

Present participles active as independent adjectives or nouns: Many present participles active have become accepted usage in everyday speech as independent adjectives, though as a rule the form is much more commonly found in the written language. They are also sometimes used as nouns. The main point is to be able to recognize them, and *the letter -щ- before the soft adjectival ending is your guide.*

Declension: They follow the declension of soft adjectives and the rule of spelling as in **хоро́ший,** which see on page 99, 129.

No predicative forms: Note that the present participles active do *not* have any short forms.

Participles in general: They are a *literary* form to be recognized when met in printed matter or letters, and need never be used by the foreigner in speaking. In speech, the relative pronoun **кото́рый** followed by a verb in present or past tense is preferable. Thus:

ма́лчик, чита́ющий кни́гу＝the boy reading the book: (*literary*).
ма́лчик, кото́рый чита́ет кни́гу＝the boy who is reading the book: (*speech*).

Present participles active are found in dictionaries when they are in fairly common use as adjectives or nouns. Otherwise, as a logical form of the verb, they may be omitted. You must therefore be able to recognize them from the rules of formation or from the TABLE on page 289. Those given with this Lesson are of frequent occurrence, especially in writing, and should be memorized.

Past participles active:

говори́вший (*who was*) speaking

чита́вший reading

писа́вший writing

гуля́вший strolling

у́мерший dying

ше́дший going on foot

ве́дший leading

вы́учивший finishing study

жи́вший living

зна́вший knowing

обраща́вший(ся) 1. turning. 2. treating

обрати́вший(ся) changing. 2. addressing

пода́вший giving, presenting, serving (*of food*)

поня́вший understanding

Past participles active as nouns or adjectives

сумасше́дший, (*adj*) insane; (*noun*) madman (**с ума́ сойти́** to go off one's head)

бы́вший (*adj*) (*noun*) the former (*from* **быть**)

проше́дшее (*noun*) the past

сумасше́дшая (*noun*) madwoman

PAST PARTICIPLES ACTIVE: These express the (past) action of the person or thing responsible for it: *who* or *that was* doing something.

Formation: Past participles active derive from both imperfective and perfective verbs and in the same ways:

I. By dropping the final -л of the past tense and then adding the suffix -вш- + the attributive soft adjectival endings -ий, -ая, -ее ; -ие. Thus:

Чита́ть: чита́(л) — чита́ + -вш- + -ий = (1) чита́вший, в *before* ш, *pronounce* ф.

Говори́ть: говори́(л) — говори́ + -вш- + -ий = (2) говори́вший, в *before* ш, *pronounce* ф.

    (1) = (*who was*) reading. *Or* who (*had been*) reading.
    (2) = (*who was*) speaking. *Or* who (*had been*) speaking.

II. If the past tense of a verb ends in a consonant other than л, then only -ш- + the adjectival endings are added after that consonant. Thus:

везти́ *to carry. Past:* вёз + -ш- + -ий = вёзший *having carried.*

III. Some past participles active are formed by replacing the л of the past tense with д or т (д is often found in the present stem of -ти verbs) then the suffix -ш- + the adjectival endings are added. Thus:

Infinitive	Present tense	Past	Past participle active
вести́ to lead	веД(у́)	вёл	вéДший having led
идти́ to go	иД(у́)	шёл	шéДший having gone

The forms II and III are less common than I.

Perfective and imperfective: Russian writers use these participles when they wish to be precise and concise. You have, first, to remember that the imperfective aspect expresses *uncompleted action*, and that the past participle active of an imperfective verb is generally used to express some action that was *going on continuously*, or *was not completed in the past*. On the other hand, the perfective past participle active expresses a *fully completed action in the past*. Thus:

    Imperfective: чита́вший = *who was in the process of reading*
    Perfective: прочита́вший = *who had finished reading*

Relative clause + verb in the past tense: In speech this is always preferable for the foreigner. Excepting a few past participles active that are used as adjectives or nouns (note those given at the head of this Lesson), always use the relative clause with кото́рый. Thus:

    (1) *In the written language:*
Я спроси́л ма́льчика, стоя́вшего у двéри. I asked the boy who was standing at the door.

(2) *In everyday speech:*

Я спроси́л ма́льчика, кото́рый стоя́л у две́ри.   I asked the boy who was standing at the door.

Declension: Past participles active are declined like **хоро́ший** for which see page 99.

Reflexives: The reflexive particle **-ся** (*never* **-сь** after a vowel) is added throughout the declension.

Stress: In past participles active, this is usually the same as that on the infinitive, but in **-ти** verbs it is on the root syllable.

Past participles active are not always given in dictionaries. You must therefore be able to recognize them from the rules of formation given here, or from the TABLE on page 289. And you should memorize the examples in these pages; they are all fairly common in popular publications.

ТАМА́НЬ

По́лный ме́сяц свети́л на камышо́вую кры́шу и белые стены моего́ но́вого жили́ща; на дворе́, обведённом огра́дой из булы́жника, стоя́ла избоча́сь другая лачу́жка, менее и древне́е первой. Берег обры́вом спуска́лся к морю почти у самых стен ее, и внизу́ с беспреры́вным ро́потом плеска́лись темно-си́ние во́лны. Луна́ тихо смотре́ла на беспоко́йную, но поко́рную ей стихи́ю, и я мог различи́ть при свете её, далеко от бе́рега, два корабля́, кото́рых чёрные сна́сти, подобно паути́не, неподви́жно рисова́лись на бле́дной черте́ небоскло́на. «Суда́ в при́стани есть, — подумал я: — завтра отпра́влюсь в Геленджи́к».

При мне исправля́л до́лжность денщика́ лине́йский каза́к. Веле́в ему вы́ложить чемода́н и отпусти́ть изво́зчика, я стал звать хозя́ина — молча́т; стучу́ — молча́т . . . что это? Наконе́ц из сене́й вы́полз мальчик лет 14-ти.

«Где хозя́ин?» — «Не-ма». — «Как? совсе́м не́ту?» — «Совсим». — «А хозя́йка?» — «Поби́гла в слобо́дку». — «Кто ж мне отопрёт дверь?» — сказал я, уда́рив в нее ного́ю. Дверь сама отвори́лась; из ха́ты повея́ло сы́ростью. Я засвети́л се́рную спичку и поднёс её к но́су ма́льчика: она озари́ла два белые гла́за. Он был слепо́й, соверше́нно слепо́й от приро́ды. Он стоял передо мно́ю неподви́жно, и я начал рассма́тривать черты́ его лица́.

Михаи́л Ю́рьевич Ле́рмонтов (1814–1841)

A full moon shone on the rush-thatched roof and white walls of my
new lodging; in the yard, surrounded with a wall of (cobble-)stones,
stood another hovel leaning to one side, smaller and more ancient than
the first.   The shore dipped steeply to the sea almost from its very walls,
and down below with uninterrupted murmur the dark blue waves
splashed.   The moon calmly contemplated the restless but obedient
element (the sea) and I could make out in her light far from the shore two
ships whose black rigging, like a spider's web, was outlined motion-
lessly against the pale line of the horizon.   "There are ships in port", I
thought, "to-morrow I'll leave for Gelendzhik."

A line-unit Cossack was doing duty for me as batman.   Telling him
to put out my suitcase and dismiss the driver, I began to call out for the
owner (of the house).   Silence; I knock(ed)—(only) silence . . .
What was this?   At last out of the porch crept a boy of about fourteen
years (of age).

"Where's the master of the house?"—"There isn't one."   "What?
No (master) at all?"   "None at all."   "What about the mistress of the
house?"   "She's gone round to the village (nearby) (suburb)."   "Who
will open the door for me?" said I, giving it a kick.   The door opened
of itself; from the hut wafted dampness.   I lit a sulphur match and
moved it near to the boy's nose: it showed up two white eyes.   He was
blind, completely blind from birth.   He stood before me motionless,
and I began to study the features of his face.

ме́сяц = moon.   **свети́ть** (II) (**по-**) = to shine, light up.   **камышо́-
вый** = made of rushes (thatch).   **кры́ша** = roof.   **стена́** (*pl* **сте́ны**) =
wall.   **жили́ще** = dwelling.   **двор** = yard, court.   **обведённый** *past
participle passive of* **обводи́ть** (II)/**обвести́** (I) = to surround.   **огра́да**
= fence, wall.   **булы́жник** = cobble-stone.   **избоча́сь** = leaning to
one side.   **лачу́жка** = hovel.   **дре́вний** (*comp* **древне́е**) = ancient.
обры́в = precipice.   **спуска́ться** (I)/**спусти́ться** (II) = to descend.
почти́ = almost.   **беспреры́вный** = incessant.   **ро́пот** = murmur.
плеска́ться (I) = to splash.   **волна́** (*pl* **во́лны**) = wave.   **поко́рный**
= obedient.   **стихи́я** = element.   **различа́ть** (I)/**различи́ть** (II) =
to distinguish.   **кора́бль** (*m*) = vessel.   **снасть** (*f*) = tackle, *pl* rigging.
подо́бно (+*dat*) = like.   **паути́на** = spider's web.   **неподви́жно** =
motionless.   **рисова́ться** (I **-у́юсь**) = to be drawn, outlined, to pose.
бле́дный = pale.   **черта́** = line, feature.   **небоскло́н** = the sky above
the horizon.   **су́дно** (*pl* **суда́**, *gen pl* **судо́в**) = vessel.   **при́стань** (*f*) =
landing stage; wharf, haven.   **отправля́ться** (I)/**отпра́виться** (II) =
to set off.   **исправля́ть** (I) = to carry out *also* to repair.   **до́лжность**
(*f*) = duty, function.   **денщи́к** = batman.   **лине́йский** = belonging to
a unit of the line.   **выкла́дывать** (I)/**вы́ложить** (II) = to lay out,
put out.   **отпуска́ть** (I)/**отпусти́ть** (II) = to dismiss, to let go.
изво́зчик = driver, cabby.   **хозя́ин** = master of the house, host.

стучáть (II)/по-=to knock. сéни (*pl*)=porch. выползáть (I)/выползти (I *like* ползти́)=to crawl out. не-ма (*dialect*)=не имéем ; хозя́йка=mistress of the house. побíгла (*dialect*)=побежáла ; слобóдка (слободá)=suburb; neighbouring village. отпирáть (I)/отперéть (I отопру́, отопрёшь, *past* отпёр, отперлá)=to open (a door). удáрив *past verbal adverb of* ударя́ть (I)/удáрить (II)=to hit, strike. отворя́ть(ся) (I)/отворúть(ся) (II)= to (be) open(ed). вéять (I)/по-=to blow, waft. сы́рость (*f*)= dampness. засветúть (II) (*pf*)=to light up, to strike (a match). сéрный=sulphur (*adj*) (сéра *no*). подносúть (II)/поднестú (I)= to bring, hold up to. озаря́ть (II)/озарúть (II)=to light up, illumine. приро́да=nature, kind. неподвúжно=motionless. рассмáтривать (I)/рассмотрéть (II)=to examine.

A

любúмый (be)loved, favourite

вúдимый visible, apparent

слéдуемый deserved, due

двúжимый moved, movable

*исполнúмый (*adj*) practicable (*from* исполнить *pf*)

B

невúдимый invisible

неделúмый indivisible

неисправúмый incorrigible

неминýемый inevitable

необходúмый (+*dat*) indispensable

неоценúмый invaluable

неутомúмый indefatigable, untiring

невыносúмый unbearable

C

уважáемый, -ая, -ое ; -ые respected, dear, esteemed

многоуважáемый much respected, etc.

глубокоуважáемый deeply respected, esteemed

A are present participles passive implying *possibility*, *feasibility*.

B with не- imply *impossibility*.

C are often used as opening forms of address in letters to somebody who is not an intimate friend, merely an acquaintance. (See also pages 288, 290).

PARTICIPLES contd. : See page 147. A verb is said to be in the "passive" when it denotes that the person or thing suffers (*receives*) an action that comes from some other person or thing. The subject of the sentence is or has been acted *upon* by some other agent.

There are two passive participles in Russian: present and past. Here we shall deal with the present. Only *transitive* imperfective verbs form a present participle passive.

Formation of present participle passive : It is formed from the first person plural of imperfective verbs by adding the hard adjectival (attributive) endings -ый, -ая, -ое ; -ые. This -м ending in both conjugation I and II verbs corresponds to the present participle passive suffixes: **-ем-, -им-**. Thus:

Conjugation I: **читáемый, -ая, -ое ; -ые**

Conjugation II: **вúдимый, -ая, -ое ; -ые**

Short (predicative) form: This is made by adding the short form adjectival endings, except in the masculine which remains without an ending. Thus:

	masc	fem	neut	plural
Conjugation I:	читáем	читáема	читáемо	читáемы
Conjugation II:	вúдим	вúдима	вúдимо	вúдимы

Declension: Attributive (long) form present participles passive are declined like hard adjectives ending in **-ый, -ая, -ое ; -ые**. See **нóвый** page 93.

Use of present participle passive: It is used in the long form as an adjective. The short form is always used predicatively and the neuter is used as an adverb.

Моя́ любúмая кóшка. = *My favourite cat.*

вúдимо = *visibly, evidently; it is evident.*

Present participle passive followed by instrumental case: The person or thing responsible for the action—the agent—is put in the instrumental case:

Кнúга, читáемая мáльчиком, скучнá = *The book being read by the boy is boring.*

Note the commas.

Present participle passive used to form tenses: The infinitive of a verb in the passive can be formed with **быть**+the instrumental of the attributive present participle active: **быть любúмым** = *to be loved* All other forms of the passive verb may be in either the short form predicative *or* long form instrumental. No link verb (auxiliary) is used in the present tense. Thus:

When a man speaks: **я любúм**
When a woman speaks: **я любúма** } *I am loved*
A man is spoken to: **ты любúм**
A woman is spoken to: **ты любúма** } *you are loved* } = *present tense passive*

Past tense: (*m*) **я был любúм** *I was loved*
(*f*) **ты былá любúма** *you* (fam) *were loved*
(*n*) **онó бы́ло любúмо** *it was loved*
(*pl*) **мы бы́ли любúмы** *we were loved*

Future: (*m*) **я бýду любúм** *I shall be loved*
(*f*) **ты бýдешь любúма** *you* (fam) *will be loved*
(*n*) **онó бýдет любúмо** *it will be loved*
(*pl*) **вы бýдете любúмы** *you will be loved*

Present participles passive are usually found in dictionaries only in the categories A, B and C listed on page 285 (and then not always). Memorize these words and the rules for formation. You should be able to recognize both attributive and predicative forms, and the TABLE on page 289 will help.

Infinitives	Attributives	Predicatives in :
-нуть, -нять, -ыть :	**-тый**	**-т, -та, -то ; -ты**
взять to take	взя́тый *(which was)* taken	взят, -а́, -о ; -ы
забы́ть to forget	забы́тый forgotten	забы́т, -а, -о ; -ы
закры́ть to close	закры́тый closed	закры́т, -а, -о ; -ы
заня́ть to occupy	за́нятый occupied, engaged	за́нят, -а́, -о ; -ы
мыть to wash	мы́тый washed	мыт, -а, -о ; -ы
наде́ть to put on	наде́тый put on	наде́т, -а, -о ; -ы
наня́ть to hire, engage	на́нятый hired, rented	на́нят, -а, -о ; -ы
нача́ть to begin	на́чатый begun	на́чат, -а, -о ; -ы
откры́ть to open	откры́тый opened	откры́т, -а, -о ; -ы
поня́ть to understand	по́нятый understood	по́нят, -а́, -о ; -ы
приня́ть to accept	при́нятый accepted	при́нят, -а, -о ; -ы
скрыть to hide	скры́тый hidden	скрыт, -а, -о ; -ы
-ать, -овать :	**-анный**	
вы́брать to choose	вы́бранный chosen	вы́бран, -а, -о ; -ы
сде́лать to do, make	сде́ланный done, finished	сде́лан, -а, -о ; -ы
услы́шать to hear	услы́шанный heard	услы́шан, -а, -о ; -ы
прода́ть to sell	про́данный sold	про́дан, -а́, -о ; -ы
прочита́ть to read through	прочи́танный read	прочи́тан, -а, -о ; -ы
сказа́ть to say, tell	ска́занный said, told	ска́зан, -а, -о ; -ы
Ending :	**Ending :**	
-ить :	**-енный**	**-ен, -а, -о ; -ы**
ко́нчить to finish	ко́нченный finished	ко́нчен, -а, -о ; -ы
купи́ть to buy	ку́пленный bought	ку́плен, -а, -о ; -ы
получи́ть to receive	полу́ченный received	полу́чен, -а, -о ; -ы
пригото́вить to prepare	пригото́вленный prepared	пригото́влен, -а, -о ; -ы

PAST PARTICIPLE PASSIVE : For the purposes of this book it is not necessary to treat this part of the verb in great detail. But, as the past participles passive listed above are in fairly common use, they should be memorized. The past participle passive is recognizable by its two principal endings: (1) **-нный** which is most frequently met; and (2) **-тый**. Short forms **-н** and **-т**.

Formation of past participle passive: Past participles passive are nearly always made from *transitive* and *perfective* verbs. When the form is made from intransitives and imperfectives it is used only as an adjective and not as a verb. (1) Drop the **-ть** of the infinitive and add the endings **-нный, -ая, -ое ; -ые.** Or (2) drop the **-ь** of the infinitive and add **-ый, -ая, -ое ; -ые.**

As regards (1) **-ать** verbs have **-а-** before the participle ending, and **-ить** verbs change **и** to **-е-** making the ending **-енный**.

As regards (2) there are some simple verbs of one syllable which form their past participle passive in this way (**бить** *to strike;* **петь** *to sing;* **жать** *to reap;* and all verbs in **-нуть.** Note two verbs which form this participle from their past tense: **тереть** *to rub* and **запереть** *to lock* (past tense respectively **тёр** and **запер**), so the participles are: **тёртый, запертый.**

Conjugation II verbs with mutations in the *first pers sing* use this stem for the past participle passive. See above

купленный = *bought,* **приготовленный** = *prepared.*

Predicative form: The hard adjectival forms ending in **-ый** form predicatives in the same way and with the same uses as short form adjectives (see pages 134–7). But in this form they have only one **-н.** Thus:

читать : читанный, -ая, -ое ; -ые : читан, читана, читано ; читаны.

кончить : конченный : кончен, -а, -о ; -ы. закрытый : закрыт, -а, -о ; -ы.

The neuter short form can be used as an adverb.

Declension: Past participles passive are declined like long form (attributive) adjectives ending in **-ый.** See **новый** page 93.

WRITING LETTERS : The sender's address is usually written on the top right-hand side and below it the date. Thus:

МОСКВА MOSCOW
Улица Горького, 67, 67 Gorky Street,
6-го октября 1963 г. 6th October, 1963.

The date is always given as the genitive of the ordinal:

шестого октября = *the 6th of October*

The year is given in cardinal numerals (not declined) for all but the final component, which is an ordinal and must be declined:

тысяча девятьсот шестьдесят третьего года = 1963

Openings : (1) The most widely used and correct form at all times,

SUMMARY OF PARTICIPLES: FORMATION

	Active		Passive	
	Imperfective	Perfective	Imperfective	Perfective
PRESENT	**-Щ-**⋆ Drop **-т** of *3rd pers pl* add **щ** + **-ий, -ая, -ое, -ие**	None	**-М-**⋆ (*ending of* 1st *pers pl*) to which add: **-ый, -ая, -ое ; -ые** *Short form:* (*m*) **-м** ; (*f*) **-ма** ; (*n*) **-мо** ; *pl:* **-мы**	Very few
PAST	**-ВШ-, -Ш-**⋆ Drop **-л** of past tense, add **-вш** or **-ш** + **-ий, -ая, -ее ; -ие**	**-ВШ-, -Ш-** Formation similar to that of *ipf*, but from *pf* verbs	**-НН-, -Т**⋆ (1) Drop **-ть** of *inf*, add **-нн** or **-т** + **-ый, -ая, -ое ; -ый** *Short form:* one **-н**. Verbs in **-нуть** have short form in **-т**	**-НН-, -Т**⋆ Formation similar to that of *ipf* but from *pf* verbs

⋆The suffixes at the head of each participle are the signs which indicate which participle it is. This brief summary is intended only to help you to *recognize* participles. You do not have to learn to use them, but you must know what they mean.

both to Soviet Russians and to emigrés, is the **и́мя-о́тчество** preceded by the adjective **многоуважа́емый** = *much esteemed*:

Многоуважа́емый Ива́н Ива́нович! = Dear Ivan Ivanovich,
Многоуважа́емая А́нна Васи́льевна! = Dear Anna Vasilievna,

Always use the exclamation mark after the opening! This is more or less the equivalent of the English opening "Dear Mr/Mrs . . ." Remember that there is absolutely nothing informal or intimate about using **и́мя-о́тчество**; it is essentially a *formal* mode of address. For a less formal, but by no means intimate opening, use **дорого́й** instead of **многоуважа́емый.** On the other hand a more formal effect is achieved by using **глубокоуважа́емый** = *deeply respected*.

(2) If the **и́мя-о́тчество** is not known, Soviet and emigré usages differ. The Soviet usage is simply to use the forms given above, substituting **граждани́н** + surname (**фами́лия**) for the **и́мя-о́тче-ство**. Thus:

Многоуважа́емый граждани́н Петро́в! = Dear Citizen Petrov,
Многоуважа́емая гражда́нка Петро́ва! = Dear Citizeness Petrova,

The form **Дорого́й това́рищ!** = Dear comrade, for both sexes, is also much used.

(3) Amongst emigrés the correct forms, if the **и́мя-о́тчество** is not known, are:

Ми́лостивый госуда́рь! *literally* = "Gracious Lord"
Ми́лостивая госуда́рыня! *literally* = "Gracious Lady"

This opening is the equivalent of *Dear Sir/Madam.*

(4) An intimate opening:

Дорого́й Серге́й! = Dear Sergei,
Дорога́я (*or* **Ми́лая**) **Та́ня!** = Dear Tanya, (*dim* of Tatyana)

ми́лый = *sweet*, *nice* and, used with a diminutive, implies an established, intimate friendship.

Endings: (1) Formal are:
С соверше́нным почте́нием,
С соверше́нным уваже́нием, } Correspond to our *Yours faith-fully* or *Yours truly.*

(2) Less formal, friendly, and much used among people who respect one another but may not know one another very intimately:

Пре́данный Вам, = *lit:* "devoted to you" and corresponds to our *Yours ever.*

(3) Intimate endings:
Either **Пре́данный Тебе́,** referring to addressee, *or* **Твой, Твоя́,**
Note also:

уважа́ть (*ipf* I) = to respect. **уважа́ющий Вас** = respectfully yours,
лю́бящий (*from* **люби́ть**) = loving. **Ва́ша лю́бящая** (*f*) = your loving,

Note: Capital letters are used for pronouns and *poss adjs* referring to addressee.

ORDER OF WORDS IN A SENTENCE: Little in the way of practice *into* Russian has been given in this book up to this point. The reason is that experience shows that it is desirable for beginners to acquire a fair mastery of (*a*) *vocabulary* and (*b*) the "*mechanics*" of the language so as to be able *to read and understand Russian* fairly well before attempting much more "into Russian" than was expected of the learner in Part I. Indeed, if it is your intention to do, or to have to do much "into" Russian, you would be well advised to go again through the PRACTICES in Part I, covering up the Russian text, and translating all the English into Russian. In so doing, you will observe that much more latitude is permissible in word-order in Russian than in English and, note this well, that there is in Russian a word-order which is both easy to master and much used. One may call it the "standard order of words". It applies to all simple, direct statements. Here it is:

I   The subject in a sentence comes before and near to the predicate.

II   Attributes that demand agreement (*full-form adjectives, numeral words, possessive and all other declined pronouns which agree in case, gender and number with their nouns*) are usually placed before their nouns.

III   The object (usually) follows the predicate.

IV   Adverbs are (usually) placed before their verbs.

V   To emphasize a word, place it first in the sentence.

VI   A number placed before a noun expresses *exact* quantity. A number placed after a noun expresses *approximate* quantity (=*more or less* or *about*).

VII   Word-order may be varied in the interests of style, but until the learner knows the language well, he should keep to the word-order suggested, which is for straightforward, *direct* statements.

VIII   Do *not* write long sentences! A dozen words should be the maximum. The shorter a sentence is, the less scope for errors! If your Russian is not up to what you wish to express, try to simplify *ideas*.

A letter in Russian: Example

Москва́,

13-го января 1960 года.

Многоуважа́емый Гео́ргий Петро́вич!

Я получи́л Ва́ше любе́зное письмо́ с приложе́нием партиту́ры моего́ „Кузнеца́", перело́женного на то́ник соль-фа. Я с велича́йшим увлече́нием пыта́лся изучи́ть эту табулату́ру, но поско́льку я не име́ю о́пыта в бы́стром её прочте́нии, я не могу́ вы́сказать Вам своего́ положи́тельного или отрица́тельного отноше́ния к э́той систе́ме в це́лом.

Меня́ о́чень интересу́ют Ва́ши сно́ски на музыка́льный слова́рь Гро́ва, статьи́ кото́рого я постара́юсь внима́тельно изучи́ть с тем, чтобы лу́чше прони́кнуть в са́мую суть э́той систе́мы. Бою́сь то́лько, что на мой взгляд она́ ока́жется для меня́ сли́шком сло́жной и тру́дной, поско́льку в э́том направле́нии у меня́ нет никако́го о́пыта. Мне бы́ло-бы чрезвыча́йно ле́стно услы́шать от Вас необходи́мые для меня́ указа́ния, как приступи́ть к изуче́нию систе́мы тоник соль-фа и, кста́ти, я о́чень проси́л-бы Вас подели́ться со мной впечатле́нием, производи́мым на слу́шателей э́тим мои́м сочине́нием. Я зна́ю, что Ва́ши хо́ры стоя́т на исключи́тельно высо́ком у́ровне и если-бы у Вас была́ грамофо́нная за́пись и́ли магнетофо́нная ле́нта, то я был-бы Вам чрезвыча́йно призна́телен, если-бы Вы сочли́ возмо́жным пересла́ть мне оди́н экземпля́р э́той за́писи.

В ожида́нии Ва́шего любе́зного отве́та, прошу́ ве́рить в и́скренность моего́ к Вам высо́кого уваже́ния.

Пре́данный Вам

Богда́н Орло́в.

For part of this Letter in Russian handwriting, see page 20.

NOTES

приложе́ние=enclosure, appendix. **партиту́ра**=musical score. **кузне́ц**=blacksmith (note that **-e-** is *not* dropped in oblique cases). **перекла́дывать** (I)/**переложи́ть** (II)=to shift, transpose. **увлече́ние**=enthusiasm. **(по)пыта́ться** (I пыта́юсь, пыта́ешься)=to try, attempt. **поско́льку**=so far as, insofar as. **о́пыт**=experience.

прочте́ние = reading (*no*).   выска́зывать (I)/вы́сказать (I) *like* сказа́ть) = to state, express.   положи́тельный = positive.   отрица́тельный = negative.   отноше́ние = relation, attitude.   сно́ска = reference, note, footnote.   (по)стара́ться (I) = to try, attempt.   внима́тельно = attentively.   с тем, что́бы = in order that.   проника́ть (I)/прони́кнуть (I), *past* прони́к) = to penetrate.   суть (*f*) = essence, the core of a matter.   ока́зываться (I)/оказа́ться (I) = to turn out to be, to prove to be.   сло́жный = complex, complicated.   чрезвыча́йно = extremely, extraordinarily.   ле́стно = flattering (*adv*).   указа́ние = indication, instruction.   приступа́ть (I -а́ю, -а́ешь)/приступи́ть (II приступлю́, присту́пишь) = to set about, to start.   кста́ти = opportunely, to the point, by the way.   (по)дели́ться (II) = to share.   впечатле́ние = impression.   производи́мый *pres part pass* of производи́ть/произвести́ = to produce.   слу́шатель (*m*) = hearer.   сочине́ние = composition.   хор = choir.   за́пись (*f*) = entry, record, recording.   ле́нта = ribbon.   магнетофо́нная ле́нта = recording tape.   призна́тельный = grateful.   счесть (I сочту́, сочтёшь, *past* сочёл, сочла́, -о́ ; -и́) a *pf* form of счита́ть = to count, consider.   пересыла́ть (I)/пересла́ть (I) = to send on.   экземпля́р = copy (of a book, recording).   ожида́ние = expectation.   и́скренность = sincerity.

TRANSLATION:

Moscow,
13th January, 1960

Dear Georgi Petrovich,

I have received your kind letter together with the score of my "Smith" transposed into the tonic sol-fa.   I have been attempting to master this notation with the greatest interest, but since I lack experience in reading it quickly, I cannot give you my reaction, positive or negative to this system as a whole.

I am very interested in your references to Grove's Musical Dictionary, the articles of which I shall try to study attentively, in order to delve more deeply into the very essence of this system.   The only thing I am afraid of is that, in my opinion, it will prove too complex and difficult for me, inasmuch as I have no experience in this direction.   I should be extremely flattered to receive (*lit: hear*) from you the necessary instructions as to how I should set about studying the tonic sol-fa system and, by the way, I should very much like to ask you to share with me the impressions of those that hear this composition of mine.   I know that your choirs are of an exceptionally high level and if you had a gramophone recording or a recording on tape, I should be extremely grateful to you, if you would consider it possible to send me a copy of this recording.

In expectation of your kind reply, I ask you to believe in the sincerity of my high respect for you.

Yours ever,
Bogdan Orlov.

An O. Henry anecdote

ПОЧЕМУ КОНДУКТОРА НЕОБЩИТЕЛЬНЫ

Трамвайных кондукторов бестактная публика часто выводит из себя. Но им запрещено возражать и тем облегчать свою душу. Вот рассказ одного из кондукторов о случае, имевшем место несколько дней назад.

В числе пассажиров — а вагон был переполнен — находилась чрезвычайно изящно одетая дама с маленьким мальчиком.

— Кондуктор, — сказала она томно, — дайте мне знать, когда будет Роу-стрит.

Когда вагон поравнялся с этой улицей, кондуктор дернул вереку звонка и остановил вагон.

— Роу-стрит, мэ'эм, — сказал он, проталкиваясь ближе, чтобы помочь даме выйти.

Дама поставила маленького мальчика на колени и указала ему на дощечку с названием улицы, прикрепленную к забору.

— Посмотри, Фредди, — сказала она, — вот эта высокая прямая буква со смешной завитушкой вверху — «р». Постарайся запомнить. Можете пускать вагон, кондуктор. Мы выходим в Грей-стрите.

О. Генри
(Перевод с английского)

кондуктор (*pl* **кондуктора́**) = conductor. **(не)общи́тельный** = (un)sociable. **трамва́й** = tram. **трамва́йный** = tram (*adj*). **беста́ктный** = tactless. **пу́блика** = the public. **выводи́ть** (II)/ **вы́вести** (I) (**из себя́**) = to lead out (to drive out of one's mind). **запрещён, -а́, -о́ ; -ы** *short form past participle passive of* **запреща́ть** (I)/ **запрети́ть** (II **запрещу́, запрети́шь**) = to forbid. **возража́ть** (I)/ **возрази́ть** (II) = to object, to answer back. **облегча́ть** (I)/**облегчи́ть** (II) = to facilitate, make easier, to relieve. **душа́** = soul.

расска́з = story. слу́чай = event, happening. име́ть ме́сто = to take place (име́вший *past participle active*). пассажи́р = passenger. ваго́н = train *or* tram car. перепо́лнен, -а, -о ; -ы *short form past participle passive of* переполня́ть (I)/перепо́лнить (II) = to overfill, overcrowd. чрезвыча́йно = extremely, extraordinarily. изя́щно = elegantly. оде́тый *past participle passive of* одева́ть (I одева́ю, одева́ешь)/оде́ть (I оде́ну, оде́нешь) = to dress. то́мно = languidly. дава́ть/дать знать = to let (one) know (+*dat*). поравня́ться (I) (*pf only*) = to come alongside. дёргать (I)/дёрнуть (I) = to tug, to pull. верёвка = cord, string. звоно́к = bell. остана́вливать (I)/останови́ть (II) = to stop (*tr*). прота́лкиваясь *present verbal adverb of* прота́лкиваться (I)/протолкну́ться (I) = to push through. помога́ть (I)/помо́чь (I помогу́, помо́жешь) = to help. ста́вить (II)/по- = to place in an upright position. коле́но (*pl* коле́ни) = knee. ука́зывать (I)/указа́ть (I укажу́, ука́жешь) = to indicate. дощё́чка = little board, name plate. назва́ние = name, title. прикреплё́нный *past participle passive of* прикрепля́ть (I)/прикрепи́ть (II) = to attach, to fasten. забо́р = fence. смешно́й = funny. бу́ква = letter (*of alphabet*). завиту́шка = curl, flourish. запомина́ть (I)/запо́мнить (II) = to memorize.

TRANSLATION:

WHY CONDUCTORS ARE UNSOCIABLE

The tactless public often takes tram conductors out of themselves (= exhausts their patience). But it is forbidden to (=for) them to answer back and thereby unburden their souls. Here is a story (told by) one of the conductors (which) took place a few days ago.

Among the (number of) passengers—the vehicle was overcrowded—there was (found) an extremely elegantly dressed lady with a small boy.

"Conductor," she said languidly, "let me know when it will be (= when we come to) Rowe Street."

When the car came up beside this street, the conductor pulled the bell-cord and the vehicle stopped.

"Rowe Street, ma'am," he said, pushing through (=his way) nearer (to her) in order to help the lady to get out.

The lady put the little boy on her knee and showed (pointed out to) him the small notice board attached to the fence with the name of the street.

"Look, Freddy," she said. "Now this high straight letter with a funny curl on top is 'R'. Try and remember it. You can let the car go (on), conductor. We're getting off at Grey Street."

Note: The Russian text of this anecdote is a translation from O. Henry, published in Же́нский календа́рь, 1960. The literal translation given above is from this text.

LESSON No. 42.　　　　УРОК № СÓРОК ДВА

RUSSIAN VERBAL SYSTEM

I. The system of conjugation

The parts of a Russian verb derive from two basic forms (*a*) the infinitive stem and (*b*) the stem of the conjugated tense (*pres* of *ipfs*, *fut* of *pfs*).　The parts are formed from (*a*) by word-formation, and from (*b*) by inflexion.　Example:

Infinitive: ipf звать/pf позвáть.　*Stem:* -зва-.
Conjugated tense: зовý, зовёшь ; -ýт.　*Stem:* зов-.

(*a*) From infinitive stem зва- by word-formation

Past tense звал, -а, -о ; -и
Past participles:
　(i) *active* звáвший
　(ii) *passive* звáнный
Past verbal adverb (по-)звав, (по-)звáвши
Compound future я бýду звать
Cond/sub я бы звал

(*b*) From present stem зов- by inflexion

Pres (ipf) зовý, зовёшь . . .
Future (pf) позовý, позовёшь . . .
Present participles:
　(i) *active* зовýщий
　(ii) *passive* зовóмый (*irr*)
Present verbal adverb зовя́
Imperative зови́, зови́те

The infinitive and present stems may be the same or different.　If you know both (these you *must* learn) you can build all other forms of *any* regular verb.

Past tense: This springs from an old ʻpast participle active, now disappeared, adjectival by nature, and used with **быть.**　Only the form of a short (predicative) *adj* remains, and it is conveniently formed by adding suffix **-л** to the infinitive stem, with **-а** (*f*), **-о** (*n*); and **-и** for all genders plural. See page 56.　And so we have:

　　Sing: я, ты, он, онá, онó, звал, звалá, звáло
　　Pl: мы, вы, они́ звáли

Other parts: These are more fully treated elsewhere on pages 246–8 and 279–88, but, for convenience of reference, are here summarized:

Summary of verbal endings

Imperatives   -й (те)   -и (те)   -ь (те)

Imperatives
reflexive } -йся (-йтесь)   -ись (-итесь)   -ься (-ьтесь)

		masc	*fem*
Pres part	*acc*	-щий(ся)	-щая(ся)
	pass	-мый	-мая
Past part	*acc*	-(в)ший(ся)	-(в)шая(ся)
	pass {	-нный	-нная
		-тый	-тая
ipf verbal adv		-я(сь), -а(ся); *and a few* -ючи, -учи.	
pf verbal adv		-в ; -вши, -ши(сь)	
Short form	*pres*	-м	-ма
participles {	*past*	-н, -т	-на, -та

		neut	*pl: all genders*
Pres part	*acc*	-щее(ся)	-щие(ся)
	pass	-мое	-мые
Past part	*acc*	-(в)шее(ся)	-(в)шие(ся)
	pass {	-нное	-нные
		-тое	-тые
Short form	*pres*	-мо	-мы
participles {	*past*	-но, -то	-ны, -ты

For reference

II. CLASSIFICATION OF VERBS: SUMMARY

As many verbs deviate slightly from the regular, a rational classification to embrace all but the few really irregulars is given:

	Conj (I) "**е**" *Verbs*			*(II)* "**и**" *Verbs*
	Class I	**Class II**	**Class III**	**Class IV**
Endings of conjugated tense shows classification	-у	-ну	-ю	-ю (-у)
	-ешь	-нешь	-ешь	-ишь
	-ет	-нет	-ет	-ит
	-ем	-нем	-ем	-им
	-ете	-нете	-ете	-ите
	-ут	-нут	-ют	-ят (-ат)

CLASS I VERBS

Conjugated tense in **-у, -е-шь ; -ут.**

Group 1	**Group 2**
No suffix **-а-** in infinitive	With suffix **-а-** in infinitive
Verbs end in **-ти́, -ть, -чь**	Verbs end in **-ть**
нес-ти́ *to carry*	рв-а-ть *to tear*
реве́-ть *to bellow*	бр-а-ть *to take*
бере́-чь *to look after*	зв-а-ть *to call*
etc. See pages 301–2.	пис-а́-ть *to write*
	иск-а́-ть *to seek*
	etc. See pages 302–3.

CLASS II VERBS

Conjugated tense in **-ну, -не-шь ; -нут.**

Group 1	**Group 2**
Lose suffix **-ну-** in the past tense (*Imperfectives*)	Retain suffix **-ну-** throughout the past tense (*Perfective*)
мёрз-ну-ть *to freeze*	дви́-ну-ть *to move, set in motion*
зяб-ну-ть *to be cold*	
etc. See pages 303–4.	etc. See pages 304–5.

CLASS III VERBS: primary and secondary verbs

Conjugated tense in **-ю, -е-шь, -ют.**

Primaries

Group 1

No suffix in infinitive or
conjugated tense
 сме-ть *to dare*
 бри-ть *to shave*
 мы-ть *to wash*
etc. See page 305.

Group 2

Infinitive has suffix **-а-** (**-я-**
after a vowel)
 дрем-а́-ть *to doze*
 се́-я-ть *to sow* (a field)
etc. See page 305.

Secondaries (= derivatives)

These always have a suffix in the infinitive.
A: with scheme of infinitive and conjugated tense the same.

Group 1

Suffixes **-а-**, (**-я-**) **-ва-**,
 -ыва- (**-ива-**)
де́л-а-ть *to do, make*
обвин-я́-ть *to accuse*
пи́с-ыва-ть *to write often*
ха́ж-ива-ть *to go often*
etc. See page 306.

Group 2

Suffix **-е-**, (**-а-** after hissing
 consonant)
черн-е́-ть *to become black*
богат-е́-ть *to grow rich*
дорож-а́-ть *to get dear*
etc. See page 306.

B: with infinitive and conjugated tense differing.
 Infinitive suffix **-ова-, -ева-.**
 Conjugated tense suffix **-у(-ю).**
 рис-ова́-ть *to draw, paint*
 гор-ева́-ть *to grieve, mourn*
 etc. See pages 306–7.

CLASS IV ("И") VERBS

Conjugated tense in -ю (-у), -и-шь ; -ят (-ат)

Group 1

Infinitive has **-и-** of conjugated tense.

черн-и́-ть *to blacken*
люб-и́-ть *to love*
говор-и́-ть *to speak*
etc. See page 308.

Group 2

Infinitive has suffix **-е-** (**-а-** after a hissing consonant).

гляд-е́-ть *to look*   **леж-а́-ть** *to lie down*
гор-е́-ть *to burn*   **дрож-а́-ть** *to tremble*
сид-е́-ть *to be seated*   **бо-я́-ть-ся** *to fear*
etc. See page 308.   etc. See page 308.

Other useful "**и**" verbs on pages 308–9.

MUTATIONS : You *must* know your mutations, for which see pages 165-6.

HOW TO USE THIS CLASSIFICATION : What is being given on pages 296–309 comprises *all* types of verbs excepting the irregulars on page 301. It provides a bird's-eye view of what you have to study. You can see from it that there is a consistency of logic and a repetition of patterns. These have to be grasped—and in time mastered.

Take, for example, verbs in Class I. They are of two kinds: (1) Verbs lacking a suffix in the infinitive and ending in **-ти́, -чь, -ть.** Some of these modify consonants in the present or past: **нести́, бере́чь, реве́ть** are examples. But the modifications are usually *consistent with* MUTATIONS about which you were warned on page 165. (2) Verbs having suffix **-а-** in the infinitive form the conjugated tense in **-у, -ут.** For example, **рв-а-ть** and **бр-а-ть.** There are not many of these verbs, but they are all fairly common.

Note the terms *primary* and *secondary* on pages 305–6. Primary verbs are those which have no suffix in either infinitive or conjugated tense. Secondary verbs always have a suffix and are derived from other words: nouns or other verbs. These distinctions enable us to view the verbs in related groups for learning.

You should refer to the SUMMARY on pages 298–9 each time you approach anew "class" or "group" in the classification. The verbs to be given in classification from now onwards will be your groundwork in the whole Russian verbal system.   When you know them, and have mastered the system, you should have few further difficulties about conjugation. The system can be applied to new verbs and to the innumerable compounds made with prefixes from the verbs in the lists.   The classification and lists of verbs exemplifying it are valuable for permanent reference.

VERBAL SUFFIX: See pages 166–7 first.   You can recognize the class and group of a verb in the classification by the existence or non-existence of a verbal suffix.   The suffixes to look for are:

-a- (-я-), -ну-, -е-, -ва-, -ыва- (-ива), -ова- (-ева-), -и-.

Distribution of suffixes among classes and groups: In order to discover how a verb is conjugated, the first thing to do is look up the SUMMARY on pages 298–9 for the suffix of the Group, and then go on to the part which deals more fully with this Class and Group—as Class I verbs are dealt with below.   The rest will follow from what you have learnt.

System: Many gallant attempts have been made to simplify the complex Russian verbal system for foreign learners of the language. None fully succeeds; all are open to criticism.   But, having examined many of the most promising of these attempts, we decided to return to that expounded by M. P. Boyer in 1895, most of which was already traditional for the best Russian grammarians.   We have kept to the main lines of Boyer, but have simplified and adapted his principles for the purpose here.   **"Irregular" verbs:** Only five are so regarded: **хотѣть** (I *ipf*) to wish; **ѣсть** *ipf* to eat; **дать** *pf* to give; **бѣжать** *indet ipf* to run; **быть** to be.   They have been dealt with in the Lessons.   References to pages will be found with the verbs in the Vocabulary at the end.

VERBS WHICH DEVIATE FROM THE REGULAR IN CLASS
I with Conjugated tense:

-у, -ешь, -ет, -ем, -ете, -ут

Group 1

-ТИ́
вез-ти́ : везу́, везёшь.   *Past* **вёз, везла́, -ó ; -и́**   to convey.   See page 174.
вес-ти́ : веду́, ведёшь.   **вёл, вела́, -ó ; -и́**   to lead.   See page 174.
грес-ти́ : гребу́, гребёшь.   **грёб, гребла́, -ó ; -и́**   to row.

ид-ти́ : иду́, идёшь. шёл, шла, -о ; -и to go on foot. See page 174.

мес-ти́ : мету́, метёшь. мёл, мела́, -о́ ; -и́ to sweep.

нес-ти́ : несу́, несёшь. нёс, несла́, -о́ ; -и́ to carry by hand. See page 174.

пас-ти́ : пасу́, пасёшь. пас, пасла́, -о́ ; -и́ to graze, tend.

плес-ти́ : плету́, плетёшь. плёл, плела́, -о́ ; -и́ to plait, weave.

рас-ти́ : расту́, растёшь. рос, росла́, -о́ ; -и́ to grow.

-чь

бере́-чь : берегу́, бережёшь, берегу́т. берёг, берегла́, -о́ ; -и́ to take care of.

вле-чь : влеку́, влечёшь, влеку́т. влёк, влекла́, -о́ ; -и́ to drag, draw.

*ле-чь : ля́гу, ля́жешь, ля́гут. лёг, легла́, -о́ ; -и́ to lie down (*pf of* пожи́ться).

мо-чь : могу́, мо́жешь, мо́гут. мог, могла́, -о́ ; -и́ to be able, can.

те-чь : теку́, течёшь, теку́т. тёк, текла́, -о́ ; -и́ to flow, pour forth.

пе-чь : пеку́, печёшь, пеку́т. пёк, пекла́, -о́ ; -и́ to bake.

(за)пря́-чь : -прягу́, -пряжёшь, -прягу́т. (за)пря́г, -прягла́, -о́ ; -и́ to harness.

стере́-чь : стерегу́, стережёшь, -гу́т. стерёг, стерегла́, -о́ ; -и́ to watch over.

стри-чь : стригу́, стрижёшь, стригу́т. стриг, стри́гла, -о ; -и to clip, cut, shear.

се-чь : секу́, сечёшь, секу́т. сек, се́кла ; -и. 1. to hew cut. 2. to thrash, flog.

-ть

жи-ть : живу́, живёшь. жил, -а́, -о ; -и to live.

клас-ть : кладу́, кладёшь. клал, -а, -о ; -и to put, lay.

крас-ть : краду́, крадёшь to steal, pilfer. *Like* класть.

пас-ть : паду́, падёшь to fall, *pf of* па́дать (*like* ду́мать).

плы-ть : плыву́, плывёш. плыл, -а́ ; -и. See page 174.

реве́-ть : реву́, ревёшь to roar, bellow; to rage.

*сес-ть : ся́ду, ся́дешь. сел, -а ; -и to sit down (*pf of* сади́ться).

*Note: This is the only verb in this group stressed on the first syllable of the conjugated tense.

Group 2

бр-а-ть : беру́, берёшь. брал, -ла́ ; -ли to take.

вр-а-ть : вру, врёшь. врал, -а ; -и to tell lies.

др-а-ть : деру́, дерёшь. драл, -а́, -о ; -и to tear, strip off.

ж-а-ть : жму, жмёшь to press, pinch, squeeze.

ж-ать : жну, жнёшь to harvest.

жд-а-ть : жду, ждёшь.   ждал, -а́ ; -и́   to wait for; to expect.
зв-а-ть : зову́, зовёшь.   звал, -а́ ; -и   to call.   See page 296.
лг-а-ть : лгу, лжёшь, лгут.   лгал, лгала́ ; -и   to tell lies.
рв-а-ть : рву, рвёшь.   рвал, -а, -о ; -и   to tear, rend; to pluck.
тк-а-ть : тку, ткёшь.   ткал, -а́, -о́ ; -и   to weave.
вяз-а́-ть : вяжу́, вя́жешь.   вяза́л, -а, -о ; -и   to bind, knit.
дви́г-а-ть : дви́жу, дви́жешь.   дви́гал, -а, -о ; -и   to move.
каз-а́-ться : кажу́сь, ка́жешься, ка́жется, ка́жутся.   *Past*
    каза́лся, каза́лась, -лось, -лись   to seem.
ма́з-а-ть : ма́жу, ма́жешь.   ма́зал, -а, -о ; -и   to daub, smear,
    anoint.
пис-а́-ть : пишу́, пи́шешь.   писа́л, -а, -о ; -и   to write.
пла́к-а-ть : пла́чу, пла́чешь.   пла́кал, -а, -о ; -и   to weep.

Note: Verbs in Class I which have a guttural in the *first pers sing* and *third pers pl* of the conjugated tense, with a hissing consonant in the *second pers*, retain the hissing consonant in the remainder of the tense: бере́чь, течь, печь.   *Note* жечь/с- to burn (*tr*): жгу, жжёшь.   *Past* жёг, жгла

Learning Russian Verbs : This and succeeding lists of Classified Verbs, are given in their rational groupings so that they may be more easily memorized than if presented in a haphazard fashion.   The conjugations, as presented in these groupings, are not difficult to memorize and the verbs are nearly all very useful.   Some verbs already met will be given in their logical place in the lists.   *Note* that all Class I verbs are Conjugation I.

CLASS II VERBS : While learning the classes and groups of verbs, refer constantly to these pages until you know them, and from time to time go back over the Preliminary Notes on pages 296–7.

CLASS II VERBS :

Conjugated tense -ну, -нешь, -нет, -нем, -нете, -нут.
Class II verbs comprise all verbs ending in **-нуть**.   A distinction must be made between two groups of these verbs.

Group 1 : These have infinitive in **-ну-ть** and in the past tense lose the suffix **-ну-**.   Example: мёрз-ну-ть *to be freezing*.   These are *imperfective* verbs and the short list given below should be known.   One may then, for practical purposes, assume that *all* the verbs in Class 2 are quite regular and *perfectives*.

Group 2: These also have infinitive in **-нуть** but retain the suffix **-ну-** throughout the verb. Example: **дви́-ну-ть**, conjugated tense **я дви́-ну** *I shall move*, etc. *Past:* **дви́-ну-л** *I moved*, etc.

Note: Some of these *pf* verbs have an *ipf* form ending in **-ать** or **-еть**. The most useful are:

ipf **тро́гать**/*pf* **тро́нуть**   *to touch* ⎫ "Semelfactive"
ipf **дви́гать**/*pf* **дви́нуть**   *to move* ⎬ perfectives describ-
ipf **пры́гать**/*pf* **пры́гнуть** *to jump* ⎭ ing sudden, instan-
                                          taneous action

Others may be met in the Reading and, if so, attention will be drawn to them.

Verbs of Group 1 : imperfectives

The conjugated tense is quite regular, and only the past tense has to be memorized:

"Inchoative" verbs describing the beginning of a *PROCESS*

See pages 245-6

вя́нуть   *to fade, wither. Past* **оно вя́ло** (*and* **вя́нуло**).
зя́бнуть *to shiver, be cold:* **я (о)зя́б.**
ли́пнуть *to stick to:* **оно (при)ли́пло.**
мёрзнуть *to freeze with cold:* **я (за)мёрз.**
пу́хнуть *to swell:* **он (о)пу́х.**
сле́пнуть *to become blind:* **я (о)слеп.**
со́хнуть *to get dry, become parched:* **оно(за)со́хло.**

Note: You see that some of these past tenses are only used with a prefix.

Verbs of Group 2 : all perfectives

All these verbs are quite regular, and the stress is nearly always fixed as in the infinitive:

дви́нуть *to move:* **дви́ну. дви́нул, -а, -о ; -и**
пры́гнуть *to jump:* **пры́гну. пры́гнул**

Note: This is a big and important group of verbs (300+) which present no special difficulties. They are mostly verbs of *sudden, momentary* or *quick action* and are therefore perfective by their meaning and nature. (The Group 1 verbs in this class are small in number but important.)   See pages 243-4 for fuller treatment.

CLASS III VERBS: This is the largest class of verbs, all of them with conjugated tense: **-ю, -ешь, -ет, -ем, -ете, -ют.**

We can conveniently divide them into two sub-classes consisting of *primary* and *secondary* verbs. Primaries have *no suffix* in either infinitive or conjugated tense; or only in the infinitive. Secondaries always have a suffix, and are derivative verbs from nouns or other verbs.

Class III primary verbs

Group 1 : These primaries have no suffix in either infinitive or conjugated tense. Example: **сметь** *to dare:* **я смѣю.**

Note: Some verbs in this group present slight difficulties which must be carefully noted. In **зна-ть** *to know* the **a** is not a suffix but part of the root. Take care with the verbs ending in **-ить** and **-ыть,** in which the conjugated tense is unusual. Note the following primaries:

бри-ть *to shave. Conjugated tense* **брѣ-ю, брѣ-ешь ; брѣ-ют.**

вы-ть *to howl:* **во́-ю, во́-ешь ; во́-ют.**

кры-ть *to cover:* **кро́-ю, кро́-ешь ; кро́-ют.**

мы-ть *to wash:* **мо́-ю, мо́-ешь ; мо́-ют.**

ры-ть *to dig, burrow:* **ро́-ю, ро́-ешь ; ро́-ют.**

би-ть *to beat, strike:* **бь-ю, бь-ёшь ; бьют.**

ви-ть *to twist, curl, wave:* **вью, вьёшь ; вьют.**

ли-ть *to pour, run:* **лью, льёшь ; льют.**

пи-ть *to drink:* **пью, пьёшь, пьёт ; пьют.**

ши-ть *to sew:* **шью, шьёшь ; шьют.**

And note the five verbs in **-оть** in the list below.

Group 2 : Primaries which in the infinitive only have suffix **-a-** (**-я-** after a vowel) or **-о-.** Example: **сѣ-я-ть.**

LIST OF USEFUL PRIMARY VERBS

Group 1 : No suffix in infinitive

ду-ть *to blow. Conjugated tense:* **я ду́-ю, ты ду́-ешь ; ду́ют.**

зна-ть *to know:* **знаю, знаешь.**

сме-ть *to dare:* **смѣю, смѣешь.**

Group 2: With suffix in infinitive

Five verbs in -о-ть
- бор-о́-ться   *to struggle, fight:* бор-ю́сь, бо́р-ешься; бо́р-ются
- кол-о́-ть   *to thrust, stab, prick:* кол-ю́, ко́л-ешь; ко́л-ют
- мол-о́-ть   *to mill, grind:* мел-ю́, ме́л-ешь; ме́л-ют
- пол-о́-ть   *to weed, hoe:* пол-ю́, по́л-ешь; по́л-ют
- пор-о́-ть   *to tear, rip:* пор-ю́, по́р-ешь; по́р-ют

дрем-а́-ть   *to doze:* дремл-ю́, дре́мл-ешь; дре́мл-ют
се́-я-ть   *to sow:* се́-ю, се́-ешь; се́-ют
ла́-я-ть   *to bark:* ла́-ю, ла́-ешь; ла́-ют
сме-я́-ться   *to laugh:* сме-ю́сь, сме-ёшься; сме-ю́тся
наде́-я-ться   *to hope:* наде́-юсь, наде́-ешься; наде́-ются

CLASS III VERBS contd: the secondaries (=derivatives): conjugated tense -ю, -ешь; -ет, -ем, -ете, -ют. In these verbs the infinitive *always* has a suffix.

A: Two groups in which infinitive and conjugated tense have the same suffix.

Group 1: Verbs derived from nouns or verbs. These have suffix -а- (-я-), or -ва-, or -ыва- (-ива-). Examples: де́л-а-ть, де́л-а-ю. ка́шл-я-ть: ка́шл-я-ю. (об)вин-я́-ть: (об)вин-я́-ю. пи́с-ыва-ть: -ыва-ю. ха́ж-ива-ть: ха́ж-ива-ю.

Group 2: Verbs derived from nouns. Suffix -е- (-а- after a hissing consonant). Example: богат-е́-ть: богате́ю. дорож-а́-ть: -а́ет.

B: The infinitive has suffix -ова- (-ева-) which is dropped in the conjugated tense, the latter taking suffix -ю- (-у-), from which there is a *first pers sing* in -ю-ю or -у́-ю.

Examples: рис-ова́ть: я рис-у́-ю. гор-ева́-ть: гор-ю́-ю, гор-ю́-ешь.

Note: There is a considerable number of verbs in **-и́ровать** of comparatively recent birth, many of them of foreign origin. Such verbs can be formed almost without limit (like those German verbs in *-ieren*). They will make their conjugated tense in **-у-ю.** Examples will be found below.

CLASS III: Useful secondary (=derivative) verbs

A: Groups 1 and 2 always with suffixes comprise regular verbs which present no special difficulties. Their prototype is the regular verb **де́лать** *to do, make:* де́лаю, де́лаешь, -ет ; -ют. And so:

ка́шлять   to cough: ка́шляю, ка́шляешь.
обвиня́ть   to accuse: обвиня́ю, обвиня́ешь.
быва́ть   to happen: быва́ю, -а́ешь, -ет. быва́ло.
пи́сывать   to write often: пи́сываю, -аешь.
ха́живать   to go often: ха́живаю, -аешь.

B: -ова-, -ева- verbs, conjugated tense suffix -у-ю:
бесе́д-ова-ть   to converse: бесе́д-у-ю, бесе́дуешь.
жа́ловать(ся)   to complain: жа́луюсь, жа́луешься.
же́ртвовать 1. to endow.   2. to sacrifice: же́ртвую, -уешь.
по́льзоваться   to make use of: по́льзуюсь, по́льзуешься.
пра́здновать   to celebrate: пра́здную, пра́зднуешь.
про́бовать   to try, attempt: про́бую, -уешь.
путеше́ствовать   to travel: путеше́ствую, -уешь.
пья́нствовать   to drink heavily: пья́нствую, -уешь.
ра́доваться   to rejoice: ра́дуюсь, ра́дуешься.
сле́довать   to follow: сле́дую, сле́дуешь.
сове́товать   to advise: сове́тую, -уешь.
существова́ть   to exist: существу́ю, -у́ешь.
тре́бовать   to demand from: тре́бую, -уешь.
торгова́ть   to trade: торгу́ю, -у́ешь.
хода́тайствовать   to take steps to: хода́тайствую, -уешь.

Note: These verbs nearly all have the stress of the word from which they derive, but more often in Class III B-verbs the stress follows that of the infinitive as in **рисова́ть, рису́ю. торгова́ть, торгу́ю.**

B verbs include seven simple verbs (of which Nos. 1, 4 and 5 are seldom required in speaking):

> **блев-а́-ть**   to vomit: блю-ю́, блю-ёшь.
> **жева́ть**   to chew; chew over: жую́, жуёшь.
> **клева́ть**   to peck, bite: клюю́, клюёшь.
> **кова́ть**   to shoe a horse: кую́, куёшь.
> **плева́ть**   to spit: плюю́, плюёшь.
> **снова́ть**   to scurry: сную́, снуёшь.
> **сова́ть**   to thrust, shove: сую́, суёшь.

CLASS IV VERBS: These have conjugated tense -ю, -ишь, -ит, -им, -ите, -ят.   Note that all verbs of the preceding three classes are what have been called "Conjugation

I" ("e") verbs for convenience in the earlier stage of learning. Now, in one class, all "Conjugation II" ("и") verbs are considered together. They comprise two important groups:

Group 1 : In these the suffix of the infinitive includes the "и" which is found in the inflexions:

Examples: **черн-и́-ть**   *to blacken, darken;* **черн-ю́, чер-**
           ни́шь ; -я́т.
      люби́ть   *to love:* **люблю́, лю́бишь.**
      говори́ть   *to speak:* **говорю́, -и́шь.**

Group 2 : In these the и of the inflexions appears only in the conjugated tense, and the infinitive has suffix **-e-** (**-a-** after a hissing consonant).   Examples are:

гляд-е́-ть   *to look at:* **гляж-у́, гляд-и́шь.**
гор-е́-ть   *to burn:* **гор-ю́, гор-и́шь.**
сид-е́-ть   *to be seated:* **сиж-у́, сид-и́шь.**
леж-а́-ть   *to be lying down:* **леж-у́, леж-и́шь.**
дрож-а́-ть   *to tremble:* **дрож-у́, дрож-и́шь.**
бо-я́-ть(-ся)   *to be afraid:* **я бо-ю́-сь, ты бо-и́шь-ся.**

CLASS IV: Other useful verbs

Group 1

спеш-и́-ть   to hurry, hasten: **спешу́, спеши́шь.**
буди́ть   to wake, awake: **бужу́, бу́дишь.**
спо́рить   to argue: **спо́рю, спо́ришь.**

Group 2 : verbs with suffix **-e-** in the infinitive

верт-е́-ть   to turn: **верч-у́, ве́рт-ишь.**
ви́деть   to see: **ви́жу, ви́дишь.**
греме́ть   to make noise: **гремлю́, греми́шь.**
оби́деть (*pf*)   to offend: **оби́жу, оби́дишь.**
смотре́ть   to look at: **смотрю́, смо́тришь.**
терпе́ть   to endure, suffer: **терплю́, те́рпишь.**

Suffix -a- in infinitive

слыш-а-ть   to hear: слыш-у, слыш-ишь.

держ-а́-ть   to hold, keep: держу́, де́ржишь.

дыша́ть   to breathe: дышу́, ды́шишь.

Note: You see that some of these verbs have the stress on the final syllable of *first pers sing* of the conjugated tense, but send it back to the syllable before that in the *second pers sing*. Such verbs retain the *second pers sing* stress throughout the tense. The commonest is **люби́ть** *to love*, in which also note the **л** in the *first pers sing* after **б**:

люби́ть : люблю́, лю́бишь, лю́бит, лю́бим, лю́бите, лю́бят.

The most distinctive feature of this class of verbs is in the mutations which occur, it must be noted, in *the first pers sing only*. These all occur in accordance with the Rules of Mutation, pages 165–7. In the preceding three classes of verbs it will be noted that the third person plural is always the same as the first person singular with the addition of the letter -т. In Class IV, however, this connection does not exist and it is the first person singular alone that appears to stand apart from the others.

STRESS IN VERBS

General rule: When the infinitive of any verb is stressed on a syllable other than the final one, this stress remains fixed throughout *all* forms of the verb. Thus, the stressed **ду́-** and **де́-** of **ду́мать** and **де́лать** must be retained throughout these verbs. This rule naturally excludes verbs of one syllable, and the reflexive particle **-ся**.

*

MOTORING: Vocabulary, road signs and useful phrases

Road signs

в одно́м направле́нии   one way only

Береги́сь по́езда!   Look out for trains! (=*level crossing*)

доро́га закры́та   road closed

доро́га откры́та   road open

желе́зная доро́га   railway

круто́й подъём   steep incline

мост   bridge

у́зкий мост   narrow bridge

Заме́длите!   Go slow!

обхо́д   detour

опа́сная крива́я   dangerous bend

Опа́сность!   Danger!

Осторо́жно!   Drive cautiously!

преде́льная скоро́сть 30 км. в час   Speed limit 30 km. per hour

перекрёсток   cross roads

ремо́нт доро́ги   road repairs

перехо́ды   pedestrian crossing

шко́ла   school

Не повора́чивать (а) напра́во, (б) нале́во   No turning (*a*) right, (*b*) left

Нет прое́зда   No passage

Vocabulary

автомоби́льная ста́нция service station for cars
бензи́н   petrol, gasoline
болт   bolt
винт   screw
вы́пуск   exhaust
га́йка   nut
гара́ж   garage
газоли́н   petrol, gasoline
грязево́й щит   mudguard
карбюра́тор   carburettor
ключ   wrench, spanner
колесо́   wheel
за́днее колесо́   back wheel
пере́днее колесо́   front wheel
колпа́к   hood
ко́ломазь (*f*)   grease
насо́с   pump

ма́сло   oil (thick)
маши́на   1. engine, 2. car, automobile (*coll*)
медпу́нкт   first aid post
огни́   lights
ось (*f*)   axle
остано́вка   stopping place
отвёртка   screwdriver
проко́л   puncture
радиа́тор   radiator
ремо́нт   repair
свеча́   sparking plug
то́рмоз   brake
шофёр   driver, chauffeur
ши́на   tube, tire
ка́мера   inner tube
щипцы́   pliers, pincers

Мой автомоби́ль слома́лся.   My car has broken down.
Укажи́те мне, где здесь гара́ж.   Show me the way to a garage.
Смени́те э́ту ши́ну (э́то колесо́).   Change this tire (wheel).
Нале́йте мне . . . литра(-ов) бензи́на.   I'd like . . . litres of petrol.
Напо́лните бензи́новый бак, пожа́луйста.   Please fill up the gas tank.
Да́йте мне два ли́тра мото́рного ма́сла.   Give me two litres of motor oil.
Напо́лните радиа́тор водо́й.   Fill up the radiator with water.
Э́то пло́хо функциони́рует.   This doesn't work (function) well.
   функциони́ровать   *to function*, -ую, -уешь ; -уют. *Note this useful verb:* it can be used for all kinds of "things that go wrong".
Ско́лько вы возьмёте?   How much do you charge?
Ско́лько сто́ит ремо́нт?   How much does the repair cost?
Когда́ э́то бу́дет гото́во?   When will it be ready?
Бу́дет ли гото́в автомоби́ль че́рез . . . часа́ (часо́в)?   Will the car be ready in . . . hours?
Я приду́ за маши́ной в . . . часа́ (часо́в).   I'll come for the car in . . . hours.

★

TO TEST YOUR KNOWLEDGE OF RUSSIAN

(1) Open the book at any page where there is either Practice in both languages, or Reading matter with translation. Take a passage of not less than about twenty lines of Russian and, without looking up words or at either the English or the

Notes, translate it into English. Then compare your effort
with the literal translation into English. Do not worry if
your rendering should differ from that of the text so long as
you have caught and rendered the meaning correctly.

(2) You may find this more difficult. Try to render the
literal English translation of some of the easier passages back
into Russian. In Part I you should persist until you can get
your rendering absolutely correct. But you need not expect
to be able to do so in Part II, except perhaps in the Conversations.

Meals in the Soviet Union

(1) *Breakfast* = **за́втрак,** unless it is a continental breakfast, in which
case it is **у́тренний ко́фе (и́ли чай).**

(2) *Lunch* = **обе́д,** if one has already had **за́втрак.** But if it is a very
light lunch it is **за́втрак.**

(3) The *early evening meal* is **у́жин** if one has had **обе́д,** otherwise it
is **обе́д.**

(4) The *late evening meal* is always **у́жин.**

Tea or coffee or soft drinks with pastry or cakes may be obtained in
restaurants, and also **заку́ски,** which are snacks like *hors d'oeuvres* but
often heavier and more substantial. One can make a meal of **заку́ски,**
often delicious and always satisfying to English and American palates.

VI. RESTAURANT: **РЕСТОРА́Н**

Useful words and phrases: eating and drinking

Where is there a (good) restaurant? **Где (хоро́ший) рестора́н?**
Have you a table for . . . ? **Име́ется ли стол на . . .**
Where is the cloak-room? **Где гардеро́б?**
Here is your cloak-room ticket. **Вот ваш номеро́к.**
Where can I wash my hands? **Где я могу́ вы́мыть ру́ки?**
Where is the lavatory? **Где убо́рная?**
Is this place vacant (free)? **Здесь свобо́дно?**
This (small) table is reserved. **Э́тот сто́лик за́нят.**
Please give me the menu. **Да́йте, пожа́луйста, меню́.**
I should like . . . **Я хоте́л бы . . .**
We should like . . . **Мы хоте́ли бы .. .**
What can you recommend? **Что вы сове́туете?**
What is to-day's special dish? **Како́е сего́дня специа́льное блю́до?**
Have you *table d'hôte* lunch? (dinner? supper?) **Есть ли у вас
табльдо́т за́втрак? (обе́д? у́жин?)**

I would prefer . . .   Я предпочёл бы . . .

Give me a portion of . . .   Дайте мне одну́ по́рцию . . .

Give us two portions of . . .   Дайте нам две по́рции . . .

Bring me (us) . . .   Принеси́те мне (нам) . . .

We should like to have morning coffee.   У́тренний ко́фе, пожалу́йста.

The wine list, please.   Дайте, пожа́луйста, ка́рточку вин.

A bottle of wine, please, number . . .   Буты́лку вина́, пожа́луйста : но́мер . . .

A half bottle of wine . . .   полбуты́лки вина́.

I don't like this wine.   Мне не нра́вится э́то вино́.

I like this local* wine.   Мне нра́вится э́то ме́стное вино́.

A bottle of light (dark) beer.   Буты́лка све́тлого (тёмного) пива́.

May I have some more?   Дайте ещё, пожа́луйста.

The bill, please.   Пода́йте, пожа́луйста, счёт.

This is not correct.   Э́то не то́чно.

Please ask the head waiter to come.   Мо́жно мне поговори́ть с метрдоте́лем.

пережа́рено	overdone	недоста́точно	not enough
солёное	salt	за́нято	reserved
жёстко	(it is) tough	свобо́дно	free
сыро́е	raw	сто́лик	small table

*Georgian wine = грузи́нское вино́

THE NEXT STEPS

In *Russian for Beginners* you have, for most practical purposes, a useful general treatment of grammar and, unless you wish to become an expert translator, you should not require much more. For those who wish to pursue their studies of Russian grammer and syntax, there are two first-rate books:

RUSSIAN GRAMMAR.   By B. O. Unbegaun.   (Oxford University Press, 1959.)

RUSSIAN SYNTAX.   Aspects of Modern Russian Syntax and Vocabulary.   By F. M. Borras and R. F. Christian. (Also Oxford University Press, 1959.)

For the rest, the next step for *all* learners must be to consolidate and expand upon both the grammar and vocabulary learnt in *Russian for Beginners*. This is best done by reading Russian, and the reading should be in three phases:

I. The first phase is by using simplified and annotated Readers—of Russian classical literature.   Two authors can be recommended:

(1) Tolstoy: *Fables, Tales and Stories, including A Captive in the Caucasus,* with Notes and Vocabulary by E. Vladimirsky and V. Zaitsev (published by Foreign Languages Publishing House, Moscow, 1960).

(2) Pushkin: *The Captain's Daughter* (**Капитанская дочка**). Edited with Introduction, Notes and Vocabulary by Anna H. Semeonoff (published by Dent & Sons Ltd., London).

II. The second phase should be to read a Russian text with the aid of a dictionary.   The following can be recommended:

Толстой: Детство, отрочество, юность (Ленинград, 1960).

Пушкин: Повести покойного Ивана Петровича Белкина.

А. Ф. Конопелкин: Хрестоматия по русскому языку. 575 pp. illus. (Moscow University). A 1962 sourcebook which contains selected passages (graded) from Soviet authors, short stories, humorous pieces, folk tales, proverbs and 200 pages of nineteenth-century writers and some verse extracts.   Excellent.

Translations of some short works are available.   You may in this phase also venture into something more difficult and longer.   Here are suggestions:

Толстой: Анна Каренина.
Гончаров: Обломов (Москва, 1958).
Лесков: Рассказы (Москва, 1958).
Тургенев: Отцы и дети.
Чехов: Собрание юмористических рассказов (*A Selection of Humorous Stories. Annotated*). Edited by Bondar.   (Pitman, London.)

III. Not until you have read some of the books recommended above should you attempt Gogol's *Dead Souls*, which is not an easy book; or *anything* by Dostoyevsky. Both authors are often the despair of translators! You should consider this third phase of reading for Soviet authors. These are often difficult because they contain references and associations relating to the modern background which, unless you know it, may be lost on you. Nevertheless, in spite of these and some lexical and other difficulties, you must not neglect contemporary writing. You should certainly try:

(1) **Михаил Шо́лохов: Тихий Дон. Роман в четырёх книгах.**
(2) **Алексей Толсто́й: Хожде́ние по му́кам.**
(3) **Илья Ильф и Евгений Петро́в: Двена́дцать сту́льев.**

This delightful (comic) novel by Ilf and Petrov, very popular writers in the USSR, is not always easy reading; but it has a strong appeal. There is a translation (*The Twelve Chairs*) by John H. C. Richardson (Random House, New York).

There are translations of Sholokhov's "*Quiet Don*" in four volumes in English, but for your purpose the best is that issued by the Foreign Languages Publishing House, Moscow, under the title first used in Britain and USA: *And quiet flows the Don*. This is a magnificent novel, probably the best published in Russia since 1917. The same House issues a translation of Alexei Tolstoy's epic in three volumes with the title *Ordeal*. Tolstoy is easier reading for the foreign student than Sholokhov.

DICTIONARIES

You will require at least a Russian-English dictionary, but it is advisable to have also an English-Russian one. The following can be recommended:

SMIRNITSKY: RUSSIAN-ENGLISH DICTIONARY.
50,000 words approx.   State Publishing House of Foreign
Languages, Moscow, 1959.   A very useful dictionary,
especially for new words.
AKHMANOVA: **Русско-английский   словарь.**
20,000 words.
AKHMANOVA: **Англо-русский словарь.**   25,000
words.

IN CONCLUSION

If you have steadfastly worked through *Russian for Beginners* you must not allow the knowledge so acquired to slip
away. The best *first* way to retain it is by reading, by reading
good books for preference, but by continuing to read almost
anything in Russian.   There are many quite entertaining
ways of doing this: by reading Russian translations of English or American novels, for example.   You can read *David
Copperfield* by Dickens, and his *Pickwick Papers*.   And O.
Henry's *Stories*; and works by Jack London.

Меры предосторожности.
Рисунок Э. Змойро.

APPENDIX

I. Indeclinable nouns: List.
II. Masculine nouns ending in soft sign: List.
III. Geographical names, adjectives and nationalities: List.
IV. Summary of genitive plural endings of nouns.

WORD LISTS FOR REFERENCE

I. INDECLINABLE NOUNS

There are dozens of these in Russian, many in common use. Nouns ending in -и (not -й!), -у/-ю are indeclinable. Of these note:

ви́ски whisky
де́нди dandy
интервью́ interview
ле́ди lady
меню́ menu
ню nude
парвеню́ parvenu

Пе́ру Peru
по́ни pony
ре́гби rugby
такси́ taxi
табу́ taboo
Чи́ли Chile
я́нки Yankee

And in -o, -e:

атташе́ attache
бордо́ Bordeaux (wine)
бюро́ bureau
кафе́ café
кабаре́ cabaret
кино́ cinema
ко́фе (*m*) coffee
импреса́рио impresario

пальто́ overcoat
ра́дио radio
мада́м madame
мадемуазе́ль mademoiselle
ми́ссис Mrs
мисс Miss
фиа́ско fiasco
шимпанзе́ chimpanzee

Note that these words are derived from other languages.

II. MASCULINE NOUNS ENDING IN -Ь

Months: янва́рь, февра́ль, апре́ль, ию́нь, ию́ль, сентя́брь, октя́брь, ноя́брь, дека́брь.
Male first names: И́горь, etc.

Note: If the noun represents an animate and is obviously masculine—изда́тель *publisher*—it will not be included.

Nouns marked * are in fairly common use, and should be memorized. The others are given for reference.

*автомоби́ль automobile
ве́ксель bill of exchange
вихрь whirlwind
*го́лубь pigeon
*гусь goose
*дви́гатель engine
дёготь tar, pitch
*день day
*дождь rain

*ло́коть elbow
ломо́ть chunk, slice
монасты́рь monastery
но́готь nail (finger, toe)
ноль, *нуль nought, zero
о́кунь perch (fish)
па́сквиль libel, lampoon
патру́ль patrol
пень stump

жёлудь acorn
*измери́тель measure
имби́рь ginger
инвента́рь inventory
*карто́фель potato(es)
ки́тель tunic
ко́готь talon, claw
ко́зырь trump
*контро́ль inspection
*кора́бль ship
*ко́рень root
косты́ль crutch(es)
креме́нь flint
*Кремль Kremlin
*ла́герь camp
*ларь bin, chest
ле́бедь swan
ли́вень heavy rain

*по́лдень noon
*путь path, way, track (gen пути́, ins путём, pl -и́)
реве́нь rhubarb
*рубль rouble
*слова́рь vocabulary, diction-ary
*тунне́ль tunnel
тюле́нь seal, sea-calf
*у́голь coal
фити́ль wick
*фона́рь lantern
хруста́ль crystal
ци́ркуль compasses
щаве́ль sorrel
*я́корь anchor
я́сень ash-tree
*ячме́нь barley

Declension: In the singular, *masc* nouns in -ь differ from feminines in -ь:

	nom	gen	dat	acc	ins	prp
Sing: Masc dec:	-ь	-я	-ю	nom or gen	-ем	-е
Fem dec:	-ь	-и	-и	-ь	-ью	-и

III. LIST OF GEOGRAPHICAL NAMES, ADJECTIVES AND NATIONALITIES

I. Continents

Австра́лия Australia — австрали́йский Australian — австрали́ец an Australian
Аме́рика America — америка́нский American — америка́нец an American (*m*)
А́зия Asia — азиа́тский Asiatic — азиа́т an Asiatic (*m*)
А́фрика Africa — африка́нский African — африка́нец an African (*m*)
Евро́па Europe — европе́йский European — европе́ец a European (*m*)

II. Countries

А́встрия Austria — австри́йский Austrian — австри́ец an Austrian
А́нглия England — англи́йский English — англича́нин an Englishman
Бе́льгия Belgium — бельги́йский Belgian — бельги́ец a Belgian
Болга́рия Bulgaria — болга́рский Bulgarian — болга́рин a Bulgarian
Брази́лия Brazil — брази́льский Brazilian — бразилья́нец a Brazilian
Великобрита́ния Great Britain — великобрита́нский British — великобрита́нец a Briton
Ве́нгрия Hungary — венге́рский Hungarian — венге́рец a Hungarian
Герма́ния Germany — неме́цкий German — не́мец a German

Голла́ндия Holland	**голла́ндский** Dutch	**голла́ндец** a Dutchman
Гре́ция Greece	**гре́ческий** Greek	**грек** a Greek
Да́ния Denmark	**да́тский** Danish	**датча́нин** a Dane
Еги́пет Egypt	**еги́петский** Egyptian	**египтя́нин** ап Egyptian
Ира́н Iran, Persia	**ира́нский** Iranian, **перси́дский** Persian	**ира́нец** an Iranian, a Persian
Ирла́ндия Ireland	**ирла́ндский** Irish	**ирла́ндец** an Irishman
Испа́ния Spain	**испа́нский** Spanish	**испа́нец** a Spaniard
Ита́лия Italy	**италья́нский** Italian	**италья́нец** an Italian
Кана́да Canada	**кана́дский** Canadian	**кана́дец** a Canadian
Кита́й China	**кита́йский** Chinese	**кита́ец** a Chinese
Ме́ксика Mexico	**мексика́нский** Mexican	**мексика́нец** a Mexican
Норве́гия Norway	**норве́жский** Norwegian	**норве́жец** a Norwegian
По́льша Poland	**по́льский** Polish	**поля́к** a Pole
Португа́лия Portugal	**португа́льский** Portuguese	**португа́лец** a Portuguese
Росси́я Russia	**ру́сский** Russian	**ру́сский** a Russian
Румы́ния Roumania	**румы́нский** Roumanian	**румы́н** a Roumanian
Финля́ндия Finland	**фи́нский** Finnish	**финля́ндец, финн** a Finn
Фра́нция France	**фрапцу́зский** French	**францу́з** a Frenchman
Чехослова́кия Czecho-Slovakia	**чехослова́цкий** Czechoslovakian	**чех** Czech
Швейца́рия Switzerland	**швейца́рский** Swiss	**швейца́рец** a Swiss
Япо́ния Japan	**япо́нский** Japanese	**япо́нец** a Japanese

Сове́тский Сою́з: Soviet Union.

СССР = USSR: **Сою́з Сове́тских Социалисти́ческих Респу́блик.**
Union of Soviet Socialist Republics.

США = USA: **Соединённые Шта́ты Аме́рики.**
United States of America.

IV. SUMMARY OF GENITIVE PLURAL ENDINGS OF NOUNS

		Gen pl ending	*Examples*
1.	Masculine in hard consonant (except ж, ч, ш, щ)	-ов	студе́нт — студе́нтов
2.	Masculine in -ц	-о́в stressed -ев unstressed	купе́ц — купцо́в не́мец — не́мцев
3.	Masculine in -ж, -ч, -ш, -щ	-ей	каранда́ш — карандаше́й
4.	Masculine in -й	-ев	геро́й — геро́ев
5.	Masculine *sing* in -анин, *pl* in -ане	no ending	граждани́н — гра́ждан
6.	Masculine *sing* in -ёнок, *pl* in -ята	no ending	телёнок — теля́т
7.	Masculine and neuter *pl* in -ья	-е́й stressed -ьев unstressed	друг — друзья́ — друзе́й крыло́ — кры́лья — кры́льев
8.	Masculine and feminine in -ь	-ей	дождь (*m*) — дожде́й пло́щадь (*f*) — площаде́й
9.	Feminine in -а	no ending	кни́га — книг
10.	Feminine in -я	no ending, stem ending remains soft (-ь)	ня́ня — нянь земля́ — земе́ль
11.	Feminine in -ья́	-е́й	статья́ — стате́й
12.	Feminine in -ия	-ий	ли́ния — ли́ний
13.	Feminine in consonant +-ня	no ending, hard н soft н	пе́сня — пе́сен; ба́шня — ба́шен *but note three exceptions:* ба́рышня — ба́рышень дере́вня — дереве́нь ку́хня — ку́хонь
14.	Neuter in -о	no ending	де́ло — дел письмо́ — пи́сем
15.	Neuter in -ко	-ов no ending	о́блако — облако́в я́блоко — я́блок
16.	Neuter in -ще	no ending	учи́лище — учи́лищ
17.	Neuter in -ле, -ре	-ей	по́ле — поле́й мо́ре — море́й
18.	Neuter in -не (-ье unstressed)	-ий	зда́ние — зда́ний воскресе́нье — воскресе́ний
19.	Neuter in -ьё	-ей	ружьё — руже́й

Note: (1) That *gen pl* in -ей can never be preceded by -ь-. (2) That noun with *no ending* for *gen pl*, having a stem ending in two consonants, usually inserts fleeting **e** or **o** between the consonants.

VOCABULARY

РУССКО-АНГЛИЙСКИЙ СЛОВАРЬ

This Vocabulary is intended to be used for study as well as for reference. It contains not only words from the Lessons but very often words of the same family are added. The Vocabulary in these pages represents a very practical selection of "All-purposes" words, including those of everyday occurrence.

Verbs marked with an asterisk(*): These are of frequent occurrence; they deserve special attention and ought to be memorized for "active" use.

How to use the Vocabulary: When a word is looked up, note all the phrases or idioms given with it and memorize them. Note also any words of the same family which may be near to it in the list and memorize as many as possible. In this way the vocabulary learnt with the Lessons can be greatly extended: such words will be required as "reading" vocabulary and, with their meanings, should be recognizable for this purpose. Many words have a reference to a page on which some further explanation will be found.

The Vocabulary does *not* contain all such words of permanent utility as numerals (cardinals and ordinals), nor any but a few common geographical names and nationalities, nor all forms of pronouns, nor the days of the week, months of the year, nor many words dealing with Eating and Drinking. Some of these become known at an early stage; others will be found grouped together in the Lessons or in the Appendixes, for which see Table of Contents.

This Vocabulary consists of about 4000 words. With the words omitted here (for reasons given above) the total vocabulary in the book is of approximately 5000 words.

A

а and, but, whereas
а то or else
абсолю́тный absolute
абстра́ктный abstract
а́вгуст August
авиапо́чта air mail
  авиапо́чтой by air mail
аво́сь perhaps
авто́бус bus, omnibus
авто́бусный (*adj*) bus
авто́граф autograph
автомати́ческая ру́чка fountain pen
автомоби́ль (*m*) motor car
ага́, aha!
а́дрес address
адреса́т addressee
адресова́ть (I) to address (*letter*)
акаде́мия academy
акваре́ль (*f*) water colour
аккредити́в letter of credit
акт act, deed
актёр actor
актри́са actress
аку́ла shark
акце́нт accent
алло́, hello! (*telephone*)
алкого́ль (*m*) alcohol
алкого́льный alcoholic
алфави́т alphabet
америка́нец (*m*) an American
америка́нка American woman
америка́нский (*adj*) American
ампи́р empire (*stylistic*)
амфитеа́тр amphitheatre
англи́йский (*adj*) English
англича́нин Englishman; *see* p. 151
англича́нка Englishwoman
А́нглия England
анекдо́т anecdote
анке́та questionnaire (*form*)
анса́мбль (*m*) ensemble
антра́кт interval (*theatre*)
апельси́н orange
аппендици́т appendicitis
апте́ка chemist's (shop)
апте́карь (*m*) chemist
арбу́з water melon
А́рктика the Arctic
аркти́ческий (*adj*) Arctic
а́рмия army
арома́тный aromatic
арсена́л arsenal
артезиа́нский artesian
арти́ст artiste
архитекту́ра architecture
аспири́н aspirin
атташе́ attaché
А́фрика Africa
а́хать (I)/*pf* **а́хнуть** (I) to exclaim "ah"; *see* p. 242
аэродро́м aerodrome
аэропла́н aeroplane
аэропо́рт air port
Аэрофло́т Aeroflot (*Soviet Air Line*)

Б

ба́бушка grandmother
бага́ж luggage
бакале́йный магази́н grocer's (shop)
бакале́я groceries
балери́на ballerina
бале́т ballet
балко́н balcony
банк bank
ба́нковый (*adj*) bank
бара́н ram
бара́нина mutton
баро́кко baroque
ба́рышня young lady, "Miss"
бассе́йн basin, swimming pool
ба́тюшка dear father
ба́шня tower
*****бе́гать** (I) to run (about); *see* p. 309
  бе́гая running (about)
бегу́щий running
беда́ misfortune
бе́ден, бедна́, -о ; -ы poor
бедне́йший poorest, very poor
беднова́тый rather poor
  беднова́то rather poorly
бе́дность (*f*) poverty
бе́дный poor
бе́дствие disaster, calamity
*****бежа́ть** (*irr see* p. 85, 309) to run
без + gen without
безвре́дный harmless
безграни́чный boundless, infinite
безопа́сность (*f*) safety, security
безопа́сный safe, secure
безу́мие madness, folly
безу́мный mad, crazy

безу́мство *see* безу́мие
бе́лка squirrel
беллетри́стика fiction
бе́лый white
бельэта́ж ("*bel étage*") dress circle, grand tier (*theatre*)
бензи́н petrol
бенуа́р ("*baignoire*"), lowest tier of boxes, below "*bel etage*" (*theatre*)
бе́рег (*pl* берега́) shore, coast, bank
береги́сь! look out!
бере́чь (I) to take care of, to guard; *see* p. 302
бес demon, devil (of possession)
бесе́довать (I) to talk, chat; *see* p. 307
бесподо́бный incomparable
беспоко́ить (II)/по- to worry
беспоко́йный restless
беспо́мощный helpless
беспреры́вный uninterrupted
беспреста́нный incessant
бессо́нница insomnia
беста́ктный tactless
библиоте́ка library
библиоте́карь (*m*) librarian
биле́т ticket
биле́тная ка́сса booking office
бино́кль (*m*) binoculars, opera glass
би́тва battle
*би́ть (I) to beat, break, strike; *see* p. 305
бишь *exclamation expressing impatience*: "now"
*благодари́ть (*pf* II) to thank
благодаря́ + *dat* thanks to
благоро́дие nobility (*title*)
благоро́дный noble, generous
благоро́дство nobility, generosity
блаже́нный blissful, beatific
бланк form (*for filling in*)
блева́ть (I) to vomit, spew; *see* p. 307
бле́дность (*f*) pallor
бле́дный pale
ближа́йший nearest, very near
бли́же nearer
близ + *gen* near
бли́зкий near, nearby
бли́зко near
близне́ц twin, *pl* близнецы́
бли́зок, близка́, -о ; -и near
бли́зость (*f*) proximity

блокно́т writing pad
блю́до dish, course (*of meal*)
Бог God
богате́йший very rich, richest
богате́ть (I) to get rich, *see* p. 306 *Group 2*
бога́тство riches
бога́тый rich
бога́че richer
бое́ц (*gen* бойца́) fighter, warrior
Бо́жий (*like* тре́тий) God's
бой battle, fighting
бо́йкий lively, vigorous
бок (*pl* бока́) side
бока́л goblet
бо́лее more
  бо́лее и́ли ме́нее more or less
  бо́лее того́ moreover
  тем бо́лее all the more
  тем бо́лее, что especially as
  не бо́лее не ме́нее как actually
боле́знь (*f*) illness, disease
бо́лен, больна́, -о́ ; -ы́ sick, ill
боле́ть (I) to be sick (habitually)
боле́ть (II) to hurt, ache; *see* p. 140
болт bolt
боль (*f*) pain
больни́ца hospital
бо́льно (it is) painful, it hurts
больно́й (*adj*) sick, ill
больно́й (*noun*) invalid
бо́льше bigger, larger, more
бо́льший larger (*attributive*)
большинство́ majority
большо́й big, large
бордо́ claret, "Bordeaux" wine
борода́ beard
*боро́ться (I) to fight, struggle, wrestle; *see* p. 306
борт board (of ship)
  на борту́ on board
  за бо́ртом overboard
борщ beet soup
ботани́ческий сад botanical gardens
боти́нок (*pl.* боти́нки) shoe
бо́чка barrel
бочо́нок small barrel, cask
боя́ться (II) to be afraid of, fear; *see* p. 308
брак marriage, matrimony
брак spoilage, waste
брани́ть (II) to scold, swear at; *see* p. 189

брат brother (*pl.* **бра́тья**; *see* p. 131)

бра́тец (*dim*) dear little brother

бра́тский brotherly, fraternal

бра́тство brotherhood, fraternity

*__брать__ (I) to take; *see* p. 302

   брать на себя́ to assume

бра́ться to undertake

брести́ (I) to wander, roam; *see* p. 179

бри́тва razor

   безопа́сная бри́тва safety razor

бри́твенное мы́ло shaving soap

бри́твенные принадле́жности shaving things, kit

*__брить__ (I) to shave (*tr*); *see* p. 305

*__бри́ться__ to shave (*intr*); *see* p. 305

бритьё shaving (*noun*)

*__броди́ть__ (II) to wander, roam; *see* p. 179

броненосец battleship (iron-clad)

бро́нза bronze

брони́рова́ть (I)/за- to book (*seats*)

*__броса́ть__ (I) to throw

броса́ться to throw oneself

*__бро́сить(ся)__ *pf* of **броса́ть(ся)**

брю́ки trousers

брю́хо belly

бу́дет! (*exclamation*) enough!

буди́ть (II) to wake (*tr*); *see* p. 278

бу́дто as if

бу́дучи (*v adv*) being

бу́дущее the future

бу́дущий future

   в бу́дущем году́ next year

   на бу́дущей неде́ле next week

бу́дущность (*f*) the future

бу́ква letter (*of alphabet*)

буква́рь (*m*) ABC (*book*)

букини́ст secondhand bookseller

бу́лка loaf, roll, bun

бу́лочка (small) roll

бу́лочная bakery, baker's

булы́жник cobble stone

бульо́н bouillon, broth, stock

бума́га paper

бума́жка piece of paper, note (*paper money*)

бума́жный (*adj*) paper

бума́жные де́ньги paper money

бура́н snow storm

бури́ть (II) to bore, drill

бутербро́д sandwich

буты́лка bottle

буфе́т buffet, refreshment room

бы (б) *particle used with past tense to indicate cond/sub*: pp. 120–1

*__быва́ло__ used to (be)

*__быва́ть__ (I) to happen, to visit

бы́ло *particle indicating act not completed or abandoned*

быстре́е quicker, faster

бы́стро quickly

бы́стрый quick, fast

*__быть__ to be (*irr* pp. 50, 75, 158)

бюро́ bureau, office

бюро́ обслу́живания service bureau

бюст bust (*sculpture*)

В

в (во) + *acc* to, into (*motion*) + *prp* in, at (*place where*)

в чём де́ло? what's the matter?

ваго́н carriage, tram car

ва́жно (*adv*) (it is) important, with an air of importance

ва́жность (*f*) importance

ва́жный important

валю́та currency

валя́й! (*from* **валя́ть**) go ahead!

ва́нна bath

   приня́ть ва́нну to have a bath

ва́нная (**ко́мната**) bathroom

варёный boiled

варе́нье jam, preserve

ва́та cotton wool, wadding

ваш, -а, -е ; -и your, yours

вверх upwards (*motion*)

вверху́ on top (*place where*)

ввиду́ + *gen* in view of

вдвойне́ doubly

вдоба́вок in addition

вдова́ widow

вдове́ц widower

вдоль + *gen* along

вдруг suddenly

ве́дать (I) to know

ведь after all

везде́ everywhere

вездесу́щий omnipresent, ubiquitous

*везти́ (I) to convey by vehicle; see вози́ть p. 174

век age, century, lifetime

ве́ксель (m) bill of exchange, bankdraft

веле́ть (II) to order, command; see p. 308

вели́кий great

венча́ть (I) to crown

венча́ться/по- to be married in church

ве́ра faith, belief

*ве́рить (II) (+dat) to believe

верну́ть (I) to return (tr)

*верну́ться to return (intr)

верёвка string, cord

вероя́тно probably

вероя́тный probable

*верте́ть (II) to turn (tr) twirl

*верте́ться to revolve; to fidget about

верх top, summit

ве́рхний (adj) upper, top

верхо́м on horseback

  е́здить верхо́м to ride on horseback

верши́на summit

веселе́е more merrily

весели́ться (II) to make merry

ве́село (adv) merrily, (it is) merry

весёлый merry, gay

весе́нний (adj) spring

ве́сить (II) to weigh (intr)

весло́ (pl вёсла) oar

весна́ Spring

  весно́й in Spring

*вести́ (I) to lead, conduct (on foot); see води́ть

  вести́ войну́ to wage war

  вести́ себя́ to conduct oneself, behave

весь, вся, всё; все all whole; see p. 100

ветвра́ч vet, veterinary surgeon

ве́тер (gen ве́тра) wind. p. 152

ветерина́р veterinary surgeon

ветерина́рный veterinary

ветеро́к breeze

ве́тка branch, twig

ве́трено (it is) windy

ве́тхий old, ramshackle

ветчина́ ham

ве́чер evening

ве́чером in the evening

вече́рний (adj) evening

ве́чный eternal, everlasting

вещь (f) thing

ве́ять (I) to waft, blow (intr)

взве́сить (II) pf of взве́шивать

взве́шивать (I) to weigh (tr)

вздох a sigh

*вздохну́ть (I) pf of вздыха́ть

взду́мать (I) to take it into one's head

*вздыха́ть (I) to sigh. p. 243

взойти́ (I) pf of всходи́ть

*взять (I) pf of брать to take

  взять себя́ в ру́ки to take oneself in hand, pull oneself together. See pp. 196, 225

*взя́ться pf of бра́ться

вид view, aspect, appearance

*ви́деть (II) to see; see p.308

ви́деться to see one another. meet

ви́димый visible

ви́дя seeing

визг squeal, yelp

ви́лка fork

вино́ wine

винова́т! sorry; guilty

винова́тый blameworthy, at fault, guilty

виногра́д grapes

винт screw

*висе́ть (II) to hang (intr)

ви́ски whiskey

вить (I) to twist; see p. 305

вихрь (m) whirlwind

включа́ть (I) to include

включа́я including

включе́ние inclusion

включи́ть (II) pf of включа́ть

вкра́тце in brief

владе́лец owner

*владе́ть (I) to own, possess

власть (f) power, authority, rule

вле́во to the left

влечь (I) to draw on, involve; see p. 302

влия́ние influence

влия́тельный influential

вме́сто+gen instead of

вне+gen outside (of)

  вне себя́ beside oneself

вне́шний external

вниз downwards

  вниз по ле́стнице downstairs (motion)

внизу́ below, downstairs (*place where*)
внима́ние attention
внима́тельный attentive
вновь anew, again
вну́тренняя inner tube (*tyre*)
внутри́ inside, within
вода́ water
*води́ть (II) to lead, conduct (*on foot*) See p. 174
во́дка vodka
водолече́ние hydropathic cure
вое́нный (*adj*) military, war
*возвраща́ться (I) to return (*intr*)
возгорди́ться (II) to become proud of, *pf* of горди́ться
возде́йствие influence
возде́йствовать (I) to influence
во́здух air
возду́шный (*adj*) air
*вози́ть (II) to convey (*by vehicle*), -ся ; see p. 174
во́зле + *gen* near, beside
*возника́ть (I) to arise, come about
возникнове́ние origin, beginning
*возни́кнуть (I) *pf* of возника́ть
возража́ть (I) to object, answer back
возраже́ние objection
возрази́ть (II) *pf* of возража́ть
вой wail, wailing
война́ war
войти́ *pf* of входи́ть
вокза́л main railway station
вокру́г + *gen* around
ВОКС = Всесою́зное о́бщество культу́рной свя́зи с заграни́цей = All-Union Society for Cultural Relations with Foreign Countries
вол ox
Во́лга Volga
волк wolf
волна́ wave (*no*)
во́лос a hair
во́лосы hairs (*of head*)
во́лчий wolf's
волчо́нок wolf cub
вон! Get out! Away!
вообража́ть (I)/-зи́ть (II) to imagine

13*

воображе́ние imagination
вообще́ in general
вооружённый armed
во-пе́рвых firstly
вопль (*m*) cry, wail, howl
вопреки́ + *dat* in spite of
вопро́с question; problem
воро́та (*pl*) gate (*gen* воро́т)
во́семь eight; see p. 185
воскресе́нье Sunday. p.151 [19]
воспита́нник (*m*) ward
воспита́нница (*f*) ward
воспрети́ть *pf* of воспреща́ть
воспреща́ть (I) to forbid
воспреща́ться to be forbidden
кури́ть воспреща́ется no smoking
воспреще́ние prohibition
восто́к east
Да́льний Восто́к Far East
Бли́жний Восто́к Near East
Сре́дний Восто́к Middle East
восто́чный eastern, oriental
востре́бование claiming
до востре́бования "poste restante"
во́сьмеро eight of; see p. 203
восьмо́й eighth
вот here
вот он! here he is!
вот хорошо́! that's good!
вот как? is that so?
вошь (*m*) (*gen* вши) louse
воя́ж voyage
впада́ть (I)/впасть (I) to fall, run into
впа́дина depression, hollow
впервы́е for the first time
впереди́ in front, ahead
впечатле́ние impression
вписа́ть (I) *pf* of впи́сывать
впи́сывать (I) to enter (*writing*)
вполне́ fully
впра́во to the right
впро́чем however, but
впуска́ть (I) to let in, admit
впусти́ть (II) *pf* of впуска́ть
враг enemy
*врать (I) to tell lies; see p. 302
врач doctor (*medical*)
вре́дно (it is) harmful, harmfully
вре́дный harmful
вре́менно temporarily
вре́менный temporary

вре́мя (*n*) time; *see* p. 126
вро́де+*gen* like, similar to
все (*see* весь) everyone, all
всё (*see* весь) everything
  всё вре́мя all the time
  всё равно́ it's all the same
  всё-таки and yet
всегда́ always
вселе́нная the universe
вска́кивать (I) to jump up
вско́ре soon, shortly
*вскочи́ть (II) *pf* of вска́кивать
вслед+*dat* after, following
  вслед за+*ins* after, following
всле́дствие+*gen* owing to
всмя́тку (*adv*) soft-boiled
*вспомина́ть (I) to remember, recall
*вспо́мнить (II) *pf* of вспомина́ть
*встава́ть (I) to get up: p. 232
вставны́е зу́бы false teeth
*встать (I) *pf* of встава́ть: p. 232
*встре́тить(ся) *pf* of встреча́ть(ся)
встре́ча a meeting
встреча́ть (I) to meet (*tr*)
*встреча́ться с+*ins* to meet
встре́чный coming from opposite direction
*всходи́ть (II) to ascend, mount
всю́ду everywhere
вся (*f*) (*see* весь) all, whole
вся́кий any, every, anyone, everyone
второ́й second
ВУЗ=вы́сшее уче́бное заведе́ние university, college
вход entrance
входи́ть (II) to go in, come in
вчера́ yesterday
вчера́шний yesterday's
вчерне́ in the rough
въезд drive, carriage entrance
въезжа́ть (I) to drive in
въе́хать (I) *pf* of въезжа́ть
вы (*pl*) you
вы- *prefix expressing* "out of", always stressed in *pf*
*выбира́ть (I) to choose, select
*вы́брать (I) *pf* of выбира́ть
*вы́вести (I) *pf* of выводи́ть
вы́вод conclusion, deduction
выводи́ть (II) to lead out

*вы́глядеть (II) to appear
выгля́дывать (I) to look, peep out
*вы́глянуть (I) *pf* of выгля́дывать
*выдава́ть (I) to give out, distribute, to betray
*вы́дать (*see* дать) *pf* of выдава́ть
*выезжа́ть (I) to drive out
*вы́ехать (I) *pf* of выезжа́ть
выздоровле́ние convalescence
*вы́звать (I) *pf* of вызыва́ть
*вызыва́ть (I) to call out, summon
*вы́йти (I) *pf* of выходи́ть
выкла́дывать (I) to lay out
вы́куп ransom
выкупа́ть (I) to ransom
вы́купить (II) *pf* of выкупа́ть
вы́лет flight, take off
вылета́ть (I) to fly out, take off
вы́лететь (II) *pf* of вылета́ть
вы́ложить (II) *pf* of выкла́дывать
вынима́ть (I) to take out, extract. *See* p. 224
*вы́нуть (I) *pf* of вынима́ть
выпива́ть *ipf* of вы́пить (I)
*вы́пить (I) *pf* of пить to drink up
*вы́писать (I) *pf* of выпи́сывать
*выпи́сывать (I) to write out, to order, to subscribe to (*a periodical*)
выполза́ть (I) to crawl out
вы́ползти (I) *pf* of выполза́ть
вы́пуск output, issue
*выраста́ть (I) to grow up: p. 222
*вы́расти (I) *pf* of выраста́ть
*вы́рвать (I) *pf* of вырыва́ть
*вырыва́ть (I) to tear out
вы́ситься (II) to tower up
*вы́сказать(ся) (I) *pf* of выска́зывать(ся)
выска́зывание opinion, saying
*выска́зывать(ся) (I) to express an opinion
высо́кий high, tall
высота́ height
высо́тное зда́ние multi-storied building
*вы́сохнуть (I) *pf* of со́хнуть and высыха́ть
высоча́йший supreme
вы́ставка exhibition

вы́стрел a shot
*выступа́ть (I) to come forward, to make a speech, to perform
*вы́ступить (II) pf of выступа́ть
выступле́ние speech, performance
вы́сший higher, highest, supreme
высыха́ть (I) to dry (intr)
выть (I) to howl; see p. 305
вытя́гивать (I) to stretch out
*вы́тянуть (I) pf of вытя́гивать
вы́ход exit
*выходи́ть (II) to go out, emerge
　выходи́ть из себя́ to lose one's temper
выходно́й день day off
вы́ше higher
　вы́ше нуля́ above zero
вы́сший higher
*вы́яснить (II) pf of выясня́ть
*выясня́ть (I) to clarify, elucidate
вяза́ть (I)/с- to bind, knit
вя́нуть (I) to wither; see pp. 242-3, 304

Г

газе́та newspaper
газе́тный кио́ск newspaper kiosk
газиро́ванный aerated
газоли́н gasoline, petrol
га́йка (metal) nut
галантере́йный магази́н draper's, haberdashery
галере́я gallery
галёрка gallery (theatre), "gods"
гало́ши galoshes
гара́ж garage
гардеро́б cloak-room, wardrobe
гарнизо́н garrison
га́снуть (I)/по- to be extinguished
гастроно́м delicatessen shop
гастрономи́ческий магази́н delicatessen shop
где where
　где-то somewhere

генера́л (a) general
гео́граф geographer
геогра́фия geography
геро́й hero
ги́бнуть (I)/по- to perish; see p. 243, 303-4
гигие́на hygiene
гид guide
глава́ head, chief
глава́ chapter
гла́вный (adj) principle, chief
　гла́вный го́род chief town, city
　гла́вным о́бразом mainly
глаго́л verb
глаго́льный verbal
гла́дить (II)/по- to stroke, iron, press
глаз (pl глаза́) eye
глазно́й (adj) eye
глазно́й врач oculist
гло́хнуть (I)/о- to go deaf; see p. 243
глубина́ depth
глу́бже deeper
глубо́кий deep
глубокоуважа́емый deeply respected
глу́пость (f) folly, stupidity
глу́пый stupid, foolish
гляде́ть (II) to look, gaze; see p. 308
гнать (II) to chase, drive; see p. 307-8
го́вор talking, dialect, soundtrack
*говори́ть (II) to talk
говоря́ (v adv) talking
говоря́щий talking
год year
　про́шлый год last year
　бу́дущий год next year
　Но́вый год New Year
голова́ head
головно́й (adj) head
　головна́я боль headache
　головно́й убо́р hat, headgear
головокруже́ние dizziness
го́лод hunger, starvation, famine
голода́ть (I) to starve (intr)
го́лоден, голодна́, -о ; -ы hungry, starving
голо́дный hungry, starving
го́лос voice, vote
голубо́й sky blue

голубь (*m*) dove
   голубь мира dove of peace
Гольфстрим Gulf Stream
гонять (I) to chase
гора mountain
гораздо much, far more
гореть (I *ipf*) to burn, glow
*гордиться (II)+*ins* to be proud
гордость (*f*) pride
гордый proud
горе grief
горевать (I) to grieve; *see* p. 307 **B**.
горничная chamber maid
горный (*adj*) mountain, mining
горняк miner
город town
городить (II) to talk nonsense; to fuss
городишко nasty little town
городничий mayor
городовой town policeman
городок little town
городской municipal
горожанин (*pl* горожане) townsman, citizen
горох peas
горсовет=городской совет= town council
горчица mustard
горячий hot, ardent
Госиздат=Государственное издательство State Publishing House
господин Mr, gentleman
   pl господа gentlemen; *also* ladies and gentlemen
госпожа Mrs, Miss
гостиница hotel
государственный (*adj*) State
государство State
государыня sovereign lady, empress, madam, Ma'am
   милостивая государыня! Dear Madam
государь sovereign, emperor, Sir, Sire
   милостивый государь! Dear Sir
*готовить (II)/при- to prepare; to cook
*готовиться/при- to get ready
готовый ready; ready made (*of* clothes etc)

градоначальник city governor
градоначальство borough
градостроительство urban building
градус degree
градусник thermometer
гражданин (*pl* граждане) citizen
гражданка citizeness
гражданский civil
гражданство citizenship
   принять гражданство to be naturalized
граница frontier, boundary; limit
граничить (II) c+*ins* to border (on), verge
граничный (*adj*) border, frontier
гребёнка comb
гребец rower
греметь (II) to rattle, thunder; *see* p. 308
грести (I) to row; *see* p. 301.
гречневая крупа buckwheat
гривенник 10 copeck piece
грипп influenza, grippe
*грозить (II)/по- to threaten
грозный terrible, menacing
гром thunder
громкий loud
громко (*adv*) it is loud; loud(ly)
громоотвод lightning conductor
громче louder
грош small coin
грудь (*f*) breast, chest
грузин Georgian
грузинский (*adj*) Georgian
грязевой mud(dy)
грязный dirty
грязь (*f*) dirt, mud
губа 1. lip. 2. bay, gulf
гудеть (II) to buzz, hoot
гудок hooter, siren
гулять (I)/по- to stroll, walk
гуляющий strolling
гусёнок gosling
густой thick, dense
гусь (*m*) goose
гуще thicker

Д

да, yes
да and, but

да́бы   so that

*дава́ть (I)   to give; *also* to let, allow

дава́ть знать   to let know

дава́йте игра́ть!   Let's play

дави́ть (II)   to press, squeeze

давно́   long ago; for a long time

да́же   even

далёкий   far, distant, remote

далеко́   a long way off

даль (*f*)   distance

да́льный   distant

да́льше   further (on, away)

да́ма   lady; queen (*in cards*)

да́мский   lady's

дари́ть (II)   to make a present (of)

да́ром   gratis, free of charge

да́та   date

*дать (*irr*; *see* p. 309)   *pf* of дава́ть

два (*f* две)   two

два́жды   twice

двена́дцатый   twelfth

двена́дцать   twelve

дверь (*f*)   door

две́сти   two hundred

дви́гатель (*m*)   engine; motor

*дви́гать(ся) (I)   to move; *see* pp. 242, 303–4 .

дви́жимый   movable

*дви́нуть(ся)   *pf* of дви́гать(ся)

дво́е   two; *see* p. 203

двор   yard, courtyard

дворе́ц   palace

двубо́ртный костю́м   double-breasted suit

двуспа́льная крова́ть   double bed

де́ва   virgin

ста́рая де́ва   old maid

деви́ца   girl, maiden

де́вочка   little girl p. 151

девчо́нка (*dim*)   slattern

де́вушка   girl

дёготь (*m*)   tar

дед   grandfather; old man

де́душка (*dim*)   grandad; grandfather

дежу́рный   on duty

дежу́рная   maid on duty

де́йствие   deed, action

действи́тельно (*adv*)   really

действи́тельность (*f*)   reality

действи́тельный   real, actual; valid

де́йствовать (I)   to act, work

де́йствующий   in force

декора́ции (*pl*)   theatre scenery

*де́лать (I)/с-   to do, make

*де́латься   to become

делега́ция   delegation

дели́ть (II)   to divide

дели́ться   to be divided

де́ло   affair, business

в чём де́ло?   What's the matter?

де́ло в том   the point is

демократи́ческий   democratic

демокра́тия   democracy

наро́дная демокра́тия   People's Democracy

дэ́нди (*indec*)   dandy

де́нежный   financial, monetary

де́нежный перево́д   money order

день (*m*)   day   *See* p. 152

де́ньги (*pl*)   money   *See* p. 130

деньщи́к   batman

депута́т   deputy

депута́ция   deputation

дёргать (I)   to pull, jerk

дере́вня   the country; village

де́рево (*pl* дере́вья)   tree; wood

*держа́ть (II)   to hold, keep; *see* p. 309

держа́ть сло́во   to keep one's word

*держа́ться   to hold on to

десна́ (*pl* дёсны)   gum (*in mouth*)

десятирублёвый (*adj*)   10 rouble

десяти́чный   decimal

деся́тки   tens (of)

деся́ток   ten (of)

детёныш   the young of

де́ти (*pl*)   children; *see* pp. 130–1

де́тский   child's, children's; childish

де́тство   childhood

деше́вле   cheaper

дёшево (*adv*)   it is cheap

дешёвый   cheap

дива́н   sofa, divan

дире́ктор (*f*-ша)   director, manager.

дирижёр   conductor

дичь (*f*)   game, wild fowl

длина́   length

дли́нный   long

для + *gen*   for

днём   by day

до + *gen*   up to, as far as, until

добега́ть (I)   to run up to, as far as

добежа́ть (*irr*) *pf* of добега́ть
добива́ться (I) to seek to, strive for
доби́ться (I) to attain, p. 222
добре́е } the nicest, kindest
добре́йший
до́брый good, kind
  до́брое у́тро! good morning
дово́лен, дово́льна, -о ; -ы content, pleased
дово́льно + *gen* enough
дово́льный satisfied, pleased
дово́льствоваться (I) to be content with
догово́р agreement
доезжа́ть (I) to reach (*by vehicle*)
дое́хать (I) *pf* of доезжа́ть
дождь (*m*) rain
  дождь идёт it's raining
до́ктор doctor (*pl* -á)
до́кторша woman doctor
документа́льный фильм documentary film
до́лгий long, prolonged
до́лго (*adv*) for a long time
до́лжен, должна́, -ó ; -ы́ due, owing (*indicates obligation*); see p. 138
до́лжность (*f*) function, duty
до́ллар dollar
дом home, house
  до́ма at home
  домо́й homewards (*motion*)
дома́шний domestic
доми́ще huge house
дописа́ть (I) *pf* of допи́сывать
допи́сывать (I) to write to
допуска́ть (I)/допусти́ть (II) to admit
доро́га road, way; journey
до́рого dear
дорогови́зна high cost
дорого́й dear, expensive
дорожа́ть (I) to rise in price
доро́же dearer
дорожи́ть (II) to value
доска́ board, plank
  кла́ссная доска́ blackboard
достава́ть (I)/доста́ть (I) 1. to reach. 2. to get, obtain
*доста́вить (II) *pf* of доставля́ть
доста́вка delivery
*доставля́ть (I) to deliver; to cause

доста́точно enough, sufficient(ly)
  доста́точно умён clever enough
*достига́ть (I) to reach, achieve
*дости́гнуть (I) *pf* of достига́ть
достиже́ние achievement
до́хнуть (I)/по— to die (*of animals*) p. 243
дочь daughter; see p. 123
доще́чка (*dim*) small board; door-plate
дража́йший dearest
дра́ма drama
драмати́ческий dramatic
драмату́рг dramatist
*драть (I) to tear; see p. 302
*дра́ться to fight with
дре́вний ancient
дрейфова́ть (I) to drift; see p. 307 **B.**
*дрема́ть (I) to doze;
*дрожа́ть (II) to tremble; see p. 308
друг (*pl* друзья́) friend; see p. 131
друго́й other, another
дру́жба friendship
дру́жеский friendly
дружо́к } dear friend
дружо́чек
*ду́мать (I) to think
*ду́маться (*impers*) one would think
дура́к fool
ду́рно (*adv*) bad(ly)
  мне ду́рно I feel ill, sick
дурно́й bad
*дуть (I) to blow; see p. 305
душ shower-bath
душа́ soul
ду́шно (it is) sultry, stuffy
ду́шный stuffy, close
дым smoke
*дыша́ть (II) to breathe; see p. 309
дю́жина dozen
дя́дюшка (*dim*) uncle
дя́дя uncle

E

еда́ food, meal
едва́ hardly, scarcely
едини́ца unit; a one

еди́нственный only
ежего́дник year book
ежего́дный yearly, annual
ежедне́вно (*adv*) daily
ежедне́вный daily
е́жели if, in case
ежеме́сячный monthly
еженеде́льник weekly (publication)
*е́здить (II) to go (*by vehicle*); see p. 174
езжа́й! езжа́йте! *imperative of* е́хать to drive, ride
*езжа́ть (I) to go often
е́ле, е́ле-е́ле hardly, scarcely
ёлка fir tree; New Year's tree
Енисе́й Yenisei (a Siberian river)
е́сли if. *See* p. 121–2
  е́сли бы не but for
  е́сли не if not, unless
  е́сли то́лько provided
*есть (*irr*) to eat; see pp. 86, 309
есть (*from* быть) is, there is
е́хать (I) to drive, ride; *see* p. 174
ещё still
  ещё не not yet

Ж

жаке́т jacket
*жале́ть (I) to pity. *See* p. 116
жа́лоба complaint
жа́лобный plaintive
жа́лованье wage(s), salary
жа́ловаться (I) to complain; see p. 307 B.
жа́лость (*f*) pity
жаль pity + *dat* to be sorry for
  мне жаль I'm sorry
жа́ркий hot, ardent
жа́рко it is hot
жарко́е roast (meat)
жа́рче hotter
жать (I) (*a*) to press, squeeze; see p. 302
*жать (I) (*b*) to reap; see p. 302
*ждать (I) to wait, await; to expect. *See* p. 74
же, ж *particle* and, but, as to
же *as emphatic*, see p. 271
же = even, then. *See* p. 275
  тако́й же the same
жева́ть (I *ipf*) to chew
жела́ние wish, desire

жела́нный long-wished for
жела́тельный desirable
*жела́ть (I) to wish, desire, want
железа́ gland
желе́зный iron
  желе́зная доро́га railway
желе́зо iron
жёлтый yellow
желу́док stomach, belly
жёлудь (*m*) acorn
жёлчь (*f*) bile
жена́ wife. *See* p. 119
жена́тый married (*man*)
жени́ть (II) to marry (off)
жени́тьба marriage
*жени́ться to get married
жени́х bridegroom; fiancè
же́нский feminine
же́нщина woman
жеребёнок foal, colt
жеребе́ц stallion
же́ртва sacrifice
же́ртвовать (I) give (up), sacrifice; see p. 307
жесто́кий cruel, severe
жесто́кость (*f*) cruelty
жечь (I) to burn; see p. 303
жив, -а́ -о, ; -ы́ alive, lively
жи́во! Quickly!
живо́й alive, living; lively
живопи́сец painter
жи́вопись (*f*) painting
живо́т stomach
живо́тное animal
живу́щий living
живя́ living while
жизнь (*f*) life
жили́ще dwelling
жило́й дом tenement house
жильё living quarters
жир fat, grease
жи́рный fat(ty), rich
жи́тель (*m*) inhabitant
жи́тельство residence
  ме́сто жи́тельства place of residence
*жить (I) to live; see pp. 85, 302
жре́бий destiny, lot
журна́л magazine, journal
журнали́ст journalist

З

за behind, beyond, across, over, out of; (2) after; (3) + *ins* for;

(4) past, over; (5) at; (6) before

забáвный amusing

забивáть (I) to drive in; block up

заболевáние disease

забóр fence

забронирóванный booked (seats)

забронировáть (I) *pf* of **бронировáть**

*забывáть (I) to forget

*забы́ть (*like* быть) *pf* of **забывáть**: забу́ду, -ешь

заведéние institution

  учéбное заведéние educational institution

завéдовать (I) to manage

завéдующий manager

завúвка „перманéнт" permanent wave

завúдный enviable

*завúсеть (II) to depend (on)

зáвисть (*f*) envy

завиту́шка curl, flourish

зáвтра to-morrow

зáвтрак breakfast; lunch

*зáвтракать to breakfast, lunch; *see* p. 311

*заглáдывать(I) /заглянýть(I) to peep, look-in; to call on

заголóвок sub-title; heading

за граníцей ⎱ abroad
за граníцу ⎰

заграни́чный foreign

*задавáть (I)/задáть to set (*a lesson* etc.)

  задавáть вопрóс to put a question

зáдний back, hind

*задýмать (I) to plan, intend

*задýмываться (I)/задýматься to meditate, be deep in thought

заезжáть (I)/заéхать (I) to call on the way (*by vehicle*)

заём (*gen* зáйма) loan. p. 152

зажигáлка cigarette lighter

зажигáть (I)/зажéчь (I) to light, set fire to

*зайти́ (I) *pf* of **заходи́ть**

*заказáть (I) *pf* of **закáзывать**

заказнóе письмó registered letter

*закáзывать (I) ⎱ to order
*закупáть (II) *pf* ⎰

закóн law

закýпщик buyer

*закричáть (II) to cry out, shout

закрути́ть(ся) (II) to begin to twist, writhe

*закрывáть (I) to shut, close

*закры́ть (I) *pf* of **закрывáть**

закры́тый closed

*закýривать (I)/закури́ть (II) to light a cigarette, pipe etc.

закýска snack, hors d'oeuvre

закýсочная (snack) bar; *see* p. 311

зал hall

*заливáть (I)/зали́ть (I) to overflow, inundate

замéдлите! Go slow!

*замерзáть to freeze

замёрзнуть (I) *pf* of **мёрзнуть** *and* of **замерзáть**

замёрзши (*v adv*) frozen

замести́тель (*m*) deputy; vice-

замести́ть (II) *pf* of **замещáть** to act for, replace

замéтка note

*замечáть (I) to notice, observe

замещáть (I) to replace

замирáть (I)/замерéть (I) to stand stock still

зáмок castle. See p. 152

замóк lock. p. 152

  под замкóм locked

зáмуж marriage

*выходи́ть/вы́йти зáмуж to get married (*woman to man*)

замýжняя married woman

*занимáть (I)/заня́ть (I) to occupy, entertain. *See* p. 224

*занимáться to be engaged in

зáново anew, again

заня́тие occupation, -ия studies

зáнято occupied, engaged

занятóй busy,

заня́тный amusing

*заня́ть *pf* of **занимáть**

зáпад west

зáпадный western

*записáть (I) *pf* of **запи́сывать**

записнáя кни́жка note book

*запи́сывать (I) to write down, note

запи́сываться/записáться to register

зáпись (*f*) record

запла́кать (I *pf*) to burst into tears

*__заплати́ть__ (II) *pf* to pay

*__запомина́ть__ (II)/**запо́мнить** (II) to remember

запо́р constipation

*__запреща́ть__ (I)/**запрети́ть** (II) to forbid

запря́чь (I) to harness; *see* p. 302

зараже́ние infection

зара́за infection

зарази́ться (II) to catch an illness

зара́зный infectious, contagious

зарва́вшийся having gone to extremes

зарожда́ть(ся) (I)/**зароди́ть-(ся)** (II) to engender, be conceived

*__засвети́ть__ (II) *pf* to light up, strike a match

*__засну́ть__ (I) *pf* to fall asleep

*__засня́ть__ (I) *pf* to photograph

застила́ть (I) to cover up

застла́ть (I) *pf* of **застила́ть**

*__засыпа́ть__ (I)/**засы́пать** (I) to cover, fill up (strewing), to strew over

*__засыпа́ть__ (I)/**засну́ть** (I) to fall asleep

затем thereupon, then

зато (*particle*) instead, in return for

заты́лок back of the head, occiput

захо́д going down, setting

*__заходи́ть__ (II)/**зайти́** to call on, at

*__захоте́ть(ся)__ *impers* to want
  мне захоте́лось I wanted to

заявля́ть (I)/**заяви́ть** (II) to state

за́яц hare

зва́ние rank, title

*__звать__ (I) to call
  как вас зову́т? What's your name? *see* pp. 147–8

звезда́ star

звёздочка asterisk

зверёнок young beast

зверь (*m*) wild beast

звон peal, ringing

*__звони́ть__ (II) to ring, call up
  звони́ть по телефо́ну to ring up on the telephone

звоно́к (small) bell

звук sound

зда́ние building, edifice

здесь here

де́шний of this place, local

здоро́в, -а, -о; -ы healthy, robust

здоро́ваться (I) to greet, to say "How are you?" *See* p. 148

здо́рово! well done!

здоро́во! hello!

здоро́вый healthy, strong, wholesome

*__здра́вствовать__ (I) to be well, thrive

да здра́вствует! Long live!

*__здра́вствуй/те!__ *a general greeting*

зелёный green
  зелёный теа́тр open air theatre

земля́ land, earth, ground

земля́к (fellow) countryman

зе́ркало looking glass

зима́ winter
  зимо́й in winter

зи́мний wintry

зимо́вка winter stay; winter quarters

зимо́вщик winterer

злить (II) to anger, vex

*__зли́ться__ to be vexed, cross

злой wicked, malicious, bad-tempered

злость (*f*) ill-naturedness

змея́ snake; serpent

знак sign, symbol

*__знако́мить__ (II) **с** + *ins* to introduce

*__знако́миться__ **с** + *ins* to make acquaintance with

знако́мый (*adj*) familiar

знако́мый (*noun*) acquaintance

знамени́тейший very famous

знамени́тый famous

зна́мя banner; *see* p. 126

*__знать__ (I) to know; *see* p. 42

знать (*conj*) obviously

значи́тельный important

*__зна́чить__ (II) to mean, signify

зна́ющий knowing

зол, зла, -о; -ы angry, malicious

зо́лото gold

золото́й golden

зо́на zone

зонт, зо́нтик umbrella
зоологи́ческий zoological
зоопа́рк zoo
зре́ние eyesight
зри́тельный зал auditorium
зуб tooth
зубна́я па́ста tooth paste
зубна́я щётка tooth brush
зубно́й dental
зубно́й врач dental surgeon, dentist
зя́бкий feeling the cold; chilly
зя́бнуть (I)/**про-** to feel cold, to shiver; *see* pp. 242–3, 304

И

и and
и ... и ... both ... and ...
и тот и друго́й both
и́бо as, for, because
игра́ game
***игра́ть** (I) to play
игра́ющий playing
игру́шка plaything, toy
идёт дождь (*idiom*) it is raining
идёт снег (*idiom*) it is snowing
иде́я idea
идио́т idiot
***идти́** (I) to go on foot; *see* pp. 171, 174
вре́мя идёт time goes on
часы́ не иду́т the watch, clock doesn't go
не идёт (it) won't do
иду́чи going
Йе́мен Yemen (river)
из+*gen* out of, from
изба́ hut; peasant's cottage
***избега́ть** (I)/**избе́гнуть** (I) to avoid
изоча́сь leaning over
изве́стный well known, notorious
изве́чный ancient, traditional
извине́ние excuse
***извиня́ть** (I)/**извини́ть** (II) to excuse
***извиня́ться/извини́ться** to apologize, beg pardon
извне́ from outside
изво́зчик cab-driver; driver
***издава́ть** (I)/**изда́ть** (*see* **дать**) to publish; to utter

изда́тель (*m*) publisher
изда́тельство publishing house
***изда́ть** *pf* of **издава́ть**
изде́лие manufactured goods
из-за+*gen* from behind, because of
***измени́ть(ся)** (II) *pf* of **изменя́ть(ся)**
***изменя́ть** (I) (*tr*) to change
***изменя́ться** (*intr*) to change
***измеря́ть** (I)/**изме́рить** (II) to measure
изму́ченный exhausted
изму́читься (II) *pf* to be worn out
изоби́лие abundance
изоби́ловать (I) to abound in
изоби́льный abundant
из-под+*gen* from beneath
и́зредка occasionally, now and then
***изуча́ть** (I)/**изучи́ть** (II) to learn
изуче́ние study
изя́щество grace
изя́щный elegant
ико́на icon; image, sacred painting
иконопи́сец icon painter
ико́нопись (*f*) icon painting
иконоста́с altar screen; iconostasis
икра́ fish roe; caviar
и́ли or
и́ли ... и́ли ... either ... or ...
иллюстри́рованный illustrated
име́ние property; estate
и́менно namely
***име́ть** (I) to have, possess, own
***име́ться** there is, are; *see* p. 159
у меня́ име́ются ва́ши кни́ги I have your books
импреса́рио (*indec*) impressario
и́мя first (Christian) name; *see* pp. 38, 254–8
инжене́р engineer
инжене́рный (*adj*) engineering
иногда́ sometimes
ино́й other, another, different
иностра́нец (*f*-ка) foreigner
иностра́нный foreign
интервью́ (*indec*) interview
интере́с interest
интере́снейший most interesting

интере́сно (*adv*) interesting(ly)
интере́сный interesting
*интересова́ть(ся) (I)/за- to (be) interest(ed)
интересу́ющий (*tr*) interesting
*иска́ть (I) to look for, search; *see* p. 165
иску́сство skill, art
испа́нец Spaniard
испа́нский Spanish
исполни́мый feasible, practicable
*исполня́ть (I)/испо́лнить (II) to carry out, fulfil
*исполня́ться/испо́лниться to come true; to be fulfilled
ему́ испо́лнилось 30 лет he is 30 years of age
испра́вить(ся) *pf* of исправля́ть(ся)
исправля́ть (I) to correct, repair
исправля́ться to reform
исто́рик historian
истори́ческий historic(-al)
исто́рия history
*исчеза́ть (I)/исче́знуть (I) to disappear, vanish. *See* p. 243
исчерпа́емый exhaustible
исче́рпывать (I)/исчерпа́ть (I) to exhaust
и т.д. (и так да́лее) and so forth, on

К

к (ко)+*dat* (1) to, towards; (2) by, about; (3) for, of, to
к обе́ду to dinner
к тому́ же (*idiom*) moreover
-ка suffix which softens (imperative)
кабаре́ cabaret
кавка́зский Caucasian
ка́ждый each, every
*ка́жется (*impers*) it seems (*see* каза́ться). *See* p. 148
*каза́лось it seemed
каза́к Cossack
*каза́ться (I)/по- (*impers*) to seem
казённый official
как (1) how, what; (2) as, like
как бу́дто as if, as though
как . . ., так и . . . as . . . so . . .

как раз exactly
как мо́жно лу́чше as well as possible
како́й what, which; what kind of
како́й-либо, како́й-нибу́дь any, some
како́й-то some, some kind of
как-то somehow; one day; that is
календа́рь (*m*) calendar
калькули́ровать/с- to calculate
калькуля́тор calculator; costs clerk
калькуля́ция calculation
камени́стый stony
ка́менный (*adj*) stone
ка́мень (*m*) stone
ка́мерная му́зыка chamber music
ками́н fire-place
камышо́вый made of rushes; thatch
кани́кулы (*pl*) holidays, vacation
капе́лла chapel; choir
капита́л capital (*finance*)
каранда́ш pencil
карбюра́тор carburettor
каре́та carriage
каре́та ско́рой по́мощи ambulance
карма́н pocket
ка́рта map; card; *sometimes* menu
карти́на picture
карти́нка illustration; print
карти́нная галере́я picture gallery
картоте́ка card index
карто́фель (*m*) potatoes
ка́рточка (small) card
*каса́ться (I) to touch; *or* to concern
ка́сса pay desk, cash desk, cash register; booking-office
касси́р cashier
катастро́фа catastrophe
ката́ть (I) (*indet*) to take for a drive; to roll
*ката́ться to go for a drive
кати́ть (II)/по- to roll, wheel
кафе́ café
ка́ша buckwheat; cereal; gruel, porridge
ка́шель (*m*) cough. -ный
ка́шлять (I *ipf*) to cough

квадра́т square
квадра́тный square
кварти́ра apartment, flat
кекс cakes
кем whom
кило́ kilo
килогра́мм kilogram
киломе́тр kilometer = 0.62 mile
кино́ cinema; moving pictures
киножурна́л newsreel
кинотеа́тр cinema
кио́ск kiosk, stall, stand, booth
кисе́йный (adj) muslin
кисе́т tobacco pouch
кисея́ muslin
ки́слый sour
ки́снуть (I)/с- to turn sour. See p. 243
ки́сточка little brush, tassel
ки́тель (m) tunic
*кла́няться (I) to bow, greet
*класть (I) to put, place; see p. 302
клева́ть (I) to peck, pick; to bite; see p. 306 B
клей glue
клешня́ claw (of shellfish)
кли́мат climate
климато́лог climatologist
клин wedge; gusset
клок rag, shred
клочо́к scrap
клуб club
ключ key
ключ spring (fountain)
кни́га book
кни́жка pocket book
кни́жный book-; bookish, literary
кова́ть (I) to shoe a horse; see p. 306 B
ковёр carpet, rug
когда́ when
когда́-либо
когда́-нибудь } some day
когда́-то at one time, formerly
кого́ (gen and acc of кто) whom
ко́готь (m) claw, talon
ко́жа skin; leather
козёл he-goat. See p. 152
ко́зырь (m) trump card
кой-кому́ (idiom) to someone or other
колбаса́ smoked sausage
коле́но knee
колесо́ wheel
коллекти́вный collective

ко́локол (big) bell
колоко́льня bell tower
колоко́льчик small bell
коло́ть (I) to prick, stab; to chop; see p. 306
колпа́к hood (of car)
колхо́з = коллекти́вное хозя́йство collective farm
колхо́зник collective farmer
колхо́зный (adj) relating to collective farm
колыха́ться (I) to rock, swing
кома́нда crew, team; detachment; command
кома́ндный commanding
*кома́ндовать (I) to command
коме́дия comedy
комите́т committee
коми́ческий comic
ко́мната room
комо́д chest of drawers
компози́тор composer
компре́сс compress
комсомо́л All-Union Lenin Young Communist League (USSR)
комсомо́лец (m)
комсомо́лка (f) } a member of the Komsomol
конве́рт envelope
конди́терская confectioner's shop
конди́терский adj confectionery
конду́ктор guard; conductor
коне́ц end. See p. 152
коне́чно of course
конститу́ция constitution
ко́нсул consul
ко́нсульство consulate
конто́ра office
контра́кт contract
контро́ль (m) inspection, supervision
конце́рт concert
конце́ртный зал concert hall
*конча́ть (I) to finish, end
*конча́ться (intr) to expire, end
*ко́нчить(ся) pf of конча́ть(ся)
конь (m) horse, steed
ко́ломазь (f) grease
копе́йка (dim копе́ечка) copeck
копна́ stack, rick

кора́бль (*m*) ship, vessel
ко́рень (*m*) root
кори́чневый brown
*корми́ть (II) to feed, nurse
коро́бка box
коро́ль (*m*) king
коро́ткий short
ко́ротко (*adv*) in short, briefly
коро́че shorter
ко́рпус body, hull, case; corps
корреспонде́нт correspondent
корь (*f*) measles
коси́ть (II) to mow
косми́ческий cosmic
ко́смос cosmos
костьı́ль (*m*) crutch
кость (*f*) bone
костю́м costume, suit
кот cat, tom-cat
котёнок (*pl* котя́та) kitten
кото́рый who, which (one)
ко́фе (*m indec*) coffee
коша́чий cat's, cat-like
ко́шка cat
край extreme, border, edge;
   region
кра́йне extremely
кра́йний extreme
   по кра́йней ме́ре at least
краси́в, -а, -о ; -ы beautiful
краси́вее more beautifully
краси́вый beautiful
кра́сить (II) to paint, dye
кра́ска paint
   кра́ски colours
красне́е redder
краснота́ redness
кра́сный red; *also* beautiful
   кра́сное ле́то a beautiful
   summer
красота́ beauty
кра́ткий short, brief
красть (I) to steal, pilfer; *see*
   p. 302
кратча́йший shortest
кремль (*m*) the Kremlin
креме́нь (*m*) flint
кре́пкий strong
   кре́пким сном sound sleep
кре́пнуть (I)/o- to get stronger:
   p. 243
кре́пче stronger
кре́сло arm-chair
крестья́нин (*pl* крестья́не)
   peasant
крестья́нство peasantry
крива́я curve, bend

криво́й curved, crooked
крик cry, shout
*кри́кнуть (I) *pf* of крича́ть
   to give a cry. *See* p. 242
*крича́ть (II) to shout, cry out
крова́ть (*f*) bed; bedstead
кровь (*f*) blood
крокоди́л crocodile
кро́ме +*gen* but, except, save
кро́ме того́ moreover, besides
круг circle
кру́глый round; circular
круго́м (*adv*) around, round
крупа́ groats
кру́пный big, great
кру́то 1. sudden. 2. stern
круто́й 1. sudden. 2. steep
крыло́ (*pl* кры́лья) wing
Крым Crimea the
*крыть (I) to cover; *see* p. 305
кры́ша roof
кры́шка lid, cover
кста́ти to the point; by the way
кто who
   кто ни whoever
   кто-ли́бо ⎫ somebody,
   кто-нибу́дь ⎭ anybody
   кто-то someone, somebody
куда́ where to, whither
   куда́-нибудь ⎫
   куда́-то ⎭ to somewhere
кузне́ц blacksmith
ку́кла doll
ку́кольный теа́тр puppet
   theatre
кукуру́за maize, (indian) corn
культу́ра culture
культу́рный cultured
ку́мушка gossip; fellow god-
   parent
купа́льный (*adj*) bathing
купа́нье (*noun*) bathing
купа́ть (I) to bath, bathe
купа́ться to take a bath; to have
   a bathe
купа́ясь bathing
купе́ц merchant, trader. p. 152
купе́ческий mercantile
купе́чество merchant class
*купи́ть (II) *pf* to buy
ку́пол dome, cupola
кури́тельная smoking room
*кури́ть (II) to smoke
   кури́ть воспреща́ется
   smoking forbidden
куро́рт health resort
курс course (*of study etc.*)

курси́в italics
курси́вный *adj* italic
ку́ртка jacket (*man's, boy's*)
ку́рточка woman's jacket
куря́щий smoker, smoking compartment
    ваго́н для куря́щих smoking carriage
кусо́к piece. *See p.* 151
ку́хня kitchen; cook-house
ку́шанье food; dish
ку́шать (I)/по– to eat *or* drink; to take

Л

ла́вка shop
ла́вочка little shop
ла́вочник shop-keeper
ла́герь (*m*) camp
ла́зить (II) to climb; to get into; *see p.* 308 *Group* 1
лак lacquer, varnish
ла́комство sweetmeats, titbits
ла́мпа lamp
ларь (*m*) chest, coffer
ла́ска weasel
ласка́ть (I) to caress, fondle
ла́сковый affectionate, tender
лачу́жка hut, shanty
ла́ять (I) to bark; *see p.* 306
лгать (I) to tell lies
ле́бедь (*m*) swan
лёгкий light, easy; slight
легко́ it is easy
легкова́я маши́на automobile
лёгкое lung
лёд ice
    на льду́ on (the) ice
ле́ди lady
ледови́тый icy, glacial
*лежа́ть (II) to repose, lie down; *see pp.* 232, 308
лежа́щий lying down
ле́звие blade
лезть (I *ipf*) to climb, get into
лека́рство medicine
ле́карь (*m*) medical doctor
ле́ксика vocabulary
ленингра́дец Leningrader
ле́нта ribbon
ле́пка modelling, moulding
лес wood(s), forest
ле́стница stairs, staircase
ле́стный flattering, complimentary
лесть (*f*) flattery, cajolery

*лета́ть (I)/лете́ть (II) to fly
ле́тний (*adj*) summer
лётный flying
ле́то summer
ле́том in summer
лётчик flyer, pilot, aviator
летя́щий flying
лече́ние (medical) treatment
лечи́ть (II)/по– to treat, cure
лечи́ться to be treated, cured
*лечь (I) *pf* of ложи́ться; *see p.* 232, 302
ли *interrogative particle*
ли́бо either, or
    ли́бо . . . ли́бо . . . either . . . or . . .
ли́вень (*m*) heavy downpour
ли́верная колбаса́ liver sausage
лик image; countenance
лимо́н lemon
лимона́д lemonade
лине́йский line unit
ли́ния line
ли́пнуть (I)/при– to adhere, stick to; *see p.* 303 *Cl II Gr* 1
лиса́, лиси́ца fox
ли́сий fox's, foxy
лист (*pl* ли́стья) leaf (tree, plant)
лист (*pl* листы́) leaf (book), sheet of paper
листва́ foliage, leaves
литерату́ра literature
литерату́рный literary
лить (I) to pour
ли́ться to flow, stream; *see p.* 305 (1)
лифт lift, elevator
лихора́дка fever
лицо́ face
    лицо́м к лицу́ face to face
ли́чно personally
ли́чность (*f*) personality
ли́чный personal
лиша́йник *or* лиша́й lichen
*лиша́ть (I)/лиши́ть (II) to deprive
*лиша́ться/лиши́ться to lose, be deprived of
лишь only
    лишь бы if only
    лишь то́лько as soon as
ло́дка boat
ло́жа box (*theatre*)
*ложи́ться (II)/лечь (I) to lie down; *see pp.* 232, 302

ложи́ться спать to go to sleep (=bed)
ло́жка spoon
ложь (*f*) lie
ло́коть (*m*) elbow
ло́моть (*m*) chunk
лошадёнка (*dim*) young horse, colt
лоша́дка (*dim*) dear little horse
ло́шадь (*f*) horse
луг meadow
луна́ moon
лу́чше better
лу́чший better; the best
люби́мец favourite; pet
люби́мый favourite
*люби́ть (II) to like, love; see pp. 70, 165
любова́ться (I) to admire
любо́вь (*f*) love
любо́й any
лю́бящий affectionate, loving
лю́ди (*pl*) people; see p. 130
лягу́шка frog

M

магази́н shop; store
магнетофо́нная ле́нта recording tape
мада́м Madame
мадемуазе́ль Mademoiselle
ма́зать (I)/мазну́ть (I) to smear, daub. See p. 303
максима́льный maximum
мал, -а́, -о́ ; -ы́ small, little
мале́йший slightest, least
ма́ленький small, little
ма́ло+*gen* not much; only a few; not enough
ма́лый little
малы́ш small child, "kid"
ма́льчик boy
мальчи́шка urchin
маникю́р manicure
мани́ть (II) to entice
марина́д pickle(s)
ма́рка (postage) stamp; trade mark
маслёнка butter dish
ма́сло butter; oil
ма́сляные кра́ски oil colours, paints
ма́сса mass; a lot of
масса́ж massage

ма́стер (*f*:-и́ца) skilled workman; foreman
мастерска́я workshop
мастерство́ skill, craftsmanship
материали́зм materialism
мате́рия matter; material
ма́тушка (*dim*) mother; mummy
мать mother; see p. 126
*маха́ть (I)/махну́ть (I)+*ins* to wave; to flap; see p. 303
маши́на machine; automobile
маши́нка typewriter; *also* clippers
мая́к lighthouse
ме́бель (*f*) furniture
мёд honey
медве́дица she-bear, the Great Bear
медве́дь (*m*) bear
медве́жий of a bear; ursine
медвежо́нок (*pl* -а́та) bear's cub
ме́дик medical man, medico
медо́вый ме́сяц honeymoon
медсестра́ *see* медици́нская сестра́
медици́на medicine
медици́нский medical
    медици́нская сестра́ nursing sister
ме́дленно slow(ly)
ме́дленный slow
медпу́нкт first aid post
меж ⎱ between, inter-
ме́жду ⎰
междунаро́дный international
    междунаро́дное письмо́ letter for abroad
мел chalk
ме́лкий shallow
ме́лочь (*f*) trifle; small change
мелька́ть (I)/мелькну́ть (I) to flash, gleam
ме́нее less
    тем не ме́нее nevertheless
ме́ньше less, lesser; smaller
ме́ньший lesser
меню́ menu, bill of fare
ме́ра measure
    по кра́йней ме́ре at least
    по ме́ньшей ме́ре at least
мерзлота́ frozen ground
мёрзнуть (I)/за- to freeze; see pp. 303-4
мертве́ц dead man

мёртвый dead
мести to sweep; see p. 302
место place
месяц month; moon
месячный monthly
металл metal
металлический metallic
метеоплощадка meteorological post
метеоролог meteorologist
метро underground railway
мечта dream
*мечтать (I) to dream
*мешать (I)/по- 1. to mix, stir. 2. to hinder, prevent
мешок bag, sack
мигрень (f) headache
милиционер militiaman; policeman
миллион million
миллионный worth millions
милый nice, lovable
милостивый gracious, kind
милый мой my dear fellow
мимо + gen by, past
минерал mineral
минеральный mineral
минимальный minimal, minimum
минимум minimum
минута minute
мир (1) peace
мир (2) world
мираж mirage
Мисс Miss
Миссис Mrs.
младенец infant, baby
младший younger
   самый младший the youngest
мнение opinion
много + gen much, plenty of
многоуважаемый much esteemed
модель (f) model
может быть may be, perhaps
можно one can, may
мозг brain
мой, моя, моё; мои my
мокнуть (I)/про- get wet; see p. 243
-мол suffix = it is said
молод, -а, -о ; -ы young
молоденький (dim) very young

молодняк young animals
молодой young
молодость (f) youth
моложе younger
молоко milk
молот hammer (big)
молоток hammer (small): p. 152
молоть (I) to grind, mill; see p. 306
молотьба threshing
молча silently
*молчать (II)/за- to be silent
молчать! Silence! (command)
монастырь (m) monastery
монета coin
море (pl моря) sea
морем by sea
мороженое ice cream
мороз frost; also = it's freezing
морозный frosty
морфология morphology
москвич (no) Moscovite
московский of Moscow
мост bridge
мох moss
мохнатый shaggy
*мочь (I) to be able to; see p. 302
мрамор marble
мрачный gloomy
мстить (II) to revenge oneself; мщу, мстишь.
муж husband; see p. 131
мужской male, masculine
мужчина man
музей museum
музыка music
мука torment
мука flour
мультипликационный фильм animated cartoon (film)
мундштук cigarette-holder
мчаться (II)/по- to speed along
мы we
мыло soap
мысль (f) thought
*мыть (I) to wash; see p. 305
*мыться to wash oneself
мягкий soft, gentle
мягонький (dim) nice and soft
мягче softer
мясник butcher
мясная butcher's shop
мясной (adj) meat
мясо (no) meat
мяч ball

Н

на + *acc* = motion to *or* during; +
  prp = place; (1) on; (2) in; at;
  (3) towards, to; (4) by, in;
  (5) during

на́ день for the day

на ме́сяц for the month

набира́ть (I)/**набра́ть** (I) to
  gather, collect, recruit

набира́ть но́мер to dial,
  get a number (*telephone*)

наблюда́тель observer

наблюда́тельный observant

наблюда́ть (I) to watch, observe

наблюде́ние observation

наве́рно for certain

наве́рх up, upwards; upstairs

наверху́ above, upstairs

навстре́чу + *dat* towards

над(о) + *ins* over, above

надвига́ться (I)/**надви́нуться**
  (I) to move upon

наде́жда hope

наде́яться *pf* to hope (*impers*)

наде́яться на кого́-либо to
  rely upon somebody

надлежа́ть (II) *impers* must,
  ought; *see* p. 308

мне надлежи́т I must, ought
  to

на́до it is necessary. *See* p. 118

на́добность (*f*) necessity

надоеда́ть (I)/**надое́сть** (*irr see*
  есть) to bother, trouble, bore

наеда́ться (I)/**нае́сться** (*irr see*
  есть) to eat one's fill

наём hire

наёмный hired

наёмный труд hired labour

наза́д back(wards)

тому́ наза́д ago

назва́ние name

назва́ть *pf* of **называ́ть**

называ́ть (I)/**назва́ть** (I) to
  call, name

называ́ться/назва́ться to be
  called

наизу́сть by heart

наилу́чший the very best

наиху́дший the very worst

найти́ *pf* of **находи́ть**

наказа́ние punishment, penalty

нака́зывать (I)/**наказа́ть** (I)
  to punish

накану́не eve, the day before

накле́ивать (I)/**накле́ить** (II)
  to lay, put on; *pf* to stick on

наклоня́ть (I)/**наклони́ть** (II)
  to bend, bow

наклоня́ться/наклони́ться
  to bend over, bow

наконе́ц finally; at last

нале́во to (on) the left

налега́ть (I)/**нале́чь** (I)
  to apply oneself to

нали́чные (де́ньги) cash, hard
  cash

нало́г tax

наме́рен, -а ; -ы willing, in-
  tending

нанима́ть (I) to hire. *See*
  p. 224

наня́ть (I) *pf* of **нанима́ть**

наперегонки́ racing competitively

напива́ться (I)/**напи́ться** (I)
  to drink one's fill

написа́ть (I) (*pf* of **писа́ть**) to
  write; *also* to paint

напи́ток (*pl* -тки) drink(s)

напомина́ть (I)/**напо́мнить**
  (II) to remind

направле́ние direction

направля́ть (I)/**напра́вить** (II)
  to send direct

напра́во to (on) the right

наприме́р for example

напро́тив opposite; on the contrary

наро́д people

наро́дность (*f*) nationality

наро́дный people's, national

нарочи́тый deliberate

наро́чно on purpose; for

наслажда́ться (I)/**наслади́ть-
  ся** (II) to enjoy

наслажде́ние enjoyment

на́сморк cold in the head

насо́с pump

насто́лько so

насто́лько наско́лько as
  much as

настоя́щий real; present

насчёт as regards, concerning

насчи́тывать(-ся) (I) to number

нату́ра nature

науга́д haphazardly

нау́ка science

находи́ть (II)/найти́ (I) to find; to consider

находи́ться to be found, situated; *see* p. 174

на́ция nation

нача́ло beginning

нача́льник chief, boss

нача́ть (I) *pf* of начина́ть

начина́ть (I) to begin

нашёптывать (I) to whisper

не not; no, none

   не́ за что (*idiom*) Don't mention it

   не говоря́ о not to mention . . .

небе́сный heavenly

не́бо sky, heavens

небольшо́й small; short

небоскло́н sky above horizon

небо́сь no doubt

нева́жно never mind; it doesn't matter

нева́жный unimportant; bad

невероя́тный incredible

невесо́мый weightless

неве́ста bride, fiancée

неви́нность (*f*) innocence

неви́нный innocent

негр, негритя́нка negro, negress

неда́вно lately, recently

неде́ля week

   на э́той неде́ле this week

не́жели than

незада́чливый hapless

нездоро́виться (II) (*impers*) not to feel well. *See* p. 148

неиме́ние absence, lack of

не́когда at one time

не́когда no time

не́который (a) certain; some

некраси́в, -а, -о ; -ы not beautiful, plain

некраси́вый plain

некуря́щий non-smoker

   ваго́н для некуря́щих non-smoking carriage

нельзя́ it is forbidden; it is impossible; one can't

нема́ло not a little, not a few

неме́дленно immediately

неме́дленный immediate

не́мец German (*man*)

неме́цкий German

не́мка German (*woman*)

немно́го+*gen* a little, a few

немно́жко just a little

немо́й dumb; dumb man

   немо́й фильм silent film

неподви́жный motionless‹

непра́в, -а́, -о ; -ы (in the) wrong

непреме́нно without fail

неприя́тность (*f*) unpleasantness

неприя́тный unpleasant

нерв nerve

неру́сский non-Russian

несваре́ние indigestion

не́сколько a little, a few; somewhat; *see* pp. 156, 250

несмотря́ на in spite of, despite

нести́ (I) to carry, bear; *see* p. 174

нести́сь to rush along

несча́стный unforunate

неся́ carrying

нет, no (are)

нет (*impers*) there is not, no

*неугомо́нный indefatigable; restless

неуда́ча failure

неуда́чный unsuccessful

неуже́ли really ? can it be ?

не́хотя reluctantly; unwillingly

неча́янно accidentally

нечи́стый unclean

ни neither, not

   ни . . . ни . . . neither . . . nor . . .

   ни оди́н none

   ни гугу́ not a word

нигде́ nowhere

нижа́йший lowest; most humble

ни́же lower

   ни́же нуля́ below zero

ни́жний lower; under

   ни́жний эта́ж lower floor (=ground)

низ lowest part, bottom

низ- (нис-) *prefix*=downwards

ни́зенький (*dim*) very low, inferior

ни́зкий base, mean

низлага́ть (I)/низложи́ть (II) to dispose

ни́зменность (*f*) lowland

ни́зость (*f*) meanness

ни́зший lowest

никогда́ never

никто́ no one, nobody

никуда́ (to) nowhere

ниско́лько not at all

ничего́ nothing; no matter! never mind!

нищета́ poverty, misery

ни́щий (*adj*) (1) pauper; (2) poverty-stricken

ни́щий (*noun*)

но but (*contrast*)

нове́е newer

но́вый new
   но́вого, что? What's new?

но́готь (*m*) (*pl* но́гти) nail; toe-nail

нож knife

но́жницы scissors; *see* p. 131

ноль (*m*) nought, zero

но́мер (1) number; (2) size; (3) item; hotel room №

нос nose

*носи́ть (II) (*see* нести́) to carry; to wear: p. 174

носи́ться see нести́сь

носо́к (*pl* носки́) toe; sock

*ночева́ть (I) to spend the night

ночле́г night's lodging

ночь (*f*) night
   но́чью by night; in the night

*нра́виться (II)/по- to please
   он мне нра́вится I like him

ну! Well! Well now!

ну́жен, нужна́, -о; -ы́ necessary. *See* p. 138

ну́жно it is necessary
   мне ну́жно I must, I have to

ну́жный necessary

нуль (*m*) zero; ноль (*m*) zero

Нью-Йо́рк New York

*ню́хать (I)/по- to smell

ня́ня nurse, nanny

О

о (об, обо) (1) concerning, about; (2) against, on, upon

о́ба (*f* о́бе) both

*обвини́ть (II) *pf* of обвиня́ть

*обвиня́ть (I) to accuse, charge; *see* p. 307

обводи́ть (II)/обвести́ (I) to surround

обе́д dinner

*обе́дать (I)/по- to dine

*оберну́ться (I) *pf* of обора́чиваться to turn; to wrap oneself

*обеспе́чивать (I)/обеспе́чить (II) to provide; to secure

обеща́ние promise

*обеща́ть (I) to promise

оби́деть(ся) (II) *pf* of обижа́ть(ся)

оби́дно offended
   мне оби́дно I'm offended

оби́дный offensive

оби́дчивый touchy

обижа́ть (I) to offend, hurt

обижа́ться to take offence

облада́ние possession

*облада́ть (I) to possess

о́блако (*pl* облака́) cloud

о́бласть (*f*) region, district

облегча́ть (I) to facilitate

облегчи́ть (II) *pf* of облегча́ть

обложе́ние military investment; taxation; assessment

обло́жка cover; dust jacket

обнару́живать (I) / обнару́жить (II) (1) to discover; (2) to display

обнима́ть (I) to embrace

обнима́ться to embrace one another

обня́ть(ся) (I) *pf* of обнима́ть(ся). See p. 224

обо *see* о

обогрева́ть (I)/обогре́ть (I) to warm

обожа́ть (I) *ipf* to adore, worship

обора́чиваться (I) to turn round

оборо́тный reverse

обраба́тывать (I) to treat; cultivate, perfect

обрабо́тать (I) *pf* of обраба́тывать

*обра́довать (I) to make happy

*обра́доваться to be glad, happy. *See* p. 222

о́браз image; manner; form; icon
   о́браз жи́зни mode of life
   гла́вным о́бразом mainly
   таки́м о́бразом thus
   каки́м о́бразом? how?

образо́ванный educated, cultivated

обрати́ться (II) *pl* of обраща́ться

обраща́ться (I) to apply to, address; to treat

обры́в precipice

обслу́живание service

о́бувь (*f*) footwear, shoes, boots
обхо́д detour
общежи́тие hostel
о́бщество society
о́бщий general, common
общи́тельный sociable
объедине́ние unification
объединённый united
объе́кт object
объекти́в objective
объясне́ние explanation
*объясни́ть(ся) (II) *pf* of объ-
ясня́ть(ся)
*объясня́ть (I) to explain
*объясня́ться to have it out
with, discuss
обы́чно usually; it is usual
обы́чный usually
о́вощи vegetables
ОГИ́З Central Publishing
House; *see* p. 169, 5 (iii)
огля́дываться (I)/огляну́ться
(I) to look back
огонёк (*dim*) small light, flame
ого́нь (*m*) fire, light. *See*
p. 152
огора́живать(I)/огороди́ть(II)
to fence in
огоро́д kitchen-garden
огороди́ть (II) *pf* to fence in
огоро́дник market gardener
огоро́дничать (I) to do market
gardening
огоро́днический of market
gardening
огоро́дничество market
gardening
огра́да fence
огро́мный huge, immense
одева́ть (I) to dress, clothe
одева́ться to dress one's self
одева́ясь dressing
оде́вшись having dressed
оде́ть(ся) (I) *pf* of одева́ть(ся)
оди́н, одна́, -о ; -и́ one; alone;
see p.87-8, 130
оди́ннадцатый eleventh
оди́ннадцать eleven
одна́жды once
одна́ко however; and yet
однобо́ртный костю́м
single-breasted suit
односпа́льная крова́ть
single bed
ожида́ние expectation
*ожида́ть (I) to expect

озаря́ть (I)/озари́ть (II) to
light up
о́зеро (*pl* озёра) lake
оказа́ть(ся) (I) *pf* of оказы-
вать(ся)
*ока́зывать (I) to render
*ока́зываться to prove, turn
out to be
океа́н ocean
океано́граф oceanographer
окно́ window; *see* p. 114
о́коло next to, nearby
*окружа́ть (I)/окружи́ть (II)
to encircle, surround
окруже́ние environment
о́кунь (*m*) perch (*fish*)
омле́т omelette
он he
она́ she
они́ they
оно́ it
опа́сность (*f*) danger
опа́сный dangerous
о́пера opera
описа́ние description
описа́ть *pf* of опи́сывать
опи́сывать to describe
о́пись (*f*) list, inventory
*опуска́ть (I) to lower
*опуска́ться to fall, sink
*опусти́ть(ся) (II) *pf* of опу-
ска́ть(ся)
о́пухоль (*f*) swelling, tumour
о́пыт experience
о́пытный experienced
о́рган organ (*physical*)
орга́н organ (*musical instrument*)
орке́стр orchestra; band
ору́дие tool, instrument
ору́жие weapon; arms
осва́ивать (I) to master
осва́иваться to familiarize
oneself with
осво́ить(ся) (II) *pf* of осва́и-
вать(ся)
осёл donkey. *See* p. 152
осе́нний autumn(al)
о́сень (*f*) autumn, fall
о́сенью in autumn
осложне́ние complication
осложня́ть (I)/осложни́ть (II)
to complicate
осма́тривать (I) to examine,
inspect
осмотре́ть (II) *pf* of осма́три-
вать

особенно especially

особня́к private (detached) house

*оставáться (I) to stay, remain

*оставля́ть (I)/остáвить (II) to abandon, leave

остальнóе the rest, remainder

*останáвливать (I) to stop (*tr*)

*останáвливаться to stop (*intr*)

*остановúть(ся) *pf* of останá-вливать(ся)

остановка stopping place

*остáться (I) *pf* of оставáться

осторóжно } careful(ly)
осторóжный }

óстров (*pl* островá) island

осты́нуть (I) *pf* to cool (*intr*)

осуществлéние realization

осуществля́ть (I) / осуществ-вúть (II) to realize, ac-complish, fulfil

ось (*f*) axle

от (ото)+*gen* from (*a distance or person*)

отбивáть (I) to beat off

отбивáться to break off, separ-ate from; to resist, repulse

отбúть(ся) *pf* of отбивáть(ся)

отвёртка screw-driver

отвéт answer, reply

*отвéтить (II) *pf* of отвечáть

отвечáть (I) to reply (to), answer

*отводúть (II)/отвестú (I) to lead, take with; to draw aside, remove. See p. 174

*отворя́ть (I)/отворúть (II) to open

отвыкáть (I)/отвы́кнуть (I) to get out of the habit of. See p. 243

*отдавáть (I) to give back, re-turn

*отдáть (*irr see* дать) *pf* of отдавáть

отдéл department, branch

отделéние separation; section, compartment

óтдых rest, repose

отéль (*m*) hotel

отепля́ть (I)/отеплúть (II) to warm up; to make winterproof

отéц father See p. 152

отéчество native land

*открывáть to open; to expose

откры́тие opening; discovery

откры́тка open card, postcard

откры́тый open

*откры́ть (I) *pf* of открывáть

откýда where from, whence

откýда-нибýдь from some-where (*or other*)

*отличáть (I) to distinguish

*отличáться to differ from

отлúчно! excellent! fine!

отлúчный excellent

отмéна revocation; abolition

отменя́ть (I)/отменúть (II) to cancel, abolish

*отмечáть (I)/отмéтить (II) to mark, note

относúтельно+*gen* concern-ing, regarding

отношéние relation; attitude; *also* memorandum

*отойтú (I) *pf* of отходúть (II)

отпирáть (I)/отперéть (I) to unlock, open: *pf* отопрý, -решь; -ýт

отправúтель (*m*) sender

*отправля́ть (I)/отпрáвить (II) to despatch, send

*отправля́ться/отпрáвиться to leave for, set off

отрезáть (I)/отрéзать (I) to cut off

отрицáние denial

отрицáтельный negative

*отрицáть (I) to deny

óтрочество adolescence

отря́д detachment

*отставáть (I) to lag behind; be slow

*отстáть (I) *pf* of отставáть

отсю́да from here, hence

оттогó therefore

оттогó, что because

оттýда from there, thence

*отходúть (II) to leave, go away from

отцепúть(ся) (II) (*pf*) to get loose

отчегó why

óтчество patronymic; *see* p. 39

отъéзд departure

отъезжáть (I)/отъéхать (I) to drive away from

офицéр officer

официáльный official

официáнт waiter; steward

óчень very, very much

очереднóй next in turn; re-current

о́чередь (*f*) turn; queue, line
очки́ (*pl*) spectacles; glasses; *see* p. 130
очну́ться (I) to come to, wake up, regain consciousness
очути́ться (II) to find oneself
о́щупью by touch
ощуще́ние sensation

П

*па́дать (I) to fall
паёк ration
пай share
па́йщик shareholder
палеонто́лог palaeontologist
па́луба deck
пальто́ (*indec*) overcoat
Пами́р the Pamirs (mountains)
па́мятник monument
па́мять (*f*) memory
пансио́н (1) boarding-house; (2) boarding school
па́па papa, daddy; (the) Pope
папиро́са Russian cigarette (*with mouthpiece*)
па́ра pair, two of
парализова́ть (I) to paralyse
парвеню́ parvenu, upstart
па́рень (*m*) fellow, chap
Пари́ж Paris
парикма́хер hairdresser
парикма́херская hairdresser's
парк park, gardens
парк о́тдыха и культу́ры park of rest and culture
паро́м ferry-boat
парохо́д steamship
парте́р pit, stalls
партиту́ра musical score
па́рус sail
парфюме́рный магази́н perfumer's shop
па́спорт passport
пассажи́р passenger
пассажи́рский passenger's
па́ста paste
пасти́ (I) to tend; *see* p. 302
пасть (I) to fall; *see* p. 302
Па́сха Easter
паути́на spider's web, cobweb
*паха́ть (I) to plough, till
*па́хнуть (I)/за- to smell: p. 243
па́чка bundle; pack, packet

певе́ц (*m*) ⎱ singer
певи́ца (*f*) ⎰
педаго́г teacher; education(al)-ist
пень (*m*) tree-stump
пе́рвый first
пере- *prefix* = (1) crossing, trans-; (2) repetition; (3) separation; (4) excess
перево́д translation
*переводи́ть (II)/перевести́ (I) to translate
перево́дчик (-ица) translator, interpreter
перевя́зка bandage, dressing
переговóрный пункт trunk calls office
перегна́ть (II) *pf* of перегоня́ть
перегоня́ть (I) to outstrip, outrun
пе́ред (пред)+*ins* in front of, before
перед обе́дом before dinner
перёд front, fore-part
*передава́ть (I)/переда́ть (*see* дать) to pass, give, hand; to broadcast
переда́ча transfer, handing over; radio broadcast
переде́лывать (I)/переде́лать (I) to amend, do again
пере́дний front
пере́дняя hall, lobby
*пережива́ть (I) to experience
*пережи́ть (I) *pf* of пережива́ть
*перейти́ (I) *pf* of переходи́ть
перекладны́е stage-horses
перекла́дывать (I) (*tr*) to move elsewhere
церекрёсток cross-road(s)
переложи́ть (II) *pf* of перекла́дывать
переписа́ть (I) *pf* of перепи́сывать
перепи́сывать (I) to rewrite; to make a list
перепи́сываться с+*ins* to correspond with
переплёт book cover, binding
переполня́ть (I)/перепо́лнить (II) to overfill, overcrowd
пересла́ть (I) *pf* of пересыла́ть
пересыла́ть (I) to send on, forward

переу́лок side-street
перехо́д passage, transition
перехо́ды pedestrians (crossing)
*****переходи́ть** (II) to pass over, to cross
пе́рец pepper
пери́од period
периоди́ческий periodical
перо́ (*pl* **пе́рья**) feather, plume; pen. *See* p. 131
пе́сня song
песо́к sand. *See* p. 152
пе́тля loop
*****петь** (I)/**с-** to sing; *see* p. 141
печа́тать (I) to print
печа́ть (*f*) seal, stamp; the press
пече́нье biscuit
пе́чка *dim* of **печь** stove
печь (*f*) stove, oven; furnace
*****печь** (I)/**с-** to bake; *see* p. 302
пешко́м on foot
пиани́но (*indec*) piano
пи́во beer
пик peak
пикни́к picnic
пи́сарь (*m*) copyist, clerk
писа́тель (*m*) (**-ница**) writer, author
*****писа́ть** (I)/**на-** to write
пи́счая бума́га writing paper
писчебума́жный магази́н stationer's
писчебума́жные принадле́жности stationery
пи́сьменный writing
письмецо́ short letter
письмо́ letter
пи́сывать (I) to go on writing, to write often; *see* p. 306-7
*****пить** (I) to drink; *see* p. 305
пи́шущий writing
    пи́шущая маши́нка typewriter
*****пла́вать** (I) to swim, float; to sail
*****пла́кать** (I) to weep, cry
пла́мя (*n*) blaze; *see* p. 126
план plan
плане́та planet
*****плати́ть** (II)/**за-** to pay
плато́к shawl
плато́чек handkerchief
пла́тье dress, gown; clothes
плафо́н decorated ceiling
плач weeping
пла́чущий weeping, crying
плева́ть (I) to spit; *see* p. 307

пле́мя (*n*) tribe, clan; *see* p. 126
племя́нник (*f* **-ца**) nephew
плеск splash
плеска́ться (I) to splash
плести́ (I) to weave, spin; *see* p. 302
плечо́ shoulder
пло́мба seal; filling, stopping (*teeth*)
    поста́вить пло́мбу to fill a tooth
плоти́на dam, dike
пло́хо bad(ly)
плохо́й bad; not well
пло́щадь (*f*) square; area
*****плыть** (I) (*see* **пла́вать**); *see* pp. 174-5
по + *dat* in motion; (1) on; (2) along; (3) by, over
    по по́чте by post
    по ра́дио by radio
    по распоряже́нию by order
    по у́лице along the street
    по оши́бке by mistake
    по полу́ночи after midnight
    по-мо́ему in my opinion
    по́ два two each; **по́ три** three each
по-англи́йски, по-ру́сски in English, in Russian
*****побе́гать** (I) to run about
*****побежа́ть** (*irr*) *pf* of **бе́гать/бежа́ть** to set off running
побо́льше somewhat bigger
по-ва́шему in your opinion
*****повезти́** (I) *pf* of **вози́ть/везти́** to drive, take
    ему́ повезло́ he was lucky
*****пове́рить** (II) *pf* of **ве́рить** to believe
*****поверну́ться** (I) *pf* of **повора́чиваться**
*****пове́сить** (II) *pf* to hang
*****повести́** (I) *pf* of **води́ть/вести́** to conduct, lead
пове́стка notice, summons
повора́чивать (I) to turn
повора́чиваться (*intr*) to turn
повторе́ние repetition
*****повторя́ть** (I)/**повтори́ть** (II) to repeat
повы́шенный increased
поговори́в(**-ши**) having talked
*****поговори́ть** (II) *pf* to have a chat
пого́да weather
*****погоди́ть** (II) *pf* to wait

погодя́ waiting

по́греб cellar

под(-о)+*acc*=*motion* under;+*ins*=*place* under; for; near; eve of; *see* pp. 143–144

   петь под му́зыку to sing to music

   под дождём in the rain

   под ве́чер towards evening

   под у́тро towards morning

пода́гра gout

подаю́щий giving, serving

подборо́док chin

подверга́ть (I) to subject to

подверга́ться to be subject to

подве́ргнуть(ся) (I) *pf* of подверга́ть(ся)

подве́рженный subject to

под ви́дом+*gen* under cover of

подвижно́й, подви́жный mobile

*подде́рживать (I) to support

поде́йствовать (I) *pf* to have effect

подкла́дывать (I)/подложи́ть (II) to underlay, line garments

подкупа́ть (I)/подкупи́ть (II) to bribe; to win over

по́дле next to

подложи́ть (II) *pf* of подкла́дывать

*поднима́ть (I) to raise, pick up

*поднима́ться to be lifted, to rise; to ascend

подноси́ть (II)/поднести́ (I) to bring; to hold up to

*подня́ть(ся) (I) *pf* of поднима́ть(ся).

подо́бно+*dat* like

подо́бный like

   ничего́ подо́бного nothing of the kind

подойти́ (I) *pf* of подходи́ть

подохо́дный нало́г income tax

подписа́ть(ся) *pf* of подпи́сываться)

подпи́сывать (I) (*tr*) to sign

подпи́сываться to sign one's name

по́дпись (*f*) signature

подража́ние imitation

подража́ть (I) *ipf* to imitate

подраздели́ть (II) *pf* to subdivide

подро́бность (*f*) detail

подру́га (*f*) friend

подставля́ть(I)/подста́вить(II) to substitute

подстри́чь (I) to clip, trim

*поду́мать (I) *pf* of ду́мать

*подходи́ть (II) to come up to, approach; to suit

*подходя́щий suitable

подъе́зд entrance, porch

*подъезжа́ть (I) to drive up to

подъём ascent

подъёмник elevator, lift

*подъе́хать (I) *pf* of подъезжа́ть

подыма́ть *see* поднима́ть

по́езд train

пое́здка trip, outing; journey

*пое́сть (*irr*) *pf* of есть to have a meal, snack

пое́хать *pf* of е́хать

пожа́луй very likely, maybe

пожа́луйте please (*invitation*)

пожа́луйста please (*request*)

пожела́ние wish

*пожела́ть (I) *pf* of жела́ть to wish, desire

пожива́ть (I) to fare

   как пожива́ете? How are you?

пожира́ть (I)/пожра́ть (I) to devour; *see* p. 302 *pf* Gr 2

*позабыва́ть (I)/позабы́ть (*see* быть) to forget about

*позволя́ть (I)/позво́лить (II) to allow

поздне́е later

поздне́йший late

по́здний late

по́здно it is late

по́зже later (on)

*познако́миться (II) *pf* to acquaint oneself with

позоло́та guilding; gilt

поигра́ть (I *pf* of игра́ть) to play for a while

поиска́ть (I) *pf* of иска́ть

*пойти́ (I) *pf* of ходи́ть/идти́

пока́ as long as, while; till; for the present

пока́зан, -а, -о ; -ы shown

показа́ние evidence, testimony

*показа́ть(ся) *pf* of пока́зывать(ся)

*пока́зывать (I) to show, display. See p. 140

*пока́зываться to appear, to show oneself, seem

пока́мест *see* пока́

*покáчивать (I) *ipf* to rock slightly

*покидáть (I)/покúнуть (I) to abandon, to leave

поклонúться/-úться to revere, worship

покóй rest, peace

поколéние generation

покорнéйше most, very humbly

покóрный obedient

покрытый covered

покупáтель (*m*) buyer

*покупáть (I)/купúть (II) to buy

покýпка purchase

покýшать (I) *pf* of кýшать to take food or drink

пол floor

пол- *prefix* = half, half a
  полбутылки half a bottle
  полвéка half a century
  полгóда half a year
  пóлдень midday
  полдня half a day
  полнóчи half a night
  пóлночь midnight
  полфýнта half a pound
  полчасá half an hour
  полдюжины half a dozen

пóле (*pl* поля) field

полевóй field
  полевые цветы wild flowers

*полетéть (II) *pf* of летáть/ летéть

*пóлзать (I)/ползтú (I) to creep, crawl; *see* p. 179

полúтика politics

пóлный full

половúна half

положим, что supposing that

положúтельный positive

*положúть (II) *pf* of класть to put

пóлон, полнá, -ó; -ы full, complete

полотéнце towel

полотнó linen; canvas

полотняный linen

полóть (I) to weed; *see* p. 306

полтúна fifty copecks

полторá, *f*: полторы one and a half

полторáста one hundred and fifty; *see* p. 204

*получáть (I)/получúть (II) to receive, acquire

*получáться/получúться to come, arrive (*by post etc.*); to turn out to be

получéние reception, acquisition

*пóльзоваться (I) *ipf* to make use of, to enjoy

пóлюс pole

поляк Pole (*nationality*)

полярник polar explorer

полярный polar, Arctic
  полярный круг polar circle

помéньше rather less

помéщик landlord, landowner

помéщичий (*like* трéтий) landowning, landowner's

помидóр tomato

*пóмнить (II) to remember

пóмниться (*impers*) to be remembered. *See* p. 148
  мне пóмнится I recollect

пóмня remembering

*помогáть (I)/помóчь (I) to help

по-мóему in my opinion

пóмощь (*f*) help

понатýжиться (II) to strain (oneself)

понедéльник Monday

*понестú (I) *pf* of носúть/ нестú to bear, carry

пóни pony

понимáние comprehension

*понимáть (I) to understand

понóс diarrhoea

понюхать (I) *pf* of нюхать *trs* to smell

*понять (I) *pf* of понимáть p.224

*попадáть (I)/попáсть (I) to catch, to hit; to find
  где попáло any old place

*поплáвать (I) *pf* of плáвать to swim about for a while

поплыть (I) *pf* of плáвать/ плыть to swim, float; to sail; *see* p. 174

попросúть (II) *pf* of просúть

порá *noun* time
  давнó порá it's high time

*поработáть (I) *pf* to work

поравняться (I) to come alongside

порóть (I) to tear; *see* p. 306

порт port

портмонé (*indec*) purse

портно́й tailor
портсига́р cigarette case
портфе́ль (*m*) briefcase; portfolio
по-ру́сски in Russian
  напи́сано по-ру́сски written in Russian
по́рция portion, helping
*посади́ть (II) *pf* (1) to plant; (2) to seat, place (*tr*)
посвяща́ть (I)/посвяти́ть (II) (1) to devote; (2) to dedicate; *pf* посвящу́, -яти́шь
посеща́ть (I)/посети́ть (II) to visit
поско́льку so far as; so long as, since
поскоре́е quicker
*посла́ть (I) *pf* of посыла́ть. *See* p. 223
по́сле + *gen* after
после́дний last
послеза́втра day after to-morrow
*послу́шаться (I) *pf* of слу́шаться to obey
посме́иваться (I) to laugh softly; to chuckle
посо́бие (1) belief. (2) textbook
посове́товать (I) *pf* of сове́товать to advise
посо́л ambassador
посо́льство embassy
*поста́вить (II) *pf* of ста́вить ; *see* p. 232
поста́вка supply; supplying
поставля́ть (I) *ipf* to supply, deliver
постано́вка production (*stage*)
поста́рше somewhat older
посте́ль (*f*) bed, bedding
постепе́нный gradual
постро́енный built
постро́йка building
*поступа́ть (I)/поступи́ть (II) to act, do; to enter; to join
посту́пок act, action
по́ступь (*f*) step, gait, walk
*посыла́ть (I) to send, despatch
  посыла́ть по по́чте to send by post
посы́лка (1) sending; (2) parcel
пот sweat, perspiration
*потеря́ть (I) *pf* of теря́ть to lose
потеря́ться to be lost
поте́шный amusing

потихо́ньку stealthily
пото́м afterwards
потому́, что because
*походи́ть (II) *pf* of ходи́ть to walk about for a while
почём ? how much (is) ?
почему́ why, how; (*adv*) that's why
почёсывать (I) *ipf* to scratch
почи́нка repair(ing); repairs
по́чта post; post office
  возду́шная по́чта air mail
  на по́чту to the post
  на по́чте at the post office
почтальо́н postman
почта́мт post office
почте́ние respect
почте́нный respectable, honourable
почти́ almost
почто́вый post(al)
  почто́вый я́щик letter box
  почто́вая бума́га note paper
  почто́вая конто́ра letter office
  почто́вое отделе́ние branch post office
пошеве́ливать (I) *ipf* to stir, shake
поэ́зия poetry
поэ́т poet
поэ́тому therefore
*появля́ться (I)/появи́ться (II) to appear
по́яс belt; zone
прав, -а́, -о ; -ы right, correct, true
пра́вда truth
правди́вый truthful
прави́тельственный government(al)
прави́тельство government
*пра́вить (II) *ipf* to rule, govern
пра́во right; licence
правосу́дие justice
пра́вый right; right wing (*politics*)
пра́здник holiday
  с пра́здником with best wishes
пра́здновать (I) *ipf* to celebrate; to take a holiday
пребыва́ние stay, sojourn
превыша́ть (I) *ipf* to exceed
прегра́да barrier, obstacle
пре́данный devoted, faithful

преде́л limit
преде́льный *adj* limit
-ая ско́рость top speed
*предлага́ть (I) *ipf* to offer, propose
предложе́ние proposal, suggestion
предложе́ние sentence (*in grammar*); clause
*предложи́ть (II) *pf* of предлага́ть
предостерега́ть (I) /предостере́чь (I) to warn, caution against
предосторо́жность (*f*) precaution
предпочита́ть (I)/предпоче́сть (I) to prefer
представле́ние performance, presentation
*представля́ть (I) / предста́вить (II) to present, introduce; to produce
*представля́ться / предста́виться (1) to introduce oneself; (2) to arise
предупрежда́ть (I)/предупреди́ть (II) to notify
пре́жде+*gen* before
пре́жний former, previous
прейскура́нт price list; bill of fare
прекра́сно excellent
прекра́сный beautiful; excellent
преоблада́ть (I) *ipf* to prevail
преодолева́ть (I)/преодоле́ть (I) to overcome
при+*prp* in the presence of; in the time of; by, at, near, when, about
прибавля́ть (I)/приба́вить (II) to add
прибо́р apparatus; cover (*at table*)
*прибыва́ть (I)/прибы́ть (*see* p. 223 to arrive; to get in
прибы́тие arrival
привлека́ть (I)/привле́чь (I) to attract, draw
*привыка́ть (I)/ привы́кнуть (I) to get accustomed to; *see* p. 243
*привяза́ть (I) *pf* to fasten, attach; to bind
при́город suburb. *dim* -ка
при́городный suburban; local

приготовля́ть (I) / пригото́вить (II) to prepare
приготовля́ться / пригото́виться to prepare oneself
приду́мывать (I)/приду́мать (I) to invent
прие́зд arrival
*приезжа́ть (I)/прие́хать (I) to arrive (*by vehicle*)
прие́м reception; waiting room
прие́мник radio receiver, set
прижима́ть (I)/прижа́ть (I) to clasp, press
*признава́ть (I)/призна́ть (I) to recognize, acknowledge
*признава́ться/призна́ться to confess, admit
призна́ние acknowledgement; confession
призна́тельный grateful
*прийти́(сь) *pf* of приходи́ть(ся)
приключе́ние adventure
прикрепля́ть (I)/прикрепи́ть (II) to fasten
прилага́ть (I) *ipf* to apply; to enclose
приле́жный diligent; studious
приложе́ние supplement
приложи́ть (II) *pf* of прилага́ть
приме́р example
приме́рить (II) *pf* of примеря́ть
приме́рный exemplary; *also* approximate
примеря́ть (I) to try on; to fit
примире́ние reconciliation
примири́мый reconcilable
примо́рский seaboard
*принадлежа́ть (II) *ipf only* to belong to
принадле́жности (*pl*) accessories
*принести́ (I) *pf* of приноси́ть
принёсши bringing
принеся́ (having) brought
*принима́ть (I) to take, receive
принима́ть ва́нну, душ to take, have a bath, shower
*приноси́ть (II) to fetch, bring in
*приня́ть (I) *pf* of принима́ть; *see* p. 224
приписывать(I) /приписа́ть(I) to add to in writing; to ascribe; to attribute

приправа condiment(s); spices
природа nature
природный natural; inborn
*прислать (I) pf of присылать
пристань (f) pier, landing place
*приступать (I)/приступить
(II) to set to, start
присущий inherent
присылать (I) to send
присяга oath of allegiance
притворяться (I)/притворить-
ся (II) to pretend, feign
притихать (I)/притихнуть (I)
to grow, become quiet
приток tributary; flow
*приходить (II)/прийти (I)
to come, arrive
*приходиться/прийтись (im-
pers) to have to
мне приходится I have
to . . .
ему пришлось he had to . . .
причёска hair-style; coiffeur
пришивать (I)/пришить (I)
to sew on; see p. 305
приятель (m) friend, crony,
pal
приятельница (f) girl friend
приятный pleasant, agreeable
про + acc concerning, about
пробка cork
*пробовать (I) (по-) to try,
taste; see p. 307
пробор parting (hair)
прованское масло olive oil
проверять (I)/проверить (II)
to examine, check, verify
*провести (I) pf of проводить
*проводить (II)/провести (I)
to take, lead; to build; to
carry out
провести дорогу to make a
road
проводник guide; guard, conductor
*провожать (I) ipf/проводить
(II) pf to see off, accom-
pany
проголодаться (I) pf to be
hungry
прогулка walk, stroll
*продавать (I)/продать (irr
like дать) to sell
*продаваться/продаться to
be for sale
продавец seller; salesman
продать (irr) pf of продавать

продлить (II) pf to extend (a
visa)
продукт product
проезжать (I) ipf to pass by,
drive by
проезд passage
нет п- (there is) no passage
проект project, design
проехать (I) pf of проезжать
произведение work (lit)
избранные произведения
select(ed) works (of a writer)
*производить (II) ipf to pro-
duce, make, to manufacture
производственный процесс
process of production
производство (1) production;
(2) industry; works, factory
*произносить (II)/произнести
(I) to pronounce
произношение pronunciation
*происходить (II)/произойти
(I) to happen, occur, take
place
*пройти (I) pf of проходить
прокол puncture
пролетариат proletariat
пролив strait, sound (on map)
получать (I)/получить (II) to
obtain, get
промокательная бумага
blotting paper
промокнуть (I) pf of мокнуть
also of промокать
пронзительный piercing (cry)
*проникать (I)/проникнуть (I)
to penetrate
прописать(ся) pf of прописы-
вать(ся)
прописка registration
прописывать (I) ipf to prescribe (treatment)
прописываться to get registered
пропуск pass, permit; admis-
sion
пропускать(I)/пропустить (II)
to let go past, through; to
omit, miss
просьба request
— не шуметь! silence please!
*просить (II)/по- to ask, beg:
see p. 74
проспект avenue; also pros-
pectus
простаивать (I)/простоять(II)
to stand for long

*прости́ть (II) pf of проща́ть
*прости́те! Forgive me
просто́й simple, easy; ordinary
простоква́ша sour milk, curds and whey
просто́р spaciousness; space, room
простра́нный vast, extensive
простра́нство space
просту́да cold, chill
простуди́ться (II) pf to catch cold
просыпа́ться (I)/просну́ться (I) to wake up
прота́лкиваться (I)/протолкну́ться (I) to push through
про́тив + gen against; opposite
протя́гивать (I)/протяну́ть (I) to extend, stretch out
протя́жность (f) slowness
профе́ссор professor
прохо́д passage
*проходи́ть (II)/пройти́ (I) to walk by, past; to go
прохо́дка driving, boring (in mining)
проце́нт per cent, percentage
  плати́ть проце́нты to pay interest
проце́сс process
*проче́сть (I) pf of чита́ть to read
прочита́в(-ши) having read through
*прочита́ть (I) pf of чита́ть to read through
прочте́ние reading
прочь away
  прочь ру́ки! Hands off!
  прочь отсю́да! Get out (of it)!
проше́ствие lapse
  по проше́ствии after (the) lapse
про́шлый past
  про́шлое the past
проща́й(-те)! good bye
проща́льный parting, farewell
проща́ние farewell, leave taking
*проща́ть (I)/прости́ть (II) to pardon, forgive
*проща́ться/прости́ться to say good-bye, take leave (of)
про́ще simpler
пруд pond

*пры́гать (I)/пры́гнуть (I) to jump
пряме́е more directly
пря́мо straight (on); direct
прямо́й straight, direct
прячь (I)/за- to harness
пти́ца bird
  дома́шняя пти́ца poultry
пти́чий adj poultry; of bird
пу́блика public; audience
пу́говица button
пу́говка small button
пункт point; station; item
пурга́ snowstorm
*пуска́й + inf = to let
*пуска́ть (I)/пусти́ть (II) to let go, free.
*пусти́ть (II) pf of пуска́ть
пусто́й empty
пусты́нный deserted
пусты́ня desert
*пусть + inf = to let
пу́таница muddle
пу́тать (I) ipf to confuse
пу́таться ipf to contradict oneself; to be confused
путеводи́тель (m) guide (book)
путём by means of
путеше́ственник traveller
путеше́ствие journey
путеше́ствовать (I) ipf to travel; see p. 307
путеше́ствующий travelling
путь (m irr) way, track, path, road
пучегла́зый goggle-eyed
пу́хнуть (I) to swell; see pp. 303-4 Cl II Gr 1
пу́шка gun, cannon
пыл eagerness
пыль (f) dust
пы́льный dusty
пыта́ть (I) ipf to torture
*пыта́ться ipf to attempt, try
пытли́вый inquisitive
пье́са play, drama
пья́нствовать (I) ipf to drink hard; see p. 307
пья́ный drunk, tipsy
пята́к five-copeck piece
пя́теро five (of); see p. 203
пятирублёвая бума́жка five rouble note
пя́тка heel

Р

рабо́та work

на рабо́ту to work
на рабо́те at work
*рабо́тать (I) *ipf* to work
рабо́тник workman
рабо́тница workwoman
  дома́шняя рабо́тница
    maid, servant
рабо́чий working, worker
  рабо́чий класс working class
равни́на plain
ра́вный equal
равня́ться (I) *ipf* to be equal
  to
рад, ра́да, ра́ды glad
  я вам рад I'm happy to see
    you
ра́ди + *gen* for the sake of
радиа́тор radiator
ра́дио radio
радиопереда́ча broadcast
радиоприёмник radio set
радиоста́нция radio station
*ра́довать (I)/об- to gladden
*ра́доваться/об- to be glad,
  rejoice; *see* p. 307
ра́достный joyful
ра́дость (*f*) joy
раду́шие cordiality
раду́шный cordial
раз time (*particular occasion*)
раз one, once
  раз так if that's so
раз-, рас- разо- *prefixes* = (1)
  division, separation; (2) development
разбива́ть (I)/разби́ть (I) *like*
  бить) to break; to defeat
разбива́ться/разби́ться to
  break (*intr*)
разби́тый broken
разби́ть(ся) (I) *pf* of разби-
  ва́ть(ся)
разбо́й robbery
разбо́йник robber, bandit
разбушева́ться (I) *pf* to rage,
  storm
*разбуди́ть (II) *pf* to wake,
  call, arouse
ра́зве? really?
*разгова́ривать (I) *ipf* to converse with; *see* pp. 306–7 **A**
разгово́р conversation
разгро́м rout, defeat
раздава́ться (I)/разда́ться (*irr*
  like дать) to resound
раздева́льня cloak room
разде́л division

разделе́ние division
*разделя́ть (I)/раздели́ть (II)
  to divide, separate
раздира́ть (I)/разодра́ть (I)
  to tear up
разли́тие жёлчи jaundice
различа́ть (I) to distinguish
различа́ться to differ from
различи́ть (II) *pf* of различа́ть
разли́чный different
разложе́ние decay
разложи́ть (II) *pf* (1) to decom-
  pose (*tr*). (2) to apportion
разме́нивать (I)/разменя́ть (I)
  to change; exchange
разме́р size
  по разме́ру in extent
разме́тить (II) *pf* to mark out
ра́зница difference
разнообра́зен, разнообра́зна,
  -о ; -ы various, diverse
разнообра́зие variety, diver-
  sity
разнообра́зный various, mixed
разно́ска пи́сем delivery of
  letters
ра́зный different; various, diverse
разойти́сь (I) *pf* of расходи́ть-
  ся
разоря́ться (I) *ipf* to be ruined
разреша́ть (I) *ipf* to allow,
  permit
разреше́ние permission
разреши́ть (II) *pf* of разре-
  ша́ть
разры́в tear, rupture
разрыва́ть (I)/разорва́ть (I)
  to dig up; to turn upside
  down
разрыва́ться/разорва́ться
  to break, burst, explode
разу́мный reasonable
разъединя́ть (I)/разъедини́ть
  (II) to cut off, separate
рай paradise
райо́н district, region
райо́нный district, regional
рак crayfish; *also* cancer
раке́та rocket
раке́тка racket (*tennis*)
ракетопла́н rocket plane
ра́мка frame
ра́нить (II) *ipf* and *pf* to
  wound
ра́нний early
ра́но it is early

ра́ньше earlier; formerly

раскалённый red hot

раскаля́ть (I)/**раскали́ть** (II) to make burning hot

раскла́дывать (I)/**разложи́ть** (II) to lay out

расписа́ние time table

расписа́ть (I) *pf* to paint (pictures) all over

расписа́ться (I) *pf* of **распи́сываться**

распи́ска receipt

распи́сываться (I) *ipf* to sign for

располага́ть (I) *ipf* to arrange, place, dispose

располага́ться to settle down

расположе́ние arrangement

расположи́ть (I) *pf* of **располага́ть**

распоряжа́ться (II)/**распоряди́ться** (I) to give orders; to dispose of

распоряже́ние orders; decree

расска́з story, tale

расска́зывать (I)/**рассказа́ть** (I) to tell, relate

рассма́тривать (I)/**рассмотре́ть** (II) to examine, consider

рассмея́ться (I) *pf* to burst out laughing

расспроси́в(-ши) having asked, having made enquiries

расстоя́ние distance

расстро́йство disorder

рассчи́танный calculated, deliberate

рассчи́тывать (I)/**рассчита́ть** (I) to calculate, count; to count on

раста́пливать (I)/**растопи́ть** (II) to melt; to thaw

*расти́ (I)/**вы-** to grow; *see* p. 302

расти́тельный vegetable

расчёт calculation

*рвать (I) *ipf* to tear, pick, pull out; *see* p. 303

рве́ние zeal

рво́та vomiting

ребёнок (*pl* **де́ти**) child

ребя́та "kids", the boys, chaps

ребя́ческий childish

реве́нь (*m*) rhubarb

реве́ть (I) to roar, bellow

революцио́нный revolutionary

револю́ция revolution

ре́гби rugby (football)

реда́ктор editor

ре́дкий rare, uncommon

ре́дко (*adv*) seldom

ре́же rarer, more uncommon

режиссёр producer (*theatre*)

резви́ться (II) *ipf* to frisk, gambol

резьба́ carving

рейс trip, passage

река́ (*pl* **ре́ки**) river

религио́зный religious

рели́гия religion

релье́ф relief (*map*)

ре́льсы rails

ремо́нт repair

ремонти́ровать to repair

ре́па turnip

репети́ция rehearsal

рестора́н restaurant

реце́пт recipe; prescription

ре́чка stream

реше́ние decision; solution

реши́тельность (*f*) resolution

*реши́ть(ся) (II) *pf* of **реша́ть(ся)** to decide, resolve, determine

риск risk

*рискова́ть (I)/**рискну́ть** (I) to risk

рисова́ние drawing

*рисова́ть (I) *ipf* to draw; *see* p. 306

*рисова́ться to be drawn, sketched; to pose

рису́нок drawing

ро́вно exactly

ро́вный flat, even

род family, kin

о́троду from birth

ро́дина native land

любо́вь к ро́дине love of country; patriotism

роди́ть (II) *pf* of **рожа́ть** to give birth (to)

*роди́ться to be born

родно́й native; kindred

рожа́ть (I)/**роди́ть** (II) to give birth to

рожде́ние birth

день рожде́ния birthday

Рождество́ (Христо́во) Christmas

рожь (*f*) rye

ро́зовый pink, rose coloured

рома́н novel
ро́пот murmur
роса́ dew
роско́шный luxurious
ро́скошь (*f*) luxury
ростби́ф roast beef
роя́ль (*m*) grand piano
рубль (*m*) rouble
  -рублёвый of (so many) roubles
рука́ (*pl* ру́ки) hand, arm
рука́в sleeve
руководи́тель (*m*) leader; guide
*руководи́ть (II) *ipf* to lead, guide
ру́сский Russian; *see* p. 99
ру́чка knob, handle; penholder
ры́ба fish
ры́бий fish(y)
ры́бий жир cod liver oil
ры́бный
  ры́бный суп fish soup
ры́нок market
рыть (I) to dig; *see* p. 305
рю́мка small glass; wine glass
рю́мочка liqueur glass
ряд row, line, series; file (*mil*)
ря́дом near, close by

С

с (со)+*gen*=from, from off;+*ins* =along with
сад garden
*сади́ть (II) *det* *ipf* to plant, seat
*сади́ться (II)/сесть (I) to sit down; *see* p. 232
сажа́ть (I) *ipf* *indet* to seat, offer a seat; to put; to plant; *see* p. 232, 306 **A**
сала́т salad
салфе́тка napkin, serviette
сам, сама́, само́, са́ми -self; *see* p. 81
самолёт aeroplane
са́мый (1) the very; (2) the most. *See* p. 82
  тот же са́мый the same
санато́рий sanatorium
сара́й shed
сарафа́н peasant woman's dress (*Russia*)
сарди́ны sardines
са́хар sugar

Caха́ра Sahara
сбо́ку from *or* at the side
сва́дьба wedding
све́жесть (*f*) freshness
све́жий fresh
свёкла beetroot
сверну́ть (I) *pf* of **свора́чивать (I)**
сверх того́ furthermore
све́рху from above
све́рху до́низу from top to bottom
свет light
свет world
свети́ть (II) *ipf* to shine
свети́ться to be shining
свеча́, све́чка candle
свида́ние appointment
  до свида́ния till we meet; *au revoir*
свини́на pork
сви́нка mumps
свобо́да freedom
свобо́ден, свобо́дна, -о ; -ы free
свобо́дно fluently (*of speech*)
свобо́дный free
свой *pronoun* one's own: p. 81
свора́чивать (I)/сверну́ть (I) to displace, remove; to turn; to roll (*up*)
*свя́зывать (I)/связа́ть (I) to tie, bind, connect
связь (*f*) tie, bond
сгиба́ть (I) *ipf* to bend (*tr*)
сгиба́ться to bend (*intr*)
сгова́риваться (I) /сговори́ться (II) to agree (about something)
сгущённый thickened, condensed
сда́ча surrender; change
*сде́лать (I) *pf* of **де́лать** to do, make
сде́латься *pf* of **де́латься** to become, grow, get
себя́ *reflexive pron*=self: 145–6
сев(-ши) sowing
се́вер north
се́верный northern
сего́дня to-day
сего́дняшний to-day's
седьмо́й seventh
сезо́н season
сезо́нный seasonal
сей this; *see* p. 156

сейча́с (1) now; in a moment

секрета́рь (m) -та́рша (f) secretary

секу́нда second (of time)

селёдка herring

сели́ть (II)/по- to settle

сели́ться/по- to settle (intr)

сели́шко (dim) dirty little village

село́ village

сельдь (f) herring

се́льское хозя́йство agriculture

сельскохозя́йственный agricultural

сельсове́т (=се́льский сове́т) village council (Soviet): p. 168

се́меро seven of; see p. 203

семья́ family

се́мя (n) seed; see p. 126

се́но hay

се́ни (pl) porch

се́ра sulphur

*серди́ться (II)/рас- to be angry, vexed

се́рный sulphurous

се́рый grey

сестра́ (pl сёстры) sister

 медици́нская сестра́ nursing sister

сестри́ца (dim) little sister

*сесть (I) pf of сади́ться; see pp. 232, 302

се́тка net

сечь (I) ipf to whip, flog, slash; see p. 302

се́ять (I) ipf to sow; see p. 306

сза́ди from behind

сиби́рский Siberian

Сиби́рь (f) Siberia

сибиря́к inhabitant of Siberia

сигаре́та cigarette (without mouthpiece)

сигна́л signal; call

*сиде́ть (II)/по- to be sitting; see pp. 232, 308

си́ла strength

 вооружённые си́лы armed forces

си́лен, сильна́, -о ; -ы strong

сильне́е stronger

си́льно strongly; greatly

си́льный strong, powerful

симфони́ческий конце́рт symphony concert

си́ний (dark) blue

сино́д synod

сире́на siren

сире́нь (f) lilac

сифо́н siphon

*сказа́ть (I) pf of говори́ть to tell

ска́зка story

ска́зочный fantastic or fairy tale

сква́жина keyhole; drill hole

скве́рный nasty

сквозь through

скла́дывать (I)/сложи́ть (II) to put together, add up

сколь (adv) how much, how many

 сколь ча́сто how often

ско́лько how much, how many

 ско́лько нибудь a little

скоре́е quickly

ско́ро quickly, fast

ско́рость (f) speed

ско́рый quick, fast

 ско́рая по́мошь first aid

 каре́та ско́рой по́мощи ambulance

скрипа́ч violinist

скрипи́чный конце́рт violin concerto

скри́пка violin

скульпту́ра sculpture

скупова́тость (f) stinginess

скупова́тый parsimonious

скупо́й stingy

ску́пость (f) greed

ску́пщик buyer-up; person who "corners" something

*скуча́ть (I)/по- to be weary, bored

ску́чно bored

ску́чный dull, boring

ску́шать (I) pf of ку́шать to eat up

слабе́е, сла́бже weaker, feebler

слаби́тельное purge, laxative

сла́бость (f) weakness

сла́бый weak, feeble

сла́виться (II)/про- to be famous

сла́вный famous; coll nice

сла́дкий sweet

сла́ще sweeter

сле́ва to the left

слегка́ slightly

след trace, track

сле́довать (I)/по- to follow; see p. 307

вам сле́дует   you ought to

сле́дуемый   due, deserved

сле́дующий   following, next

слеза́ (pl слёзы)   tear

слепо́й   blind

сле́пнуть (I)/о-   to become blind; see pp. 304

сли́вки (f pl)   cream

сли́шком (adv)   too, too much, too many

слобода́   village near a town

слобо́дка   suburb, outskirts

слова́рь (m)   dictionary; vocabulary

сло́вно   as if, as though

сло́во   word

сло́вом   in a word

сложи́ть(ся) pf of скла́дывать(ся)

сло́жный   complex, complicated

слон   elephant

*служи́ть (II)/по-   to serve, wait on

слу́чай   case, instance, event; chance

*случа́ться (I)/случи́ться (II)   to take place, happen

слу́шатель (m)   hearer, student

*слу́шать (I)/по- to listen to p. 73

слу́шаю!   Hello! (on the phone)

*слу́шаться/по-   to obey

слыть (I)про-   to be reputed

слыха́ть ipf (past tense only)   to hear (about)

*слы́шать (II)/у-   to hear. See p. 73

*слы́шаться/по-   to be heard

смерть (f)   death

*сметь (I)/по-   to dare; see p. 305

смех   laughter

смешно́й   ridiculous, funny

*смея́ться (I)/за-   to laugh; see pp. 145, 166, 306

*смотре́ть (II)/по-   to look; see p. 308

смотре́ться/по-   to look at oneself

смотря́ на   depending on

смочь (I) pf of мочь   to be able

снасть (f)   tackle; pl rigging

снег   snow

снег идёт   it's snowing

снежо́к (dim)   snowflake, snowball

*снима́ть (I) ipf   to take away; to photograph

снима́ться   to be photographed

сни́мок   photograph. See p. 224

сно́ва   again, anew

снова́ть (I)   to scurry; see p. 307

сно́ска   reference, footnote

снотво́рное   soporific

*снять(ся) pf of снимать(ся)

соба́ка   dog

собачёнка   little cur; whelp

соба́чий   of dog; doggy

соба́чка (dim)   little dog; lapdog

собира́ние   collection

собира́тельный   collective

*собира́ть (I)   to gather, collect

*собира́ться   to assemble, meet together

собо́р   cathedral

собра́ние   meeting

   по́лное собра́ние сочине́ний   complete works of

*собра́ть(ся) pf of собира́ть(ся)

со́бственность (f)   property

со́бственный   one's own

собы́тие   event

сова́ть (I)/су́нуть (I)   to shove, thrust; see p. 242

соверше́нный   perfect; absolute

со́вестно   ashamed

   мне со́вестно   I feel ashamed

со́весть (f)   conscience

сове́т   council, Soviet

сове́т   advice, counsel

*сове́товать (I)по-   to advise; see p. 307

сове́товаться/по-   to consult, seek advice

сове́тский   Soviet

совреме́нный   contemporary; modern

совсе́м   quite, entirely

совсе́м нет   not at all

согла́сно + dat   according to

соглаше́ние   understanding

содержи́мое   contents

сожале́ть (I) ipf and pf   to regret, be sorry for

созва́ть (I) pf of созыва́ть

*создава́ть (I)/созда́ть (irr like дать)   to create

созда́ние   creation

созрева́ние   ripening

созы́в   convocation

созыва́ть (I) ipf   to call together, summon. See p. 224

*сойти́ (I) *pf* of сходи́ть
  сойти́ с ре́льсов to be derailed
сокраща́ть (I)/сократи́ть (II)
  to shorten, abridge.
сокраще́ние abbreviation
сокращённый shortening
сокро́вище treasure
солда́т soldier
соли́ст soloist
со́лнце sun (л *silent*)
соло́нка salt cellar
соль (*f*) salt
*сомнева́ться (I) *ipf* to doubt
сон sleep; dream. *See* p. 152
со́нный sleepy
сорва́ть(ся) (I) *pf* of срыва́ть-
  (ся) to pick, tear off; to fall, fail
соро́ка magpie
сосе́д (*m*) neighbour
сосе́дка (*f*) neighbour
сосе́дний next, neighbouring
соси́ска sausage
со́ска rubber teat
соста́в composition; *also* staff
*составля́ть (I)/соста́вить (II)
  to compose
составно́й compound; component
*состоя́ть (II) *ipf* (1) to bet;
  (2) to consist of
  состоя́ть в бра́ке to be married
состоя́ться to happen
состяза́ние contest
состяза́ться (I) to compete
со́тня a hundred; *see* p. 118–9
со́хнуть (I)/за-, вы́- to grow dry, be parched; *see* pp. 243, 296–7
социали́зм socialism
социали́ст socialist
социалисти́ческий socialist(ic)
сочине́ние work, composition
сочиня́ть (I)/сочини́ть (II) to write, compose
сою́з union; conjunction
  Сове́тский Сою́з Soviet Union
сою́зник ally
сою́зный of the union
спа́льня bedroom
спаси́бо! thank you, thanks
*спать/поспа́ть (II) to be asleep

спекта́кль (*m*) performance, show
специа́льность (*f*) speciality
специа́льный special
*спеши́ть (II)/по- to hurry; to be quick; *see* p. 308
спирт spirit, alcohol
спиртны́е напи́тки alcoholic drinks
списа́ть (I) *pf* of спи́сывать
спи́сывать (I) to copy from
спи́чка match
сплошно́й unbroken
сплошь (*adv*) continuously
споко́йный quiet, calm
  споко́йной но́чи! good night
сполна́ fully
спо́мнив(-ши)
спо́мнить (II) *pf* of по́мнить to remember
*спо́рить (II) to argue, dispute
спо́рный debatable, questionable
спра́ва to the right of
спра́вка (*pl* -ки) information
спра́вочник reference book
спра́вочное бюро́ enquiry bureau, office
*спра́шивать (I)/спроси́ть (II) to ask
*спроси́ть (II) *pf* of спра́шивать. *See* p. 192
спросо́нья sleepily
спуска́ть (I) to lower; to launch
спуска́ться to go down, descend
спусти́ть(ся) (II) *pf* of спуска́ть(ся)
спустя́ + *acc* after
спу́тник companion; satellite
спя́щий sleeping
сра́зу at once
среди́ among
сре́дний middle, average
сре́дство means; remedy
сро́чный urgent
срыва́ть (I) *ipf* to pick, tear off; to spoil
срыва́ться to fall, break loose; fail, miscarry
ссо́ра quarrel
ссо́риться/по- to quarrel
СССР (Сою́з Сове́тских Социалисти́ческих Респу́блик) Union of Soviet Socialist Republics; USSR
*ста́вить (II)/по- to put, place; to stage, produce, put on; to lay down; *see* p. 232

стака́н glass

стака́нчик little glass

ста́ло быть consequently

сталь (f) steel

стан stature; body; bodice

*станови́ться (II)/стать (I) to become, get; to take one's stand

ста́нция station

стар, -а́, -о ; -ы old

стара́тельный painstaking

*стара́ться (I)/по- try, endeavour

стари́к old man

ста́рость (f) old age

стару́ха old woman

ста́рше older

ста́рший elder, eldest, oldest

ста́рый old

*стать (I) pf of станови́ться to become, get, grow (intr); see pp. 225, 232

статья́ article, editorial

стена́ wall

сте́нопись (f) wall painting, mural

степь (f) steppe

стереофони́ческий звук stereophonic sound

стере́чь (I) to guard, watch; see p. 302

сте́рлинг sterling (£)

сте́рлинговый (adj) sterling

сти́рка washing, laundering

стихи́я element

сто́имость (f) cost; value

*сто́ить (II) to cost, be worth

стол table; also board

столи́ца capital (city)

столо́вая dining-room

сто́лько so much, so many

сто́лько ско́лько as much as

стоп! Stop!

сторона́ side; party; place

сто́я standing

стоя́нка car park; stopping place

— такси́ taxi rank

*стоя́ть (II) to stand; to be standing

стоя́ть за . . . to be, s. for . . . ;

страна́ country, land

стра́нствование wandering

стра́шен, страшна́, -о ; -ы terrible, dreadful

стра́шно it is terrible, dreadful

стра́шный terrible, dreadful

стри́жка haircut; shearing

стричь (I)/по- to cut

стри́чься/по- to have one's hair cut; see p. 302

строй system, order

строи́тельство

строи́тель (m) builder

строи́тельный (adj) building

*стро́ить (II)/по- to build

стро́иться to be built

стро́йка building (act)

стро́йно slender, slim; harmonious

стро́йный slender, slim

студе́нт student

сту́дия studio

сту́жа cold, hard frost

стул chair; see p. 131

*стуча́ть (II)/по- to knock, bang

стуча́ться/по- to knock

постуча́ться в дверь to knock at the door

стуча́щий knocking, banging

сты́нуть (I)/о- to grow cold; to freeze; see p. 243

суд court of law; trial

су́дно (pl суда́) ship, vessel

судья́ judge

*суме́ть (I) pf of уме́ть to be able; to succeed

сунду́к trunk, chest

суп soup

су́тки day and night (24 hours)

суть are (in exact definition; in science)

суть (f) essence

суть де́ла the heart of the matter

су́хо it's dry

сухо́й dry (tr)

су́ше drier

суши́лка drying apparatus; drier

суши́ть (II)/вы- to dry

существова́ние existence

*существова́ть (I) ipf to exist, be; see p. 307

схвати́ть (II) на́сморк to catch a cold

схе́ма scheme; diagram, sketch

*сходи́ть (II)/сойти́ (I) to go down; to get off, come off; to pass as

сце́на stage; scene

сце́нка little scene

счастли́вый happy, fortunate

сча́стье happiness; luck

счесть *pf of* **счита́ть** to count:
сочту́, -тешь, -тут. счёл, сочла́

счёт calculation; account, bill

счита́лка counting rhyme

*****счита́ть** (I) *ipf* to count, consider

*****счита́ться** to be considered, reputed

США = U.S.A. **Соединённые Шта́ты Аме́рики** United States of America

сын son. *See* p.131

сыни́шка little son

сыпь (*f*) rash

сыр cheese

сы́ро it is damp

сыро́й damp; raw

сы́рость (*f*) dampness

сыска́ть (I) *pf* to seek and find

сюда́ to here, hither

ся *reflexive par* pp. 146–7

Т

таба́к tobacco

таба́чный tobacco

табу́ taboo

так so; like that
так как as, since
так . . . как . . .
as . . . as . . .
так-таки́ so, in fact

та́кже also too

-таки *suffix* = and so, after all

тако́й such

такси́ taxi

тала́нтливый talented

там there

тамо́жня custom house

танцева́ть (I)/**по-** to dance

танцо́р male dancer (*ballet*)

танцу́я dancing

таре́лка plate

таска́ть (I) to carry, pull, drag; to steal; *see* p. 180

тата́рин (*pl* **тата́ры**) Tatar (Tartar)

тата́рский Tatar

*****тащи́ть** (II)/**по-** (*det ipf of* **таска́ть**); *see* p. 180

твёрдо firmly

твёрдый hard; firm

твёрже harder

теа́тр theatre

телегра́мма telegram

телегра́ф telegraph; telegram office

телеграфи́ровать (I) to telegraph, cable

телегра́фный telegraph
телегра́фный а́дрес telegraphic address
телегра́фный бланк telegram form

теле́жка small cart

телефо́н telephone

телефо́н-автома́т automatic telephone

телефони́ст(-ка) telephone operator (*m* and *f*)

телефо́нная кни́га telephone directory, book

те́ло body

тем by this, with this
чем . . ., тем . . .
the . . . the . . .
тем лу́чше so much the better
тем ху́же so much the worse
тем бо́лее (что) especially as

тёмный dark

температу́ра temperature

те́ннис tennis

тёпел, тепла́, -о ;-ы warm

тепе́рь now

тепло́ it is warm

тёплый warm

терпе́ние patience

*****терпе́ть** (II) *ipf* to bear, endure, tolerate; *see* p. 308,

те́сно crowded, cramped

те́сный cramped, tight, narrow

тётенька (*dim*) dear little auntie

тётка aunt(ie)

тетра́дь (*f*) note book

тётушка (*dim*) dear auntie

тётя aunt

техни́ческий technical

течь (I) to flow, run; *see* p. 302

тип type

типи́чный typical

типово́й standard, model, type

ти́хий quiet, calm; low

ти́хо it is quiet, calm

ти́ше! silence!

ткать (I) to weave; *see* p. 296

то that

то then
то . . . то . . .
now . . . now . . .

-то suffix = (1) *emphatic*

-то (2) *vagueness* кто-то somebody, anybody

това́рищ colleague, mate, comrade, chap

това́рищеский comradely, friendly

това́рищество association

*то есть that is

то́же also, too

толк sense; use; doctrine

*толка́ть (I)/толкну́ть (I) to push, shove

то́лстый thick; fat, stout

то́лще fatter, stouter

то́лько only

том volume (*book*)

тому́ наза́д ago

то́мный languid

то́нкий thin, slim; delicate

тону́ть (I)/по- to drown, sink (*intr*)

то́ньше thinner

топи́ть (II) *ipf* to heat; to melt

*топи́ться *ipf* to burn (*intr*)

топлёный melted (butter etc.)

то́пленный heated

торгова́ть (I) *ipf* to trade; *see* p. 307

торго́вец trader, merchant

торго́вля trade, commerce

торго́вый trading, commercial

то́рмоз brake

торопи́ть (II)/по- to hurry

торопи́ться/по- to be in a hurry

торопли́вый hurried

то́рос (ice) hummock

тот that

то́тчас instantly, at once

то́чка point, dot, full stop

точка зре́ния point of view

то́чно it is exact; precisely

то́чность (*f*) precision, accuracy

то́чный exact

тошни́ть (II) *ipf* (*impers*) to feel ill

меня́ тошни́т I feel ill, sick

тошнота́ sickness, nausea

траге́дия tragedy

тра́ктор tractor

тракто́рист tractor driver

трамва́й tram, street car

*тре́бовать (I)/по- to demand; to require; *see* p. 307

тре́боваться/по- to be required, needed

трево́га alarm, anxiety

трево́жить (II) *ipf* to alarm, disturb, trouble

трево́жный uneasy; disturbing

тре́тий third; *see* p. 202

треть (*f*) one third

*тро́гать (I)/тро́нуть (I) to touch, move

*тро́гаться/тро́нуться to start, move

тро́гаться в путь to set out

тро́е three of; *see* p. 203

тро́йка team of three horses

тролле́йбус trolleybus

тро́нуть(ся) *pf* of тро́гать(ся); *see* pp. 244, 303-4

тротуа́р side walk, pavement

труба́ pipe, tube

тру́бка pipe; telephone receiver

тру́ден, трудна́, -о; -ы difficult

трудне́е more difficult

трудне́йший being difficult

тру́дный difficult

туале́т lavatory

туда́ to there, to that place

тужи́ть (II) to worry, grieve

тума́н mist, fog

тунне́ль (*m*) tunnel

тури́ст tourist

тури́стский tourist

тут here

ту́фля shoe

ту́ча cloud

ты thou; you (*fam*)

ты́сяча thousand

тьма darkness, dark

тюле́нь (*m*) seal, sea calf

тюль (*m*) tulle

тюрьма́ prison

тяжёлый painful; difficult, hard

*тяну́ть (I)/по- to pull, draw. *See* p. 244

У

у + *gen* = possession; at the home of; by, near

у меня́ ... I have ...

*убега́ть (I) to run away

*убежа́ть *irr like* бежа́ть) *pf* of убега́ть

уби́йство murder, killing

уби́йца murderer

убо́р attire, dress

убо́рная toilet; dressing room

убы́ток loss

уважа́емый respected; dear (*in letters*)

*****уважа́ть** (I) *ipf* to respect

уважа́ющий having respect

уваже́ние respect

*****увезти́** (I) *pf* of **увози́ть** to drive, take away

увели́чивать (I) to increase, extend, augment

увели́чиваться (*intr*) to increase

увели́чит(ся) *pf* of **увели́чивать(ся)**

увести́ (I) *pf* of **уводи́ть** to lead, take away

*****уви́деть** (II) to spot, to catch sight of; *pf* of **ви́деть**

уви́дя catching sight of

увлека́ться (I) *ipf* to be carried away; to become infatuated (with)

увлече́ние passion, craze, enthusiasm

уго́дно welcome, pleasing

как вам уго́дно as you choose

что вам уго́дно? What can I do for you?

куда́ уго́дно anywhere

у́гол corner; angle. *See p.* 152

у́голь (*m*) coal. *See p.* 152

угрю́мый grim, forbidding

*****удава́ться** (I)/**уда́ться** (*irr like* **дать**) (*impers*) to be successful

ему́ удало́сь he succeeded (in)

*****удаля́ть** (I)/**удали́ть** (II) to move, remove

удаля́ться/удали́ться to retire

*****ударя́ть** (I)/**уда́рить** (II) to strike, deal a blow

ударе́ние emphasis, stress

уда́ча success

уда́чный successful

удиви́тельный amazing

удивля́ть (I)/**удиви́ть** (II) *tr* to amaze

удивля́ться/удиви́ться to be amazed

удово́льствие pleasure

с удово́льствием with pleasure

*****уезжа́ть** (I)/**уе́хать** (I) to go, (drive) away

ужа́сно terribly, awfully

ужа́сный terrible, awful

уже́ already

у́же narrower

у́жин supper

у́жинать (I)/**по-** to have supper

*****узнава́ть** (I)/**узна́ть** (I) to hear, learn, find out; to recognize, know

узо́р design, pattern

*****уйти́** (I) *pf* of **уходи́ть**

указа́ние instructions

*****ука́зывать** (I)/**указа́ть** (I) to point out, show, indicate

укла́дывать (I) to put to bed; to pack up; to keep within

укла́дываться to pack up one's things

уко́л sting, stab; injection

у́ксус vinegar

улета́ть (I)/**улете́ть** (II) to fly away

у́лица street

на у́лице in the street

уложи́ть(ся) *pf* of **укла́дывать(ся)**

улы́бка smile

*****улыба́ться**(I)/**улыбну́ться**(II) to smile

ум mind, intellect

*****умере́ть** (I) *pf* of **умира́ть**

*****уме́ть** (I) to know how (to)

умира́ть (I)/**умере́ть** (I) to die

умне́е more clever

у́мница clever person (*m or f*)

у́мный clever, intelligent

умыва́льник washstand

умыва́ть (I) to wash

умыва́ться to wash oneself

умы́ть(ся) (I) *pf* of **умыва́ть(ся)**

унести́ (I) *pf* of **уноси́ть**

универма́г = **универса́льный магази́н** universal store(s)

университе́т university

уноси́ть (II) /**унести́** (I) to carry away)

*****упа́сть** (I) to fall; *see p.* 302

уплыва́ть (I)/**уплы́ть** (I) to swim *or* to float, drift away

управле́ние management, control

управля́ть (I)/**упра́вить** (II) to manage, control

упражне́ние exercise. *See* p. 151 [20]

упражня́ться (I) to practise

Урал Urals (mountains)
у́ровень (m) level
уро́д monster, freak
уро́к lesson
урони́ть (II) to drop, let fall
уря́дник sergeant
ус (pl усы́) whisker(s)
уса́дьба farmstead, country seat
уса́тый whiskered
усе́рдие zeal
усе́рдный zealous
услыха́ть (only in past tense) pf of
  слыха́ть
услы́шав hearing
услы́шать (II) pf of слы́шать
*успева́ть (I)/успе́ть (II) to
  succeed
успока́ивающее сре́дство
  sedative
уста́лый tired, weary
устра́ивать (I) to arrange, or-
  ganize
  устра́ивает ли э́то вас?
  Does that suit you?
*устро́ить (II) pf of устра́ивать
у́стье mouth, estuary
усы́ (sing ус) whiskers
утопи́ть (II) to drown, sink (tr)
у́тренний morning
у́тро morning
  у́тром in the morning
уткну́ться (I) to bury oneself,
  to hide one's face
утю́жка pressing, ironing
*у́хо (pl у́ши) ear
уходи́ть (II) to go away, retire
уходя́ departing
уцепи́ться (II) pf to cling to
*уча́ствовать (I) to take part
  in
уче́бник textbook, manual
уче́бный educational
уче́ние teaching; studies
учени́к (m)
учени́ца (f)} pupil; disciple
учёный learned; scholar,
  scientist
учи́лище school, college.
  p. 151 [21]
учи́тель (m)
учи́тельница (f)} teacher
*учи́ть (II) pf to teach; to learn
учи́ться to study, learn

Ф

факт fact

факти́чески practically
факти́ческий actual, real, in
  fact
фами́лия surname
фантасти́ческий fantastic
фарфо́р porcelain, china
фарфо́ровый of porcelain
фасо́н style, cut
фате́ра quarters
фельето́н feuilleton
фиа́ско fiasco
фигу́ра figure; chessman, piece
фи́зик physicist
фи́зика physics
филосо́ф philosopher
филосо́фия philosophy
фильм film
фи́рма firm, house, business
фити́ль (m) wick
флот fleet; navy
фойе́ lobby, foyer
фо́кус focus
фона́рь (m) lamp, lantern
фоне́тика phonetics
фонта́н fountain
фото́граф photographer
фотографи́ровать (I) to
  photograph
фотографи́ческий photo-
  graphic
фотогра́фия photography
фотокорреспонде́нт press
  photographer
франкиро́ванный prepaid
  (letter)
францу́женка Frenchwoman
францу́з Frenchman
францу́зский French
фрукт fruit
фунт pound (lb or £)
фунт сте́рлингов pound sterling
футбо́л football
футболи́ст footballer

X

ха́живать (I) ipf to go often;
  see p. 306
ха́ос chaos
хара́ктер (adj -ный) character-
  (-istic)
харьковча́нин (-анка) person
  from Kharkov (m or f)
ха́та hut

хва́статься (I) *ipf* to boast, brag
хвастовство́ boasting
хвасту́н braggart
*хвата́ть/хвати́ть to seize, grasp
хвост tail
хи́мик chemist
хими́ческий chemical
хи́мия chemistry
хини́н quinine
хиру́рг surgeon
хлеб bread, grain
хло́поты trouble, bustle
хо́бот trunk
ход motion, speed, course; entry; move (*at chess*)
хода́тайствовать (I) *ipf* to petition, intercede; *see* p. 307
*ходи́ть (II) to go on foot, walk; to go (*of machines*); *see* pp. 171, 174, 178
ходьба́ walking
хозя́ин (*pl* хозя́ева) master, boss, proprietor; host (*inn etc.*)
хозя́йка hostess; mistress (*of house*)
хозя́йничать (I) to be the boss, manage everything
хозя́йский authoritative
хозя́йство economy
домашнее хозя́йство housekeeping
хо́лод cold
хо́лоден, холодна́, -о ; -ы cold
хо́лодно it is cold
холо́дный cold
хор chorus
хоро́шенький pretty
хоро́ший good
хорошо́ good; well
*хоте́ть (*irr*) to wish, desire
я хоте́л бы I would like
хоть, хотя́ although
хотя́ бы if only
храм temple, church
хруста́ль (*m*) cut glass; crystal
хруста́льный crystal
худо́жество art
худо́жник artist
худо́й thin, lean; delicate
худо́й bad
ху́дший worse; the worst
ху́же worse
хулига́н hooligan, rough customer

Ц

*цари́ть (II) *ipf* to reign, prevail
царь (*m*) tsar; emperor
*цвести́ (I) *ipf* to bloom: цвету́, -тешь. *pa* цвёл, ела́
цвет (1) flower; (2) colour
цвето́к blossom, flower
полево́й цвето́к wild flower
цветно́й coloured
цветы́ flowers
целе́бный curative; medicinal
цели́ться (II) *ipf* to take aim at
целова́ть(ся) to kiss
це́лое the whole
це́лость (*f*) safety
в це́лости intact, safe
це́лый whole, entire
це́лый день all day
цель (*f*) aim, goal, object
Це́льсий Celsius
по Це́льсию centigrade
цена́ price, cost
центр centre
це́рковь (*f*) church
цирк circus
ци́ркуль (*m*) compasses, dividers
ци́фра cipher
цыплёнок (*pl* цыпля́та) chick(en)
цып-цып "chuck-chuck" (*calling chickens*)

Ч

чай (*adv*) probably
чай tea
час hour
кото́рый час ? What's the time ?
часово́й sentinel, sentry
часово́й watch-, clock-
часовщи́к watchmaker
ча́сто often
часту́шка folk verse, song
ча́стый frequent
часть (*f*) part, share
часы́ clock, watch
ча́шка cup
ча́ще more often
ча́ще всего́ mostly
ча́яние expectation, hope
чего́ what, of what
чей whose; *see* p. 254
чей-нибу́дь of somebody
чей-то somebody's
чек cheque

человéк person, human being, man
человéческий human
человéчество man
чéлюсть jaw
  вставны́е чéлюсти false teeth
чем than
  чем ..., тем ... (the) more ... the more
чемодáн suitcase, bag
чéрез (чрез)+acc across, over, through; in (of time ahead)
  чéрез два часá in two hours
  чéрез час in an hour's time
чернéть (I) to become black
черни́ла (pl) ink
черни́ть (II) to blacken (tr)
чёрный black
чёрт (pl -и) devil
чертá line, feature, trait
чéтверо four (of)
чéтверть (f) a quarter, fourth
числи́ться (II) (ipf only) to be numbered
число́
чи́стить (II)/по- to clean, brush; to peel
чи́стка clean-up; purge
чи́стый clean; pure
читáльня reading room
читáтель (m) reader; see p. 169
*читáть (I)/про- to read/read through
  читáть лéкции to give lectures
читáя (while) reading
чихáть (I)/чихну́ть (I) to sneeze; see p. 243
чрезвычáйный extraordinary
чтéние reading
что what; that
  что за+nom = What kind of a ...?
чтóбы (чтоб) in order to: p. 120
что-ли́бо, что-нибу́дь something, anything
что-то something
чу́вство sense, feeling
*чу́вствовать (I)/по- to feel
чудóвище monster
чуть scarcely, hardly
  чуть ли almost
  чуть-чуть very nearly

Ш

шаг step

шаги́ footsteps
*шагáть (I) to step, stride, pace
шагáющий stepping
шáлость (f) prank
шалу́н (m) mischievous boy; -нья girl
шампу́нь (m or f) shampoo
шарлатáн charlatan, humbug
шáхматы (pl) chess
*шевели́ться (II) to move, stir
шедéвр masterpiece
шéдши going
шёлк silk
шёлковый silk(en)
шерсть (f) wool
шерстянóй woollen
шéстеро six of; see p. 203
шéя neck
ши́бкий fast, swift
ши́бко fast
шимпанзé chimpanzee
ши́на tyre (automobile)
ши́ре wider, broader
ширинá width, breadth
широ́кий broad, wide
широкó widely
широкоэкрáнный фильм wide screen film
широтá breadth, width
*шить (I)/с- to sew; see p. 305
шкаф cupboard
шкóла school
шкóльник (-ица) schoolboy, girl
шкóльный school-
шля́па hat
шоколáд (adj -ный) chocolate
шоссé highway, road
шофёр chauffeur, driver
шпиль (m) spire
шпи́лька hairpin
штат (1) state; (2) personnel
штукату́рка plaster, stucco
шум noise
*шути́ть (II) to joke, jest
шу́тка joke

Щ

щавéль (m) sorrel
щади́ть (II)/по- to spare
щель (f) chink, split
щётка brush, broom
щи (pl) cabbage soup
щипцы́ pliers

Э

экватор equator
экзамен examination
экземпляр copy, sample
экран cinema screen
экскаватор excavator; power shovel
  шагающий экскаватор walking excavator
экскурсия excursion, trip
электронный (*adj*) electronic
элемент element
энергичный energetic
энергия energy
эпоха epoch
эра era
эрмитаж hermitage
эскалатор escalator
эстрада platform
эстрадный platform
  эстрадный театр music hall
этаж floor, storey; *see* p. 189
этот, эта, это ; эти this, that

Ю

юг south
  на юг to the south
юго-восток south-east
юго-запад south-west
южный southern
юмор humour
юмористический humorous

юность (*f*) youth
юный youthful

Я

я I
яблоко apple
яблочко (*dim*) apple
*явиться (II) *pf* of являться
явление appearance
*являться (I) *ipf* to appear; + *ins* = to be
явно evidently, obviously
явный evident, obvious
язык language
яйцо (*pl* яйца) egg
  яйца всмятку soft boiled eggs
  яйца вкрутую hard boiled eggs
яичница fried eggs (*pl*)
яичный (*adj*) of eggs
якорь (*m*) anchor
яма pit
ямщик driver; coachman
январь (*m*) January
янки yankee
яркий bright
ярок, ярка, -о ; -и bright
ярус circle, tier (*theatre*)
ясень (*m*) ash, tree
ясно it is clear
ясный clear
ячмень (*m*) barley
ячмень (*m*) sty
ящерица lizard